A
SECRET
LIFE

A SECRET LIFE

THE LIES AND SCANDALS OF PRESIDENT GROVER CLEVELAND

CHARLES LACHMAN

A HERMAN GRAF BOOK
SKYHORSE PUBLISHING

Skyhorse Publishing books may be purchased in bulk at special discounts for sales promotion, corporate gifts, fund-raising, or educational purposes. Special editions can also be created to specifications. For details, contact the Special Sales Department, Skyhorse Publishing, 307 West 36th Street, 11th Floor, New York, NY 10018 or info@skyhorsepublishing.com.

Skyhorse® and Skyhorse Publishing® are registered trademarks of Skyhorse Publishing, Inc.®, a Delaware corporation.

www.skyhorsepublishing.com

10 9 8 7 6 5 4 3

Library of Congress Cataloging-in-Publication Data available on file

ISBN 978-1-62087-096-9

Printed in the United States of America

ABOUT THE AUTHOR

CHARLES LACHMAN IS the author of *The Last Lincolns: The Rise & Fall of a Great American Family* and *In the Name of the Law*. He is the executive producer of the television program *Inside Edition*.

No matter what, tell the truth.

—Grover Cleveland, 1884

I do not want strangers to come and gaze upon my face. Let everything be very quiet. Let me rest.

—Maria Halpin, on her deathbed, leaving
instructions for her funeral

CONTENTS

PROLOGUE

THE CHILD WAS born on September 14, 1874, at the only hospital in Buffalo, New York, that offered maternity services for unwed mothers. It was a boy, and though he entered the world in a state of illegitimacy, a distinguished name was given this newborn: Oscar Folsom Cleveland.

His mother was Maria Halpin, a shopgirl. His father was Grover Cleveland, ten years away from being elected president of the United States.

Two days after the birth, Dr. James E. King, who delivered Oscar, wrapped the baby in a swathing blanket and went by carriage to the apartment of his sister-in-law, Minnie Kendall.

Dr. King would not say who the baby was or how he came to be in his possession, but told Mrs. Kendall that he was going to leave the infant with her. The understandably bewildered Mrs. Kendall was pregnant herself; her due date was any day now. How was she going to explain the sudden appearance of a baby to her neighbors? Dr. King suggested that she tell everyone she had had twins.

Something else was bothering her. The baby had a sore on the top of his head. It looked like an open wound.

"I don't want to take it," she said.

Dr. King knew that Minnie Kendall and her husband, William, a horse car conductor, were strapped for cash. They had been living on a farm in Kansas before coming to Buffalo four years earlier. Now here they were, in a shabby apartment near the stockyards, with a baby on the way. Her overbearing brother-in-law told her in so many words that she had to take care of this newborn and also be his wet nurse, and she would be paid for it.

Mrs. Kendall, seeing that Dr. King would not take no for an answer, asked him what to call the baby. Jack, he told her.

Dr. King had brought the newborn's clothes with him, and Mrs. Kendall saw that his blanket and all of his outfits were monogrammed "M. H." There were also several handkerchiefs bearing the name "Maria Halpin." Dr. King scooped it all up and told Mrs. Kendall he was taking it back and she would have to replace everything. Before he left, he made it clear to her that the infant and their transaction had to be kept strictly within the family. No one could ever speak about what had happened on this day. Its exposure could have tragic consequences for all concerned.

The submissive Mrs. Kendall, full of questions she did not dare ask, could not help wondering if Baby Jack's mother, this Maria Halpin, would one day appear at their door.

Twelve days after Jack came into Minnie Kendall's life, she gave birth to her son, William Harrison Kendall.

Mrs. Kendall nursed Jack and William together, and raised them like brothers. Overtime, the sore on Jack's head healed, and he was growing into a handsome little toddler the Kendalls came to love as their own. With the extra money coming in, they moved to a nicer place on Union Street, in Buffalo proper, and did their best to "hide the traces" of Jack's existence.

One morning, Dr. King and his wife, Sarah, William Kendall's sister, showed up at the Kendalls' door. They told Mrs. Kendall to immediately gather all of Jack's things. They were taking him downtown—"to its father's office." Mrs. Kendall "rigged the child up" and climbed into a carriage for the trip to the law firm of Bass, Cleveland & Bissell in downtown Buffalo.

Everyone was crowded into Grover Cleveland's second-floor law office when an extraordinary scene took place. A woman Mrs. Kendall had never seen before suddenly came in, ran toward her, and "snatched the child out of my arms without saying a word to me." So this was Baby Jack's mother, the mysterious Maria Halpin, Mrs. Kendall thought. It seemed to her that Maria was frantic—even "crazy" with grief.

Maria looked at her son, whom she called Oscar, now fast asleep in her arms.

"Oh, my baby, open your eyes and let me see them," she whispered. "Oh, my precious baby, why don't you open your eyes once more?"

Maria kept speaking this way to the baby until Grover Cleveland, his face twisted into what Mrs. Kendall called a "rough expression," like an angry fist, said to Maria, "Give the child up to Mrs. Kendall." Maria Halpin was crying—"as though her heart would break," while Cleveland, his voice harsh and insistent, was repeatedly ordering her to turn the baby over to Mrs. Kendall.

Mrs. Kendall saw Cleveland give Dr. King a "sly wink" and heard him say, "It is all right, Doctor. Have a cigar, Doc." It upset her to see them so chummy, laughing, while Maria was in tears. She felt nothing but sympathy for the woman.

When it was time for everyone to leave the office, a veil was placed over the baby's face, and Mrs. Kendall, with her brother-in-law, walked out carrying him. The purpose of the gathering now became apparent to Mrs. Kendall: "It was to assure Maria Halpin that her child was alive and well."

Outside the law offices, on Swan Street, Mrs. Kendall remarked, "How much the child looks like his father." Before this eventful afternoon she had never heard of Grover Cleveland.

Dr. King lifted the veil and studied the baby's face. "Yes, it does look like its father."

1

BUFFALO

WHEN GROVER CLEVELAND turned seventeen, the time had come for him to go forth into the world. The year was 1854, and he was living in the tiny hamlet of Holland Patent, New York, about nine miles north of Utica; but it was too inconsequential a place to offer much of a future, so he tried Utica and Syracuse, but nobody seemed to be hiring. It was an exasperating time. Grover passed the evening hours studying Latin to keep his mind alert, but he had to admit to his sister Mary, "I am kind of fooling away my time here."

Grover had a pet name for Mary—Molly; she was the big sister he could unburden his heart to. There were nine Cleveland children in all. Stephen Grover Cleveland (he dropped the "Stephen" early on) was born on March 18, 1837, the fifth child of Ann Neal Cleveland and the Reverend Richard Falley Cleveland. Grover was closest to Mary and his big brother William, a student at the Union Theological Seminary in New York City, but William had not written in a while, and what he did write said very little.

Grover sometimes found dealing with William very frustrating. Mary, though, was giving and wise. Grover wrote her that he was "heartily sick of studying at home," that he wanted to attend Hamilton College in Upstate New York, but it was a dream he would have to defer. "How is a man going to spend four years in getting an education with nothing to start on and no prospect of anything to pay his way with?" College, he said, with some bitterness, was not going to happen. "That's gone up."

Grover set himself a deadline: Come next spring, at the latest, he was going to be out of Holland Patent.

From nowhere Grover received a message from Ingham Townsend, a wealthy local property owner with a reputation as a thoughtful benefactor who had offered financial assistance to several promising young men from Holland Patent. Townsend was also a deacon in the Presbyterian church where Grover's father had been minister. Richard Cleveland died in 1853, at age forty-nine, of acute peritonitis brought on by a gastric ulcer, and Townsend had a genuine interest in doing all he could for the Cleveland family. So it happened that Townsend met with Grover, was very impressed with him, and offered to pay the boy's way through college. There was one catch: Grover had to make a commitment to enter the ministry following his graduation. Right then, Grover had to say no. That was his father's and his brother William's calling, not his. There was further discussion, and an idea came to Grover "like an inspiration." He now presented it to Townsend. He wanted to go west, to the booming city of Cleveland, Ohio.

"It's just the place for a young man to establish himself in," he told Townsend.

Cleveland was the city founded by Grover's forebear, Moses Cleaveland, a Connecticut lawyer and Revolutionary War officer. In 1796, he led a surveying party across Lake Erie to explore the Western Reserve, territory claimed by the state of Connecticut in what is now northeastern Ohio. At the mouth of the Cuyahoga River, General Cleaveland beheld a magnificent plain and proclaimed it to be the site of a settlement. It was named in honor of the leader of the expedition.

In 1820, Cleaveland's population had reached just one hundred and fifty. By 1854, the city's name had been shortened to "Cleveland." This came about because the editor of the local newspaper thought "Cleveland" looked cleaner than "Cleaveland" on the masthead. Cleveland's population had reached thirty thousand, and the city was on its way to becoming a vital port that, via the Erie Canal, linked the West to the Atlantic Ocean.

Deciding on the city of Cleveland made sense, even if, as Grover gamely acknowledged, he knew not a single soul there. Settling in a boomtown named for a distinguished kinsman would set him apart from all the other determined young men who were flocking to Ohio.

"I was attracted by the name. It seemed that it was my town because it had my name," Grover later said.

As Townsend listened to Grover sketch out his shrewd plan, he must have admired the magnitude of the young man's ambition. Right then he offered Grover the sum of $25 to finance his way west. It was a loan, but one that Townsend assured Grover he need never pay back. There was, however, one condition; and as did anything associated with Ingham Townsend, it came positioned as an act of philanthropy.

"If you ever meet with a young man in a similar condition, give it to him if you have it to spare," Townsend said.

Townsend handed Grover the $25 and a promissory note. He would forever be grateful for the money. It was, Grover would say many years later, "my start in life." Townsend could never have imagined that the simple gesture he made that day would have such profound consequences in American history.

Grover said good-bye to his family. His mother, Ann, was a fine-boned, pretty Southern belle, the daughter of a wealthy book publisher from Baltimore, when she had married Richard Cleveland at age twenty-three. Coming north as the bride of a young Presbyterian minister had been a culture shock. Though she had been advised in no uncertain terms not to take a black servant from a slave state North, her black maid had begged to go with her, and Ann had brought her along. That, and Ann's attire, made the villagers suspicious. The maid was sent home, along with Ann's jewelry and all her dresses of colors other than black, brown, and gray.

It had been a disciplined household. Every evening the Cleveland children would gather for prayers and brace themselves to be drilled by Reverend Cleveland on the basic principles of the Christian faith. In this manner, Grover and his siblings committed to memory the entire handbook of the Presbyterian catechism. The Sabbath was strictly observed, work and any form of play were forbidden from sundown on Saturday until sundown on Sunday. On Saturday evening, the children lined up for their weekly baths; and on Sunday, all except the babies were required to attend Reverend Cleveland's two-hour sermons.

Grover boarded a barge on the Erie Canal for the voyage to Cleveland, Ohio. Accompanying him was another young man from Holland Patent who was also seeking his fortune out west. The Erie Canal was the engineering marvel of the age; some even called it the Eighth Wonder of the World. It was a long and tedious crossing—a winding, sluggish process through beautiful pasture and virgin forest as a team of horses, or sometimes mules or oxen, towed the barge 365 miles across New York State, from Albany to its terminus in Buffalo, on the shores of Lake Erie. When they reached Buffalo, Grover, exhausted and covered in dust, informed his traveling companion that he had to visit his aunt and uncle in the Buffalo suburb of Black Rock. He said he'd be back in plenty of time to make the connection to Ohio. That was fine with the other fellow, and Grover went ashore.

Lewis Allen's home was about two miles away. Grover walked straight down Niagara Street and stopped when he reached the Allen house at the corner of Ferry and Breckenridge. Four years had passed since Lewis had last seen his intense and eager nephew, and it was a jolt to see him again, for now Grover was mature and filled out.

Lewis was married to Grover's Aunt Margaret, his late father's sister. Lewis and Margaret and their two children lived on a fine estate on a bluff overlooking the Niagara River. Two great American statesmen, Henry Clay and Daniel Webster, had stayed there as overnight guests when passing through Buffalo.

Lewis was aware that the Cleveland family had its struggles. Grover's sister Susan had been born with deformed feet and was being treated by a specialist in New York City. Reverend Cleveland, a graduate of Yale, never made more than $600 a year. His sermons had been earnest, but had never dazzled. He had not sought fame, aspiring to be nothing more than a simple country cleric, what he'd called the "proper location for me." He'd walked humbly with his God. To his prosperous brother-in-law, Richard's was a life frittered away. "His modesty killed him," Lewis once reflected. "I mean, he didn't have push enough."

Grover told his uncle that he was on his way to Ohio and thinking about becoming a lawyer. Lewis always had a high regard for Grover; here was a lad who was not afraid of hard work. When he was fourteen, Grover found a job at a general store for $50 a year, plus room and board. Grover woke at five each morning to open the store, build a fire, dust off the merchandise, sweep the floor, and get everything in shape before the boss arrived at seven. At night, he slept on a plain pine bed with a mattress filled with cornhusk. His room had no stove, and the only source of heat was a pipe from the store's stove below. The privy was out back. When he was sixteen, still a boy but also a man, Grover spent a miserable year in charge of the boys' dormitory at the New York Institution for the Blind in Manhattan, a job arranged by his brother William for a "pittance" of a salary.

As Lewis listened to Grover, something seemed off. What Grover was saying sounded so random. Law schools did not exist in those days. A young man became a lawyer by apprenticing for three or four years and then applying for admission to the local bar association. Connections definitely helped.

Lewis found himself obliged to point out that Grover did not know anyone in the city of Cleveland—not a "single friend or acquaintance." Just how did he expect to find a law firm ready to take him on? Grover could not say. Then it was folly to be going there, Lewis Allen told his nephew.

Lewis tried to persuade Grover to stay in Buffalo, where it just so happened that he was embarking on a challenging project and could use a young man like Grover to help out. He owned a six-hundred-acre farm on Grand Island where he raised Shorthorn cattle. For eight years, he had been obsessively documenting the bloodline of every Shorthorn he owned—a record of his livestock would be indispensable in establishing the herd as a great domestic breed of cattle. Now he was interested in publishing the results for the benefit of farming and stockman circles.

He proposed that his nephew stay with him for five months and organize everything. The pay would be $50, plus room and board. There was something else that sealed the deal for Grover—his uncle gave him his word that he would do what he could to introduce him to Buffalo's most "eminent" law firms. It took Grover about five seconds to say yes. He thanked Lewis then tramped two miles back to port, found his friend from Holland Patent, and informed him that he was staying put. He would be settling in Buffalo. Apparently, there were no hard feelings, and the young man carried on with his voyage westward. What became of him, no one can say. He and Grover never saw each other again.

Grover moved in with Uncle Lewis, Aunt Margaret, and their two children, Gertrude and Cleveland. Gertrude was enthusiastic and always seemed to be "full of fun." Cleveland Allen had had a sickly adolescence and suffered from periodic "spells of derangement," which may have meant epilepsy.

Grover and his cousin Cleveland, who were close in age, could often be found fishing in the Niagara River. One day, the duo was admiring a giant yellow pike that must have weighed at least fifteen pounds. Generally regarded as the tastiest of all freshwater fish, yellow pike are also aggressive and predatory, as Grover learned when he tried to pry open its razor-sharp teeth with a stick. The stick slipped, the pike's mouth snapped shut on Grover's hand, and his injury was so severe he came close to losing two fingers.

The two-story Allen house, constructed of stone and rough stucco, was square and solid, with a veranda out front where the Allens gathered as a family on the warm summer evenings. Behind the house was an orchard with apple, peach, plum, and cherry trees. Beyond that flowed the Niagara River at a swift current, churning up pockets of snowy white foam. It was a splendid vista. The Breckinridge Street Church, just across the street, is where Grover sometimes joined the Allens in Sunday worship. Also on Breckenridge lived a playful little boy, Timothy J. Mahoney, who was ten years old when Grover moved in with the Allens. Timothy first saw the unfamiliar teenager picking cherries in the orchard.

"Who's the new fellow?" Tim asked the Allen family handyman.

"Name's Cleveland," the handyman answered. "Father's dead. Used to be a minister down east somewhere. Boy's come to live with his uncle and aunt."

Tim was the neighborhood mischief-maker-in-chief, always getting into some scrape. He often sneaked through a gap left by a missing plank in the Allen's picket fence and filled a basket with pears. His petty crime spree came to an end when he ensnared himself in the fence, looked up, and saw Cleveland

Allen clutching a fistful of his pants. Grover enjoyed Tim's company, and he became a sidekick of sorts.

The Allens treated Grover like a son. He accompanied his uncle to the state fair in Utica. Aunt Margaret purchased Grover a formal dress coat—it was the first one he ever owned—and got him to agree to pose wearing it. He looked stiff and uneasy in the photograph.

There were some anxious days at the Allen house when Grover developed a high fever and severe abdominal pain—classic symptoms of typhoid fever, caused by ingesting contaminated food or water and spread via substandard public sanitation. It was touch-and-go for the next four weeks. The Allen family physician prescribed the starvation diet, sometimes known as the absolute diet. It meant absolutely no food for up to three days and was meant to heal intestinal ruptures. Somehow, Grover survived.

When he recovered, Grover resumed work on the herd book. Grand Island, where Lewis Allen raised his cattle, is a thirty-three-square-mile land mass in the Niagara River that lies near the international border between Canada and the United States. In those days, Grand Island was reached by a ferry powered by horses on a treadmill. When Grover Cleveland stepped onshore, he found an island blessed with magnificent forests of white oak trees and swarming with geese, ducks, and other game birds. Hawks and eagles patrolled the sky. The water held an inexhaustible source of yellow pike, sturgeon, and bass. For someone with Grover's appreciation of nature, it was a wonderland.

Lewis Allen's farm produced more than three hundred tons of hay annually, and the island soil also proved ideal for fruit trees. Indeed, the first peaches to be grown in Western New York were picked on Grand Island. For the farmers who lived there, though, it was an isolating existence; and the wells produced bitter-tasting water high in sulfuric content, which made for "very poor tea." This was a real problem considering that the inhabitants of Grand Island were of English, Irish, and Scottish descent. Settlers had to resort to building cisterns on their rooftops to store decent drinking water from rainfall.

Grover tended to his uncle's cattle and kept the books. Eventually, more than 125,000 Shorthorns would be registered in the American Herd Book. But mostly, when he went to Grand Island to put in a full day's work in the summer and fall of 1855, he ended up fishing with his cousin Cleveland. Even so, Lewis Allen must have been pleased with his nephew's industry and work ethic because in November, when the first edition of the herd book was completed, he paid Grover $60—$10 more than the arrangement called for—for a job well done.

All this time, Grover kept pressing his uncle for those lawyer connections. Finally, Lewis delivered. Looking at the field of attorneys in the city of Black Rock, Lewis settled on Daniel Hibbard, a justice of the peace who lived on Breckenridge Street and had once served as postmaster. "Grover, you had better go up and see Hibbard," Lewis told his young charge.

Grover showed up at Hibbard's Black Rock office just down the street from the Allen house. The interview was a disaster. It seems that Hibbard treated Grover like a supplicant, or some hard-up urchin looking for a handout. Perhaps he questioned Grover's credentials; after all, the teenager had no college education. Quick to take offense, Grover found Hibbard's questions to be so "impertinent" he walked right out. When Lewis heard about what had happened, he generously let it go as one of those things. Grover, he was coming to understand, was a "high-spirited boy."

Lewis tried again. He rode into downtown Buffalo and went to the offices of Rogers, Bowen & Rogers, one of the city's leading law firms, with a notable history dating back to Millard Fillmore, the thirteenth president of the United States. He wanted to have a word with the fifty-five-year-old senior partner, Henry W. Rogers. In the pecking order of Buffalo citizenry, Rogers ranked as one of the "solid men" of the city. He was witty and acerbic and an outstanding orator before a jury. His family Bible at home chronicled the full record of his distinguished line in America, going back to Thomas Rogers, the eighteenth of forty-one signatories of the Mayflower Compact. When Lewis asked Rogers if he would hire a new boy, the cantankerous Rogers was not very keen on doing this favor, even for Lewis Allen. Then he did say that he was always interested in having "smart boys" around. It was the opening Lewis was looking for. He told Rogers there was a "smart boy at my house who wanted to come in and see what he could do." Rogers must have looked at his old friend with some resentment. Next to Millard Fillmore, Lewis Allen was probably Buffalo's leading citizen. He had founded the city's fire, marine, and life insurance companies; fought for the enlargement of the Erie Canal; had served in the state legislature in the 1830s; and regularly exchanged correspondence with some of the most admired men in America, men like Henry Clay, Daniel Webster, William H. Seward, and General Winfield Scott. To cross Lewis Allen was probably unthinkable when the favor to be granted was so inconsequential. Besides,

Rogers had an affinity for taking on the nephews of prominent people. Sherman S. Rogers, the third named partner in the firm, was his twenty-five-year-old nephew.

Rogers pointed to a spare desk tucked into the corner of his office. "Well," he said, "there's a table." An understanding was reached. For the first two months, Grover would work for no pay, but once he had proved his value, they could talk salary. No promises were made; apparently, Rogers wanted to leave all options open in the event that this Grover Cleveland did not prove to be as smart a boy as his uncle had said he was.

The law firm was located at Spaulding's Exchange, a five-story office building owned by the former mayor of Buffalo, at 162 Main Street. It was a hub of business and commerce. On the ground floor were the Bank of Attica and an array of shops and stores. The second floor held the offices of Farmers and Mechanics Bank. On the upper floor was the law firm of Rogers, Bowen & Rogers.

On Grover's first day at Rogers, Bowen & Rogers, he immediately realized that no one wanted him there. Old Man Rogers set the tone when Grover introduced himself; he responded by tossing a copy of Blackstone's *Commentaries on the Laws of England* on the desk that had been set aside for the new boy. The book was, of course, the foundation of all the laws in the United States and England. It landed on the desk with a loud *thunk* and a cloud of dust.

"That's where they all begin," Rogers informed the confounded young man and, with that, walked away. Thus was launched the legal career of Grover Cleveland. He opened the book with what must have been total bewilderment and began to read. For the rest of the morning, the other partners and clerks ignored him. Around noon, the office cleared out. Everyone went to lunch, but no invitation was extended to the new clerk on tryout. When evening came and it was time for everyone to go home, Grover waited at his desk for a summons or some signal that it would be appropriate to leave. Before he knew what was happening, the office was empty. The last man out actually locked the door. Grover was trapped inside. Whether this was another act of humiliation or he had just been forgotten, no one can say. Surely Grover felt hurt by the way he had been treated, but to his credit, he took it as another challenge. "Someday I will be better remembered," he recalled thinking that night. He was stuck in the office until the following morning.

Several days later, Lewis Allen asked his nephew, "How are you getting on at the office?"

"Pretty well, sir. Only, they won't tell me anything."

The next time Lewis came face-to-face with Rogers, he repeated his nephew's complaint.

"If the boy has brains, he'll find out for himself without anybody telling him" was Rogers's crusty response, but it belied the realization he was coming to that the boy was worth mentoring. He told Lewis that Grover could stay on. As for salary, Lewis told Rogers to pay his nephew what they could afford. It came to $6 a week, which Grover found to be "very satisfactory."

Grover was at his desk one Thursday afternoon in mid-October, bleary-eyed from work and feeling a little out of sorts because he had received just one letter from his family in two weeks. So he put Blackstone aside and wrote a letter to his sister Mary, who had recently given birth to her first child who, in jest, Grover called "little what's-his-name." For the most part, Grover wrote, he was feeling "pretty well encouraged." Things had settled down at Rogers, Bowen & Rogers; he had full access to the firm's law library for his studies, and his physical presence in a thriving practice allowed him, through continual exposure, to absorb the law. He was proving his worth, he told Mary, and the lawyers at the firm, above all Dennis Bowen, were "very kind to me." They were even promising him a promotion, but he was worrying about his finances, which, he complained, left him in a state close to poverty. The work was piling on at the firm, but Grover said he didn't mind—"the more I do, the more I learn." He told Mary that he was looking to find a room to rent before he overstayed his welcome at the Allen house. He had also had enough of trudging two miles to work and two miles back every day, so he wanted a place of his own close to the law office. He was going to check out another boardinghouse when he got off work that evening.

A month later, Grover finally found a place to live that fit his budget, and moved into the dreary $40-a-week room in a second-class hotel at 11 Oak Street in town. Like any robust young man just starting out, he tried to keep his spirits up, even if his pocket was feeling "light."

New Year's Eve 1855 found Grover in a contemplative mood. Buffalo had been hard hit by a wicked northeaster that had slammed the Mid-Atlantic states before heading into New England. The streets were slicked over with ice, and gentlemen with plans for the evening were cautioned to wear cork-bottomed heels for traction, particularly if they intended to drink wine or hard liquor. Apparently, the nineteen-year-old lad had no plans for New Year's Eve, which he dismissed "as any other day to me and no better." He sat in his room all night, feeding anthracite into the heater to ward off the "dreadful" chill. On the bustling street outside his hotel room, Grover could hear the steady jingle of sleigh bells. In the distance came cannon fire and the celebration of the New Year. He was already lamenting the slow decay of his once-lithe frame, owing mainly to his overindulging himself at meals and his steady consumption of beer, which would have truly upset his father. He missed his siblings; his brother Cecil had not written in months, and Grover had no idea where he was. On the whole, he wrote Mary, he was trying to be happy—"though sometimes I find it pretty hard."

One year later, Grover was living at the Southern Hotel at Seneca and Michigan Streets. He had a roommate, though they were so poor the only room they could afford was a low-ceilinged cockloft. Christmas held no special meaning for Grover; not one relative or friend had sent him a gift. He spent a pleasant New Year's Day attending a performance of acrobats at a Buffalo theater, and then, to his relief, the holidays were over. He found himself back at work on a Sunday, January 3.

Grover's grievances started piling up the moment he entered the office at 9:00 AM and found it to be as cold as an icebox. He was entering the second year of his apprenticeship at Rogers, Bowen & Rogers, and Henry Rogers and Dennis Bowen, he told Mary, were assuring him that if he continued doing well, "I'll make a lawyer." Under the new arrangement with the firm, he was now being paid $500 a year—an "enormous sum," he acerbically called it.

"O God! That bread should be so dear, and *work should be so cheap*," Grover wrote Mary. It was getting under his skin. He had come to the conclusion that the partners at Rogers, Bowen & Rogers were exploiting his hard labor.

"I am so ashamed of myself after allowing such a swindle to be practiced upon me. It shows how selfish the men I have to do with are, and how easy it is to fool me." As he thought more about the deal, his irritation grew. "From the bottom of my soul I curse the moment in which I consented to the contract." For extra cash, Grover had arranged to take a brief leave from the law firm to assist Uncle Lewis in the publication of the next annual edition of the *Shorthorn Herd Book*. He dreaded going to Black Rock because it diverted him from his legal work, but "for the sake of the pay," he had agreed to help out. Grover finished his disheartened letter to Mary with the pronouncement that his fingers were growing so numb from the cold in the office he could not write another word.

In May 1859, after three and a half years of devoted learning, Grover Cleveland went before the New York State Supreme Court, presented his credentials and letters of recommendation, and was admitted to the bar. He was twenty-two years old.

Grover stayed on at Rogers, Bowen & Rogers, but now in the bumped-up position of managing clerk, at an annual salary of $1,000. Good son that he was, each month Grover tucked what extra cash he could spare into an envelope and mailed it to his widowed mother in Holland Patent. Ann Cleveland was the glue that bound the far-flung Clevelands together as a family. Even as his relationship with his other kin, even Mary, grew more distant, Grover worshipped his mother. "The truth is I have a great deal to do nowadays and am getting quite out of the habit of writing letters," he informed Mary. Grover also cut his ties with another beloved relative, his uncle Lewis Allen. His regular visits to Black Rock had dropped off, and after he received his law license, it ceased altogether, except when Grover had important family news to communicate that made the trip absolutely necessary. The great issue of slavery, which was tearing North and South apart, was crushing Grover's attachment with the uncle who had done so much to launch his career.

Grover was a partisan Democrat. To him, abolitionists were extremists, and the Democratic Party was solid and conservative— values that held real appeal for him and also happened to match his personality. In 1856, he marched in the torchlight procession that celebrated the victory of James Buchanan in the presidential election. Under the guidance of Dennis Bowen, who had once served as a Democratic alderman from the tenth ward, he started taking an interest in politics, volunteering as a ward heeler. It was pound-the-pavement machine politics at the street level. Assigned to Buffalo's second ward, a neighborhood populated by German immigrants, Grover was handed a list of reliable Democratic voters and issued instructions to lead them to the polls on Election Day. Going door-to-door was humbling, but for a young lawyer keen on making his mark in local politics, it was compulsory work.

As Lewis Allen watched Grover's political stance take shape, he mourned; it was like experiencing a death in the family. Lewis was a proud Yankee who had presided over the first Republican Party convention in Erie County in 1855. For him, the Fugitive Slave Act was a hateful piece of legislation. Remarks he made thirty years later indicate that his nephew's political evolution still rankled: Allen stated that he was a "pronounced opponent" of Cleveland's position. "Politically, we differed," he simply said.

In the transformational presidential election of 1860, Grover Cleveland supported the Democratic Party standard-bearer, Stephen A. Douglas, over the candidacy of Abraham Lincoln. Lincoln won the election and took New York State's thirty-five electoral votes. Buffalo also went for Lincoln. The nation now stood on the brink of civil war.

President-elect Lincoln bade Springfield, Illinois, farewell on a wet and bitterly cold morning and embarked on a twelve-day journey via railroad to his inauguration in Washington. On Saturday afternoon, February 16, the train pulled into Buffalo for a tumultuous reception at the railroad depot. Crowd control was nonexistent, and for a few terrifying moments, it was feared that Lincoln was in physical danger from the crushing throng; but he was able to make his way to the balcony of the American Hotel, and there he delivered a speech advising his countrymen to "maintain your composure" in these perilous times.

As Abraham and Mary Lincoln shook hands with hundreds of local residents later that evening, Lincoln seemed grave and "sad in the eye," weighed down by the Southern rebellion. One elderly gentleman who was presented to the President-elect was heard to say in a trembling voice: "You must save the Union. May God help you do it." The next day, in a gesture of national unity, former president Millard Fillmore escorted the Lincolns to Sunday services at the Unitarian church where he worshipped. Fillmore, who was known for sympathizing with the "just rights of the South," was showing the citizens of his state that in this time of national crisis he stood with the Union.

On April 13, 1861, Fort Sumter came under fire by rebel forces, triggering the Civil War. In Buffalo, a huge crowd gathered outside the Metropolitan Theatre. That day Democrats and Republicans spoke with one voice. Millard Fillmore rose and said the country faced an emergency in which no man, however low in rank, had a right to stand neutral.

"Civil War has been inaugurated, and we must meet it. Our government calls for aid, and we must give it."

By April 18, hundreds of Buffalo's men had come forward to sign up for two years of military duty. Fillmore was elected captain of a company of volunteers. On May 11, the entire city, with cheers and tears, turned out to bid the regiment Godspeed as they marched off to war.

The four Cleveland boys took different paths. In New York City, Grover's brother Lewis Frederick Cleveland, who was known as Fred, heard the call to arms and fought for two honorable years, mustering out a first lieutenant. Cecil Cleveland, living in Indiana when war broke out, served with Generals Fremont and Grant in the Western Theater, and rose to the rank of second lieutenant. William Cleveland, now an ordained Presbyterian minister in Southampton, Long Island, had just gotten married and made the choice that in his situation, family came before country. To complicate matters, William's wife was from Georgia, and he was "lukewarm" to the notion of doing battle against the South. Grover Cleveland also made up his mind to sit this one out.

Grover would later try to explain himself, saying his priority was supporting his widowed mother and sisters, who were now solely dependent on him for financial assistance. Of his two eldest sisters, Anna Cleveland Hastings was a missionary in faraway Ceylon, and Mary Cleveland Hoyt was raising a family. But Susan was eighteen and entering college, and Grover had promised to pay her tuition; Rose, the baby of the family, was fifteen and living with their mother in Holland Patent, but she was a bright student and also aspired to attend college. It was a daunting financial burden for a young man like Grover, who was just starting out. That, at least, was the story Grover later put out for public consumption. Apologists for Grover Cleveland added assertions that Mrs. Cleveland was "filled with anxiety for the fate of her two boys" who had gone to war, and that Grover remained his mother's "greatest earthly comfort" in those troubled times. It was also said that the four Cleveland brothers drew straws from the family Bible to determine by lot who would stay home and who would go to war—but even Grover Cleveland said that was a myth.

The war dragged on, and the Union Army faced hard fighting. In Buffalo, a steady line of soldiers strode out of Fort Porter behind drum and bugle and marched down Delaware Street to the railroad depot on their way to the front lines. News of an important battle down South sent civilians surging to the offices of the *Buffalo Daily Courier*, the *Buffalo Commercial Advertiser*, and the other newspapers where casualty lists were posted. Hundreds of families in Western New York were in grief over the loss of loved ones. As casualties mounted, enthusiasm for enlisting waned, which was only natural. Both sides were suffering appalling losses. Union and Confederate killed or wounded at the Battle of Shiloh came to 23,000 in just two days of fighting. Gettysburg was even worse—50,000 men killed, wounded, or captured.

Facing a profound shortage of volunteers, in 1863, Congress passed the first conscription act in American history. It made all able-bodied men between eighteen and thirty-five (forty-five if unmarried) eligible for the draft. A furor arose due to a provision in the act that permitted draftees to secure exemption from national service if they paid a commutation fee of $300. Or they could arrange for a substitute to take their place. It was now a rich man's war and the poor man's fight. At least that was the perception.

Grover followed the grim news from his desk at Rogers, Bowen & Rogers. With his legal career finally taking off, he ran for ward supervisor from Buffalo's second ward and was elected by 509 votes. When Buffalo elected a Democrat as district attorney, Grover was offered the post of assistant DA; but he had a lot to think through before he could accept the job. His salary at the district attorney's office would be $500 a year—half the salary he was pulling in at the law firm. Dennis Bowen did not want to lose Grover, but he was also urging his young associate to see the big picture and take the prosecutor's position. One other factor moved Grover to finally say yes. The new DA was Cyrenius C. Torrance, already an old man when he won the election by 1,700 votes. The major focus of his life was operating a mill he owned in a village outside Buffalo, so in all likelihood, he would be an absentee DA. Grover would pretty much have a free hand in running t' ⸲ office. He was sworn in as assistant district attorney on New Year's Day 1863.

Seven months later, in July 1863, the Civil War draft began. The names of eligible recruits were written on small pieces of paper and then stuffed inside a drum-shaped box that was turned on an axle. The local enlistment board drew the names at the provost marshal's office. These came from the so-called first class of eligibility—unmarried men from twenty to forty-five years of age, and married men from twenty to thirty-five. Erie County's quota came to about 2,000 men. Just his luck, Grover Cleveland's name was pulled on the first day.

Buffalo was a tinderbox. Just a week earlier, riots had erupted on the docks between Irish laborers and black longshoremen. One antiwar politician was accused of inciting the rabble to drive out every Negro and "black Republican." The city braced for an outbreak of violence.

When Fred Cleveland heard that his brother Grover had been drafted, he sent word offering to take his place. But Fred, who had mustered out of the army two months earlier, had "done enough," Grover decided. Besides, Grover said, "I have my man."

George Beniski was thirty-two years old when he met Grover Cleveland for the first time. Beniski was a sailor on the tugboat *Acme*, which carried cargo of flour, pork, lard, and other goods from Buffalo to Detroit, across Lake Erie. A Great Lakes sea captain, George Reinhart, had heard that Grover was looking for a conscript to take his place in the Union Army. Reinhart knew it was a knotty problem and suggested George Beniski. On August 20, 1863, six weeks after Grover was drafted, Reinhart took Beniski to see Grover in his grimy little prosecutor's office at the Erie County courthouse. When Grover was introduced to Beniski, he must have thought, here was the perfect man. The Polish-born Beniski had immigrated to the United States in 1851, spoke English with a thick accent, and stood just under five foot four. He had a round face, big ears, a low forehead, and elaborate tattoos on his hands. Beniski was illiterate and had no family. He could not even spell his name—he wrote the letter *X* as his mark.

Cleveland got right down to business. He offered to hire Beniski for $150 to serve as his substitute in the war. Beniski definitely got the impression that Grover had borrowed the money from Reinhart, and the sailor may have been illiterate, but he knew how to drive a bargain. "I knew that the bounty then was three hundred dollars," Beniski later recalled. So he asked Grover for better terms. "I told him if he would . . . help me out if I came out alive, I would go for him. This he agreed to." Beniski also asked Grover to "get an office or something for Captain Reinhart" as a sort of finder's fee.

The next thing Beniski knew, the three of them shook hands on it and were out the door, headed straight for a swearing-in ceremony. Perhaps Grover did not want to risk Beniski changing his mind if he had time to think things over. After Beniski took the oath of allegiance, Grover gave him the $150. Then it was off to Fort Porter, a military encampment overlooking the Niagara River; but first Grover suggested they stop for a beer. That was fine with Beniski. When Grover paid for the drinks, he showed Beniski what was in his wallet.

"There, George, do you see how little you've left me?"

That was true, Beniski thought, but at least this Grover Cleveland got to stay home while he went to war in his stead. He kept these sentiments to himself.

Fort Porter was a scene of frenetic activity, with raw recruits on the parade grounds drilling and training and adjusting to army discipline. Beniski went before a three-man enlistment board, which certified that he was able-bodied and sober. The conscript was presented with a Substitute Volunteer Enlistment form, on which he committed to three years' military service as a proxy for Grover Cleveland. He signed his mark, *X*.

Cleveland always held to the belief that Beniski was entirely aware of what he was getting into, and he never expressed regret for dodging the draft. Almost twenty-five years later, Cleveland was still arguing that Beniski had made out well. After all, plenty of substitutes were being hired at "even less" than the $150 he had paid out. Cleveland also insisted that he had never struck a side deal with Beniski promising the man a bonus should he survive the war.

"The terms . . . were distinctly repeated by me and perfectly understood. There was no hint or suggestion of anything more being paid or of any additional obligation on my part."

Cleveland put forward a curious defense. "Being then the assistant district attorney of Erie County, I had abundant opportunity to secure without expense a substitute from discharged convicts and from friendless persons accused of crime if I had wished to do so." Certainly, such a deed would have been a gross ethical, and perhaps criminal, violation, even by slipshod 19th-century standards. But Grover Cleveland never saw it that way. And neither have his biographers, who sought to excuse the hiring of Beniski as an act of altruism, namely Cleveland's commitment to his mother and sisters. Allan Nevins, who won a Pulitzer Prize in 1933 for his biography of Grover Cleveland, spun Cleveland's war record from the most benevolent perspective imaginable. As for the Polish immigrant, Nevins wrote that Beniski had an "uneventful" history in the war.

"He served briefly . . . injured his back, was then detailed to orderly duty in the military hospitals of Washington, and was never in any important battle as a combatant." In other words, there was not much more to say about the hapless George Beniski.

The truth was, George Beniski's Civil War experience ruined him.

Beniski served as a private in F Company, 76th New York Regiment. Less than a week after he enlisted, he was shipped out by rail and found himself in Virginia, on the shores of the Rappahannock River, the natural barrier that divided Union and Confederate forces. Eight months earlier, the Rappahannock had been the scene of the ferocious Battle of Fredericksburg, a big victory for the South.

Beniski was ordered to unload a wagon filled with fresh supplies for the troops. What happened next was one of those stupid little accidents that can happen in war. It may even have seemed unimportant at the time, but it changed a man's life in a flash. As Beniski was lifting a carton of provisions, he apparently made too abrupt a motion to the left and felt something pull. He knew immediately that it was a serious injury. Writhing in agony, he had to be lifted into an ambulance and transported to a military hospital in Washington, where he remained for two weeks. Then he was transferred to DeCamp General Hospital, on David's Island off the coast of New Rochelle, New York. It was a vast hospital facility set on seventy-eight acres. Prisoners of war were also treated there, wounded Southern fighting men who made a pathetic picture, landing at David's Island barefoot and in rags, looking "frightfully filthy," and infected with lice.

Beniski's medical records show that he had apparently suffered a testicular torsion; his spermatic cord had twisted around his left testicle. Doctors now understand that a testicular torsion is an acute medical emergency that must be treated within hours, not weeks. Beniski was almost certainly liquored up before surgery, probably lasting no more than thirty minutes, to cut out his testicle. Primitive as it was, the procedure probably saved his life from the onset of gangrene, and Beniski was declared "unfit for duty." For him, after just ten days of military service, the war was over. He was put on medical furlough and permitted to go home to recuperate.

Beniski returned to Buffalo—not the conquering hero, but a lonely convalescing soldier weighed down with worry about his future. Somehow, Grover Cleveland heard about the injury suffered by his substitute in war and stopped by to see how Beniski was doing. Certainly Beniski appreciated the gesture. At this point, no one really knew how much damage had been done to Beniski's body, or whether the operation had rendered him sterile. He stayed in Buffalo for eight days then returned to David's Island. From there, he was sent to Fort Wood on Bedloe's Island in New York City Harbor, then back to Washington. An alarming word started making its way into Beniski's medical records: *invalid.*

It is here that Beniski disappears from the annals of Grover Cleveland's life story. But he would resurface many years later, with harsh consequences to Cleveland's good name and place in history.

2

THE BACHELOR

MARIA HOVENDEN WAS a talented dressmaker with bright blue eyes, bow-shaped Cupid lips, a thin waist, and a full womanly figure. Statuesque, she stood just under five foot eight and carried herself with a proud and regal countenance. She lived with her family in the Williamsburg section of Brooklyn, which was then an independent city on the other side of the East River from Manhattan.

Her father, Robert Hovenden, was an officer in the Brooklyn police department. Sometimes he would work sixteen-hour shifts, and one night, on routine patrol at two in the morning, he saw someone trying to break into a dry-goods store at Graham Avenue and North Second Street. Hovenden gave chase, but the out-of-shape cop was no match for the fleet-footed burglar. After two blocks, Hovenden did not have the energy to continue the pursuit. All he could make out was the thief's coattails vanishing around the corner of Powers Street. It was just as well. In those days, police officers were not authorized to carry personal firearms. The only weapon Hovenden wielded was a twenty-six-inch-long nightstick made of solid oak, which could be used to bring down a perpetrator or to send a signal to other officers on patrol by rapping it against a curbstone.

Maria Hovenden's beau was a young man from the neighborhood, Frederick Halpin, whose father, also named Frederick, was a portrait engraver from Worcester, England. The Halpins had immigrated to the United States in 1842, when Frederick Junior was seven, and had settled in Brooklyn. The elder Halpin was regarded as one of the finest engravers in America. He specialized in steel plate etchings, which even in the 1850s was considered a dying craft. His engraving of the great scholar Noah Webster remains an iconic image to this day. Halpin once presented Fletcher Harper, a founder of the Harper & Brothers publishing empire, with an engraving that he had stippled for a book Harper & Brothers was publishing. Harper, who supervised all illustrations for the company, was impressed. "It is a very fine piece of work, Mr. Halpin. What is your bill?"

Halpin hesitated a moment before finally saying, "One hundred and fifty dollars."

"Is that all?" Fletcher Harper paid the bill before adding, "I wish for your sake it was more."

It must have delighted Police Officer Hovenden to see his daughter being squired by the son of such an important English gentleman. But Hovenden was also apprehensive. For one thing, Frederick Halpin Jr. appeared to have inherited none of his father's aptitude with the graver. Frederick was learning to be a bookbinder, which was a fine and respectable craft, but he always seemed to be ailing, with a chronic cough and a pallid hue to his skin. In general, he was in "poor health," and it made Hovenden wonder whether this was the right match for his daughter.

The dark clouds of war were passing. The South had surrendered, slavery was abolished, and the Union had been preserved, but at a staggering cost—620,000 dead. That is more than the combined number of American casualties in the two world wars that were to come in the 20th century. Confederate soldiers staggered back to their homes, and the 1-million-warrior-strong Grand Army of the Republic that had saved the Union was disbanded. The nation now faced an uncertain peace.

After these four lost years of blood-soaked conflict, family life resumed. Maria Hovenden married her beau from Brooklyn, and in quick order, first came a son, Freddie, born in 1863; and two years later, a daughter, Ada.

The Halpins were settling in and raising their children when Freddie, at age four, became seriously ill. A photo taken of Freddie in 1867 shows the boy in distress. In that era it was a ritual for a child who was facing death to be dressed for a photo in his or her Sunday best so that, should the worst happen, the little one's memory would be preserved. In Freddie's photograph, he is in misery—so fragile and bent it looks as though he could slip off the chair. He's wearing knickers fluffed up at the knees, and significantly, his high-button shoelaces hang untied. According to Halpin family lore, Maria could not tie them because Freddie's feet were so swollen, which may suggest that he was suffering from acute rheumatic fever, which can sometimes lead to kidney damage and edema in the legs. On the back of the photo is written, "Sick and expected to die." By some miracle, Freddie pulled through, and Maria Halpin was able to breathe again.

As Maria was raising her family, three hundred miles away in Buffalo, Grover Cleveland was enjoying the freedom of confirmed bachelorhood.

As he had predicted, his appointment as Erie County assistant district attorney to the elderly and infirm Cyrenius C. Torrance had left him de facto in charge of the office. For the three years that Cleveland stayed on as prosecutor, his workload was intense. Cleveland personally tried half the criminal cases that went to trial in Erie County. It was common to find Cleveland toiling at his desk in the county courthouse until three o'clock in the morning, preparing for trial, and then see him come in at 8:00 AM, ready to argue the case before a jury. In 1865, the ineffectual Torrance was forced into retirement by party power brokers, and Cleveland was awarded the nomination for district attorney.

At age twenty-eight, Cleveland was still living at the Southern Hotel, though he was now sharing a room with another gifted young lawyer, Lyman K. Bass. They were the same age, and like Grover Cleveland, Bass came from humble roots; his father owned a hardware store in Buffalo. Politically, however, they played in different arenas. A few days after Cleveland informed his roommate that he was running for district attorney as a Democrat, Bass came home with some news of his own.

"Well, Cleve, I have been offered the nomination for district attorney against you."

"Well," responded Cleveland, "why don't you take it?" And Bass did, running on the Republican ticket.

The roommates enjoyed each other's company and remained steadfast friends, getting together on many occasions to hoist a few beers even during the heat of the campaign. At one of these sit-downs, Cleveland and Bass made a gentlemen's agreement to restrict their consumption of beer to just four glasses a night from then to Election Day in November. One summer evening, after yet another round of drinks, the two men, behaving more like college frat brothers than candidates for district attorney, reached the conclusion that four beers was far too meager a ration. Thereafter, they settled on a new agreement that permitted them to "anticipate" (borrow from, really) consumption of the beer they'd allotted for every sitting to come for the duration of the campaign. Not too many boozy days passed before Bass said, "Grover! Do you realize we have by now 'anticipated' the whole campaign?"

The next night, the issue was settled: Cleveland and Bass met for drinks, and each ordered a glass—but the "glass" was a capacious German stein. So four glasses of beer was fine, as long as each glass was the size of a tankard, which in the 19th century was about forty eight ounces. In this manner, they could consume well over a gallon of beer a night.

Bass was a brilliant orator and debater, but Cleveland, after three years as a prosecutor, was the better-known candidate. Even so, this was 1865, and with the North rejoicing in victory, Cleveland's political timing was all off. Running as a Democrat, he found himself on the wrong side of history and went down to defeat by 600 votes. Although Cleveland outpolled his roommate in seven of Buffalo's thirteen wards, Bass's electoral strength lay in the towns outside Buffalo's city limits. There were no hard feelings; Cleveland offered his congratulations to Bass and cleared out his desk at the district attorney's office. Part of him was probably relieved; now he could go about the business of building a lucrative law practice. He opened a firm in partnership with a politically connected lawyer, Isaac K. Vanderpoel, who had been state treasurer of New York from 1858 to1859.

With all that drinking, Cleveland's weight had ballooned, and he grew a large paunch. Folks who knew him back when remarked on how "husky" he had grown, and his friends took to calling him "Big Steve"—a throwback to his birth name, Stephen Grover Cleveland. Most of his socializing took place at German beer halls, and it was said that he also knew the "inside of dozens of saloons." A perfect evening for Cleveland was playing poker or pinochle or the popular card game euchre with the boys. Everything about saloons he found irresistible: the lusty male camaraderie, the thick fog of cigar smoke, and the crunch of sawdust under his boot. His memory held a library of jovial drinking songs. A favorite was, "There's a hole in the bottom of the sea."

In this atmosphere of swaggering spirits and alcohol, brawls were inevitable. After one genial evening at a saloon, Cleveland was heading home when he got into an argument over Democratic Party politics with one of his drinking companions, Mike Falvey. When Falvey called Cleveland a liar, the future president squared off against the Irishman. Falvey raised his fists, but Cleveland landed the first punch. Then they went at it hammer and tongs. The fight spilled down Seneca Street, with Cleveland and Falvey raining blows on each other, and they did not call it quits until they reached Swan Street. At that point, the breathless brawlers had had enough. They dusted off their hats, shook hands, and everyone adjoined to the nearest saloon, Gillick's, whereupon the armistice was sealed with drinks to everybody's health.

Cleveland usually took his meals at local saloons. A scruffy place called the Shades, at Main and Swan, was a favorite watering hole. It had no bar, no chairs, and not even a bartender. You stood as you ate and drew your own liquor. There were clean glasses on one table and linen and silverware on another, and the place was run on the honor code. You left money in a pot on a counter in the center of the tavern and made your own change. The absentee bar owner claimed that not one of his patrons had ever cheated him. Another bar, Boas's, had better accommodations, but not by much; it had five chairs, but the proprietor discouraged his customers from sitting on them.

"Boas used to say he preferred to have his patrons take one drink and then take a walk," said John C. Level, who owned a livery stable that served as a local hub for political gossip.

There came a time when Cleveland tried to cut back on his drinking and pub crawling, and when he found himself missing the hand-rolled cigars available at his favorite German beer garden, he had the owner send a box of them to his room. Cleveland lit one up. As always, he positioned it on the left side of his mouth—the chewing side. He inhaled deeply, then let the smoke linger in his lungs. But something was strangely bland about the cigar. Nothing seemed different about the tobacco— it still had that premium woodsy aroma, but it just didn't taste the same. He lit another, and another, and eventually, after he had gone through the entire box, the problem finally dawned on him. Everything about the cigar was the same; it was the ambiance of the beer garden that was missing. Cleveland went back to drinking. There were times, he later had to admit, when he got so wasted he was forced to "lose a day."

A SECRET LIFE

After the Civil War, when Grover Cleveland was in his late twenties, something of a social revolution began to take hold. It was the dawning of the Age of the Bachelor. Young men were moving to boomtowns like Buffalo and finding solidarity and companionship with other unmarried young men. In some cities, bachelors constituted as much as 50 percent of the male population between twenty-five and thirty-five years old. At that time, toward the end of the 1860s, the trend was a shocking departure from the social order, and bachelors like Grover Cleveland came to be regarded as outcasts. Far from being seen as the male counterpart of the lonely spinster, an object of pity, almost every portrayal of bachelors in popular culture was negative. They were pariahs, indifferent to the bonds of holy matrimony, dangerous, and possibly even degenerate.

During this period of Cleveland's life, there is no record of his having pursued women or ever having a serious relationship. One must reach back to Valentine's Day 1856, when he was nineteen, for evidence of a budding romance. On that day, in the morning mail, he received a charming little card of embossed lace from a lady admirer. It was apparently unexpected, but common courtesy required Cleveland to reciprocate, so he had to scramble to send her his valentine before the end of the day. It was a hectic day for him because he had sent a flirty little verse to another young lady that began, "How doth the little busy B," but at least he was certain that one of his two cards would "hit the mark." Yet, whatever interest he might have had in women and the rituals of courtship, it seemed to have faded as time went on. The physical presence of women seemed to make him uneasy, possibly because he had little tolerance for small talk and was lacking in the social graces. There was also misogyny in his way of thinking, as is later revealed. As to the inevitable question of Cleveland's sexuality, there is no evidence that he was a suppressed homosexual. There is, nevertheless, little doubt that he preferred the company of men.

Every year, the premier society ball of the season was held at the Genesee Hotel for the Charity Organization Society of Buffalo. Against his better judgment, Cleveland allowed his friends to twist his arm to attend; it may well have marked the "end as well as the beginning" of his high-society social life.

The night of the ball, Cleveland seemed to be in fine spirits. Many of the eligible young bachelors in attendance had taken dance lessons at the Cobleigh Dancing Academy in the polka and other popular formal dances, like the lancer. If you didn't know the moves, the best advice was to steer clear of the floor.

Cleveland, who had never had a dance lesson in his life, found his friend the lawyer George Sicard and said jovially, "Let's dance the step-over."

"Who'll be your pard?" Sicard asked uncertainly.

Proceeding with confidence, Cleveland stepped forward and found a willing young lady to be his dancing partner. Apparently, his moves were pitiful. A leading Buffalo socialite with a gift for mockery even wrote a verse about the spectacle of observing Grover Cleveland on the dance floor. It was the last time he attended the ball.

At least Cleveland could still enjoy the easy congeniality of his male friends. He found true contentment with his band of bachelor brothers.

Observing all this with a disapproving eye was his Aunt Margaret, Uncle Lewis's wife. Her nephew had stopped attending church and was associating himself with some very "queer people," she remarked. (At that time, *queer* meant "odd," not "homosexual," just as *gay* would have meant "carefree.") Margaret found everything about her nephew's personal life offensive. From her home in Holland Patent, Ann Cleveland was distressed to hear these reports of her son, the incorrigible bachelor. She herself sometimes found his personality inflexible, and she also noted with "pain" that of all her nine children, Grover alone was capable of being rude.

Cleveland and his law partner, Vanderpoel, rented out space at the old post office at Seneca and Washington streets and hung up their shingle. John C. Level, the livery owner, gave the firm its first $100 retainer.

"They needed it too," Level said. Level was one of those local political players who were considered a "good man to know." He was in and out politics, at various times serving as chief of detectives, United States marshal, and Overseer of the Poor. But mostly he ran the livery stable.

Those early days were a struggle. Cleveland's former boss, Dennis Bowen, tried to throw a little business his way and arranged for him to handle the estate sale of a house owned by a man suffering from a mental disorder—a "lunatic" in Cleveland's estimation. The work netted Cleveland a $15 referee's fee, but when the payment was late, Cleveland had to write Bowen to expedite it, saying, "I am a trifle hard up today."

He detested taking on criminal cases. It was said that he would never accept a retainer from a client he knew to be guilty—and he absolutely refused to defend murderers. Cleveland preferred civil litigation and negotiating settlements. A lawsuit was like a gun, he once said—a dangerous instrument that could go either way without "lock, stock or barrel." When a wealthy grain dealer sued the editor of the *Buffalo Commercial Advertiser* newspaper for libel, Cleveland took the case and won. He had an impressive aptitude for crystallizing legal issues and articulating the law in a common-sense style that jurors found genuine and believable. It was said that he could work through the night, take a bath at dawn, wake himself up with a pot of hot coffee, and make a first-rate presentation in court.

Cleveland was still sending his mother and sisters whatever spare change he could when he finally scrounged up the $25 to repay Ingham Townsend, his kindly benefactor from Oneida County who had loaned him funds when he was a teenager to set out for the west. It may have taken twelve years, but it was a matter a pride for Cleveland to take care of the debt, with interest. He wrote Townsend a letter.

My Dear Mr. Townsend:

I am now in a condition to pay my note which you hold given for money borrowed some years ago. I suppose I might have paid it long before. But I never thought you were in need of it, and I had other purposes for my money. . . . The loan you made me was my start in life, and I shall always preserve the note as an interesting reminder of your kindness.

Yours respectfully,

Grover Cleveland

Cleveland had moved out of the Southern Hotel and was now living in a boardinghouse at 47 Niagara Street. It had once been the mansion of William G. Fargo, cofounder of the great stagecoach and banking concern Wells Fargo & Company. Fargo had built the ornate brick Italianate mansion in 1851, and it was now a boardinghouse, run by a widow, Alison B. Ganson, with the help of her comely daughter Alice. If Cleveland was interested in Alice Ganson, he failed to pursue the young lady, and Alice ended up marrying another boarder. Cleveland tried to make the room his own in small ways; above his bed he hung a framed proverb from Deuteronomy that his mother had given him for comfort: "As thy days are, so shall thy strength be."

Mrs. Ganson ran a tight ship. No cooking was permitted in the rooms. Dinner was served at a certain hour in the formal dining room downstairs. All the boarders had to adjust their eating habits to the schedule of the landlady. As a prominent lawyer in town, Cleveland held an honored position at the head of the long common table. To his left sat Edward Hawley, a well-liked insurance salesman and volunteer fireman. After dinner, Cleveland and the other bachelors gathered in the drawing room to smoke cigars—just about every man smoked. There in the wood-paneled parlor they relaxed and engaged in casual conversation about politics or current events. In other words, all the comforts of home without the wife.

By 1870, when Grover Cleveland was thirty-three, there was talk of him running for Congress, but when Erie County Democrats held their convention in late September, party elders, put off by Cleveland's identification with saloons and what was called the "livery-stable set," steered the congressional nomination to a retired railroad executive, David Williams. Cleveland was awarded a consolation prize: the nomination for Erie County sheriff, and he surprised everyone by accepting. Sheriffs were responsible for enforcing the local gaming and liquor laws—vices Cleveland was certainly acquainted with, so in that regard, he was eminently qualified. But his heart did not seem to be in the race, and he ran a feeble campaign. Part of the problem was his opponent, the war hero John Weber. At age nineteen, Weber had enlisted as a private in the Civil War. By war's end, he had attained the rank of colonel, serving with the Eighty-ninth Colored Infantry. Perhaps deep inside Cleveland considered Weber the more deserving candidate, because he made just five campaign speeches. But Cleveland had the backing of party loyalists and the *Buffalo Daily Courier*, which called him the "most popular man in the Democratic Party of the county. . . . so true a gentleman, so generous, modest, and lovable a man, that we have never heard of anybody's envying him." Cleveland could not have asked for a heartier endorsement had he paid for a full-page ad himself.

Electioneering in those days required candidates to solicit votes where men congregated in packs. That meant saloons. Cleveland was at a saloon in the twelfth ward when he declared an open bar, on his tab.

"Come on up, boys, have a drink with the next sheriff. My name is Cleveland, and I want you all to vote for me."

Just as he said this, a gentleman strolled into the saloon. Cleveland saw him and said, "Come on up, little fellow, have a drink with me."

The man came over to Cleveland. "Who did you say you were?"

"I am Grover Cleveland."

"I am the other fellow." It was Cleveland's opponent, John Weber. The two candidates had never met before.

Cleveland burst into laughter and said, "Well, let's have a drink together."

The year 1870 was a Democratic year in New York. When the votes were tabulated, Cleveland squeaked past Weber by just 303; but although he won, he came in last among the Democrats running for office in Erie County. Once again, the base of his popular support had come from the German American wards. They had taken to Grover Cleveland as if he were one of their own.

Cleveland took office on New Year's Eve 1871. His predecessor had invited all his friends over for a big send-off, and Cleveland took the oath of office in an atmosphere of revelry and high spirits—liquor and cigars for everyone. He had his work cut out for him; Buffalo, it was said, had more saloons and taverns per head than any other city in the world. It seemed there was a bar on every corner—more than six hundred saloons for a population of less than 150,000. Sailors, canal hands, and roustabouts working the city's ports roamed the tenderloin district looking for a good time. Brothels operated in the open seven days a week. Buffalo was a "sink of iniquity," with more "social eyesores" than any other city of its size in America.

The undersheriff in office when Cleveland took over was William L. G. Smith, a Democratic lawyer who had earned a national reputation as the author of *Life at the South, or "Uncle Tom's Cabin" as It Is*, a pro-slavery plantation novel published in 1852 as a "refutation" of Harriet Beecher Stowe's famous book.

In Smith's work, slaves were loyal and content and their masters benign. The villain was an abolitionist from the North who worms his way into the confidence of Tom the black slave and convinces him to escape to Canada. Tom realizes the error of his ways and returns to "good Old Virginia." Somehow Cleveland was able to look beyond Smith's politics and see an able, if fussy, administrator who could keep the sheriff's office running like an efficient machine. "You could set your watch by the time he arrived and departed from the office," went one depiction of Smith—"precise in every word and action." So exacting were his daily routines that it was said Smith would never deviate from the number of steps it took him to get from his house to the office. It was the same every day—"without clipping off an inch."

Cleveland reappointed Smith, and it may have been a shrewd thing too, because Cleveland seemed to have very little interest in the routine duties of the sheriff. He delegated most of the day-to-day administration to the under-sheriff; meanwhile, he played. Weather permitting, he would go hunting or fishing with a buddy, usually Oscar Folsom, a young lawyer he came to feel as close to as a brother. If Folsom was busy, Cleveland rounded up Louis Goetz, owner of a Buffalo pub known as the Dutchman's. Goetz's saloon was located behind City Hall, at 194 Pearl Street, in the heart of the county office buildings and across the street from Democratic Party headquarters. The geography made the Dutchman's a favorite hangout for Democrats.

Goetz served steak at the saloon, but the specialty of the house was bluefish when it was in season, sent directly from the Fulton Fish Market in New York City. Sometimes, after Cleveland and

Goetz went fishing, they would return to the saloon, and Cleveland's catch would be served for dinner.

Goetz worshipped the new sheriff and called him what sounded like "Grofer" in his German accent. He even hung a full-length portrait of Cleveland in the saloon, directly above the grill. During Cleveland's tenure the Dutchman's became a kind of annex of the Erie County Sheriff's Office. In the back room, Cleveland's cronies would gather for ale and song, and Cleveland himself, using a stein as a baton, would lead the chorus. In his rich baritone, he would begin, "There's a hole . . ."

"There's a hole," the choir answered.

"There's a hole," sang Cleveland.

"There's a hole," responded the choir.

"There's a hole in the bottom of the sea," went Cleveland.

They could go on for hours like this. And the song would not end until everyone had emptied their steins.

The legal closing hour in Buffalo was 1:00 AM, but rank had its privileges, and for Cleveland, Goetz's would remain open until the wee hours. Soon, so would the other saloons where Sheriff Cleveland took his ale. He was playing cards at Blume's saloon with Oscar Folsom and two other lawyers when the proprietor pointed to the clock. It was two in the morning.

"Now, boys," Blume said, "take one more drink—on the house. I have got to close up, or the police'll be after me."

Cleveland, as the chief law enforcement officer in Erie County, had a good laugh over that one. Then he raised his mug and started singing—what else!—"There's a hole in the bottom of the sea." They had the next round on the house, and several more after that.

Sometimes, Louis Goetz failed to appreciate Cleveland's brand of humor. One time, around midnight, Cleveland dropped by the Dutchman's and found Goetz asleep. No one else was there. It was almost too good to be true. First, Cleveland set the clock ahead two full hours. Next, he found two Buffalo cops on patrol outside the saloon and asked them to play along. Then Cleveland returned to the Dutchman's, woke Goetz up, and ordered a drink. A few minutes later, in walked the cops. Pointing to the clock, they informed Goetz that he was under arrest for illegally keeping his bar open past closing hours. Goetz turned to his friend.

"Grofer," he said and pleaded with the sheriff to come to his rescue.

Cleveland shook his head. "Can't do it, Louis. Look at the clock. The officers are doing their duty."

Only when Goetz's simmering temper came to a boil did Cleveland let him in on the practical joke.

The frat-boy atmosphere of the sheriff's department took a solemn turn when Cleveland had to hang a man—Erie County's first public execution of a prisoner in six years. The crime was matricide.

Patrick Morrissey was born in County Tipperary in Ireland. His parents took him to America, and they settled in Buffalo. As a youngster, Morrissey got into a few scrapes; and when he was eleven, he was sentenced to six months in the Western House of Refuge, the first prison in the United States built for juvenile delinquents. When he was fourteen, he ran away from home and signed on to a schooner as a roustabout. First he sailed the Great Lakes, and then the world—Brazil, Liverpool, the West

Indies, Amsterdam, Sicily, St. Petersburg, and many other ports of call. Aboard the clipper *George Peabody*, he made a voyage that took 122 days—from New York to San Francisco, around Cape Horn—the sailors' graveyard. In June 1872, back in Buffalo on one of his occasional visits home, he went to see his mother.

Patrick Morrissey was short, about five foot four, with wavy chestnut hair and light blue eyes. Ann Morrissey, fifty-five years old, ran a waterfront saloon and boardinghouse at No. 7 Pratt's Dock, near the Erie Canal. She was a hard woman and a heavy drinker, with a "most savage and ungovernable temper." Mrs. Morrissey was cutting cold meat with a sharp carving knife, preparing dinner for her boarders and saloon patrons, when her wayward son came in drunk. He demanded money from her. Harsh words were exchanged; she called him a bastard and ordered him to leave, threatening to send for the police if he did not get out immediately. Enraged, he threw her to the floor. "You had better kill your mother and be done with it," she spat.

Morrissey wrestled the knife from his mother's hand and plunged the seven-inch blade into her left breast. Five minutes later, she was dead. Her final word was "Oh!" as her son stabbed her.

Morrissey made no attempt to escape. When the police arrived, they found him slumped over in a chair. He never denied the killing, only that it was not premeditated. He told police he would "give the heart out of his body" if he could only bring his mother back to life.

Justice moved swiftly in those days. The trial was held three weeks later. Testimony lasted a single day. The verdict, rendered on July 10, 1872, was guilty. Sentencing was immediate. The judge told Morrissey he was to be "hanged by the neck until you are dead" on September 6. Morrissey's lawyers appealed for a new trial on grounds that a member of the jury had fallen asleep during important testimony and that another juror was over the age of sixty. The appeal was denied, and when the governor of New York, John Hoffman, refused to grant a respite, Morrissey's fate was sealed.

The Morrissey saga gripped the city. An immigrant son stabbing to death the mother who bore him—it had all the elements of a Greek tragedy, by way of Buffalo. The buildup to Morrissey's date of execution was covered in every vivid detail. It was Grover Cleveland's responsibility as sheriff of Erie County to carry out the hanging. He found it so detestable a responsibility he actually considered resigning. How he resolved his conflicted state said much about him as a man.

Grover journeyed to Holland Patent to talk things over with his mother, now sixty-six years old, and it felt good to be home. Ann Cleveland was still living in the parsonage of her late husband's church. The bighearted parishioners had pulled together after Reverend Cleveland's death in 1853 and told the widow that she could remain in the house indefinitely, rent free.

Grover never attended church in Buffalo, but he made an effort to accompany his mother to services whenever he stayed in Holland Patent. Mrs. Cleveland considered everything there was to know about the Patrick Morrissey case. As a good Christian, she told Grover, she could not countenance the execution of a man, even someone who had murdered his own mother. She advised her son to delegate the hanging to a subordinate.

But this was one time when Grover had to disagree with his mother.

Even though the law gave Cleveland the authority to appoint a surrogate in his place as executioner, for a $10 fee, he returned to Buffalo determined to carry out his duty himself. He ordered the gallows to be constructed in the courtyard of the county jail, which took only an afternoon. On the night before the hanging, Morrissey read the Bible, prayed, and fell into a fitful sleep at one in the morning on September 6. He awakened four hours later and got dressed. At 9:00 AM, onlookers started to gather for the hanging. Some parents brought their children. But a force of twenty-five police officers arrived and sent everyone home. To his credit, Cleveland had done everything he could to make sure the hanging did not degenerate into a public spectacle.

Morrissey's three sisters and a brother-in-law had pooled their funds to buy a beautiful black walnut coffin. It was delivered to the jail. Eerily, there was already a silver plate on the coffin's lid with the following inscription:

Patrick Morrissey
Died Sept. 6, 1872
Aged 28 Years

That morning, Cleveland appeared grim, even despondent—"not his old self." He looked as if he had not slept all night. For ten weeks, since Ann Morrissey's murder, he had known this day was coming. A deputy, Richard Harris, pulled Cleveland aside and informed him that instead of breakfast that morning, he had drunk several glasses of brandy. Slurring his words, he said he was volunteering to take Cleveland's place and send the condemned man to eternity. The task was something that he could perform without having it haunt him for the rest of his life, Harris said.

"That job's up to me, Mr. Sheriff," Harris insisted.

Cleveland, with a cluster of deputies surrounding him, listened, met Harris's eyes, and shook his head: "No, I have to do it myself. I am the sheriff."

At 11:43 AM, Morrissey was taken from his cell and escorted down the corridor toward the yard. On his way, he bid farewell to the other prisoners; and when he reached the cell of John Gaffney, he stopped and begged the deputies to let him embrace his friend. They shared an exceptional connection; in just twenty-one days, Gaffney was to be hanged for shooting a gambler to death during a game of draw poker. It was Morrissey's last request. Everyone looked at Undersheriff Smith for guidance. He silently nodded his consent. Gaffney's cell door was opened, and he stepped out. The two condemned men embraced and sobbed, kissing as they held each other until they were pulled apart.

The execution was set for noon. At 11:57 AM, Cleveland led Morrissey into the yard, where sixty witnesses, appointed by Cleveland, were waiting. The noose was already around the prisoner's neck. A Catholic priest, Father Malloy, stood at Morrissey's side and chanted the death service: "Even though I walk in the valley of death, I shall fear no evil . . ." Cleveland took his place at the foot of the gallows, his hand resting on the lever that would unbolt the trapdoor. When Morrissey was asked whether he had any last words, Father Malloy handed him a folded sheet of paper. Morrissey opened it and read.

"I have no words but these to say. I am about to die on this scaffold, and God above knows how guilty I am. I hope my sad end will be a warning to all young men and determine them to keep away from liquor, to abandon all evil associations, and attend to their religious duties." It certainly sounded as if a priest had written it. Then Morrissey whispered, "I am ready to go now. Good-bye. God bless you all."

A deputy pinioned Morrissey's hands and feet. At 12:09 PM, a black shroud was drawn over the prisoner's eyes. One minute later, the signal was given. The future president of the United States pressed the lever, which pulled out the iron pin on which the trap rested. Morrissey fell through the trapdoor. His neck broke, and his body hung there, dangling in the breeze. He died without a struggle.

Some of the witnesses turned away from the ghastly sight; others looked on in morbid fascination. The gallows had been constructed, to Cleveland's specifications, in such a way that the sheriff would not have to see the prisoner hanged. At 12:13 PM, a doctor came forward and found no pulse on the prisoner. Morrissey was officially pronounced dead at 12:17 PM. His body remained hanging for a total of twenty-five minutes. It was then cut down and placed in the coffin.

Cleveland found the entire experience "grievously distasteful," and was in utter anguish. And the next execution was just three weeks away.

Fred and Cecil, the Cleveland brothers who had served with distinction in the Civil War, were now in the hotel business together. Fred owned Fairfield House, a summer resort in Connecticut. He, like Grover, was strong-willed. He had one policy at Fairfield House that was strictly enforced, no exceptions. Employees were forbidden from accepting tips. When Fred discovered that a waiter had pocketed a Christmas gift from an appreciative woman guest, he immediately had him fired.

"I will not have those in my house who are unable or unwilling to fee the servants put to any disadvantage," Fred thundered. (Tips were called fees in those days.)

Only after the guest begged Fred to relent did he grudgingly take the waiter back—but only on the condition that he refund the money.

In 1872, Fred purchased from the British colonial government the lease for the Royal Victoria Hotel, the finest hotel in the Bahamas. During the Civil War, the Royal Victoria had been a haunt of Confederate spies and smugglers and had quite the reputation as a place for tropical bacchanals and skullduggery. The Blockade Runners' Ball, a notorious party honoring smugglers, was once held there, and some 350 magnums of champagne were consumed. Now, in these days of peace, wealthy American tourists were sailing to the Bahamas and staying at the Royal Victoria Hotel for the winter. The hotel was said to be the most splendid ever to be built in the tropics, and Grover Cleveland's brother was the new manager and leaseholder. Fred invited his brother Cecil to go with him and help him open the hotel for the season, and Cecil, who had been struggling to find his niche in business, jumped at the opportunity.

On their way to New York City to link up with the steamship that would take them to the Bahamas, Fred had an ominous premonition.

"I do not know how it is, but I have an impression that I cannot get rid of, that this will be my last voyage," he said.

Accompanying the Cleveland brothers was a large contingent of staff they had hired to work at the Royal Victoria. On a Friday morning in October, everyone boarded the steamship *Missouri*—in all, ninety-eight passengers. Most were traveling to Havana, but others, like Fred and Cecil and their staff, were disembarking at Nassau in the Bahamas.

From day one, there were problems: Some boiler malfunction made the ship start and stop, slowing down the voyage; and the winds from the north were light before they picked up on the third day. There was a heavy sea. Four days out, on October 22, 1872, as Fred and Cecil and the other passengers were eating breakfast, the call "Fire!" rang out. Crewmen filled buckets with water and headed for the engine room. In those early moments, everything seemed under control.

"It is nothing but a box of matches, and all is out," the chief steward assured the passengers.

But just as he said this, flames were seen bursting out of the engine room. Pandemonium followed. Everyone ran to the main deck, and the captain ordered all engines stopped and the lifeboats lowered. The conduct of the crew was disorganized and shamefully inept. The blaze spread across the ship, creating an impassable barrier of flames between bow and stern. The lifeboats were so carelessly lowered over the side one actually fell into the ocean, bottom up. As another lifeboat was lowered on the port side, passengers saw that only nine crewmen were occupying it; they said the boat "belonged to them." Still another lifeboat, afloat under the command of the ship's assistant engineer, John Freaney, immediately took on water and began to sink. Freaney rowed to a lifeboat commanded by crewman James Culmer and demanded that his passengers be transferred to Culmer's more seaworthy vessel. Culmer refused, saying he had enough on board.

"Your boat could hold more," Freaney called out. Culmer responded by throwing a bucket to Freaney and leaving him and his passengers to their fate. Everyone aboard started bailing. They had the bucket and four oars.

What followed was utter hell. In the lifeboat they were sitting in, water was waist deep, and there was nothing to eat or drink. It was like this for four unbearable days. A crewman died of thirst; two others, suffering from dehydration and hypothermia, went "crazy" and jumped overboard, never to be seen again. Another man, in a state of delirium, tossed the bailing bucket overboard. Now they were left with nothing but two hats to bail with. On the fifth day, they made a sail out of their life preservers. At last, on the eighth day, they sighted land: Abaco, the northernmost island in the Bahamas archipelago. In a state of exhaustion, they landed on the beach and came upon a spring of fresh water and a deserted house. They discovered a few tomatoes that they boiled in a pot. This was their first taste of food since the *Missouri* had gone down. On the tenth day, they were about to give up and surrender to death when they saw a sloop cruising off the island. Freaney hoisted his clothes on the oar and signaled. They were rescued—Freaney and the three other crewmen who were left alive.

The disaster at sea was huge news in America. In total, sixty-six souls had been lost. When the first telegrams reporting the calamity reached Buffalo, Grover Cleveland rushed to Holland Patent to comfort his mother. He arrived at a scene of hopeless misery. Five of his siblings were there too—his brother Reverend William Cleveland and his sisters Mary, Louise, Susan, and Rose. Only the eldest, Anna, the missionary in Ceylon, was unaware of the family misfortune. All of Holland Patent was in mourning. A woman from the village named Mary, who had been hired by Fred and Cecil to work at the Royal Victoria Hotel, had also been on board the *Missouri*. Like the Cleveland brothers, she too was unaccounted for.

Ann Cleveland was a beloved figure in the village – an "estimable lady," in the words of the *Utica Morning Herald*. Fred and Cecil were also popular and respected, not only for their wartime service to the nation but also for their devotion to their mother. Just the past summer, they had spent several weeks with Mrs. Cleveland, keeping the elderly widow company. For three weeks, Grover and the others waited for word of them, praying for a miracle.

Then, on November 21, the steamship *Morro Castle* arrived in New York City. It had left Nassau four days earlier and carried fifteen *Missouri* survivors. These included "a servant of Mr. Cleveland, the lessee of the R. V. Hotel, who was on board the *Missouri* at the time of her loss," *The New York Times* reported. Grover must have read the newspaper report with cold fury. The article quoted crewmen as saying the *Missouri* had been "hastily prepared" for the voyage and that the boilers in the engine room had been improperly fitted with insulation. That could explain the cause of the fire: Heat from the boiler would likely have ignited the ship's woodwork.

"The responsibility for this catastrophe indisputably rests on those who sent the *Missouri* to sea in the condition she was in," the *Times* reported.

It sounded like pure negligence on the part of the ship's captain and the owner, the Atlantic Mail Steamship Company.

It was distressing beyond words for the Cleveland family to read the account of suffering and panic on board. Mrs. Cleveland was said to be in a state of despair—a "stricken mother in her untold, unfathomable grief." Perhaps the only solace for Grover and his family was the touching depiction of Cecil's and Fred's final moments. In the chaos and panic on board the *Missouri*, with the ship ablaze, Cecil and Fred were observed on deck assisting the terror-stricken passengers as the lifeboats were being lowered. "When the boats were filled, there was no room for them, and together they went down." The Cleveland brothers died heroes.

3

MARIA

MARIA HALPIN COULD see that she was losing her husband. His symptoms were chillingly recognizable to any woman of the 19th century: flushed cheeks, pale skin, fever, and swollen red eyes sensitive to bright light. Most of all, there was the bloody cough. He had tuberculosis. In Maria's time, it was called consumption. With a mortality rate approaching 80 percent, more often than not, it was a death sentence.

Consumption was a relentless fading-away of the patient. Perhaps because so many famous artists and poets died from it in the prime of their lives, in Maria's time, the disease was romanticized; suffering from consumption had a hauntingly transcendent aura about it. The great composer Chopin died of tuberculosis at age thirty-nine, and the philosopher Henry David Thoreau succumbed at age forty-four. Emily Brontë, the author of *Wuthering Heights*, was dead at age thirty from consumption; her sister Charlotte Brontë followed her to the grave six years later, also from tuberculosis. In the final throes of the disease, women were said to be enchantingly alluring and men brilliantly lucid.

Maria found nothing romantic about consumption. Frederick Halpin was clearly dying of it, and he was dying slowly. When her husband succumbed, in 1870, Maria was thirty years old. Her son Freddie was seven, and her daughter Ada just five.

The Halpin family did what they could. For a time, Maria moved in with her in-laws, in Jersey City, New Jersey—never a perfect state of affairs for a young widow. The engraver Frederick Halpin was now seventy, and his wife, Elija, sixty-five. A widow like Maria was expected to remain in a period of deep mourning for a minimum of a year plus a day. Two of the best-known widows of the era, Queen Victoria and Mary Todd Lincoln, made a public spectacle of their deep mourning that went on for the rest of their lives. Of course Maria Halpin did not go to that extreme, but she did wear black, including a black crepe veil, and she followed the rituals and etiquette that were laid out in *Godey's Lady's Book*, the premier women's magazine of the Gilded Age.

With two children to feed, Maria found it necessary to look for a job. A woman working outside the home was becoming progressively widespread, mainly because the Civil War produced thousands of widows who were forced to support themselves and their children for the first time.

Maria was hired by A. T. Stewart & Co. to work as a saleslady in the company's flagship department store, the Iron Palace, on Broadway and 9th Street in New York City. Alexander Turney Stewart was an innovative Irish-born entrepreneur who had started in business as a bag boy. Later, assisted by a $5,000 inheritance from his grandfather, he became a wealthy merchant and, in 1862, opened the Iron Palace.

Stewart focused on pleasing the lady customer of the carriage-trade class. His formula for building a successful retail store and encouraging repeat business was paying attention to the smallest details, offering his customers great deals, and connecting with them on a personal level. Hiring the right saleswomen was fundamental, and Maria, with a background in dressmaking and her natural gifts as a conversationalist, was eminently qualified. That she also spoke fluent French made her eminently qualified and then some.

When Maria walked into the Iron Palace for the first time, the commotion she encountered jolted her. Two thousand men and women were employed there. It was Alexander Stewart's showcase, the largest department store in the world, with eight floors of specialty shops—for silks, dresses, carpets, toys, furs, bedding, carpets, glass, china, even sports—nineteen departments in all. Unlike the brick or thick masonry of competing stores, the Iron Palace had a cast-iron façade. The innovative architecture allowed Stewart to open up the store to passersby with huge plate-glass windows, which also flooded the interior with natural light. Music came from an organ while the world's first fashion models posed in the latest designs from Europe. It made going to Stewart's an event.

Less than a year had passed when Maria was faced with what must have been the hardest choice of her life.

It so happened that a dry-goods store was opening in Buffalo, and through a Halpin family friend who was cofinancing the new venture, Maria was offered a sales position. Getting in on the ground floor of a good business was a once-in-a-lifetime prospect, a rare entrepreneurial opportunity for a woman in the 19th century. But it meant quitting her job at the Iron Palace, leaving her in-laws, and moving to another city.

In 1871, Maria found herself on the train to Buffalo with but one of her children—little Freddie. She'd left her daughter behind with the Halpins in Jersey City, thinking that Ada would be happier staying with her grandparents until things got settled. The reality was that without a family support structure in place in Buffalo, Maria would have found it impossible to work full-time and take care of two little ones. Her quandary was not unlike that of any 21st-century woman struggling with the challenges posed by single motherhood.

Maria and Freddie arrived in Buffalo like all newcomers to a strange city, a little awed and probably a touch terrified. The first order of business was finding a place to live. One of the best boardinghouses in the city was run by Mrs. J. C. Randall, at 39 Swan Street. Mark Twain, under his birth name, Samuel Clemens, had lived there in 1869 when he served as an editor of the *Buffalo Express* newspaper, whose office was conveniently located down the street at 14 East Swan. Maria found Mrs. Randall's rooming house to be clean and respectable, and a chief benefit was the neighborhood. Next door stood the magnificent St. John's Episcopal Church, the third oldest Episcopal congregation in Buffalo, cofounded by the businessman William Fargo. Maria joined the St. John's community and was soon mingling with the finest and most prominent families in the city's Protestant establishment.

Maria struck anyone who encountered her in 1871 as someone special. One of her neighbors, Mrs. William Baker, took note of her "remarkable beauty and rare accomplishments," adding that she was, "beyond suspicion." Maria's knowledge of French gave her an exotic air of sophistication that certain men in Buffalo apparently found enticing. Later, her fluency in the language would come back to haunt her in the court of public opinion.

Of those early days in Buffalo Maria would later say that her personal character was "pure and spotless." Mrs. Baker was awed by Maria's special gifts. She could talk to the most educated man or woman in Buffalo and come across as clever, but genuine. She was a born saleswoman. Pushed to say something provocative about her, Mrs. Baker finally acknowledged that her friend was deficient in one quarter—she was a "bad housekeeper."

When Maria came to live in Buffalo, even though her period of deep mourning for her husband, with its rigid requirements, had passed, she was still wearing widow's black. She now entered the next stipulated stage of widowhood—half mourning; that meant she was no longer wearing a veil. Nor was she limited to wearing all black; patterned fabrics and dark colors such as gray, mauve, violet, and lavender were permissible, as long as black was included.

In the early 1870s when Maria moved to Buffalo, it was a city of contrasts—flourishing but vulnerable, thriving yet paradoxically fighting for survival.

Canal Street, running parallel to the Erie Canal, was known as the "wickedest street in America," with a reputation for vice and debauchery unmatched in America. Across the oceans, in the waterfront saloons of far-flung ports of call, when Buffalo came up in conversation, the question was always the same: "Is it true what they say about Canal Street?" Even the good citizens of Buffalo who brimmed with civic pride took to calling Canal Street "the Infected District."

There were ninety-three saloons on Canal Street alone, serving their rotgut liquor, and 60 percent of the buildings housed brothels. A certain social pecking order defined the prostitutes: Women working Canal Street regarded themselves as upmarket "ladies of the evening," a cut above those who walked the towpath alongside the Erie Canal—these ladies were deemed to be "dirty whores." Buffalo's prostitutes wore Mother Hubbard dresses—which, with their long sleeves and high neck, covered as much skin as possible—with nothing underneath. The garment had once symbolized girlish innocence; now a woman wearing a Mother Hubbard dress on Canal Street was immediately identified as a hooker.

Life was cheap on Buffalo's waterfront. It was so dangerous that no cop dared patrol it alone; police went out in squads of three—one up front and two covering his back. Street brawls were constant. Great Lakes sailors spoiling for a fight were hostile to the "canawlers" who plied the Erie Canal, and vice versa. One sea captain compared Canal Street to the violent mining towns of the Wild West, only worse.

"Bring out your dead," came the call each morning as death carts went up and down the waterfront collecting the departed. Bodies would be loaded onto the wheelbarrows and lugged to Buffalo police headquarters, where the remains would be thrown down a chute, worn smooth from constant use.

The Erie County Jail, run by Sheriff Grover Cleveland, was reputed to be one of the harshest jails in America. Years later, when the writer Jack London was eighteen years old, down and out, and passing through Buffalo, he was jailed for vagrancy. The thirty days he served in the Erie County Jail left London a lifetime of painful memories.

On his first day in jail, young Jack London found his bunk alive with bedbugs, hundreds of them, so brazen that they were swarming over his cell in broad daylight. Dinner that night was a hunk of bread and soup—hot water and a "lonely drop of grease" floating on the surface. London, rather than eat the bread, chewed it into the consistency of putty and used it to cork the crevices between the bricks where the bedbugs teemed. He worked at it for several hours and would not quit until he'd plugged every cranny. He asked a guard how he could go about arranging for a lawyer; the guard burst out laughing. A decade before he found fame as the author of *The Call of the Wild*, Jack London saw things in that jail that he called "unbelievable and monstrous."

Vice found new expressions in Buffalo: The Only Theater at Canal and Commerce Streets was infamous for its exhibition of orgiastic sex. Prostitutes sat on the laps of the sailors who filled the concert hall every Sunday, and in full view of everyone, lifted their Mother Hubbards to expose a "bare posterior," and the men pumped away.

Crime was seasonal and was generally rooted in desperation rather than passion. Murder rates peaked in December, when the Erie Canal froze over and men were out of work; they were at their lowest in July, when everyone was busy and money flowed.

Disease was omnipresent. Cholera was the scourge of the age, and periodic epidemics of it hit Buffalo like the outbreak of a war. The first symptom appeared as diarrhea; it was followed within one to four hours by complete physical collapse. In the most severe cases, the patient would be dead by the end of the day. Cholera could afflict anyone, even the daughter of a former United States president. Mary Abigail Fillmore died of it at age twenty-two during the epidemic of 1854. Buffalo's doctors, like physicians everywhere, were at a loss as to what to do. They advised citizens to eat their vegetables, promoted cleanliness in the streets, and urged everyone to become more hygienic in their personal habits at home.

Buffalo's streets were filthy. At the rear of the horse stables on Erie Street, manure was piled forty feet high, alive with swarms of flies and mosquitoes and the movement of a million maggots feeding on it.

The Fourth of July was a day the city went a little crazy. The festivities would begin on the second and not end until the fifth. Revelers would get so drop-dead drunk they would have to be hauled by their feet into the back rooms of saloons and laid out side by side until they sobered up. And it wasn't just on the waterfront. During one July 4 fireworks celebration, a rocket hit the steeple at St. John's Episcopal Church, where Maria now worshipped, and set it ablaze. Fortunately, the loss was covered by insurance, and St. John's was rebuilt.

When Maria and her son settled in Buffalo, its population had more than doubled since Grover Cleveland had arrived as a teenager two decades earlier. It was the third largest city in the state, after New York City and Albany and, nationally, ranked below San Francisco, then the tenth largest city in America.

Buffalo simmered with tension. Protestants dominated the legal, medical, and business professions. Their newspaper of record was the *Commercial Advertiser*, which once conveyed concern about the city's immigrant poor, whether they could survive the harsh Buffalo winter to come, with the words, "What shall be done with these poor creatures," before condescendingly pointing out that after all, immigrants required plenty of help because their "reasoning and moral faculties are limited." The paternalism and arrogance of the ruling class was also communicated by that other mouthpiece of the Protestant establishment, the *Buffalo Express*, which disdainfully suggested that Catholics might want to consider spending less money on their churches, for if they did, perhaps they could manage to feed their hungry.

The Irish who were employed as unskilled laborers on the waterfront lived mainly in the first ward, on the city's south side, close to the terminus of the Erie Canal. Their voices were heard in the pages of the *Catholic Sentinel*, which proclaimed the Irish American's respect for law and order while noting that an empty stomach can sometimes drive reason away. German immigrants resided in small-framed houses on the east side, in the fifth, sixth, and seventh wards, where the principal language spoken was the mother tongue. These German Americans were the tradesmen of the city—shoemakers, tailors, blacksmiths, butchers, clock-makers, and bakers. Racially, Buffalo was strictly segregated: A small community of black people lived east of Main Street; there were two black churches, and prior to the Civil War, blacks were required to send their children to a special "African School."

Severe winter weather made Buffalo an uninviting place for many newcomers. In the summer, the daily struggle of life eased up. For relaxation, families attended church bazaars and cruised Lake Erie or took in the natural splendor of the 350-acre parkland designed by the great landscape architect Frederick Law Olmsted, fresh from his triumph of creating Central Park in New York City. Of course, there was also Niagara Falls, straddling the U.S.-Canadian border, and already a popular destination for honeymooners. There was no public library system, but the Young Men's Association maintained a library of twenty thousand volumes available to all.

Entrepreneurs were making fortunes. Jewett and Root's Stove Factory employed more than two hundred men, the Buffalo Iron and Nail Works manufactured fifteen thousand pounds of nails a day, and Ketchum's Mowing Machine produced the nation's first mechanical lawn mower.

Mansion Row along Delaware Avenue was the location of the city's most magnificent residences. There, shaded by towering elms and great stretches of lawns, lived the elite. At the top of the social pyramid stood Millard Fillmore. His gothic mansion at No. 52 was a residence so immense that upon his death, in 1874, it was combined with another mansion and converted into a hotel.

Buffalo was the preeminent inland port in America, a key hub for pioneers heading west, and, from the other direction, shipping wheat east to New York City and beyond, to the great capitals of Europe. In this regard, Buffalo was indispensable to national commerce. And yet, with all this trade, the city was vulnerable and stood on the razor's edge of obsolescence. Unforgiving winters meant frozen lakes and the end of marine traffic until the spring thaw. The Erie Canal—the source of the city's prosperity—was slow and inefficient when measured against the locomotive. Those with foresight were already aware that the city had a gun pointed at its heart.

In the beginning, Maria Halpin had a rough time of it. The new store that had brought her to Buffalo failed, and she now found herself looking for work. Main Street was the prime shopping district in the city, and one store in particular, Flint & Kent, drew most of the carriage-trade class; this is where Maria found her first real job in Buffalo. The store had been founded in 1832, selling wholesale dry goods at 188 Main Street. By 1871, it had moved to a more desirable location up the block at 261 Main Street.

With Maria's sales experience at the celebrated Iron Palace in New York City, Flint & Kent was a natural place of employment for her. The store sold only first-class merchandise that appealed to the well-to-do customer and was recognized for its ambiance of decorum and courteous hospitality. About thirty people worked there when Maria was hired. In no time, she came to realize that the store was a place where the city's elite came not just to shop but also to socialize.

The busiest time of day at Flint & Kent was the period called the "proper hours," between 11:00 AM and 1:00 PM. Any shopping before or after was considered vulgar. Gloves were a big sale items, along with hosiery, underwear, elegant plaids, damask napkins, and Irish poplin wraps in all the best makes. In those days, the business of ready-to-wear clothing, mass-produced in predetermined sizes, was still in its infancy. Most women made their clothes at home from patterns, which they copied from *Godey's Lady's Book*. Or a customer could buy fabric from a bolt and take it to her own dressmaker.

The founding partner, William Flint, lived on Mansion Row, at 600 Delaware Avenue, and was sixty-five when Maria was hired. Flint's background was unremarkable; he'd clerked in a little general store in New Hampshire and at age forty moved to Buffalo, where he achieved success as a merchant prince. Modest, and with a reputation for unimpeachable integrity, Flint was the perfect partner. He preferred a low profile, content to keep the books in the office and leave the glamorous sales operation to Henry M. Kent.

Kent also lived in a mansion on Delaware Avenue. Even in 1871, he was old-fashioned in business matters. He wanted to stick with what he knew: bolts, lace, and hose. Notions or knickknacks—the buttons, trims, embroidery, braids, and ornamentation so necessary in accessorizing clothing—were sold as incidental items at a small counter on the first floor. When a shrewd young store manager suggested expanding the line, Kent responded dismissively, "Send them to Barnum's." Barnum's was Flint & Kent's down-market competitor on Main Street.

Maria excelled at Flint & Kent. The customers in what was still a frontier town appreciated her big-city sophistication, and she was an intriguing fresh face—"beautiful, virtuous and intelligent." She had started in the collar-making department, but it was obvious that she was going places.

"I always felt that I had the confidence and esteem of my employers," Maria said of Messrs. Flint and Kent.

Through her work, Maria got to know many of Buffalo's leading citizens, one of whom was Emma Folsom, the pretty wife of the lawyer Oscar Folsom, Grover Cleveland's best friend. Maria's familiarity with Oscar Folsom would later become an issue in the scandal that marked her history. On this point, Maria was utterly certain: "I never spoke a word to that man in my life. I know his wife because she traded with me in Buffalo."

Because Maria worked in the men's department at Flint & Kent, Grover Cleveland may have first encountered her when she waited on him from behind the counter. Perhaps Emma Folsom, trying to make a match, spoke to him of this eye-catching young widow who spoke fluent French. Grover Cleveland was attracted to the tall and slender saleswoman, and Maria said of him, "He sought my acquaintance and obtained an introduction to me from a person in whom I had every confidence, and he paid me very marked attention."

Maria never divulged the identity of the person who made that formal introduction, but she said that Cleveland was "persistent" in his desire to meet her, which was not in his nature. As a widow and congregant of St. John's Episcopal Church, Maria made the necessary inquiries and determined that her suitor's character "so far as I then knew, was good, and his intensions I believed were as pure and honorable."

Grover Cleveland had one more onerous duty to perform before his term of office as sheriff was over, and that was the public execution of yet another prisoner.

Jack Gaffney was a hard case. He had coal-black hair and a mustache, very pale skin, and blue eyes. He stood five foot eight and had a well-built and slender physique. Gaffney grew up in the slums of Buffalo and ran with the Break-o'-day Johnnies, a notorious Irish street gang. His criminal record was shocking for its depth of wickedness. For no apparent reason, he had shot a woman in the hip as she sat at her window. He shot a minstrel singer on the street without the slightest provocation. He bashed in the skull of a saloonkeeper with a stone. He grabbed a silk hat off a stranger's head on Canal Street, for which crime at least the law came down on Gaffney; he was fined $10. As his first wife lay on her deathbed, she told him she was glad to be dying just to be rid of him.

Justice finally caught up with Gaffney when he turned twenty-seven. It was four in the morning, and he was playing draw cards at Sweeney's saloon, a dive on Canal Street near the waterfront, in the heart of the "vilest of the vile sections of the city." He was in a foul mood, down $8, all the money he had, when he pulled out a pistol and shot a sailor named Patrick Fahey in the head. No one mourned for Fahey, who, it was said, was a "loafer, vagrant, thief" and apparently preferred to earn a living in any manner other than honest labor. In any event, Gaffney, while sticking to his story that he had had nothing to do with the murder, said of Fahey: "Dead or alive, he's a son of a bitch." The appeals judge really let Gaffney have it when the sentencing was affirmed.

"John Gaffney, stand up. There is blood on your hands, and there is blood upon your soul, and we do pray you go to the only source by which you can be purged." His hanging was set for September 27, 1872.

Gaffney pulled every trick in the swindler's handbook to delay his day of reckoning. Then, during a jailhouse visit, his brother-in-law said, "Why, Gaffney, you look as if you was crazy, and I believe you are crazy." It gave Gaffney an idea. He went to sleep, and when he woke up, he complained about hearing "bees in my head." That morning and for days thereafter, his ravings and profanities startled even the hardened deputies working at the Erie County Jail. No one believed for a minute that Gaffney was really insane, but Sheriff Cleveland, in concurrence with the county judge, appointed a twelve-man jury of inquiry to determine whether he should be certified a lunatic—grounds for a reprieve in New York State. Under Cleveland's name, a telegram was sent to the governor, John Dix, requesting a stay of execution until the issue of Gaffney's sanity could be determined. Clearly, Cleveland was doing what he could to sabotage the execution. The sour experience of springing the trap at Patrick Morrissey's hanging was still fresh in his memory. That and the drowning of his brothers on the *Missouri* had brought enough death into Cleveland's life, and he wanted to be spared another hanging.

Dr. John Gray came in from Utica, where he was superintendent of the New York State Lunatic Asylum, to observe Gaffney in his cell. With him was Dr. Samuel Vanderpoel, chief quarantine surgeon of New York. Dr. Gray conducted a physical examination of the prisoner and noted that everything looked normal, from his tongue to his skin, which showed no evidence of being feverish or flushed. The two physicians studied Gaffney as he ranted on about cockfighting, swore, and paced his cell like a madman.

"How unlike insanity this is," Gray remarked to his colleague.

Vanderpoel had to agree. He came from an old Dutch family in which his grandfather, father, and two uncles were also physicians. Locking eyes with the prisoner, he said, "Gaffney, you're a miserable bungler."

After listening to the expert testimony, the jury of inquiry deliberated for half an hour before ruling that Gaffney was of sound mind. Construction of the gallows in the northeast corner of the jail yard commenced, and once Gaffney realized his fate was sealed, all his symptoms of mental illness disappeared, and he prepared to meet his maker. He engaged in a rational and thoughtful conversation with Cleveland. Then his son and daughter were permitted a final visit.

"Johnny," Gaffney told the youngster, "Papa's going to die. I want you to promise me these things: that you will not drink any spirituous liquors, that you will never play cards, that you will never swear and never break the Sabbath, that you will go to church and Sunday school, that you will not be out nights and keep bad company as Papa has done."

Johnny Gaffney listened to his condemned father and replied with all the gravity he could muster, "Papa, I'll do as you tell me."

Gaffney had similar words of counsel for his daughter, and the little girl also promised to always remember what he said.

Execution day was set for the second Friday in February 1873. By tradition, hangings were always held on Fridays. It just so happened that this year the second Friday fell on Valentine's Day of all days. Gaffney's last meal was a breakfast of poached eggs, toast, and coffee. He ate with relish. Fifteen minutes before the clock struck noon, Cleveland, Undersheriff Smith, and two priests escorted the doomed prisoner to the gallows.

Gaffney wore a black cap and a black gown that covered his body. The noose was already around his neck, and in his left hand he clenched a crucifix. He mounted the scaffolding with a steady step, without flinching. Undersheriff Smith read the death warrant, and Gaffney was asked if he had anything to say before his execution was carried out. He made some rant about how his friends had abandoned him and had stolen his money. He rambled on about the circumstances of the shooting that had led him to the gallows. Then Gaffney said he grieved for his second wife and children.

"I hope and pray to God that you will believe me and forgive me. I beg your pardon for all the crime I have done, and I forgive all who have injured me."

Those were his final words. The black cap was drawn over his eyes, and his legs and arms were pinioned. Then the signal was made to Sheriff Cleveland that all was ready. Cleveland did not hesitate. The next moment, he pressed the lever, and the trap-door dropped.

Gaffney's body twitched. The five-foot drop broke his neck. But somehow, strangely, Gaffney still clutched the crucifix in his left hand. What followed was the realization of Cleveland's worst fears.

The sheriff thought he had done everything to ensure Gaffney's merciful and humane death, but five minutes after the trapdoor had dropped, a physician took his vital signs, and he was still alive; his pulse read 145. At ten minutes, his pulse rate was 69. Finally—twenty-three minutes into the hanging—Gaffney's heart ceased to beat, and he was pronounced dead.

Grover Cleveland had never been opposed to the death penalty. And as a hunter and fisherman, it was said that he did not have a squeamish bone in his body. But this execution left him in profound angst. He ordered the seventy witnesses to clear the yard. Then Gaffney's body was cut down and placed in a rosewood coffin lined with white velvet and merino—the finest and softest wool in existence.

4

"WITHOUT MY CONSENT"

CLEVELAND'S TERM AS sheriff was coming to an end. On his last full day in office, New Year's Eve 1873, he had a beefsteak dinner at Weber's restaurant with his political crony, the livery owner John C. Level. The new sheriff was to be sworn in the following day, relieving Cleveland of the burden of a job he'd never wanted. Cleveland was in a cheery mood as he and Level sat down for a celebratory feast.

Beefsteak dinners on New Year's Eve were a New York political tradition, and part of the custom was that men ate only with their fingers, caveman-style. Typically, an enormous quantity of food was ordered. For starters, hamburger, lamp chops, and kidneys wrapped in bacon. That was just the appetizer. The entrée consisted of a huge broiled steak, washed down by copious amounts of beer.

Cleveland, his lips perhaps loosened by alcohol, was unexpectedly open about his tenure as sheriff of Erie County.

"Grover told me that night that during his three years in office, he had cleaned up $20,000," Level said. It was a gross undervaluation; others would later put Cleveland's actual take as sheriff at $60,000, all in legal revenues. For every writ that was executed and summons served in Erie County, payment of a fee to the sheriff was required, and Cleveland took his fair percentage. As sheriff, he had also supervised the sale of fore-closed properties, and evictions; and for every such service he received a commission. It was grubby and squalid work, which was why the shrievalty was traditionally a magnet for dishonest political hacks. The office may have been beneath Cleveland's dignity, but it had left him, at age thirty-five, on a solid financial footing for the first time in his life.

Returning to private practice, Cleveland had started a new law firm with his old bachelor roommate, the former district attorney Lyman K. Bass. The third named partner in the firm was a bright newcomer, Wilson S. Bissell, a Yale graduate. On the night Cleveland and Level were enjoying their beefsteak dinner, Bissell was celebrating his twenty-sixth birthday. Cleveland and Bissell had a lot in common. Physically, both were large in stature, and Bissell also appreciated a good joke.

Meanwhile, Bass was continuing his steady climb in politics. Having just been elected to the House of Representatives as a Republican, he was spending half the year in Washington. It was also an eventful time in his personal life. His days of confirmed bachelorhood were almost surely coming to an end. He was squiring one of Buffalo's prettiest socialites, Frances Metcalfe, the twenty-two-year-old daughter of James Metcalfe, president of the First National Bank. The Metcalfes were celebrated in

Buffalo for their sophisticated parties and social events, and Frances lived in her family's Italianate villa on Mansion Row. The works of Shakespeare, Dickens, Thackeray, and Goethe filled their magnificent library; and come the first sign of winter, servants would light its huge fireplace, which would remain lit until spring.

The firm of Bass, Cleveland & Bissell rented space in a five-story brick office building at the corner of Main and Swan known as the Weed Block. The National Weather Service also had an office in the building, as did a popular bookstore, and the Buffalo branch of Manufacturers and Traders Bank. The offices at Bass, Cleveland & Bissell were on the second floor. There was nothing lavish about them; their walls were lined with books, and in the main room there was a conference table and a cast-iron barrel stove resting on a large zinc plate. The space was illuminated with gas fixtures.

Cleveland's living arrangements could not have been more convenient. In the back of the Weed Block, he found a small third-floor apartment with windows that faced south onto Swan Street. It required less than two minutes of exertion to get to work, down a flight of stairs and up another. Cleveland decorated his suite of rooms with all the predictable accoutrements of a well-to-do bachelor: deep easy chairs; a well-stocked library with books on history and law and some fiction, indicating a taste for literature; a collection of fishing and hunting trophies; and a humidor to keep his stash of cigars moist. Curiously, scattered about the apartment were photographs of youngsters—an indication, according to an authorized biography published in 1884, of his "fondness for children."

A young law clerk from the firm took care of Cleveland's laundry, and every morning the milkman left a quart of milk outside his door. A new favorite eating place was Gerot's, a French restaurant just a block away. Sunday mornings he usually had breakfast with a friend, Major Milton Randall, at a restaurant where the specialty of the house was turtle. Cleveland's Sunday evenings were set aside for sausages and sauerkraut at Schenkelberger's.

Every so often a relative would visit Cleveland, for one, his nephew Cleveland Bacon, the son of his sister Louise and the architect from Toledo, Ohio, she had married. Uncle Grover's drinking and consumption of fatty red meat diet had ballooned his weight to almost three hundred pounds; and young Bacon, who had a tart tongue, mocked him with the sobriquet "Uncle Jumbo." Bacon was well aware that his uncle ate all his meals out, so he was surprised to see an icebox in the apartment. He asked Cleveland what was in it.

Cleveland's eyes twinkled. "Watermelons!"

The bonds of affection Cleveland developed with his male comrades could be profound, even romanticized, but there was no man, not even Bass, whom Cleveland held in as much esteem as he did his best friend, Oscar Folsom. Like Cleveland, Folsom was tall and stout—"built in about the same mold." Cleveland and Folsom were inseparable; and sometimes, when they stood next to each other, it was hard to tell them apart.

Impossibly handsome, Folsom was Cleveland's ideal of what a man should be. Women found him debonair and roguishly charming, but he also excelled in hunting and fishing; so in that regard, Folsom was a man's man. For a brief period before

Cleveland ran for sheriff, he and Folsom had been law partners. Folsom had a fine mind, and even if he was not entirely studious, his contemporaries described him as a naturally gifted lawyer. One day, Folsom asked Cleveland for advice on a matter of law.

"Go look it up," Cleveland told him, "and then you'll remember what you learn."

Sound advice, but Folsom begged to differ. "I want you to know that I practice law by ear, not by note." Cleveland roared with laughter. Only Folsom could get away with a crack like that.

Folsom radiated a swashbuckling aura wherever he went, and Cleveland found him a joy to be around—except when he had to watch Folsom driving a rig. Folsom worshipped fast trotters and could be incredibly reckless with his mare, White Cloud, who was celebrated in Buffalo for her speed. Time and again, when Folsom was holding his buggy's reins, Cleveland warned him to show some common sense.

Politically, Cleveland and Folsom were ideological twins. The night of the 1872 presidential election, hundreds of Democrats gathered at the party's headquarters in Buffalo to await the returns. Folsom, with his natural stage presence, was given the honor of reading the returns as they poured in. The incumbent, Republican candidate Ulysses S. Grant, was running for reelection against Horace Greeley. When Folsom was handed a bulletin with some early returns, he glowered, then crunched the paper in his hand and proclaimed, "Grant's reelected, and the country's gone to hell." It was a landslide victory for the Civil War hero. Horace Greeley, broken in mind and body, died twenty-four days later.

Folsom had grown up in a Federal-style house in Cowles-ville, a small town thirty miles outside Buffalo. His family was so prominent locally that the town was sometimes informally known as Folsomville. He attended the University of Rochester and met his wife, Emma Harmon, in 1859 at a Fourth of July picnic, where he delivered the keynote address. Folsom married Emma in 1863, when he was twenty-six and she twenty-three. Their daughter Frances Clara Folsom was born on July 21, 1864; they gave her the pet name Frank, or Frankie.

Several weeks after Frances's birth, Cleveland and Lyman K. Bass paid a congratulatory call on the proud parents. They were living in a picturesque little red brick house on Edward Street, just north of downtown, on the border of a Buffalo neigh-borhood known as Allentown, named after Cleveland's uncle Lewis Allen. Cleveland arrived bearing a generous gift—a baby carriage for Frances, an adorable child with a perfectly round head and deep violet eyes. Cleveland was utterly charmed by this enchanting little creature and, it was said, beheld her in wonder as she lay in her crib.

Over the years, Cleveland watched Frances blossom into a charming young lady, popular with her classmates and "very pleasing in appearance." Cleveland visited the Folsoms frequently and doted on the girl, who called him Uncle Cleve.

Once when Cleveland's sister Susan Cleveland Yeomans was nagging her bachelor brother, she asked him whether he had ever thought of getting married.

"A good many times," Cleveland said, "and the more I think of it, the more I think I'll not do it." Susan did not find his answer amusing.

Several years passed, and during another conversation with her brother, Susan again pressed him on the subject of marriage. Would he ever consider it? She really wanted to know. This time Cleveland had a different response.

"I'm only waiting for my wife to grow up," he told her. At the time, it seemed an off-the-cuff dodge, which, though a little creepy, was not to be taken seriously. One wonders how Susan would have responded had she realized that Grover was not teasing; he was speaking the literal truth.

Frances was seven when Cleveland became sheriff, and ten years old when he returned to private practice. Tall for her age, she was an agile and healthy child with a generous personality, and she shared her father's enthusiasm for sports. Frances preferred the name Frank, though once it caused confusion on the school roster when she was misidentified as a boy. On that occasion, she grudgingly consented to being called Frances. She spent her summers at her father's family farm in Folsomville, her favorite place in the world. It was a happy home.

Maria Halpin was doing well in Buffalo. After her bosses at Flint & Kent had started her off making shirt collars, they'd realized her worth and promoted her to head of the cloak department. She also had a wide circle of fashionable friends, mainly through her affiliation with St. John's Episcopal Church; and after two years in Buffalo, she seemed content with her new life.

On December 15, 1873, all around Buffalo, friends were getting together to celebrate the Christmas holiday season. On this evening, Maria, still living with her son Freddie in rented rooms at Mrs. Randall's boardinghouse, had been invited to a birthday party for a friend, Mrs. Johnson. She left her apartment and was walking down Swan Street when she ran into Grover Cleveland, who lived just a block and a half away. In those days, Cleveland was always correct in his dress, in the office and out, which meant he was almost certainly wearing black broadcloth and a top hat. They exchanged friendly greetings. Cleveland had been courting her for several months now, and it was obvious that he was interested in getting to know her better. Physically, they looked good together. Cleveland was thirty-seven; Maria was a year younger. The bulk on Cleveland's six-foot frame projected a figure of unusual might and virility. Maria was a worthy complement to an outsized man like Cleveland. She had matured into her beauty, with a cascade of dark hair set against pale skin, a rounded chin, and a mouth cut into a seductive arc. And her robust figure harmonized perfectly with Cleveland's body type.

Maria explained that she was on her way downtown to Mrs. Johnson's birthday party at the Tifft House. The Tifft House on Main Street was the city's finest hotel, with two hundred spacious rooms and a first-class bar with a choice selection of wines and liquors. In the year 1873, in Buffalo, it was unrivaled for grandeur and handsome accommodations. The Tifft House was also like a second home to Cleveland. There he presided over the "seven bachelors' table," the corner power table that looked out over the entire dining room, surrounded by other prominent bachelors, including Powers Fillmore, the eccentric son of the former president.

Now, still chatting on the street, Cleveland invited Maria out to dinner. She could not possibly, Maria responded, saying that Mrs. Johnson and the other guests were waiting for her. Cleveland refused to take no for an answer and suggested that they head off to the Ocean Dining Hall & Oyster House, a popular restaurant that had opened the year before down the block at No. 11 West Swan Street. He was "persistent," "urging" her to accompany him, and obviously persuasive. Maria decided to forget about Mrs. Johnson's birthday party and go to dinner with Cleveland.

Their meal together must have been a pleasant one. The Ocean Dining Hall was popular with Buffalo's business community and local politicos. It had an extensive wine list and offered an assortment of English ales and porter and domestic and imported cigars. The he-man menu was a pure Grover Cleveland bill of fare: green turtle soup, oysters in the shell for 20¢, little neck clams, scallops, and sirloin steak for 50¢. For greens, it was just the basics: radishes, lettuce, and green peas.

After dinner Maria and Cleveland walked back to Mrs. Randall's rooming house. On past social occasions, Maria acknowledged, Cleveland had "frequently" escorted her to her apartment, so he was also aware that her son Freddie, now ten years old, "lived with me."

What happened next, Maria said, came as a complete shock. Once they were alone in her apartment, Cleveland got on top of her and, she claimed, "by use of force and violence and without my consent" had intercourse with her.

"Up to that hour my life was as pure and spotless as that of any lady in the city of Buffalo," Maria said. There was not the "slightest shadow of suspicion over me."

Now, she said, she was a "ruined" woman.

When Cleveland was finished with her—in Maria's arched words, "after he had accomplished his purpose"—she apparently threatened to report his crime to the police. Cleveland went into a rage.

"He told me that he was determined to ruin me if it cost him $10,000, if he was hanged by the neck for it. I then and there told him that I never wanted to see him again and would never see him and commanded him to leave my rooms, which he did."

As a lawyer and former assistant district attorney, of all people, Cleveland would have appreciated how improbable it would be for him to ever face criminal charges. In the 19th century, a woman claiming rape faced extraordinary challenges in bringing her assailant to justice.

No case so vividly laid out the issues as the attempted rape of a woman outside Eureka, California, in 1874.

Julie Dow was riding a horse on a public road with her sister-in-law when they came upon a scoundrel named F. A. Brown. This lowlife started following them, and Mrs. Dow kicked the horse into a gallop. At some point, the animal, carrying the two women on its back, became exhausted, and Mrs. Dow had to climb off and walk beside it. Seizing the moment, Brown grabbed Mrs. Dow and wrestled her to the ground. There was a fierce struggle. Mrs. Dow's sister-in-law came to her aid, "clobbering" Brown with a stick, to no avail. Brown pulled Mrs. Dow's drawers down to her knees and forced her legs apart. Then he pulled out his private parts. When Mrs. Dow's sister-in-law ran screaming for assistance to a nearby farmhouse, Brown finally climbed off the victim without having completed the act.

A Humboldt County jury convicted Brown of assault with intent to rape. Justice seemed served, but on appeal, the California supreme court overturned the verdict. Mrs. Dow was a "large, young, vigorous woman," the court found. There had been "no violent struggle." Mrs. Dow had dismounted her horse voluntarily, and during the thirty-minute struggle, Brown said not a word to her and made "no threats of bodily harm." Mrs. Dow failed to resist to the utmost of her ability, and consequently, she was inviting Brown to persist in his conquest of her. The court said that Brown did not commit attempted rape: "It was an act of "'seduction.'" And Mrs. Dow, by climbing off the horse and failing to resist Brown's advances to the utmost of her ability, showed herself to be, in the words of Brown's defense lawyer, a woman of "easy virtue."

The presumption in the 19th century was that a woman who truly wanted to preserve her honor could repel any rape, unless it was a gang rape. She could use her hands or draw back her legs and physically thwart the insertion of a man's penis into her body. If the act of sex was consummated during rape, it was because the woman "did not earnestly resist it."

Another rape case that received attention illustrated the prevailing view in 1870s America. Twenty-year-old Orilla Vincent was employed as a maid in Vermont when a neighbor, John Hartigan, came to the door on a Sunday morning when the family Orilla worked for was at church. Hartigan forced Orilla into the pantry and got her on the floor. She testified she could not cry out because Hartigan was pressing his mouth against hers. She tried to fight him off, but he pinned down her arms and raped her. When he was finished, Hartigan told Orilla that if she would not speak a word about the rape, he would give her a silk wrap. Orilla refused the offer, and Hartigan tossed a

25¢ piece at her feet and ran off. When Orilla's employer, Mrs. Rockwell, came home from church, she found clear evidence of a vicious assault: bruises all over her maid's body and hand imprints on her arms where Hartigan had held her down. Orilla also turned over to Mrs. Rockwell the 25¢ Hartigan had thrown at her.

It seemed to be a straightforward case of rape. Yet Hartigan was not convicted of rape, but of the lesser charge of assault with intent to rape. The jury found that when Hartigan had taken hold of the maid by force, at first she had resisted; but then she "ultimately yielded" to having sexual intercourse with the defendant.

According to the customs of the time, it was fine for a man with normal biological urges to use a "certain degree of violence" when engaging in sex. As the law saw it, even if the woman put up a struggle, that was foreplay.

The circumstances surrounding Cleveland's alleged assault on Maria made it highly unlikely that she would file charges against him.

For one thing, Maria had accepted Cleveland's invitation to dinner—tendered on a city street as she was on her way to a birthday party. That would not have been deemed the conduct of a chaste woman. Then she had permitted Cleveland to escort her to her rooms, which certainly would have portrayed her as a woman of questionable morality whose purpose in doing so was to encourage his base desires. The legal doctrine of utmost resistance meant that to prove rape, Maria would have to show that she had tried to fend off her attacker to the "fullest extent of her abilities," which would require more than her sworn testimony.

There had to be physical evidence of a fierce struggle. As far as we know, Maria had no black eye, cuts, or bruises, or any other conspicuous evidence of having been violently assaulted. The law would have presumed that even if she had resisted Cleveland's aggressive conduct, the consummation of sex was evidence that, in the end, she had willingly surrendered to her ravishment. And consent—even partial consent—meant that, under the law, she had not been raped.

There was another important factor for Maria to consider. As the former sheriff of Erie County, Cleveland would undoubtedly have had the connections to crush or derail any official investigation.

Six weeks after the assault, Maria became aware that she was pregnant.

Being pregnant and unmarried in the 19th century did not give her many options. She was now a fallen woman. To induce abortion, she could swallow poison or overdose on herbs and such plants as snakeroot, cohosh, or tansy. Surgery was an alternative, but society viewed it as a crime against God and nature— the "evil of the age," as *The New York Times* put it. Maria ruled out telling her father, the retired police officer Robert Hovenden, who still lived in Brooklyn. She was determined to keep the knowledge of her "shame," as she put it, from him and also from her sisters. More likely than not, the Hovenden family would have disowned her. She was in this alone.

Since the night of December 15, Maria and Cleveland had gone their separate ways. She had not spoken to or tried in any way to communicate with Cleveland. But then her "condition" made it "necessary for me to send for him . . . to inform him of the consequences of his actions." She was determined to deal with Grover Cleveland directly—"he being the proper person to whom I could tell my trouble."

Maria wrote Cleveland a note demanding that he come see her at Mrs. Randall's. When he arrived at her rooms, Maria was in "despair," and laid everything out: She told him she was pregnant, and insisted that he marry her.

Cleveland must have realized he was facing the worst jam of his life. He was apoplectic.

"What the devil are you blubbering about? You act like a baby without teeth."

When Cleveland had calmed down and considered everything Maria was saying, he accepted some of the responsibility. According to Maria, Cleveland "told me that he would do everything which was honorable and righteous" and "promised that he would marry me." Cleveland would later deny he said any such thing.

For the next several weeks, Maria seemed at peace. She truly believed that Cleveland was going to become her husband and their child would be born legitimate. He even supported her with small stipends. For a time, there was the illusion of a family coming together. But Cleveland hemmed and hawed. Maria sent her son Freddie to Jersey City to stay with her in-laws. Then, by mutual agreement with her bosses, she resigned from her job at Flint & Kent. The idea of standing behind the counter with her growing belly was unthinkable; it would be the talk of the town. Now was the time to disappear.

Maria gave up her apartment at Mrs. Randall's boardinghouse and moved into rooms at 11 East Genesee Street, five blocks north of Cleveland's apartment. There she met Mrs. William Baker, who lived on the same floor. Mrs. Baker was impressed with Maria, finding her "ladylike and intelligent"; she became a trusted confidante—and an eyewitness to the drama that would follow. During those long afternoons as winter turned to spring and Maria awaited the birth of her third child, she and Mrs. Baker talked endlessly. Maria unburdened her heart to her new neighbor. She told Mrs. Baker plenty, but not everything.

"Was she there at Mr. Cleveland's expense?" Mrs. Baker was asked years later. In other words, was Cleveland paying the rent?

"Well, she wouldn't say," Mrs. Baker replied.

Maria also sought the counsel of her church. Reverend Charles Avery, her pastor at St. John's Episcopal Church, had a genial smile and a kindly manner. He had taken over St. John's just the year before, on Easter Sunday 1872. In his first sermon following his installation, Avery thoughtfully informed the three hundred families who made up his congregation, "I cannot ask your love in advance, but only that you will allow me to hope I may win it, which I fear I never can." Avery came from the small village of Fredonia in Chautauqua County, so Buffalo was a huge step up for him, though he came to understand that making the case for temperance in the big city was a daunting challenge. Not surprising, given that Buffalo's mayor at the time also owned the city's largest malting center.

When Maria went to see Avery, she told him she was pregnant and that Grover Cleveland was the father. He was shocked. Scandal had come to his church. Listening to every detail of what he later called the "circumstances of her intimacy" with the former sheriff of Erie County, Avery's response was immediate and authoritative.

"He must marry you," he told Maria.

That was what Maria had hoped he would say.

The young minister did not know Cleveland, but his law partner was a parishioner of St. John's, so there was that connection. Avery reached out to Cleveland, and when they met, the hulking lawyer "acknowledged his fault" and said he would be willing to make financial provisions for Maria. Man to man, however, he told the minister that he was uncertain whether he was the father of the unborn child. It could be his. Or it could one of the other men Maria was having relations with. That, at least, was how Cleveland saw it. According to Cleveland, Maria had fixed on him because he was the only bachelor among her paramours; the others involved in the "scrape" were all married.

Assailing Maria's morals clearly resonated with the minister; Avery emerged from the meeting agreeing with Cleveland that marriage would be "impossible." "Doubtful paternity" had reversed Avery's decision.

Later, he explained his reasoning. "I do not wish to palliate his offense, but I must say that I think he did nobly, far more than most men would have done under the circumstances. I am of the belief that when a man acknowledges an error, and does everything in his power to atone for it, he is entitled to forgiveness and respect. If it were not so, what kind of a world would this be?"

Now Maria came to the realization that it was over with Cleveland. There was no chance of a wedding. The impending birth of her child put her in a state of depression mixed with intense anxiety. Meanwhile, Cleveland made arrangements. He approached the city's premier obstetrician, Dr. James E. King, who agreed to attend Maria at the delivery.

The child was born September 14, 1874, at Buffalo's only hospital for unwed mothers, St. Mary's Lying-In Hospital, and he was named Oscar Folsom Cleveland, after Cleveland's best friend.

"Mr. Cleveland wanted him to have that name," said Mrs. Baker.

As Maria recovered from the physical ordeal of giving birth, a plan was hatched. Dr. King had a sister-in-law by marriage, Minnie Kendall, who lived with her husband, William Kendall, in a grungy apartment in East Buffalo near the stockyards. Dr. King had decided he would hire Minnie to take care of the newborn, and as she was about to give birth herself, she would also be the wet nurse.

Two days after Oscar was born, Dr. King arrived at the Kendalls' apartment carrying the baby in his arms. Dr. King said he had come directly from the hospital to make an arrangement with Mrs. Kendall and leave the baby with her.

Minnie Kendall's antennae went up; something about the whole business was putting her on edge. The sore on the top of the baby's head was also troubling.

"I don't want to take it," she said.

Dr. King was adamant. He was expecting the Kendalls to take the baby. When she asked the baby's name, "They told me to call him Jack," Mrs. Kendall said. Dr. King gathered the blanket and all the baby clothes monogrammed with the initials "M. H." or the full name "Maria Halpin" and said the Kendalls had to replace everything. He also told them never to speak about this day again.

Twelve days later, Mrs. Kendall gave birth to her son, William Harrison Kendall.

Mrs. Kendall met Maria Halpin once, when Dr. King instructed her to bring the baby to Grover Cleveland's law offices (see Prologue). Mrs. Kendall was dismayed to see her brother-in-law joking and in cahoots with this Grover Cleveland while Maria Halpin stood there in tears. Mrs. Kendall also got the strong impression that some kind of business transaction was being conducted between Cleveland, King, and Maria.

Mrs. Kendall returned home with Oscar, or Jack, as she continued to call him. For the next year, she nursed and raised the boy. One day, a gift arrived for him—a tiny pair of cotton stockings, knitted by Maria Halpin for her son. Attached to the stockings was a personal note from Maria, addressed to Minnie Kendall. A short time later, another gift was delivered, a strange one: a little knit cap with a photo of a man inside that looked like Grover Cleveland. When Mrs. Kendall removed the picture from the cap, she saw that two words had been written on the back: "Baby's papa."

Another full year passed. Then came the news that Mrs. Kendall had feared. Dr. James E. King and his wife Sarah Kendall King once again appeared at Minnie Kendall's apartment on Union Street in a state of "alarm" and frantic haste. The baby was being returned to Maria Halpin. They told Mrs. Kendall to gather all of Jack's things in a hurry. Everything had been arranged, and it had to be done right now. Maria was expecting her. She would be waiting for Mrs. Kendall outside her apartment. The transfer of the baby must take place outdoors, Mrs. Kendall was informed. On no account was she to enter the building. "It was a bad house," she was told.

"They cautioned me on this point over and over again," Mrs. Kendall said. There was one other important set of instructions. Under no circumstances, she was warned, could she let Maria know where she lived or where the baby had been raised the past year.

Mrs. Kendall and the child stepped into a waiting carriage. A driver, hired by Dr. King, took the carriage along a deliberately circuitous route to an address deep in the city. Apparently, for whatever reason, Dr. King was trying to keep his sister-in-law from remembering where she was going or how she got there. When Mrs. Kendall finally reached her destination, she learned it was Maria Halpin's apartment, at 11 East Genesee Street. An elderly woman came out of the building—it may have been Maria's neighbor, Mrs. Baker—and told Mrs. Kendall to bring the baby in. Maria was expecting her.

"Dr. King told me not to go in," Mrs. Kendall dutifully replied.

The woman returned to the apartment to consult with Maria Halpin, and when she came out several minutes later, she said, "You must carry the child in and place it in its mother's arms."

Mrs. Kendall thought it through and decided she had to ignore Dr. King's instructions and go along with Maria's demands.

Carrying Jack, Mrs. Kendall entered the "bad house" and found waiting for her the woman she had first encountered in Grover Cleveland's office. Mrs. Kendall was struck by Maria's physical beauty. She was very "ladylike," and she still had her figure. She was also weeping hysterically.

"Are you the baby's mother?"

"Yes," she answered. "I am Maria Halpin, the baby's own mother."

Maria took the child from Mrs. Kendall and held Oscar Folsom Cleveland in her arms, hugging and kissing him. She could not stop crying, and the child became alarmed by her behavior. After all, she was a stranger to him, and he was old enough to sense something was wrong. Mrs. Kendall took Oscar back and gave him her breast, which quieted down the fretful little fellow. Maria took everything in—this woman was nursing her biological son, and it must have hit her hard. She insisted that Mrs. Kendall tell her where she lived. But Mrs. Kendall stayed true to her word to Dr. King.

Suddenly, Maria began to spew venom—aimed not at Mrs. Kendall but at Grover Cleveland and Dr. James E. King. Her own obstetrician had stolen her baby, Maria declared. King was a "villain." So was Cleveland (although she never once uttered his name). They were both evil.

When Maria and Mrs. Kendall parted ways at the door, it seemed that Maria did not bear this woman any ill will. In spite of everything, there was a special bond between them—their shared love for the boy. Maria gave Mrs. Kendall $2 for her troubles. She also tried to give the driver $3 if he would go back to Mrs. Kendall's house and retrieve Oscar's cradle, but Mrs. Kendall saw this as a ruse to find out where she lived; so on the way back, she asked the driver not to give Maria any information about her home address. In all his years driving a hack around Buffalo, the driver had never seen anything like what he had just witnessed.

"My god," he said, "whose child is that that they are making so much fuss about?"

Mrs. Kendall said not a word in response. As the driver steered his carriage to Union Street, once again he took a circuitous route so that his passenger could not remember where Maria Halpin lived.

When Mrs. Kendall arrived home, Dr. King was waiting for her. She briefed him on what had happened. Then the good doctor informed her that it made sense for her family to get out of town.

"He was very anxious to have us leave Buffalo," she said. Mrs. Kendall could not believe it. Dr. King was so eager to hasten their departure he announced that he had even found a job for his wife's brother William Kendall—working for a railroad in Ontario, Canada, of all places. Dr. King could not wait for them to go. "He charged us over and over again never to tell what we knew about Maria Halpin's child, and used all manner of means to intimidate us and compel us to keep the matter quiet," said Mrs. Kendall. Still, the Kendalls vacillated. Then one day their apartment was burglarized. All their belongings were turned "topsy-turvy," and when the Kendalls inventoried everything, they realized that the only items stolen were Baby Jack's trinkets. These included the little booties Maria had sewn for him and the photo of Grover Cleveland with the words "Baby's papa" written on the back. That did it. The Kendalls decided for their own personal security that it was time to go. They settled on moving to Concord, New Hampshire, where William and his sister Sarah King had grown up on the family farm. William had found employment there at a wool factory, and Minnie could work part-time at a Concord shoe factory.

Just before they left, Minnie Kendall and Sarah King got together for a final farewell. By now, the two sisters-in-law were barely speaking to each other. Minnie refused to even call Sarah by her first name; now she was simply "Dr. King's wife." Before they parted, Sarah said something that Minnie found haunting and truly unsettling.

"Maria Halpin has got that child now, but I will get him, and then she will never see him again."

Sarah Kendall King was thirty-eight, and had recently suffered a terrible loss—the death of her daughter, Mary, at the age of ten, just seven months before Maria Halpin had given birth. Sarah was now childless. Though Minnie Kendall did not fully understand what was going on, she didn't want to stay in Buffalo to find out. She wanted to get as far away from these people as she could.

5

THE ORPHAN

IT WAS A Friday afternoon, July 23, 1875, and Oscar Folsom was calling it a day. His wife, Emma, and daughter, Frances, were out of town, vacationing for the summer with Emma's mother in Medina, New York. Just two days earlier, Frances had turned eleven.

Folsom climbed into his buggy. With him was his friend, the lawyer Warren F. Miller. Folsom steered his mare, White Cloud, down the river road and came to a stop when he reached the home of Charles E. Bacon, a wealthy Buffalo businessman. The trio spent about four hours socializing and drinking. Then, around eight at night, it was time to go.

Folsom climbed into the right-hand seat and took the reins while Miller got in from the other side. Lickety-split, Folsom drove up Amherst Street and was just turning the corner at Niagara when he saw a streetcar up ahead. A sensible man would have slowed down, but Folsom flicked White Cloud's reins to try to pass the streetcar on the right. The buggy's rear wheel hit a farmer's wagon parked in front of a saloon, and Folsom was thrown from the buggy headfirst. When he landed, the rear wheel of his own carriage ran over his chest. Miller grabbed the reins, pulled White Cloud over, and jumped out. He ran to where Folsom was lying, unconscious, on the street. A few men from the large crowd that had gathered carried Folsom to the saloon while Miller got back in the buggy and drove as fast as he could to get help.

When Miller returned, he had with him Dr. W. C. Phelps, the city's public health physician. Two other doctors were already examining Folsom when Phelps strode in and took charge. Folsom's skull was fractured, and he was paralyzed from the neck down. His condition was mortal.

When news of Folsom's accident reached him, a shaken Grover Cleveland rushed to his friend's side. Again and again Cleveland had warned him about his aggressive driving. Now, ten months after Oscar Folsom Cleveland had been born, Cleveland got there in time to see the man his son had been named after take his last breath. It was 9:45 PM.

Assembled in the back room of the saloon were Folsom's cousin Benjamin Folsom and two other well-known lawyers, Henry Box and Charles Thomas. The county coroner was called, and Folsom's body was lifted into a wagon and transported to the Tifft House, where Folsom had rented an apartment for the summer while his family was away.

A telegram was sent to Emma Folsom at her mother's estate in Medina. It arrived after midnight. Frances was immediately awakened and informed of her father's death. Many years later, she would recall how she sat on the steps in the hallway taking it all in. Her father was gone, and she could see her mother sitting on the porch, reading and rereading the telegram by the light of a lantern. It was as if she could not quite believe what had happened, that at age thirty-three she was now a widow.

Emma returned to Buffalo the next day and found a city in mourning. Her husband's accident was the lead local story in the *Commercial Advertiser*.

"There is no one among the prominent young men of this community whose death would be more deeply mourned than is that of Oscar Folsom," the article said, heaping praise on Folsom for being "true as steel to his friends." The paper also conceded, in so many words, that Folsom had had a reputation for recklessness with a horse and buggy when it took note of his "quick and impulsive" nature. The *Morning Express* said the city had lost a citizen whose place "cannot be refilled. Oscar had not an enemy in the world." Of course the tension surrounding the illegitimate birth of Oscar Folsom Cleveland was kept in the strictest privacy. Not a word about it appeared in print. Only the most intimate friends of Grover Cleveland and Maria Halpin knew that the enmity between them was mounting.

Cleveland was given the honor of delivering the eulogy at Oscar Folsom's funeral—a stirring address, spoken from the heart, and considered by those who were there to be the greatest speech of his life. Emma was present, as was Folsom's grieving father, Colonel John Folsom. He had now lost his wife, a daughter, and two sons in the span of just nineteen months. Death seemed to be stalking John Folsom's family, which had been virtually wiped out by disease and hard luck. The adolescent Frances, who was considered to be too young to attend the funeral, remained in Medina with her grandmother.

Oscar Folsom left no will—a surprising lapse for someone in the legal profession but characteristic of his irresponsible nature. Dying intestate meant Folsom's assets had to be processed through probate court, and Grover Cleveland was appointed administrator of the estate. Everyone agreed that Cleveland's veneration of the dead man and his affection for Emma and Frances Folsom made him the perfect choice.

Oscar Folsom left a sizable estate of an estimated $250,000, the rough equivalent of $5 million in modern currency. Financially, Emma and Frances had no worries.

For a time, they stayed in Medina, where Frances continued her education at the Medina Academy for Boys and Girls. Then they tried living with Emma's sister Nellie in St. Paul, Minnesota, thinking that a new life in another city might be just the thing to cheer them up, but they disliked St. Paul; and six months later, they were back in Medina.

Grover Cleveland was a continuous presence in Frances's life. Given that her mother was still alive, the girl did not require a legal guardian, but Cleveland effectively took over that role and was advised on every important aspect of her upbringing. There was talk that Cleveland and Emma were destined to marry. It did seem inevitable that the widow of Oscar Folsom and his bachelor best friend would one day wed.

Grover Cleveland, however, was in a serious predicament: what to do about Maria Halpin. She was the stone in his shoe that would not go away.

Oscar Folsom Cleveland was now two and a half years old. After spending the first year of his life in the care of Dr. King's sister-in-law, Minnie Kendall, Oscar was back living with his mother on East Genesee Street. Maria Halpin had won that skirmish, and Cleveland was realizing that this department store clerk made a formidable foe. She was relentless in pursuing her purpose: to salvage her family name. Remarkably, that meant marrying the man she claimed had raped her. From Maria's perspective, marriage was the "only step possible to even partially repair the wrong he had done." Marriage would save her son from shame, relieve her of her "misery," and eradicate the "stain on her honor." Maria made one more appeal for Cleveland to do the right thing. Cleveland was unwavering; he said no.

Cleveland's communications with Maria were thorny at best; at times he even interpreted her statements to be threats to his life and the boy's. He was "haunted" by the crisis with Maria Halpin and Oscar. There were days at work when he could think of nothing else. Sensing that a public scandal might erupt at any moment now, he became thoroughly alarmed.

Cleveland had not become as powerful as he was by waiting for things to happen. He focused on a chink in Maria's armor. She had always appreciated a glass or two of wine at dinner, but now, he heard, her drinking was becoming a serious concern. Even her supportive neighbor, Mrs. Baker, had to agree.

"After the birth of her child she led a blameless life until her misery drove her to drink," Mrs. Baker told a reporter in 1884. She said she understood the source of Maria's problems: "She took to drink to drown the grief that was consuming her." Whatever the rationale, this was the information Cleveland needed to finally go on the offensive.

His years in the district attorney's office and as sheriff of Erie County had left him with innumerable law enforcement contacts. His first move was to seek out the services of the police, but in a strictly private capacity. He went to see John Byrne, the superintendent of the Buffalo Police Department.

Byrne was born in Ireland and came to America when he was five. In his teens, he was apprenticed to a carriage and coach manufacturer. He was twenty-two when the Civil War broke out, and was an authentic war hero with the battle scars to prove it. In an assault on the enemy works at the Spotsylvania Court House in Virginia, Byrne, then a major in the celebrated 155th New York State Volunteers Irish Regiment, was shot in the head with a bullet that entered his temple, blew apart the back of his eyeball, and exited his cheek. He not only survived but became a regimental legend when, after just ten weeks of convalescence, he returned to the field wearing patches on his wounds to take command. A month later, Byrne was captured by Confederate forces and spent six months in a POW camp before he was released in a prisoner exchange. At war's end, he mustered out of the army having achieved the full rank of colonel.

Byrne was appointed Buffalo's first police superintendent in 1872, and brought military discipline and professionalism to a force reputed to have been one of the most "untrustworthy" in the nation. On the day Cleveland went to see him about Maria Halpin, Byrne still bore his disfiguring war wounds. His left eye was gone, and he no longer had a sense of taste or smell.

Cleveland told Byrne about Maria Halpin's drinking and threats and asked the police superintendent to assign some men to keep her under surveillance. Despite their political differences—Byrne was a Republican—and whatever Byrne may have privately thought of Cleveland for sitting out the war, the police superintendent said he would see what he could do.

Byrne assigned two of his sharpest men to investigate Maria: Robert Watts, a dependable detective whose father had served as a cavalry captain in the War of 1812, and Police Officer Thomas Curtin, another steady hand, currently assigned to special duty at the Third Precinct. Curtin was thirty-six, the son of Irish immigrants. (Police work ran in his blood: His brother John was a detective with the Pinkerton National Detective Agency in New York City.)

Thomas Curtin had been an ironworker until he was twenty-five, then switched careers and found work as a clerk in the Buffalo tax receiver's office. In 1872, he joined the police force, where he developed the reputation of having an "eagle eye" for ferreting out crime; it was said that he could "tell a culprit on sight quicker than any man in America." He was a big man, just under six feet and weighing two hundred pounds, with a muscular physique, a florid complexion, and brown hair with matching mustache. He was also a politically connected Democrat, and a rising star in the police department.

Cleveland met with Watts and Curtin and told them he had two goals in procuring their services. One was to "divine the woman's intentions"; the other was to "work some scheme by which she and her child could be separated and removed."

When Watts and Curtin went to see Maria at her apartment on East Genesee Street, they encountered a woman of culture and determination—not what they had expected. Some civilians might find a dressing-down by two police officers intimidating, but Maria made no concessions and refused to give any ground.

Watts and Curtin reported to Cleveland that "they could find nothing out from the woman and could do nothing with her." Cleveland was disappointed, and was even said to be in a state of "desperation" at the report; but in his mind, he had already begun to formulate the next stage in his campaign to eradicate Maria Halpin from his life.

Cleveland decided to seek the advice of Roswell L. Burrows, a judge whose four-year tenure on the Erie County Court bench had just come to an end. Now in private practice, the fifty-five-year-old Burrows lived on Franklin Street with his wife, Marie; four children; and a maid who went by the peculiar name Thankful Brum. Burrows was the son of a former New York State senator and had served on the Buffalo Sanitation Commission during the great cholera panic that swept the city in the early 1850s. Most significantly for Cleveland, Burrows was also a trustee of the Buffalo Orphan Asylum. Cleveland asked Burrows to see if he could reason with Maria Halpin.

Burrows went to Maria to plead his case. He must have caught her in a vulnerable moment because whatever words he used somehow resonated with her. The former judge was able to persuade Maria that it would be best for everyone if she went away for a while and placed Oscar in a home where he could be looked after. Naturally, he recommended the Buffalo Orphan Asylum. He added that Grover Cleveland had agreed to pay $5 a week for the child's board at the orphanage. Cleveland would funnel the money to Burrows, who would see to it that the orphanage was paid. That way, the Cleveland name would never have to be associated with the boy. There was something in it for Maria too: Burrows told her that Cleveland was willing to support her in a business start-up—she could open a dress shop in Niagara Falls.

Perhaps Maria was exhausted by the endless conflict with Cleveland. Maybe she truly bought into the accusation that she was neglecting Oscar and endangering his welfare with her drinking. Whatever the reason, to her shame, she agreed to everything. Burrows presented her with legal papers in which she agreed to "surrender" all rights and claims to her son and to turn him over to the custody of the Buffalo Orphan Asylum. In doing so, she had to pledge to not interfere with the child's "management." Visitation would be permitted only with the consent of the orphanage. Maria signed the documents.

On March 9, 1876, Oscar Folsom Cleveland, under the name Oscar Halpin, was officially placed in the orphanage. Archival records document in plain language what must have been a heartbreaking moment for Maria: "Received from MB Halpin; mother. Rate of board—$5.00." After she deposited her son at the Buffalo Orphan Asylum, Maria was off to Niagara Falls to start a new life.

It took her just a few days to realize what an error in judgment she had made. Desperately lonely, she buckled under the weight of her guilt. She also probably realized that Cleveland and Burrows had manipulated her into surrendering her legal rights as Oscar's mother. Maria returned to Buffalo and set about the task of recovering her son.

At age two and a half, Oscar Folsom Cleveland, the biological son of a future American president, found himself unwanted by his father, and, for the time being at least, dumped by his mother at the Buffalo Orphan Asylum. It stood at 403 Virginia Street, a two-story brick building with adjoining wings and an attic. It was lit by gas, heated by steam, and administered by a board of trustees of important Buffalo citizens like Roswell Burrows, who were drawn from the city's leading Protestant churches, even though most of the orphans were Catholic.

On his first day at the asylum, Oscar was given a bath and thoroughly cleaned with soap and hot water. As a precaution against lice, his hair was almost certainly cut short, and his clothes were probably consigned to the flames, as was routine procedure. Oscar was in better physical condition than the other woebegotten orphans, many of whom arrived there in a state of such filth due to exposure and neglect that it was sometimes hard to tell what color their hair was. Oscar was issued a uniform, numbered and tagged with his name, which would be replaced only when it was deemed to be "past repair."

Breakfast was oatmeal with cream and sugar, and bread and butter on the side. Dinner, on alternate days, was roast beef with brown gravy, potatoes, beet pickles, bread, syrup, and milk. The fruits offered—apples, pears, plums, and berries, almost always stewed—depended on the season and were grown on the asylum grounds. For a charitable institution, the diet at the Buffalo Orphan Asylum was generous and nutritious.

There were 139 orphans living at the asylum when Oscar arrived. The average age was about eight, and the oldest was twelve. As one of the youngest "tots," Oscar was awakened at 6:30 AM. Nap time was from 10:00 AM until noon. The older children pitched in with housekeeping, and everyone was expected to make his or her bed. The ceilings in the orphanage were low, and the beds were set close together, but at least the sheets were neat and snowy white. The older orphans were required to attend Public School No. 14 next door, but they were also taught a trade. The girls learned to sew and knit and make patchwork, darn stockings, and mend clothes. The boys were trained to sew buttons and weave rag carpets, for which they were paid a penny a pound.

Discipline was sometimes enforced with a spanking. "I seldom ever have to punish a child," the superintendent of the asylum once informed a state inspector. "When I do, it is by spanking with the hand or by using a switch. I never put a child in a dark room. Some simple and not hurtful means of correction is usually resorted to, like making a child go to bed out of its regular hours."

Towels in the bathroom were communal—there were not enough of them to supply every child with one. Hairbrushes also had to be shared, but each girl had her own comb. There were four tubs in the bathing room in open view, affording no privacy. Once a week, the older children had to take a bath and on that occasion were issued clean underwear and socks. The tots were bathed more frequently, when required by necessity.

At the first symptom of an infectious disease or an epidemic, aggressive steps were taken. The orphan in question was immediately isolated; special attention was paid to cases of conjunctivitis. The year Oscar was there was abnormally lethal. Five children who were confined to the sickroom lay at the "point of death," and two died.

Each youngster at the Buffalo Orphan Asylum had a sad story to tell. About 10 percent of them had lost both parents, but most were so-called half-orphans, meaning one of their parents was alive but unequipped or unwilling to assume the responsibilities of parenthood. The superintendent had nothing but contempt for the parents who—in her words—were "poor and shiftless," though the staff recognized that sometimes decent families could be overtaken by some disaster and require a helping hand. They also made efforts to place orphans in good Christian households. A letter of recommendation from a pastor or a family physician or some other prominent person was required of anyone interested in adopting. A three-month trial period followed. If a home inspection revealed some issue of cruelty or neglect, the adoption contract would be declared void, and the orphan would be returned to the asylum. Some of the children stayed in touch with the staff and each other after they were adopted, either from gratitude or a desire to communicate with a sibling who remained behind.

"I will send my likeness, and you will please send it to my dear little sister," one girl beseeched.

"I often think of you all, and wonder if any of the boys I knew are there yet," wrote one boy.

Corresponding from her new home, a youngster reported, "I like my new Pa and my new Ma very much, and they are very kind to me."

Overcrowding was a serious problem. There was not enough land to offer the children a playground that was more than a patch of earth covered with gravel. On rainy days, the children were shuffled into the basement where the laundry was done. In 1876, the year Oscar entered the orphanage, two children managed to escape, apparently never to return; fifty-two were returned to their parents, and thirty-five ended up adopted. In general, the Buffalo Orphan Asylum received good marks on its state inspection reports.

When Maria Halpin reappeared in Buffalo, Grover Cleveland once again found himself thwarted by this headstrong woman. She went to the orphanage and demanded to see her son. After Cleveland consulted with Judge Burrows, he tolerated her visits there for the time being, but he must have issued some word of warning to the staff, because the attendants kept a watchful eye on Maria, always hovering nearby when she strolled the grounds of the asylum, holding hands with Oscar, in the spring of 1876.

As the weeks wore on, the staff relaxed their guard when, in their opinion, Maria seemed to be "reconciled to the separation" from her son—but it was a feint. On April 28, forty-eight days after Oscar was sent to the orphanage, when no one was looking, Maria scooped Oscar up and fled with him. In the words of the incident report submitted by the supervisor on duty, Oscar had been "stolen by M. B. Halpin – mother."

Cleveland, in a panic, leaped into action. Local law enforcement agencies went on the hunt, but quietly, without the public's knowledge. They checked out the place in Niagara where Maria had been living, and her apartment at 11 East Genesee Street, but there was no trace of her or Oscar. They even grilled Mrs. Baker and all of Maria's other friends. No one knew—or admitted knowing—where Maria and Oscar were hiding out.

In those days, the Overseer of the Poor was an elected post, the fifth ranking office in municipal government, after mayor, controller, assessor, and corporate counsel. Cleveland must have felt himself blessed with good fortune because it so happened that in the year 1876, it was his political crony and drinking companion John C. Level who had just been elected the Overseer of the Poor who administered the Erie County Almshouse.

Level had narrow gray eyes, prematurely graying hair, perfect posture, and was of medium build. An expert horseman—he sat in the saddle with an easy grace, and astride his horse with his shoulders thrown back—he made a splendid sight. His livery stable had once served as Cleveland's political clubhouse, so that even though Level had been elected as a Republican, Cleveland felt comfortable confiding in him. He told him the entire sad story of the birth of Oscar Folsom Cleveland, explaining that he wanted him, once he was found, removed from Maria's custody. Because of her purported drinking, he informed Level, the child's life was in danger, and steps had to be taken to rescue him without delay.

Level, forty-three, liked to boast that he had never attended a day of school in his life. Born in Kentucky in 1833, he had moved to Buffalo in 1852 and, at the age of nineteen, went into the flour and feed business. He later opened his livery and, during the Civil War, signed up as a field agent for the Bureau of Military Information, the precursor agency of the Secret Service. Following Abraham Lincoln's assassination, Level was one of the bodyguards selected to escort the body across the United States for burial in Springfield. At war's end, Level returned to Buffalo and became a private detective. He had an effortless gift for making friends and telling amusing stories. Not surprisingly, he drifted into politics.

Level listened to Cleveland, but was wary. He let Cleveland know that being Overseer of the Poor gave him no right to remove any minor from his mother without a court order. Cleveland took a law book from Level's shelf and found the section of state law that empowered the Overseer of the Poor to seek custody of a child whose life was in imminent danger. That was good enough for Level, and he signed the necessary papers. Level may not have been a lawyer, but he was perceptive enough to understand that Cleveland wanted to avoid the "attendant publicity" that might come his way should Maria file a civil lawsuit.

Sometime in July, Cleveland received information that Maria was back on East Genesee Street, and Oscar was with her. He ordered Detective Watts and Officer Curtin to return to Maria's apartment. Ominously, a third man joined them—Dr. James E. King, the obstetrician who had delivered baby Oscar.

The three men arrived at Maria's building in two hired carriages on the night of July 10, 1876. Curtin waited outside while Watts and Dr. King strode up the flight of stairs. Detective Watts "surreptitiously" broke into the apartment and, with Dr. King, found Oscar playing on the floor. Maria, stunned to see them there, particularly the "evil" Dr. King, picked up her son, and a violent struggle ensued. Maria was "forcibly seized" and Oscar "torn" from her arms. Maria, "stubborn and resistant," was "violently dragged" down the staircase and hauled into the waiting carriage.

Roused by Maria's "shrieks . . . and the heartrending cries of her baby," Mrs. Baker and some of the other neighbors emerged to investigate the commotion. What they saw happened so swiftly, and in the dead of night, that it left them in a state of disbelief. Had they witnessed a kidnapping? Or was it some lawful arrest by the police? As a reporter wrote eight years later, "The work of abduction was so brutally and speedily done by Cleveland's hired men that they got their victim off before the people got any notion of what the unusual proceedings meant."

Watts would later defend his role in Maria's seizure, claiming that when he broke into her apartment, evidence that Oscar was being neglected was "not lacking." He asserted that Maria had been drinking that evening, and when she was informed that he and Dr. King were not leaving without Oscar, she screamed out, "I'd rather kill the child than have it snatched from me."

"It was a hell of a time," the detective recounted, and it wasn't something he had bargained for. He said that overpowering Maria had taken all of his nerve and physical strength. For their work this night, Cleveland paid Watts and Curtin the sum of $50.

With the hired driver at the reins, the carriage bearing Maria Halpin and the two detectives drove off. Maria, having no idea where she was being taken, was hysterical.

Dr. King, who was left in charge of Oscar Folsom Cleveland, climbed into the remaining carriage with the child and told the driver to take them to 403 Virginia Street.

Less than an hour later, when the carriage slowed down, Maria Halpin found herself on the far outskirts of the city. The carriage turned into the private entranceway of the Providence Lunatic Asylum and came to a stop. Maria was told to climb out, and, with Watts and Curtin on either side of her, she was escorted into the lobby and directed to the admitting office on the first floor. There she was registered as patient no. 1050. Her medical chart declared her to be suffering from *onomania*, a now-arcane medical term that a 19th-century medical guide for doctors and lawyers described this way: "A peculiar form of insanity, in which the patient breaks out into paroxysms of alcoholic excess, attended with violence, strange, or even indecent acts, due apparently to uncontrolled impulses." The medical entry log recorded on the night of Maria's admittance indicates that she was also suffering from dementia tremens, or DTs—that is, she was exhibiting tremors and other physical symptoms of withdrawal from alcoholic abuse.

Maria was taken to a private room to spend the night. She must have wondered, as she tried to fall asleep, how it had come to this. Years later, she would explain that she had never intended to go public with her accusations against Grover Cleveland, believing that she had as much at stake as Cleveland did in avoiding a public scandal and in keeping her shame a private matter. But this terrifying night brought her face-to-face with the reality: Cleveland was the unseen hand that had ripped her son from her arms and thrown her into a mental institution. From then on, she would later tell her family, she utterly "loathed" the man.

In the morning, Maria got a sense of her surroundings. The Providence Lunatic Asylum was set on twenty-three acres, at Main Street and Kensington Avenue. It was a gracious four-story yellow brick farmhouse situated on the highest point of land within Buffalo's city limits, chosen partly because it offered a delightfully cool breeze in the summer. In the years to come, the name of the institution would be changed to the Providence Asylum for the Insane and Inebriate, and still later, to the more benevolent-sounding Providence Retreat. But for now, it was the Providence Lunatic Asylum, in the domain of the Sisters of Charity, a Catholic order dedicated to serving the poor. It could only have been to Maria's relief that she was in the asylum and not incarcerated next door, at 3399 Main Street. That was the Erie County Almshouse, or Poor House—a true snake pit, notorious for chaining inmates half naked to benches and posts. Rosaline Brown, the Sister Superior at the Providence Lunatic Asylum, had once walked through the almshouse and found that the inmates "resembled wild animals rather than human beings."

Sister Rosaline had raised the $8,000 needed to build the Providence Lunatic Asylum in 1861, and during those early days, accommodations were of the "poorest kind." The mattresses were made of straw; water had to be carried in enormous casks from a mile away; and there was no money for oil lamps, so light was provided by handmade tallow candles. Sister Rosalie often told the other sisters, "Pray that I may meet some good soul who will give me money for today's marketing. I have not a dollar in my purse." Most of the patients were destitute, under treatment for hysteria or nervous prostration, for which the asylum billed the city or county $2.50 a week per patient. Private patients filled the other beds. These were alcoholics or opium and morphine addicts who could afford their own board and were charged $10 a week, income that defrayed the cost of running the institution.

Like other progressive 19th-century advocates for the rights of the mentally ill, the Sisters of Charity held to the belief that insanity could be cured through peace and quiet and a bucolic setting. Consequently, the grounds of the Providence Lunatic Asylum were beautified with shrubbery for shady walks and private contemplation. A dairy and a hennery supplied abundant fresh milk and eggs. People were treated humanely, and private rooms were even available, except for inmates who required twenty-four-hour watch—as a "guarantee against destructive tendencies." The report of a state official who inspected the asylum offers a firsthand account of life there as Maria Halpin would have experienced it. When the inspector arrived on a stormy day in March 1884, he found 273 inmates, about equally divided between men and women.

"I went through all the halls and rooms and saw all of the patients," he wrote. "There were several noisy cases . . . but no extremely violent ones." This inspector found a suicidal state pauper handcuffed in leather "muffs," and two boys and a girl—"epileptic and feeble-minded"—living in the institution. The walls had been freshly whitewashed and the closets and bathrooms all redone. The patients were "comfortably clothed" and the bedding in overall good condition. The staff consisted of a part-time medical director, a laundress, a cook, an engineer, and his assistant. But the Sisters of Charity were in charge of everything.

On the morning of Maria's first full day of incarceration, she was taken to the office of Dr. William Ring.

Dr. Ring was beloved in Buffalo. He was the first student to graduate from the Buffalo Medical College, in 1847, and it was said that he offered as much care for the underprivileged as he did for his wealthiest patients, and treated them with the same zeal. No physician did as much to benefit the sick and poor. On the day that Maria Halpin came into his office, Ring was fifty-two years old and had been affiliated with the Providence Insane Asylum since it had first opened its doors to serve fifteen impoverished patients. He came to the asylum once a week to offer his services gratis as attending physician. Standing at his side on these missions of mercy were his adolescent sons, William and Charles. Their visits to the asylum must had made a deep impression on the boys, because they both became doctors.

Like any good diagnostician, Dr. Ring was a keen observer of human mannerisms and conduct. He notes in his initial evaluation of Maria Halpin that she had been drinking—he would later use the word *boozy* to describe her disposition—although he could not yet tell whether she was a habitual abuser. But she seemed very "ladylike," and there was nothing frenzied or manic about her behavior. It made Dr. Ring question the diagnosis of onomania and DTs. As he listened to Maria's story and came to understand the powerful legal and political forces that had been arrayed against her, Ring grew indignant. This woman, he was beginning to realize, had been thrown into the asylum "without warrant or form of law." Obviously, she was "not insane," and the Providence Lunatic Asylum, he determined, had "no right to detain her." He advised Maria to remain in the asylum for a few days—"long enough to get straightened out." But after that, he refused to admit her as a patient. She was free to go.

On the morning of July 21, Maria felt well enough to leave. Her three days at the asylum had cleared her head, and now she was determined to find her son.

Milo A. Whitney was at his desk in his law office, pondering the woman seated across from him. Maria Halpin's account was almost impossible to believe, and yet his lawyerly instincts told him she was telling the truth.

Whitney was forty-eight years old and stood five foot eight. He had light hazel eyes set above a prominent nose, was bald except for a fringe of gray hair, and had a mustache. Physically, Whitney was unimpressive, his features, by his own account, "ordinary."

Taking on Grover Cleveland, one of the most admired lawyers in Buffalo, was something Whitney would have to think about. After all, the bar association of Erie County was a tight-knit professional organization of power brokers, influential insiders. Then there was the matter of linking Roswell Burrows to this messy scandal and the deceased lawyer Oscar Folsom; involving Folsom's good name in it, however remote his connection, could backfire. And Roswell Burrows was more than a highly regarded former judge—he was also a neighbor who lived just a few doors down the street from Milo Whitney at 476 Franklin Avenue.

It was Maria's good fortune that Whitney, a native of Vermont, was by nature a flinty New Englander. As he listened to her story, he became indignant, like Dr. Ring. If Maria was to be believed, Whitney later recalled, then Cleveland had "plotted" her abduction and "hired the men to carry it out." It was clear to the lawyer that Cleveland was trying to get her out of the way by throwing her into an insane asylum, which Whitney deemed "outrageous." Just four months before, Whitney's wife, Mary, had given birth to the couple's first child, Grace. Maria Halpin's determination to take any measure necessary to reclaim her son surely moved this caring new father.

Whitney told Maria that he would have to investigate her allegations, but if everything she said held up under scrutiny, he would take the case and institute legal proceedings against "all concerned in the assault and abduction." He was inclined to disregard her claims regarding breach of promise, for now.

Bluntly, he informed Maria, the evidence was weak and open to dispute. Alleging kidnapping and false arrest would make for a far more muscular case.

The death of Sarah Kendall King and Dr. James E. King's only child, Mary, age ten, in March 1874 had left Sarah bereft in her grief. The Kings lived in a grand house at 93 Niagara Street, but a grand house without a little one to raise was an empty and lonely place for a woman yearning to be a mother again.

Sarah was born in Pembroke, New Hampshire, in 1841. Her father, Prescott Kendall, was an early follower of the biblical prophet William Miller, who predicted the Second Coming of Jesus Christ sometime between March 21, 1843, and March 21, 1844. When March 21, 1844, turned into a day like any other day, Miller, upon further biblical analysis, prophesized a new date—April 18, 1844. He tried again with October 22, 1844. When this day also passed into night, the Millerites "wept till the day dawn" over what became known as the Great Disappointment. Prescott Kendall remained a disciple and lived to the ripe old age of ninety-five, even after his doctor had given up all hope, because, it was said, he wanted to live to see the Second Advent of Christ.

Sarah's sister, Elizabeth, or Lizzie as she was known, left New Hampshire in 1850 to seek her fame and fortune as a dancer and actress. When she returned, she had banked enough cash to rescue the Kendall family farm from foreclosure. Then she went back on the road, this time accompanied by Sarah and another sister, Jenny. Appearing under the name the Misses Kendall, the sisters were a sensation, performing at theaters as far west as

Chicago, usually as second billing to such Irish farces as "How to Pay the Rent," and the saucy comedy "Day After the Wedding." Sometimes their brother Charles Kendall, who played the fiddle and banjo, accompanied the Misses Kendall.

Their reviews were excellent, and always emphasized the correctness of their performance in an era when many women in the theater were considered to be one step from the gutter. A Philadelphia critic called them "young, beautiful and graceful," and wrote that they were blessed with a fairy-like grace. Appearing in Chicago in 1856, the Kendall Sisters were praised for their "deportment in their public and private life." The backstory of how they had saved the family farm through hard work and talent added to their popularity.

Jenny was the sister with the blushing rosy cheeks; Elizabeth, who danced with the tambourine, had a "dazzling gaze"; and Sarah, the youngest of the three, walked out on the act and married Dr. James E. King.

King was born in 1821, in Warren, Pennsylvania, and settled in Buffalo, seventy miles to the north, after earning his medical degree. He shunned romantic entanglements, telling friends he was too busy building a medical practice to worry about raising a family. He was in his late forties when he saw Sarah Kendall onstage and became besotted with her fine figure and exquisite face. She had the natural poise and melodious voice of a born performer. Whatever uncertainty Sarah may have harbored about their twenty-year age gap, at least James offered the young dancer a lifetime of prosperity and social position. The esteemed Reverend Dr. Alexander Hamilton Vinton married James and Sarah at St. Paul's Church in Boston on New Year's Eve. Then

James King brought his lucky catch of a bride back with him to Buffalo, and Sarah was welcomed into Buffalo society. Dr. King's mother, Betsey, who was in her eighties, lived with them, as did a servant from Norway, Dorothea Johnson, who helped around the house.

Their daughter, Mary, was born in 1864 and died in 1874, seven months before the birth of Oscar Folsom Cleveland. Mary's death had been a crushing blow, and Sarah wanted another child, but for whatever reason—perhaps medical— whether she could conceive again was uncertain. For Sarah King, Oscar Folsom Cleveland's birth came as a blessing. She had been one of the schemers who had arranged to have her sister-in-law Minnie Kendall (her brother William's wife) nurse Oscar from birth. Now, with Oscar's return to the custody of the Buffalo Orphan Asylum and with his mother Maria under siege, Sarah was consumed with bringing into her life this child who, so incongruously, seemed to be wanted by everyone and no one.

Maria was finally coming to the realization that if she were to succeed in winning custody of Oscar, she needed her family's support. Throughout the tumult of her life in Buffalo, she had kept the Halpins and her father, Robert Hovenden, in the dark about Grover Cleveland. They knew nothing of her pregnancy or the birth of Oscar. It was time to brace them for the news.

Simeon Talbott, now the titular head of the Halpin family, was Maria's brother-in-law, having married Maria's late husband's sister, Lizzie Halpin. Talbott was born in Brooklyn, and Maria had gotten to know him when he was courting Lizzie. Now the

Talbotts were living in Jersey City and taking care of Maria's two adolescent children, Freddie and Ada. The entire clan resided in the sprawling home of the master engraver Frederick Halpin Sr., sixty-six years old in the year 1876 and in failing health. When Talbott heard from Maria, he was beside himself, to say the least. Without delay, he boarded the train for Buffalo to manage the crisis.

Talbott was a good-looking traveling salesman with an outsized walrus mustache that looped over his entire mouth like a furry bandage. He worked for a New York City wholesale leather dealer, Henry Arthur & Co., and his business kept him on the road for most of the selling season, taking him as far west as Indiana.

As Talbott heard Maria's story straight from her lips, he came to the conclusion that this Grover Cleveland was a "seducer" of vulnerable women, who had made his sister-in-law a "positive promise of marriage." The more he learned about Cleveland, the more a quiet fury built within Talbott. He came to believe that the man was a "notorious libertine and kept a regular harem in Buffalo"—or at least those were the stories he was hearing from Maria.

Even so, Talbott remained levelheaded. He didn't appreciate the fact that Maria had hired a lawyer. Above all, he told Maria, scandal must be avoided and the Halpin name protected. After listening to everything Maria had to say, the best advice he could offer her was to forget about the boy, leave Buffalo, and return to the bosom of her family downstate. From Talbott's point of view, Oscar Folsom Cleveland was a bastard child born out of a rape, and not fit to live with the Halpins. If Cleveland wanted to assume financial liability for the boy and pay the $5 fee required by the orphanage, then let him take the responsibility.

There was the added factor of Maria's children, Freddie and Ada. Freddie was now thirteen, Ada eleven. They needed their mother. Wasn't it about time Maria started looking out for their interests? Come home, Talbott told Maria, and connect with the family again. In the meantime, he would personally meet with this Grover Cleveland and see what could be worked out.

Over at the law offices of Milo A. Whitney, preparations for *Maria Halpin v. Grover Cleveland* were proceeding at a quickening pace. Whitney seemed to be looking forward to the litigation; he thought it was shaping up to be an exceptionally strong case. Then one day, on the eve of filing the lawsuit, Maria Halpin came to see him. Accompanying her was a gentleman Whitney had never met before, her brother-in-law, Simeon Talbott. It quickly became evident to Whitney that his client was taking direction from Talbott, that the traveling salesman from Jersey City was calling the shots.

Talbott informed Whitney that there had been a change in strategy. There would be no litigation. The case was over. The Halpin family was not willing to risk a "public scandal." Talbott said "innocent parties"—presumably meaning the Halpins and Maria's two children—would be "bowed down in an exposure of Maria's shame." Before Whitney could absorb this extraordinary statement, he was handed another shock: a signed agreement made between Maria Halpin and Grover Cleveland. Talbott had done all the negotiating, and everything had been worked out. Cleveland would pay Maria the single lump sum payment of $500. In return, Maria Halpin agreed to "surrender her son,

Oscar Folsom Cleveland, and make no further demands of any nature whatsoever upon his father."

Whitney could not believe it. As he examined the settlement accord, he saw that it had been written in Grover Cleveland's own hand. The crafty Cleveland had settled the case out of court without even the knowledge of Maria's own attorney. And from Whitney's point of view, it had been settled for a ridiculously low figure.

Right then, Whitney realized, even if he still believed Cleveland to have committed an egregious abuse of power, the lawsuit had been irrevocably "compromised." His representation of Maria Halpin "ceased as soon as he saw that agreement." The litigation had ended before it was ever begun.

As Whitney watched Maria Halpin and Simeon Talbott walk out of his office, his compassion for Maria was unchanged. Evidently, the poor woman had "yielded" to unrelenting family pressure, which left Whitney in a state of profound distress. He also had to wonder about the other pathetic victim in the case. What would be the fate of the orphaned boy, Oscar Folsom Cleveland?

New Year's Day 1877 was marked by great events across the globe. In Delhi, in the fortieth year of her reign as British monarch, Queen Victoria was proclaimed Empress of India. At the stroke of midnight at Trinity Church in Manhattan, under a crisp cold sky, and to the solemn strikes of the belfry clock, an immense throng welcomed the New Year. In London, a British astronomer issued a warning to humanity that the sun could one day "blaze up" and destroy the earth. And in Washington, President Ulysses Grant, holding court at the Executive Mansion, received the diplomatic corps in their brilliant decorations and official regalia. Outside, a blinding snowstorm had begun in the nation's capital; by nightfall, a foot of snow would render the streets impassable.

On this same day, January 1, 1877, in the city of Buffalo, a little boy departed the grounds of the Buffalo Orphan Asylum for the final time. Archival records indicate that he was "taken by his guardian." The record is silent on the name of the guardian. It could have been Judge Burrows. It might have been Grover Cleveland. We do not know who took the youngster by the hand that day, but we do know where he was ultimately delivered: To 93 Niagara Street, the home of Dr. James E. King and his wife, Sarah.

Oscar must have been bewildered as he took in these splendid surroundings and got to know his new parents. It was a clapboard house with a front porch and veranda and a picket fence. This was the first real house he had ever experienced; until now he had lived only in dank apartments and boarding rooms. Perhaps Dr. King informed the boy of their exceptional connection. He, Dr. King, had been present at his birth. He had delivered the boy into the world.

At some point, the boy was informed that he would now be known by another name. He had been born Oscar Folsom Cleveland. For the first year of his life, the woman who was his caregiver had called him Jack. Henceforth, the puzzled little boy was told he would be known as James. From this day on, he was James E. King Jr., the doctor's son.

6

PATH TO THE PRESIDENCY

GROVER CLEVELAND COULD never have imagined that as he swung open the doors of Billy Dranger's saloon he was taking the first step on a journey that in just three years would catapult him from a lawyer unknown outside the city of Buffalo to the presidency of the United States.

It was October 22, 1881, around seven thirty on a Saturday evening. Cleveland was forty-four years old. Five years had passed since that unpleasant business with Maria Halpin, an episode in his life that, as far as he was concerned, was now ancient history. The Halpin woman had vanished from the city of Buffalo; Cleveland had no idea where she was living. From what he gathered, his biological son, now known as James E. King Jr., was doing well, although whispers of the boy's true heritage and his link to Grover Cleveland remained a steady undercurrent of gossip. For all its big-city complexity, Buffalo fundamentally remained a small town.

Cleveland walked into the saloon at Eagle and Pearl, positioned his large belly against the bar, and ordered a drink. Off at a corner table, some men were talking in raised voices. Cleveland turned and saw they were five Democratic Party leaders having a drink and a bite to eat. One of them was Warren F. Miller, the lawyer who was in Oscar Folsom's buggy that terrible summer night in 1875 when Folsom was killed. They hailed Cleveland over. He sat down, wondering what had brought them to Dranger's.

It turned out that Miller and the others made up the search committee that county chairman Peter Doyle had appointed to find a Democratic candidate to run for mayor, preferably an eminent businessman with an unblemished record. They had a short list of top men and had first called on the banker Stephen Clarke. They moved on to businessman Delavan Clarke and the merchant prince Stephen Barnum. Then to Charles Sweet, president of the Third National Bank, and Charles Curtis, president of the Board of Trade. They had started at the top of their list, and offered all of them the nomination. Every one of them had turned it down. It had been a day of mounting frustration, and with just three days left before the Democrats of Erie County were to hold their convention, this was shaping up to be a huge embarrassment for the party. In short, the first contender to answer in the affirmative would have the nomination.

As they vented, Cleveland listened. Republicans outnumbered Democrats in Buffalo; in this election cycle, Buffalo's citizens were expected, as usual, to go Republican. The mayor earned a salary of $2,500 a year—for a job with so many headaches,

Cleveland totally understood why these estimable businessmen had all said no.

Then somebody on the committee had an inspiration. The solution to their problem was staring them in the face. Grover Cleveland was the man!

Cleveland shook his head and told them not a chance. He had zero interest in running for elective office again. Besides, he told them, he was a lawyer, and the mandate from Doyle was to find a rich businessman whose integrity and reputation for honesty could not be questioned. But the more Miller and the others thought about it, the more Cleveland seemed like the perfect candidate. Plus, they *were* desperate. Cleveland protested vigorously; then he started to waver. This buoyed the committee. Everyone knew Cleveland as a proven vote-getter, and he had been elected sheriff with the support of independents and Republicans, a coalition he would need to cobble together to win the mayoral race.

Finally, Cleveland said, "All right, I'll run, but only on condition that the rest of the ticket is made up to suit me."

He wanted John C. Sheehan, the incumbent city comptroller, booted off the ticket. Sheehan had a reputation for shiftiness and political malfeasance, and Cleveland refused to have him as his running mate. On this issue, he was unyielding.

"I'll be damned if I'll run with that Irishman," he said.

Three days later, when the convention was called to order at Tivoli Hall, Cleveland was still dithering. Three party honchos were delegated to track him down and inform him that all his conditions had been met: Sheehan was done for, and in his place the nominee for comptroller was Timothy J. Mahoney. This was the same neighborhood rascal who in his youth had sneaked into Lewis Allen's orchards to pilfer peaches. Mahoney had joined the police force, and political connections had aided his rise through the ranks, to captain and then inspector. All that time, he had stayed in contact with Cleveland. He was now the city auditor. Given the ethnic politics in play, with his Irish name, he made a credible replacement for Sheehan.

The committee caught up with Cleveland in court, where he was arguing a case before New York State Supreme Court Justice Albert Haight. They pulled him aside to inform him of his man Mahoney's nomination. Cleveland listened to the news, then went over to Justice Haight. Cleveland and Haight had been friends since 1872, when Cleveland was sheriff and Haight, at age thirty, had been elected to the county bench. Back then, he had been known as "the Boy Judge."

Nodding at the three men hunched over in the corner, Cleveland told the justice, "This is a committee from the Democratic city convention, and they want to nominate me for mayor. They've come over to see if I'll accept. What shall I do about it?"

"I think you'd better accept," Haight replied. "Your chances may be pretty good."

"But I'm practicing law, and I don't want it interfered with."

"The mayoralty is an honorable position," Justice Haight countered. "You haven't any family to take care of. I'd advise you to accept."

Cleveland pondered what Haight had to say, but just didn't know what to do. Was a life in the public spotlight really for him? He asked the justice to adjourn the case to give him a chance to think things through.

"Court stands in recess for half an hour," Justice Haight announced.

While the committee waited, in the courtroom Cleveland reviewed the pros and cons for a final time, then said, "Go back and place me in the running." In the interest of party harmony, he added, "Make up the rest of the ticket to suit yourselves." With that, at 4:30 PM, a keyed-up committeeman ran back to Tivoli Hall to break the news to the "great unwashed," as a Republican newspaper referred to the packed convention hall. He elbowed his way through the throng and announced, "He's accepted, boys! He's accepted! Let's have a drink!"

Meanwhile, Cleveland had made his own way up Washington Street to Tivoli Hall. When he strode in at 5:00 PM, wild cheers erupted. He took the stage and announced, "I accept the nomination tendered to me." Then he put forth his vision of low taxation and integrity in government. Right after his brief remarks, Cleveland returned to his case in Justice Haight's courtroom and picked up his argument where he had left off.

During that mayoral campaign of 1881, Cleveland hoisted many a stein of beer. Most of the electioneering took place in the city's saloons, where men congregated in large numbers. (Women's suffrage was still four decades away.) Cleveland made his stump speech standing not behind a rostrum but atop a beer barrel. He rallied the citizenry under the banner of good government, striking a bipartisan tone of contempt for machine politics: "A Democratic thief is as bad as a Republican thief," he said.

The *Courier* and other pro-Democrat newspapers in Buffalo conspired to assist Cleveland in discreet ways. When he spoke at a rally at Diebold's Saloon in the first ward, the *Courier*, mindful that conservative church elders might take offense at the venue, altered it to Diebold's Hall. Those in the know had a good laugh when they read the article the next day, though the mischief went over the heads of the Episcopalian churchmen, who knew nothing of life in the Irish first ward.

Naturally, the Republican papers were doing their utmost to prop up their candidate, Milton E. Beebe, a mild-mannered architect who served as an alderman and was deemed to be in the pocket of the shady political ring that ruled City Hall. In the final weeks of the campaign, the *Commercial Advertiser*, crowning Beebe as the "workingman's friend," published the entire Republican ticket on its front page every day. The paper also took special pleasure in assailing Cleveland—"Grove" as he was scornfully called—for his "lordly manners." He was derided as a "wealthy old bachelor and white-vested aristocrat" who "carries his head so high, as a rule, that he cannot see ordinary persons." Cleveland's draft-dodging days came up in another story, this one told by a veteran who said that after he had hounded Cleveland for a donation to send a delegation of soldiers to Yorktown for the centennial celebration of the British surrender, Cleveland sputtered, "I am sick and tired of this old-soldier business. You fellows have been well taken care of, and I am opposed to it on principle." That was either a tactless stand or a gutsy one, depending on one's point of view: Cleveland seemed to be taking a shot at the Grand Army of the Republic, the fraternal organization of nearly half a million Union Army veterans, known for its political clout. It was said that no Republican candidate could be nominated for president without the endorsement of the GAR. Yet for whatever reason, Cleveland's scorn for the veterans' vote failed to gain traction.

The first ward was shaping up to be key to a victory. It was typically a Democratic stronghold, but Cleveland was concerned that his ouster of John Sheehan from the ticket would lead to a tepid turnout, or even worse, outright sabotage by Sheehan's legions of followers. The *Commercial Advertiser* tried to stir things up yet again with the accusation that Cleveland had "ostracized" the entire Irish American population from jury duty when he was sheriff and, this time, had refused to run on the ballot with "that Irishman Sheehan." The Saturday night before the election, Cleveland poured all his resources into campaigning in the bars along the waterfront. His last stop was Schwabl's saloon, right on Sheehan's home turf.

Election Day fell on the first Tuesday in November. In those days, there were polling booths at police precincts, but more often than not, they were in private houses scattered around the city; a voter in the fourth ward, for example, had to cast his ballot at No. 62 E. Huron Street, the home of Frederick Schottin, a bookbinder. A Buffalo policeman stood outside each polling station, and as soon as the votes were tabulated, the officer ran to the nearest telegraph office to send the results to police headquarters.

The final returns gave Grover Cleveland a solid victory, 15,080 to Beebe's 11,529. Jubilant Democrats were so appreciative of the coverage they had received in the *Courier* they marched in a procession with a band to the newspaper's editorial offices, lit a huge bonfire, and serenaded the staff. It was, the *Commercial Advertiser* sourly reported, a "waste of good kindling." For Republican mouthpieces such as the *Commercial Advertiser*, the election of Grover Cleveland and the Democrats was a "disaster," which it blamed on the "treachery" of those Republicans who had switched party allegiance.

In truth, Cleveland was swept into office on a wave of revulsion over machine politics and the conduct of a clique of grafters known as the Ring who ran City Hall. Democrats and Republicans were deemed equally crooked. Cleveland's platform of good government and his reputation for pugnacious honesty connected with the electorate. Plus, the German voters really delivered.

In Holland Patent, Ann Cleveland sat down at her desk and composed a letter to her son. Mrs. Cleveland had misgivings about Grover entering politics. "But now that you have taken upon yourself the burdens of public office do right, act honestly, impartially and fearlessly," she wrote him.

Cleveland was inaugurated on New Year's Day 1883, and immediately set the tone of his frugal new administration by refusing to hold a formal inaugural ceremony. The next day, he got down to business and sent the sixteen Republicans and ten Democrats who sat on the Common Council a stern message that hit them right in the collective solar plexus. The clerk started to read Cleveland's address at 2:00 PM.

First, the new mayor took aim at the "shameful neglect of duty" in the office of the street commissioner. How was it possible, Cleveland thundered, that the network of streets and sidewalks constructed by the city was in such deplorable condition and yet the city's ten street inspectors could offer no record whatsoever of actually conducting a single inspection? And why did the city charge 26¢ per foot for the construction of plank sidewalks when private citizens were able to hire construction crews for 15¢? Henceforth, Cleveland demanded, as a blanket rule, that all city contracts be awarded to the lowest bidder.

One Republican alderman was so affronted he rose and moved that any further reading of the mayor's address be dispensed with at once; he had heard enough. Perhaps curious about what was to follow, the council voted him down, and the rest of the mayor's communiqué was read into the record. The aldermen listened as Cleveland went on to declare that he was "utterly unable to discover any valid reason" why municipal offices were closed at 4:00 PM when the city work force was paid to work until five. That policy was ending as of now.

The aldermen just sat there stupefied; they had never heard anything like this. Then they swiftly got back to the practice of business-as-usual machine politics.

A piece of legislation was passed creating the position of city mortician; the bill was sent to the mayor's desk for his routine signature. Mayor Cleveland quickly surmised that the council was once again crafting a do-nothing patronage job for a political hack, to be named later. As Cleveland saw it, it was just another measure to bloat municipal government. It became his first veto.

More drama followed. A routine city contract came before the council: a politically connected businessman, George Talbott, was awarded a five-year contract to clean all paved city streets and alleys for $422,500. The curious thing was that Talbott was the *highest* bidder. A rival sanitation company with a perfectly acceptable history of honest work had put in a bid for $313,000 for the same contract. Another curious thing: Talbott's original bid had been $372,000; he had *raised* it by $50,000. Everyone knew what was going on. It was so transparent it was almost laughable. Talbott was lining the pockets of the aldermen to win the contract. Even so, it took some horse trading to corral the necessary votes, but when it came before the council, it was awarded to Talbott, 15 to 11.

"This is time for plain speech," Mayor Cleveland told the aldermen. "I regard it as the culmination of a most bare-faced, impudent, and shameless scheme to betray the interests of the people." Cleveland's language in vetoing the deal whipped the citizenry into a populist frenzy. Who could have imagined that the veto of a street-cleaning contract could galvanize the public?

John Weber, who lost the race against Cleveland for sheriff in 1870, would later recall it as "nothing short of a popular revolt. I cannot remember a time when interest in any municipal matter reached such a height," he said. "Groups of men could be seen on the street, discussing it to the accompaniment of waving arms." Weber watched in genuine amazement as the coverage of the scandal spread across the state, and as it did, he wondered if it would make Cleveland governor.

Cleveland had nothing against George Talbott. Actually, Talbott was a former law client and a drinking buddy. At the height of the hullabaloo over the veto, Cleveland took Talbott aside. "This is neither a personal nor a legal matter," he said. "While I was your attorney, I was loyal to your interests. Now the people are my clients, and I must be loyal to them."

A storm of public outrage was heaped on the Common Council, leading one alderman who voted for the contract to mutter, "I have made the greatest mistake of my whole life." In the wake of Cleveland's veto, when Talbott's street-cleaning contract came before the body again, the humbled aldermen voted it down 23 to 2.

Cleveland detested the ceremonial duties associated with the mayoralty. On a scorching day in May, when he laid the cornerstone at the new YMCA building, he found it a "ridiculous thing for me to do." Through some foul-up, the *Express* city desk had neglected to send someone to cover the event. Frank Severance, a bright cub reporter, was told to track down the mayor and obtain a copy of his YMCA speech. It was a tricky assignment. In all his dealings with Cleveland, Severance had found him to be as "gruff as a mastiff." Every Cleveland veto message to the Common Council came larded with sarcasm.

Severance went to City Hall, but Cleveland was not in the office. On a hunch, he went down to Gerot's, the French restaurant on Main Street that was known to be a favorite of the mayor's. Sure enough, he found Cleveland alone at a table before an enormous pile of food. Severance gulped and approached him, uttering a stream of abject apologies for intruding on his meal, but the *Express* really needed a copy of the speech for the edition that was going to press. Cleveland locked eyes with Severance; the young man braced for a rant.

"Had your supper?" Cleveland asked.

"No, Mr. Mayor."

"Sit down."

Severance got his story—and the food was delicious.

Around this time, the *Buffalo Times*, in an otherwise-friendly sketch of the new mayor, wondered whether Cleveland's "prejudices" against married people had induced him to select a fellow bachelor, Harmon S. Cutting, as his chief clerk.

Cleveland read the scandalous innuendo in a cold fury, suspecting that it was the handiwork of the City Hall grafters, sniping at him any way they could. He never forgave the *Times* publisher, Norman E. Mack.

Just as the street-cleaning veto was ebbing, another ruckus erupted—this one over sewage—with the shady aldermen on the Common Council once again stirring the pot.

For decades, the city had let raw sewage flow directly into the Erie Canal at Hamburg Street, where in the summer it would bake under the hot sun until it became a revolting stew of germs and offensive odors. This was a grave issue for the citizens of Buffalo. In 1881, more than a third of the city's four thousand recorded deaths were due to typhoid and other epidemic diseases. On taking office, Cleveland declared that a modern municipal sewage system was now a priority. What he proposed seemed to make sense: the naming of an independent commission to supervise the planning and construction of the sewer line. That way the taxpayers of Buffalo would be assured of the "best available engineering skill."

The machine politicians on the Common Council immediately screamed holy hell. Where Cleveland envisioned a state-of-the-art sewage system befitting a great and growing city, the aldermen saw the opportunity of lining their pockets slipping away. The last thing they wanted to do was to hand over control of the most expensive public works project in Buffalo history to an independent agency beholden to the mayor.

When Cleveland submitted the names of his five commissioners, the council rejected every one by a vote of 14 to 12. It was war. Cleveland's retort was ruthlessly straightforward: He resubmitted every name, contemptuously informing the aldermen that their rejection must have been the "result of haste and confusion." All the major newspapers in the city, Democrat and Republican, lined up behind Cleveland; and the aldermen were compelled, under threat of civil insurrection, to capitulate. The five independent sewer commissioners were confirmed by a vote of 17 to 8. It was a triumph for Cleveland, particularly when the costs of the sewer system came in at $764,000—previously estimated by the Republican-controlled council at an inflated $1.5 million.

All of Western New York watched the unfolding drama. In the late 19th century, public sanitation was such a life-and-death concern that faint stirrings of a Cleveland-for-governor movement began to appear in the Buffalo press. Even the publisher Norman Mack joined the campaign.

In the seventh month of his administration, as July came around, Cleveland prepared to go on vacation. As usual, he planned to visit his mother in Holland Patent. Then a telegram arrived with unsettling news: Ann Cleveland was close to death. The forty-five-year-old mayor hurried to Holland Patent. All the surviving Cleveland children once again gathered, even Anna Cleveland Hastings. She lived in Ceylon with her missionary husband and happened to be on one of her rare visits home when her mother was stricken.

The matriarch of the family lingered for several days, and the Cleveland siblings remained at her bedside until the end. Mrs. Cleveland was seventy-six when she died on July 19, 1882. Grover was disconsolate. Of all her children, he held a special place in her heart. She died without ever knowing that her bachelor son had fathered a son.

Cleveland sent a telegram to Harmon Cutting, notifying his clerk of his mother's death. The *Express*, almost certainly after a briefing by Cutting, reported that the mayor "has always been devotedly attached to her, and will feel her loss deeply." Holed up in a room at his mother's house, Cleveland said he could only imagine "the desolation of a life without a mother's prayers." He conducted what city business he could and answered telegrams and letters of condolences. He poured his heartache into the inscription he composed for her memorial stone: "Her children arise and call her blessed."

Mrs. Cleveland was buried in the same cemetery where a monument—inscribed with the legend, "Loving and pleasant in their lives, and in their death they were not divided"—had been erected for the two Cleveland brothers lost at sea in the *Missouri* disaster of 1872.

Holland Patent had not changed much since Grover's departure nearly thirty years before, and he got a chance to get reacquainted with his siblings. Reverend William Cleveland had moved to Oneida County, not far from his late father's parish. Mary Cleveland Hoyt was still in Fayetteville, and Louise Cleveland Bacon lived in Ohio. Susan Cleveland Yoemans was raising a family near the Canadian border. Only the gifted youngest sister, thirty-six-year-old spinster Rose, remained in their mother's house.

In Albany, Edgar K. Apgar was following the reports out of Buffalo with genuine curiosity. The Yale-educated Apgar was a leading Democratic political operative and the deputy treasurer of New York State. With shoulders so slender he looked like a boy, the forty-year-old made an improbable political boss. He weighed just one hundred pounds, ate two meals a day, and shunned sleep. "I shrink from it every time with just the same reluctance you would feel in surrendering yourself to the influence of ether in a dentist's chair," he once said. Until the end of his brief time on earth, he was cursed with a malfunctioning digestive system that one friend said left him at the mercy of a "capricious stomach."

Apgar read all the state's major dailies to keep on top of local political developments. He saw how the street-cleaning contract in Buffalo was erupting into a major scandal that was galvanizing the citizenry of Buffalo. He followed every aspect of it. One day, he went to see his friend Daniel S. Lamont, the chief clerk of the New York State Department of State. Like Apgar, Lamont was a young functionary who served on the Democratic Party's central committee. Apgar asked Lamont if he knew of a "Grover Cleveland of Buffalo." Lamont answered that he did not. Apgar said this Cleveland was the new mayor of Buffalo, and his intuition was telling him that Cleveland was someone worth considering for statewide office. An "ugly-honest man," Apgar called him, with "undaunted courage." Apgar even wondered whether Cleveland would make a dark-horse candidate for governor in the election of 1882, which was just around the corner.

Apgar told Lamont that he was going to start paying careful attention to Grover Cleveland.

The next few weeks were electrifying. Apgar found himself consumed with the news out of Buffalo. Grover Cleveland was averaging two or three vetoes a week! Whenever he had to go out of town on state business, Apgar made sure his staff saved the

Buffalo newspapers, and on his return, he voraciously consumed the stack of back issues.

Finally, on August 23, Apgar took the plunge. He wrote a letter to Cleveland, introducing himself and saying he had a matter to bring up that was perhaps presumptuous but of vital importance to Cleveland's political future. "I deem it right, though I have not the honor of your personal acquaintance, to place before you some suggestions which seem to me worthy of your consideration," Apgar wrote.

The condition of the Democratic Party, he informed Cleveland, was bleak. The party had lost the confidence of the people. It had "abandoned its principles and made dishonest alliances for the sake of temporary success, which even in most cases it has failed to secure." Apgar asked Cleveland to come to Albany and meet with Daniel Manning, chairman of the Democratic state committee.

"Men come here daily from all parts of the state—active, earnest and influential men. They come not to receive orders from a boss but to consult one whom they look upon as representing their views," Apgar told Cleveland. An alliance between Manning and Cleveland, Apgar said, would guarantee Cleveland the gubernatorial nomination on the first ballot at the state convention coming up in Syracuse in two months.

When he read Apgar's letter, Grover Cleveland was intrigued. He had returned to Buffalo after burying his mother to find his political allies in a state of exhilaration and the editorial pages of the Democratic newspapers in the city urging him to run for governor. Cleveland wrote his response to Apgar on August 29.

"I am gratified with the interest you take in my candidacy. . . . You are quite right in believing that I am not actively seeking the nomination for governor. The efforts of my friends and neighbors in that direction were begun in my absence from the city." While he found the attention to be "extremely pleasant," Cleveland said he would regrettably have to decline meeting with Manning in Albany. It would be impossible to keep such a get-together private, Cleveland explained, and a Cleveland-Manning sit-down would inevitably lead to stories that "an understanding had been arrived at between us, and pledges which make me his man." The Cleveland boom, such as it was, hinged on his reputation as a reformer of uncompromising integrity. He could not be labeled as another politician angling for higher office.

Apgar read Cleveland's response in his office in Albany. It was written on gray paper in purple ink. Cleveland's handwriting was small and delicate, surprisingly feminine for such a burly drinking man. An hour after opening the letter, Apgar showed it to another cunning Democratic Party operative, William Gorham Rice. Rice studied it and asked Apgar what he thought. Apgar had to admit that it was disappointing. Cleveland was not going to publicly declare. But as Apgar thought it through some more, he came to understand the shrewdness of Cleveland's position. He was more convinced than ever: Here was a new type of politician he had been searching for—"a man for the hour."

Back in Buffalo, Cleveland, with a wink and a nod, set to work marshalling his forces. He was in his office at City Hall when he sent word that he wanted to see the comptroller. Timothy Mahoney bounded upstairs to the mayor's office, where Cleveland laid out the plan for his old neighborhood sidekick.

"Captain Tim, I want to be the Democratic candidate for governor this fall. I'd like your help."

"You've already got it," Mahoney answered.

"I understand that you are prominent in the Catholic Mutual Benefit Association?" The CMBA was a fraternal organization composed mainly of Irish Americans, and loosely modeled on the Freemasons.

"That's right," Mahoney said. He was the supreme vice president.

"Some of its members in this part of the state are prominent in the Democratic Party and are delegates to state conventions?"

"They are," agreed Mahoney.

"I'll have Erie County solid for me, of course. But other counties around here will have to be rounded up. Would you write your fraternal friends and—"

"I'll do that, and better," Mahoney said. "I'll have them call on you at City Hall, and you can talk to them face-to-face."

Over the next three weeks, Cleveland quietly drummed up support. Thanks to Mahoney's lobbying efforts, he won pledges from sixty-six delegates, most of them Irish Americans from Buffalo and Rochester affiliated with the Catholic Mutual Benefit Association. Western New York was an isolated region that had a long history of political inferiority because no United States senator and only one governor had ever been elected from there. Western New York delegates rallied around Cleveland as their favorite son.

It would take 193 delegates to win the nomination. The front-runners were Congressman Roswell P. Flower of upstate

Watertown and Major General Henry W. Slocum of Brooklyn. Slocum was a by-the-book military commander ridiculed for indecision at the Battle of Gettysburg, where he had earned the insulting epithet "General Slow Come." Flower and Slocum could count on 100 delegates each. Snubbed by Cleveland, state party chairman Daniel Manning had thrown his support behind Slocum. In the Byzantine world of New York politics, Manhattan Democrats were split between reformers and Tammany Hall. The reformers backed Flower, even though Cleveland in theory would seem a natural partner. Tammany Hall, under the domination of Boss Jim Kelly, who had taken leadership after the incarceration of the notorious Boss Tweed, was noncommittal. Strategically, Boss Kelly was determined to serve as kingmaker at the convention. He was playing the waiting game.

Cleveland's candidacy was front-page news in Buffalo and other cities in Western New York, but downstate he was essentially ignored. As *The New York Times* dispatch put it, "Only one candidate is mentioned who resides West of Albany, and that is Mayor Cleveland of Buffalo. . . . No one here expresses any confidence in his nomination."

William C. Hudson, a reporter who covered state politics for *The Brooklyn Eagle* under the pen name Seacoal, was sent to Buffalo to evaluate the candidate. Hudson was the kind of correspondent who always knew more than what he reported. That discretion earned him access because politicians could rely on Hudson never to publish anything they didn't want to see in print. As a journalist once said of Hudson, "Deposits placed in his mind were as safe as those made in a bank, and more safe, because they were never, even indirectly, put into circulation."

Charley McCune, the owner of the *Courier*, escorted Hudson to Cleveland's law office, where the reporter was introduced to the dark-horse candidate for governor. Wilson Bissell was also present. Everyone knew that Hudson was a plugged-in guy. They also suspected that as the representative of *The Brooklyn Eagle*, he was a Slocum man. But Hudson surprised everyone in the room when he said he thought Cleveland had a decent shot at the nomination, provided he stayed "aloof" from the internecine divisions tearing the party apart. The smartest move for Cleveland was to sit back and wait until the "inevitable break," at which point the entire convention would rally around him.

Cleveland listened more than he spoke. It just so happened that Hudson's tactic fit his own, so the two men clicked. He asked Hudson to join him for a carriage ride the next day when they could talk some more.

Cleveland sounded glum about his chances when he and Hudson were alone in the carriage the following afternoon.

Hudson begged to differ. "Mr. Cleveland, you will be the nominee. I can see no other outcome of the situation."

Cleveland wasn't buying it. He tried to explain how he had found himself in this fix. "Sometime ago," he told Hudson, "my mother was taken seriously ill. She is dead now. I was sent for. Laying everything aside, I hastened to her and remained with her to the end. When all was over and she was laid away, I returned to Buffalo to find that in my absence the boys had started a campaign for me for governor. It had such an impetus that it was difficult to stop it." Then Cleveland surprised Hudson by saying he had very little interest in serving as governor. His experience as mayor of Buffalo, he said, "has not put me in love with executive administration."

His true ambition, he confided to Hudson, was to be named a state supreme court justice.

Hudson pondered everything Cleveland had to say. "Well, Mr. Mayor," he said, "when a man plunges into the political stream, he soon becomes subject to its current."

Two nights before the opening of the convention, Daniel Manning's brother John paid an unexpected call on Cleveland at City Hall. John Manning owned four breweries in Buffalo, so he had clout in town. He came as an emissary from his brother, the state party chairman. In his talk with Cleveland, he used the word *treachery* without directly accusing Cleveland. But the insinuation was in the air. There was no way Cleveland could prevail, John Manning informed the mayor. Slocum was too famous and Flower too rich. Why not settle for the nomination of a congressman-at-large from New York State?

Cleveland just sat there. But the moment Manning left his office, Cleveland hurriedly wrote a letter to his law partner, Wilson Bissell, who was already in Syracuse at the state convention corralling delegates. It was one in the morning.

"John B. Manning has been in to see me tonight," Cleveland reported. "Now do just as I tell you without asking any questions." He instructed Bissell to track down Daniel Lockwood and Samuel Scheu—Cleveland's floor managers—and have them find Daniel Manning in Syracuse and "urge with the *utmost vehemence* my nomination.

"Never mind what he says—have them pound away." It had to be drilled into Manning's head that Cleveland was unswerving, and that he was not going to be "placated" with a run for Congress.

Meanwhile, the Cleveland forces, such as they were, gathered in Syracuse. Tim Mahoney, accompanied by a brawny aide, pulled into the train depot carrying armloads of Grover Cleveland lithographs, which were distributed to all the delegates, to the derision of a *New York Tribune* correspondent, who reported that the posters were causing "considerable merriment." It was all a big joke to the sophisticates from downstate.

But Mahoney was chipping away. "He's our kind of people," he assured all his friends from the Catholic association. Bissell was also making the rounds of the delegates. Many of them seemed receptive to Cleveland but wanted to meet the candidate in person. Bissell and the other floor managers "inundated" Cleveland with telegrams pleading with him to come to Syracuse. Cleveland was never much for pressing the flesh. Even so, he heeded their advice and took the next available train, stewing the entire time. "It was almost beyond my understanding what to do, or for what purpose I was needed at Syracuse," he complained.

At dusk, he reached Syracuse, where he was greeted with "bombshell" news.

Word had come down that the Republican convention in Saratoga had denied the incumbent governor, Alonzo Cornell, the nomination for reelection. It was a huge shock to everyone. In his place, U.S. treasury secretary Charles J. Folger had been given the nod. The robber baron Jay Gould was seen as the invisible hammer behind the power play, acting with the connivance of President Chester A. Arthur and former New York senator Roscoe Conkling. Cornell and Conkling hated each other. It all reeked of machine politics at the highest national level.

In Syracuse, Democrats realized that the ham-fisted Republicans had committed an act of self-immolation. A Democratic politician with a clean record of independence could actually win the statehood. It was as if the stars had aligned for Cleveland.

In the lobby of his hotel, on an unusually hot night for Upstate New York in late September, the habitually proper Cleveland was dripping with sweat. He took off his coat and rolled up his sleeves as Bissell and Mahoney rounded up one delegate after another and introduced them to the bachelor mayor from Buffalo who was causing such a stir. It gave them, Cleveland said, a "chance to look me over. I came rather to enjoy it."

Reporters from the New York City newspapers also got to check out this intriguing new figure in politics. Watching him in action in the hotel lobby, the correspondent from *The New York Times* sent a dispatch describing Grover Cleveland to the citizens of the largest city in America:

> His features are regular and full of intelligent expression. His eyes are dark and penetrating in their glances. He wears no beard, but a heavy dark mustache completely covers his mouth, and underneath is a square, firm chin. In his movements Mr. Cleveland is deliberate, dignified and graceful.

Finally, after Cleveland had finished his politicking in the hotel lobby, he went to pay his respects to the state chairman, Daniel Manning. It was the first time they had met.

In his hotel room, Manning shrewdly checked his temper. Maybe Edgar Apgar was right and Cleveland did represent the future of the party. Considering everything that was at stake,

Cleveland left Manning on gracious terms. Definitely they could do business together down the road.

As far as Cleveland was concerned, his work was done. At 2:00 AM, still shaking his head at the "novel experience" of his Syracuse adventure, he boarded a train back to Buffalo and was back at his desk at City Hall the same morning, where he awaited the outcome of the vote.

The convention at the Grand Opera House was called to order at 10:20 AM. Poor lighting, combined with great clouds of cigar smoke, made it almost impossible to see from one end to the other. Dan Lockwood placed Cleveland's name in nomination. He delivered a frosty speech that apparently did his candidate no good. Fortunately for Cleveland, the slender figure of Edgar Apgar made its way to the rostrum to second the nomination. Apgar spoke from the heart. He pointed to Cleveland's machine-busting record as mayor. Here, at last, was a politician who was free of all political entanglements. Cleveland was beholden to no one. And he was the only candidate among the Democrats who Republicans would feel comfortable voting for. When Apgar was finished, the audience cheered.

"He had achieved that rare result in a political convention— he had changed votes."

The delegates were called to order, and the balloting began. Tim Mahoney had cunningly packed the balcony with his Irish American chums, and when the first vote was recorded on the Grover Cleveland column, on cue, every Mahoney man bellowed their approval. The convention floor shook with the applause of the Clevelandites. At least from the peanut gallery, Cleveland was top choice.

The forces of Daniel Manning held solid. Every single one delivered for Slocum.

When the votes on the first ballot were tabulated, it went as predicted: Slocum had 98 and Flower 97. Cleveland's support stood at 66. Another hundred votes were scattered among lesser candidates and favorite sons.

On the second ballot, Slocum and Flower gained, each polling 123. Cleveland garnered only 5 additional votes. The convention stood at a deadlock. But all the zeal seemed to be for Cleveland. Each new vote added to the Cleveland column produced scenes of pandemonium in the gallery. The people—at least Mahoney's people—were screaming for a new kind of politics.

Still confident of victory, Congressman Flower buttonholed a Cleveland delegate from Buffalo and demanded to know which way Erie County would go once it was realized the Cleveland candidacy was doomed.

"Grover Cleveland," came the response.

Flower blinked. Perhaps the chap did not understand the question. "But after you're satisfied he can't win, after you get through voting for him, who next?"

"Grover Cleveland."

On the third ballot, the pendulum started to swing Cleveland's way. The first break came when Columbia County was called and the nephew of the revered former governor of New York, Samuel J. Tilden, switched his vote from Slocum to Cleveland. To the audible groans from Slocum delegates, two other men from Columbia joined young Mr. Tilden.

Down the alphabetical lineup of counties went the roll call. Then came the turn of New York County, the largest in the state. Manhattan was split between the forces of reform and those aligned with Tammany Hall, alienated from each other, and barely on speaking terms. All thirty-eight reformist delegates switched to Cleveland. That did it. Boss Kelly of Tammany Hall gave his men a stiff nod of assent, and 23 votes were suddenly swung for Cleveland. Kelly became the convention's kingmaker, even if he loathed the politics of the king he had just crowned.

Pandemonium reigned. Delegate after delegate rose and demanded to be recognized so that they too could switch their votes to Cleveland. It was a stampede.

At 4:00 AM, the final tally came in: Cleveland, 211 and Slocum, 156. Flower's support had gone up in smoke. He ended with only 15 votes.

The band struck up the "Red, White and Blue." In the gallery, Mahoney shouted himself hoarse with joy and watched in pure bliss as a Cleveland lithograph he had brought with him to such mockery was unfurled on the platform.

News from the convention reached New York City during one of the most drenching rainstorms in the city's history— more than six inches of water fell in the deluge, rinsing the filthy streets of mud and garbage until the water looked as pure as a mountain stream. Old-timers said they could not recall a day when New York seemed so cleansed. Over at Grand Central Depot, the rain-delayed train from Syracuse pulled in two hours late. Boss Kelly, wearing a white straw hat, alighted from the drawing-room car with his crew of Tammany warriors, grinning like a "conqueror" and declaring that Cleveland was sure to win the big race in November. The Tammany boss was last seen that night getting into a carriage that went rattling down the cobblestone streets to his home on Madison Avenue.

In Buffalo, the telegraph service flashed word of the Cleveland victory with these words from Bissell: "You are nominated." A cheering mob of Democrats awaiting the results at City Hall moved en masse to Billy Dranger's saloon, where they heard that Cleveland was having a drink. Dranger's was known locally as the Sewer, for the restaurant in the basement.

Cleveland saw the horde spilling into the streets outside the saloon. He went to the balcony, where everyone could have a good look at him.

"My friends . . . I cannot but remember tonight the time when I came into your midst, friendless, unknown, and poor. I cannot but remember how, step-by-step, by the encouragement of my good fellow citizens, I have gone on to receive more of their appreciation than is my due, until I have been honored with more distinction, perhaps, than I deserve."

The crowd roared.

7

THE GODDESS

FRANCES FOLSOM HAD been only eleven when her father died, and ever since, Grover Cleveland had been a guiding force in her life. She called him Uncle Cleve, and he called her Frank. He was always there for her, like a second father.

Cleveland showered Frances with generous gifts, the most memorable being a frisky bull terrier puppy; and on warm summer days, he took her to Beaver Island. Reachable only by steam launch, this small jut of land, a thousand acres or so off the head of Grand Island, was where Cleveland and other prominent citizens of Buffalo had organized a social community of movers and shakers known as the Beaver Island Club. The Jolly Reefers, as they called themselves, were used to seeing Cleveland holding the chubby little girl by the hand as he showed her around the island's rose garden and towering trees or brought her to a picnic or a clambake. They were aware that in Cleveland's capacity as executor of the Oscar Folsom estate, he was involved in Frances's life, and it was also taken for granted that he would one day marry the widow Emma Folsom. Even Emma thought so.

When Frances reached the end of her childhood, Cleveland stood ready to offer her his guidance on the major choices that confront every adolescent girl. She was an excellent student with a genuine curiosity about things, whose teachers appreciated the extra effort she put into her schoolwork. Tall, about five foot seven, she had rich chestnut hair that cascaded onto her shoulders, and dreamy violet eyes. She had blossomed into a young lady of indisputable glamour and what her cousin Isabel Harmon had called "witchery."

Frances had just begun her senior year at Central High School in Buffalo, the city's preeminent public high school, when she became besotted with Mr. Charles Townsend. A few weeks later, she dropped out, announcing that she was getting engaged to young Townsend. This hit Cleveland like a swift kick in the teeth.

Frances's departure from school upset Cleveland for several reasons, not least of which was that he had suggested she enroll at Central High, so he took her failure to graduate personally. Then there was this Townsend fellow.

Charles Townsend came from solid stock: His grandfather, also named Charles Townsend, had founded the Buffalo Savings Bank and been one of Niagara County's first sitting judges. Eight years older than Frances Folsom when they announced their engagement, Charles had lived with his parents in Europe for five years during which he studied in Belgium, Switzerland, and Germany. He had a wry sense of humor, and in his breezy writing style, he wrote articles that he submitted to travel magazines and the Buffalo newspapers. After his father's death in Germany, Townsend returned to Buffalo to study at the Auburn Theological Seminary with the intention of becoming an ordained Presbyterian minister when he asked Frances to marry him.

The wedding of Frances Folsom and Charles Townsend would have been deemed a fine match between two socially connected Buffalo families. Alas, their engagement lasted just a few weeks before Frances sent her fiancé a "Dear Charles" letter. In the envelope, she also sent back the ring. As breakups go, it was amicable, and Townsend never bore a grudge. What role, if any, Grover Cleveland may have played in the drama remains a mystery, but with young Townsend out of the picture, the way was clear for Cleveland to pursue an unambiguously romantic relationship with Frances Folsom. (Townsend, it seemed, could never escape Cleveland's shadow. When he died in 1914, Townsend's address was 55 Cleveland Street in Orange, New Jersey; and on his deathbed, he officiated at the wedding of his daughter Gladys to a Mr. Guy Cleveland—no relation to Grover.)

It was decided that Frances would attend college. Cleveland pulled a few strings and obtained certification from Central High School that Frances had completed her studies in good standing. Then, with Cleveland's encouragement, she settled on Wells College on the eastern shore of Cayuga Lake in Auburn, about 120 miles from Buffalo. Cayuga Lake is one of a chain of lakes in New York's Finger Lakes region, so named for their similar shape.

Frances satisfied the language requirements, passing entrance exams in Latin and German (she also spoke French), and in February 1882, although she had dropped out of high school and skipped the entire fall semester of college, she was admitted to Wells as a freshman with "advanced standing."

In those days, Wells College enrolled only women and was run like a finishing school though it boasted a respectable liberal arts curriculum. Every afternoon the students, in long formal dresses, gathered to sip tea from china cups. Frances played the piano and took classes in painting and photography, but she also took challenging courses in botany, geometry, trigonometry, astronomy, geology, and logic; and she was close to being a straight-A student.

Her roommate, Ms. Katherine "Pussy" Willard, had a beautiful singing voice, spoke fluent German, and was the niece of the famous suffragette Frances Willard, who was president of the Woman's Christian Temperance Union. As Cleveland was vehemently opposed to prohibition and to women getting the right to vote, he and Frances may have had some lively discussions about one or both issues. It was pure luck that Frances and Katherine were reputed to be the only Democrats on the entire Wells College campus and happened to be assigned to the same room. They shared something else: Like Frances, Katherine knew what it was like to lose her father; she was twelve when Oliver Willard died.

Not long after she settled in at Wells College, Frances received a shipment of fresh-cut red roses; when they died, another shipment arrived, and then another—a fresh bouquet every week, filling their room with the fragrance of roses. They were from her beau, she said, but would never utter the gentleman's name. She could never let it be known that her admirer was Grover Cleveland, twenty-seven years her senior.

At some point, Cleveland wrote Emma Folsom to ask her what he should do with a treasured Folsom family heirloom that had come into his possession, a sword that had once been owned by her late husband, the sword that Oscar Folsom had carried when he fought in the Civil War. In the letter, he also, just in passing, asked Emma for permission to write to Frances. He may have felt a little uncomfortable doing so, but he was in a bind because Wells College required parental consent to permit correspondence with its students. Emma gave her blessing, presumably considering Cleveland's request the innocent gesture of a guardian who wanted to keep in touch with his ward who had gone off to college.

During Cleveland's entire six-week campaign for governor, the acceptance speech he delivered from the balcony of Billy Dranger's saloon turned out to be the only formal address he gave. Having refused to travel the stump circuit, the only electioneering he did was in the form of two letters he wrote for publication and a pamphlet extolling his virtues, which was published by the Democratic state committee and distributed throughout New York. He was coasting to victory on a wave of history. What was the point of campaigning when his triumph was a foregone conclusion? Cleveland's Republican opponent, Charles Folger, had had to acknowledge that his nomination had come about through "fraudulent practices," and even his friends were calling on him to withdraw. Major Republican newspapers bemoaned the corruption that had sullied the party of Lincoln and were openly advocating Cleveland's election. At a Republican rally, America's most renowned clergyman, Henry

Ward Beecher, said that he would see his right arm "wither" before he would vote for Folger.

"I will vote for Mr. Cleveland," Beecher declared.

On Election Day, Cleveland cast his vote in the morning, then went to his office at Buffalo City Hall. He was alone except for an artist from *Frank Leslie's Illustrated Newspaper* who was rendering a sketch of the man of the hour for an article that was to run in the following week's edition. Cleveland seemed at ease, but in fact, he missed his mother very much. In this pensive state, seated at his desk, Cleveland penned a letter to his brother William.

"I have just voted," he wrote. "If Mother were here, I should be writing to her." He wrote William that he was "certain" of success in the election. But something was vexing him; the middle-aged bachelor was aware that once he was ensconced in the governor's mansion in Albany, an active "social life" would be expected of him. Balls, dinner parties, receptions, social teas were obligatory for a governor. Who would serve as his first lady? The matter was giving him much "anxious thought," and Cleveland wrote William that he was thinking about cutting back on some of the "purely ornamental" duties of the office.

"Do you know that if Mother were alive I should feel so much safer? I have always thought her prayers had much to do with my success."

Then suddenly his office became the scene of frenzied activity: Wilson Bissell, the newspaper publisher Charley McCune, and Cleveland's old law partner Sherman S. Rogers were running in and out, wishing him well and handling last-minute political matters. The Mutual Union Telegraph Company strung a wire in his office, and around six o'clock, the returns started coming in. It was a rout. His victory was ensured.

In New York City, a sea of humanity had gathered at the cluster of newspaper offices on Park Row to await the results, but an eerie silence hung in the night air. People seemed dazed by the votes being posted for Cleveland, wondering if the figures could be trusted. A steady murmur began about Cleveland advancing to the front row of candidates for president in 1884, just two years away.

When the final tally came in, Cleveland's total came to 535,318 to Folger's 342,464. Cleveland's margin of nearly 200,000 votes was the largest majority ever recorded from any state in American history up to then.

Even Cleveland took pity on Folger, finding it preposterous that someone with as distinguished a career as the treasury secretary's could suffer such a humiliating defeat at the hands of a politician "wholly unknown outside my own small community." Twenty-five years later, his victory still confounded him. Looking back, Cleveland said he was "unable to understand it."

Cleveland now faced six weeks of relentless activity. His first order of business was to tender his resignation as mayor, which he did on November 20, after serving only eleven months. He then turned over his law partnership to Bissell and the firm's junior partner, George Sicard. Everything was happening so fast he had to candidly admit that he needed help. He reached out to Daniel Manning and asked the party chairman to recommend someone smart who knew Albany inside and out. Manning suggested Daniel S. Lamont, the clerk of the state assembly. Lamont was a former correspondent for the *Albany Argus* newspaper, which was owned by Manning. Like Edgar Apgar, Lamont had total command of the political and bureaucratic apparatus of the state government. He knew where all the bodies were buried. Manning directed Lamont to give Cleveland a hand, and when he arrived in Buffalo and introduced himself to the governor-elect, there was an immediate connection. Cleveland found the thirty-two-year-old Lamont to be just as smart as Apgar. Together they worked on policy and personnel for the incoming administration. There were just three weeks to go before the inauguration.

All this time, Cleveland continued to fret about the social life awaiting him as governor. For a while, he considered naming his sister Rose his official hostess. Since the death of their mother, Rose Cleveland had been living alone at the Cleveland homestead in Holland Patent. Now thirty-six, she was just like her brother, intellectually gifted but something of a misfit in social situations. Cleveland realized right away that it would not be a good fit. Then he came up with a temporary fix, at least in terms of running the mansion. William Sinclair was chief steward at the City Club in Buffalo. Everyone liked Sinclair. He'd be perfect. The two men sat down for a discussion, and Cleveland made him a nice offer. The next thing Sinclair knew, he had quit his job at City Club to serve as Cleveland's valet and manservant.

In early December, Cleveland took a break from the transition to go to New York City for a reception in his honor at the elite Manhattan Club. Accompanied by Bissell, he left Buffalo by train on a Monday evening and pulled into Manhattan the following day at 11:00 AM.

The reception at the Manhattan Club at 96 5th Avenue was shaping up to be a major event. It was Cleveland's coming-out party, and the first opportunity for Democratic big shots on the national level to have a good look at the politician who was generating so much attention.

All the furniture in the Manhattan Club's parlor had been taken out to accommodate the swarm of guests—it was "denuded," went one description. Nevertheless, it was so crammed with power brokers it became almost impossible for anyone to move, and the orchestra had to be stationed one flight up to make room. A carriage was sent to the Windsor Hotel to pick up Cleveland, and at nine thirty, he was ushered in to thunderous applause.

Cleveland took off his overcoat and was at once encircled by well-wishers. There were eight hundred people in all, including General Winfield Scott Hancock, the defeated Democratic nominee for president in 1880, thus the titular head of the party, and the philanthropist Peter Cooper, whom Cleveland took particular pleasure in meeting. Supper was an informal buffet, and when the guests were seated in the dining hall, the club's president, Aaron Vanderpoel, clanged his champagne glass for attention and offered a toast.

"I propose the health of Governor Grover Cleveland and wish him a most successful and honorable administration."

Cleveland returned to Buffalo to pack his bags while a thousand little details still had to be attended to—plus, he had to write his inaugural address. He hired a stenographer and had a printing press standing by to copy it. William Sinclair—Cleveland called him his "colored servant"—was about to set out for Albany to take charge of the executive mansion; and Cleveland's sister Mary Cleveland Hoyt volunteered to help out with the housekeeping. Cleveland notified Daniel Lamont that he would be on the 8:00 AM train for Albany that would get him to the state capital at 4:30 PM on December 30, and that he would like Lamont to meet him at the depot.

When Cleveland arrived in Albany and strolled the snowy streets of the state capital with Bissell and Lamont at his side, he went unrecognized. As a courtesy, Governor Alonzo Cornell had already vacated the Executive Mansion so Cleveland, who called it Cornell's "surrender," moved right in even though he was not yet officially governor. That night, Cornell, the son of the founder of Cornell University, came by to wish Cleveland well.

Cleveland and Cornell had met once before, and detested each other. A month after Cleveland had become mayor of Buffalo, he had journeyed to Albany to make a personal appeal to Cornell to commute the death sentence of a laborer who had been convicted of the stabbing murder of his plant foreman. Cornell listened as Cleveland and a delegation of Buffalo lawyers argued that the jury had failed to take into account the defendant's drunken state as a mitigating factor. After two hours, Cornell had had enough and exploded in anger. How much longer was this going to take? he wanted to know.

Cleveland sprang to his feet. "We come to you as the king, pleading for mercy. It is your duty to hear us and hear us to the end." Public executions always touched a raw nerve in Cleveland, a former Erie County sheriff who had presided over two hangings; while Cornell was taken aback by Cleveland's ferocity. They stared each other down in a test of wills between two men who were used to being in absolute command of their domain.

Cleveland rattled on for another fifteen minutes while Cornell stewed and, in the end, did the right thing: He commuted the Buffalo defendant's sentence to life.

Years later, Cornell recounted, "I was so impressed with the sincerity and the legal cocksureness of the man that I commuted the sentence."

Over brandy and cigars on the eve of Cleveland's inauguration, Cornell generously offered him whatever assistance he could provide.

Cleveland spent an uneasy first night in the mansion, which was just too enormous to suit his simple bachelor taste. It had been erected in 1856 as a two-story Italianate at 138 Eagle Street, on a bluff overlooking the Hudson River. The furniture was heavy and traditional, the library paneled in rich black walnut. An excellent greenhouse offered a daily supply of fresh-cut flowers, and there was an arched porte cochere that was of little use to Cleveland as he owned neither horses nor a carriage; he intended to walk to work. For a man who had spent his adult life residing in boardinghouses and hotels, it was all too much, and he let it be known that he wanted to move out and establish himself at a hotel so he could "live the same bachelor life as in Buffalo."

Cleveland's advisors howled in protest. William Dorsheimer, a former lieutenant governor, told him flat-out that abandoning the governor's mansion would send the wrong signal and "offend" the people of New York, who had provided their chief executive with an official residence that was a perk of the office. Unpersuaded, Cleveland insisted on moving to a hotel. Only after Dorsheimer, for whom this was confirmation of Cleveland's "utter disregard of the trappings and glory of the office," pointed out that Cleveland would be "overwhelmed" by citizens and lobbyists who would take advantage of the easy access his hotel living offered did the governor-elect finally relent.

On the morning of the inauguration, Cleveland was escorted into the Senate Chamber behind a squad of police who drove a wedge through the crowd. Everyone made way for him. At his side was Alonzo Cornell.

Cornell, speaking first, put past issues aside and had only the kindest words for his successor. Like Cleveland, he was a big man with an oversized head and hulking physique. Side by side, the outgoing and incoming governors could have passed for siblings. Cornell wished Cleveland Godspeed and left the stage to him.

Governor Cleveland's inaugural address impressed everyone, not so much for its content but for his delivery. Cleveland had an extraordinary capacity for total recall of the written word, and had committed his entire speech to memory. Not once did he look at his prepared text. Speaking in a clear and deliberate voice, and enunciating every word with perfect diction, he praised Cornell as a "tried and trusted" public servant and acknowledged that the people of New York had taken a giant leap of faith in electing as governor someone "yet to be tried." In his inaugural address, all those years of honing his communication skills before Erie County juries came together.

The next day, Cleveland got down to the business of running a great state. As Buffalo's mayor, he had been venerated for governing on the principle that every citizen had the right to visit him in his office at City Hall and have a chat. Word got out in quick order that Cleveland was bringing the same open-door policy to Albany; it disgusted his lieutenant governor, David

Hill, who, along with William Hudson, watched helplessly as a "throng" of citizens wandered the halls of the Executive Chamber seeking out the new governor. The former *Brooklyn Eagle* reporter had left journalism to join the Cleveland administration as a political aide.

Hill grumbled that it was a waste of energy. "The governor might just as well place his desk on the grass in front of the capitol." At least, he said, it would have the "advantage of the fresh air." He told Hudson, "It must be stopped."

Hudson had to agree. These were tourists or the idly curious who had no business being there.

In due time, Cleveland came to realize that he could not operate effectively without setting limits on access to his office. This, after all, was the state capital, not frontier land in Buffalo.

Daniel Lamont was proving himself to be indispensable, but he found Cleveland a tough boss to work for—obstinate, and almost impossible to dissuade once he had formulated an opinion. Lamont learned that the best way to deal with him was to avoid direct "combat," and instead maneuver and sometimes deploy harmless trickery to accomplish his objectives. One day, Cleveland was interviewing a politician from Syracuse who was seeking the appointment of superintendent of a vast tract of state-owned property known as the State Salt Reservation. Cleveland took "enormous fancy" to this fellow, who was handsome and engaging and a great communicator. Lamont did some checking with his contacts in Syracuse and concluded that the man in question was an "undesirable citizen . . . not guided by rules of morality." What that meant was anybody's guess; nevertheless, Cleveland announced his intention to nominate him.

Lamont was alarmed, worried that the appointment would be a "blunder of great dimensions" that could bring embarrassment to the new administration. He sought out Lieutenant Governor Hill, and together they scripted a gambit. Cleveland was at his desk in the Executive Chamber when Hill wandered in for a friendly chat. Lamont, having been appointed Cleveland's private secretary and military secretary, with the honorary rank of colonel, was at his desk at the other end of the office. Secretive, shrewd, and of "infinite tact" in Cleveland's opinion, Lamont had been heaven-sent. "I never saw his like. He has no friends to gratify or reward and no enemies to punish."

"Good afternoon, Governor," Hill began and, with a wink and a nod, turned his attention to Lamont. "Good afternoon, Dan. I see your old friend from Syracuse was here today."

Playing out his part, Lamont said, "Yes, he was here."

"Was he sober?"

Cleveland's head shot up in surprise. Now they had his full attention.

"Seemed to be," Lamont said.

"How did he get here?" When Lamont replied by train, Hill said that would have required money. "Who'd he borrow it from?"

"I don't know."

"Did he go away sober?"

"I don't know. Didn't see him after he left here."

"How did he get back? Didn't borrow money from you, did he?"

"Oh, no," answered Lamont. "I kept out of his way."

With a snort, Cleveland resumed his work, but he had taken everything in. It had all gone according to the script, and the disreputable gentleman from Syracuse never got the appointment.

In Buffalo, Cleveland had been known as the Veto Mayor; now he was becoming known as the Veto Governor. The scale of Albany's corruption proved as institutionally deep-rooted as Buffalo's, and then some. A young reform-minded Republican assemblyman, Theodore Roosevelt, estimated that a third of his fellow legislators were agreeable to putting their votes up for sale—sometimes on the floor of the state assembly chamber itself.

Cleveland set a new standard: Every bill that was up for passage had to meet the standard of good government; otherwise it was dead. The veto that aroused the biggest hullabaloo concerned the railroad fare. Tammany Boss John Kelly—the so-called friend of the workingman—led the fight to reduce the ten-cent fare on the 6th Avenue and 9th Avenue elevated railroads in Manhattan to a nickel. Naturally, it was a popular piece of legislation, and the senate passed it by the overwhelming vote of 24 to 5. Cleveland, knowing that a tempest would come his way, showed real political courage in vetoing the measure on solid business and constitutional grounds. He was getting ready for bed after he had sent his veto message to the senate when he thought to himself, *By tomorrow at this time, I shall be the most unpopular man in the State of New York.*

Cleveland woke up at seven the next morning, had his breakfast, and walked to the office with the weight of the world on his shoulders. He dared not look at the stack of New York City newspapers that he knew for certain would have launched full-scale attacks on his young administration. As he went through the morning mail with Dan Lamont, still thinking about those newspapers, in as casual a tone as he could muster, he asked Lamont, "Seen the morning papers, Dan?"

"Yes."

"What have they got to say about me, anything?"

"Why, yes," said Lamont, "they are all praising you."

Cleveland was stunned. "They are? Well, here, let me see them." Cleveland scooped up the papers and read—in the *Tribune*, *World*, *Mail*, and *Express*—that they were solidly in his corner. Even the *Sun*, which had urged passage of the five-cent fare, was extolling Cleveland's pluck. The governor exhaled a deep sigh of relief.

Tammany Hall, whose support for Cleveland at the Democratic state convention in Syracuse had put him over the top, now demanded a "few crumbs" of political patronage from him. Boss Kelly's puppet in the state senate, Tom Grady, sent the governor a note asking that, as a special favor, Cleveland name a former Tammany Hall alderman, Bryan Reilly, harbormaster of New York City.

"I hope that you will kindly make the appointment for me as it will place me in a most humiliating position with my people here if . . . I should fail."

Grady was notorious for patronizing Albany's slimiest whorehouses and saloons; Cleveland could not abide the man. It gave him pleasure to reject the Reilly appointment, and the political consequences be damned. That Cleveland refused to throw Tammany Hall such a piddling spoil of war spoke volumes:

Under the Cleveland administration, Tammany could not even count on obtaining a lowly night watchman's position for one of its own.

Observing all this downriver in Manhattan was Tammany's boss, the cunning John Kelly, who was getting the message that Cleveland was no pushover. Kelly had become a wealthy man—although "no one quite knew how." He was also Irish American royalty. When he had been elected to Congress in 1855, at the height of the Know Nothing movement, he was the only Catholic in the House of Representatives. After his wife died, he solidified his regal position in American Catholicism by taking for his bride the niece of John Cardinal McCloskey, who in 1875 had been chosen by Pope Pius IX to be the first American cardinal.

In October 1883, Cleveland shot yet another arrow at Tammany. In a letter he drafted to Kelly, he began by saying that he wanted to be "entirely frank," then went on to demand that the disreputable Tom Grady be kicked off the ballot in the coming fall elections, just three weeks away. He showed the letter to Lamont, who disapproved. Why pick a fight with Tammany now? The presidential campaign was around the corner, and Cleveland would need Tammany's cooperation.

"Well," said Cleveland after considering what Lamont had to say, "I'm going to send it." And he did.

Kelly held on to the letter for more than two weeks, while it seemed to beburning a metaphorical hole in his pocket. For him the issue was the Catholic working class versus the Protestant Anglo-Saxon establishment as represented by Cleveland. The governor, of course, never saw it as sectarian warfare, just straightforward good government. Kelly never responded to

Cleveland's letter, but he did leak it to his friends at the *New York World.*

Kelly had begun to hate Cleveland with a "sleepless vindictiveness."

As a hard frost swept over New York State that winter of 1883, Frances Folsom had boys on her mind. The dorm room she shared with Katherine Willard was decorated with photographs of Frances's beaus, and apparently there were several. Two proposals of marriage came her way during a single memorable visiting day in her sophomore year at Wells. She rejected one and said yes to the other, but after a few weeks made it clear to her new fiancé that it was not meant to be. Charles Townsend now had company.

"When I marry, it must be someone more than a year older than I am," she wrote her mother, indicating that she was looking for maturity in a husband. The man she would marry, Frances said, had to be "someone I can look up to and respect."

Contact with young men and communication with the outside world was strictly supervised at Wells College. The dean, known as the lady principal, was Helen Fairchild Smith. Not much got by Miss Smith, who maintained the list of "approved correspondents" for Wells students. The daughter of the president of Wesleyan College in Connecticut, at Wells, she also taught English literature. It was said that she ruled her students with a just and steady hand, and though the girls sometimes chaffed under her stern restrictions, they idolized her.

Ice-skating on the frozen surface of Cayuga Lake was a favorite winter sport at Wells, and sometimes an excursion with the good-looking cadets from the Cayuga Lake Military Academy would be arranged—but always under the eagle eye of Miss Smith or another chaperone she so designated.

At Wells everyone dressed for dinner, and formal evening-wear was required at all concerts and evening lectures. It was not acceptable for a student to show any leg, so proper attire, meaning a long dress, was expected, even to play bridge.

Frances was a leading lady on campus. With her authentic stage presence and lovely voice, she almost always landed a principal role in the college's Shakespearian productions. She also had a naughty sense of humor. Once, when the campus was buzzing with excitement over the double wedding of two alumni, Frances found a white robe and a black shawl and parodied the ceremony; playing the part of the bishop, she read from the actual vows, and everybody howled.

Frances was also a skilled debater for the Phoenix Society, the campus debating club, which tackled such serious subjects as free trade, the tariff and protectionism, and all the hot-button political topics of the day. On every issue, ever loyal to her guardian, Grover Cleveland, she took the official Democratic Party line. Politics was second nature to her.

Deemed the most beautiful student on campus, in the art studio above Morgan Hall, Frances posed for a photograph as Urania, goddess of astronomy, which was turned into a poster to promote an evening of mythology and revelry. Without any other student who came close to matching her goddess-like physical beauty, it was perfect casting. And her whimsical fondness for her masculine pet name *Frank* seemed to add to her charm.

The dorm room of Frances Folsom and Katherine Willard resounded with giggles and the innocent girlish commotion of young women always running in and out. Sometimes Frances entertained her friends with stories of her life back in Buffalo as the ward of the newly elected Governor Grover Cleveland. And her stories would be even more entertaining when he became a potential candidate for the presidency.

Helen Smith never missed a thing. In a college packed with girls who came from wealth and upper-class privilege, at some point she recognized how exceptional Frances was, and undertook the mission of educating the teenager. Whether through insight or intuition, she saw the unique role Frances could play in American history. The word on the Wells College campus—heard "more than once"—was that Miss Smith was preparing Frances "specifically for the White House."

8

STIRRINGS OF A SCANDAL

IN THE EARLY months of 1884, politicians began to gear up for the presidential election. A wave of momentum was building for the former governor of New York, Democrat Samuel J. Tilden, who had been robbed of the presidency in what was called the Crime of '76, the most disputed presidential election in American history.

Tilden had won the popular vote over Rutherford B. Hayes by 250,000 votes, but after some double-dealing in the Electoral College, it was Hayes who ended up in the White House. When it seemed that the United States was tottering on the brink of another civil war, Tilden earned the esteem of history by graciously accepting defeat. Having sacrificed his presidential ambitions for the sake of national harmony, he retired a political martyr and was living as a recluse at his country estate, Greystone, outside Yonkers, New York. Such was the enduring bitterness over the 1876 election it was thought that Tilden could have the Democratic nomination with a snap of his fingers—if he truly desired it.

A sympathetic journalist who went to interview the Sage of Greystone found him in failing health: Would Tilden throw his hat in the ring? he asked him. Tilden smiled meekly and said, "My boy, don't you see it is impossible?"

Whether Tilden would declare was a touchy subject within the party. Daniel Manning, state party chairman, owed his political career to Tilden and would not offend him under any circumstances. Grover Cleveland not only appreciated Manning's position, he also concurred with it, and was ambivalent about seeking the nomination anyway. Like most of the other potential Democratic nominees, he was willing to step aside should the great Tilden declare he was a candidate for the office he had been cheated out of eight years before.

As the party convention loomed, one day when Manning thought Cleveland aide William Hudson was becoming too aggressive in promoting his boss's standing on the national stage, he warned, "Cleveland is not yet a candidate, and Tilden is not out of the way."

But even Manning began to understand that the time had come for Tilden to formally announce or make way for fresh blood. Such a mission was fraught with delicacy and required diplomacy. And it had to be done in person.

Tilden lived with a coterie of servants in a hundred-room stone villa. On warm spring days, he could be found on the veranda gazing out at his commanding view of the Hudson. The former governor suffered from colic and a stomach bloated with gas; unable to tolerate solid foods, he lived on broth. On a bad day, a bit of toast could bring on a spasm of vomiting and diarrhea. He had a weak heart and walked with a cane. One arm was useless, and he could barely make it to the top of the staircase without the assistance of his valet, Louis.

"What makes me puff so?" he would ask Louis.

Tilden was seventy years old when Manning went to see him. The party chairman found the rumors of Tilden's failing health to be all too true. He was shocked at Tilden's physical deterioration. Tilden's good hand shook with palsy, and his facial muscles trembled, and his lower jaw drooped—the consequence of a paralytic stroke. His voice was a barely audible whisper. It was obvious that he did not have long to live. Yet his eyes—at least the one eye he could still see out of—still sparkled with intellect.

Manning laid everything out. He explained that he had met with Grover Cleveland the week before, and that Cleveland wanted to assure Tilden of his anti-Tammany credentials and commitment to the great principles of reform and good government. Manning also wanted Tilden to know that should Cleveland be elected president, he, Tilden, would have a hand in naming his cabinet.

Tilden hesitated—in part the natural objection an old man would have to being pushed, however gently, out the door and into oblivion. He said he did not want to be seen as favoring Cleveland or any other candidate, plus, he had "profound" questions about Cleveland's credentials. Was this man really prepared to govern 60 million Americans? Tilden said he wanted to think about it for a day or two. Actually, it only took a day.

"I ought not to assume a task which I have not the physical strength to carry through," he wrote Manning in a letter that was promptly made public. Tilden said his life in public service was now "forever closed."

In Albany, Cleveland reached an understanding with Manning. He would stand as a candidate for national office, but only if President Chester Arthur or former secretary of state James G. Blaine of Maine secured the Republican nomination. Manning did not appreciate Cleveland's hesitancy. "It's difficult to understand the governor's attitude," he confided to William Hudson. Privately, he was peeved and wondered whether Cleveland had the fire in the gut that it took to play politics at the national level.

Cleveland tried to explain his position to one of his closest allies in Albany, New York—state comptroller Alfred Chapin. In the strictest confidence, Cleveland informed Chapin about the "woman scrape" he had gotten himself into back in Buffalo almost a decade before. He could only pray that it would not come out.

In early June 1884, Dan Lamont, William Hudson, and other key Cleveland advisors were gathered around a telephone in the Executive Mansion in Albany. All the ardent and ambitious men who were there that day were under forty, and they had hitched their wagons to the governor's rising star. They were waiting for news from the Republican Party convention taking place in Chicago. It stood deadlocked between President Arthur and Blaine. Senator George Edmunds of Vermont was also in contention. At Exposition Hall the fourth ballot was under way.

Seated at the other end of the long table, busying himself with paperwork, was Grover Cleveland, utterly indifferent to the outcome of the political drama unfolding in the Windy City. Two months earlier, he had unburdened his heart to his sister Mary, telling her how he felt about running for president.

"I wish I might not hear my name mentioned in connection with it again," he wrote her.

Cleveland, holding up a printed copy of a bill he was considering vetoing, called out for Hudson, who couldn't believe it. History was being made, and Cleveland wanted to debate some minor piece of legislation no one cared about. Hudson couldn't take his eyes off that phone.

"It does not appear to me that you are giving me your attention," Cleveland complained.

"Good heavens, Governor, how can you potter over these bills when any moment the announcement may be made of an event that will force you into the Democratic nomination for president?"

Cleveland gave Hudson a knowing smile. "Oh, neither Blaine nor Arthur will be nominated," he said. He sounded certain. "The Republican situation demands the nomination of Edmunds. Edmunds will be nominated." Blaine had a reputation for shady political wheeling and dealing. And Arthur was president by accident, having assumed the office following the assassination of President James Garfield in 1881. On the other hand, Edmund Edwards had an unblemished reputation as the squeaky-clean intellectual of the Senate.

At that moment, the telephone came to life. It was over.

"Blaine's nominated!"

Everyone howled for joy, surrounding Cleveland, when Hudson saw something that unnerved him: Grover Cleveland's face took on a "hard" expression; then a wave of gloom seemed to engulf him. The suggestion of a tear appeared at the corner of his eye.

"Now we'll have you for the Democratic nominee," someone shouted. The Democratic National Convention was just four weeks away.

Cleveland grabbed a pile of paperwork on his desk. "Go away, boys, and let me do my work as governor. You're always trying to get me into a scrape."

One month later, everyone would know just what Cleveland meant.

Dr. George W. Lewis could still remember the day when Maria Halpin came to see him. It had been eight years before, in 1876. Dr. Lewis was seeing patients in his medical office in Buffalo when Maria Baker, a regular patient of his, walked in with Maria Halpin. She told Dr. Lewis that her friend Mrs. Halpin needed his wise counsel.

Maria Halpin told Dr. Lewis her story: Grover Cleveland had raped her, and the son that had been conceived had been forcibly taken from her and placed in an orphanage. Cleveland had had her thrown into an insane asylum and wanted to run her out of town.

Lewis had gently explained that as a physician, there were limits to what he could do about her situation, and sent Mrs. Halpin and Mrs. Baker on their way. That was his first and last encounter with Maria Halpin.

Over the years, Dr. Lewis had said nothing about the episode. He had stood by when Grover Cleveland became mayor of Buffalo, and had kept his silence after Cleveland was elected governor of the state. Now Cleveland stood on the verge of winning the Democratic Party's nomination for president.

Dr. Lewis came from a colorful family; it was not in his nature to live timidly. His brother, Dr. Diocletian Lewis, was a well-known homeopathic physician who was prominent in the national temperance movement. Another brother, Loren Lewis, was a judge in Buffalo. All three Lewis brothers were fitness fanatics who worked out with dumbbells in an era when staying in top physical condition was unusual and considered a little eccentric. Judge Lewis's wife, Charlotte, had founded the Ingleside Home for unwed mothers, so the Lewis family was disposed to assist women in trouble.

In July 1884, Dr. Lewis decided the time had come to let somebody know about Maria Halpin and Grover Cleveland. He set his sights on a leading Buffalo churchman, Reverend George H. Ball, pastor of the Free Baptist Church on Hudson Street. Dr. Lewis told Ball everything he knew about Mrs. Halpin. The Baptist minister found the story truly unsettling. Could it be that the nation stood on the verge of electing a depraved libertine to the White House?

Ball was sixty-five years old and had a distinguished pedigree: He was a descendant of George Washington's mother, Mary Ball. George Ball had grown up in Ohio, and as a young principal, he had taught a future president, James Garfield. He had gone to Buffalo in 1850 to preach on the docks. He found a vacant building and built a church. Over the years, while he and his wife raised five children, he earned a national reputation as a theologian and author of *The Story of Jesus*. He was also in a roundabout way responsible for one of the great industrial fortunes in American history. In 1880, Ball had loaned his enterprising nephews Frank and Edmund $200 to go into business selling tin containers for storing paint, varnishes, and kerosene. The company came to be called Ball Brothers Glass Manufacturing Company and became a huge success when it added glass jars for canning fruits to its production line. Ball State University in Muncie, Indiana, is named after the family.

George Ball knew Grover Cleveland. In 1882 he had gone to see then-Mayor Cleveland to request a donation to build a new church. Cleveland wrote a check for $50. Politically, however, Ball and Cleveland were polar opposites. Ball had served as a delegate to the first Republican National Convention in 1856 and had been active in the antislavery movement. That Cleveland had dodged the Civil War draft and was now threatening to end a quarter century of unbroken Republican rule in the White House since Abraham Lincoln's momentous victory in 1860 made Ball ideologically prepared to think the worst of Cleveland.

After Ball had listened to everything Lewis had to say about Cleveland and Maria Halpin, and taken notes, he was determined to investigate the story. And he had plenty of leads to pursue.

Ball went to see William Flint and Henry Kent, the owners of the Flint & Kent department store where Maria Halpin had once worked. The last thing in the world the merchants needed was to get caught up in a sex scandal, but they did confirm for Ball the essence of Maria's claim that she had been let go after becoming pregnant with Cleveland's child.

Next, Ball sought out Maria Baker and the attorney Milo Whitney. He also spoke with Dr. William Ring, medical director of the Providence Lunatic Asylum where Maria had been placed following her seizure by two off-duty Buffalo police officers. So far, everything was checking out.

After that, Ball went to Vine Alley in Buffalo in search of a Mrs. McLean. She had been Grover Cleveland's janitress at the Weed Block apartment building, where he'd lived before moving to Albany. Vine Alley—or the Alley as it was called in local parlance—had a notorious reputation, second only to Canal Street's, as a tenderloin district of infamy. It was claimed that more bottles of wine were opened nightly on Vine Alley than on any other street in America, with the exception of Broadway in Manhattan. Thunderbolt Smith, a boxer of national repute, ran a popular saloon on the Alley.

Vice was more or less condoned by police, so for his personal safety, George Ball asked another minister, E. S. Hubbell, to accompany him. These two elderly gentlemen of the cloth poking around disreputable Vine Alley must have made an amusing spectacle, but they managed to find Mrs. McLean's apartment. They asked the cleaning lady what she knew about Cleveland, but she had nothing incriminating to offer.

Ball followed every lead he got but could not locate Maria Halpin. No one seemed to know where she was living, only that she had left Buffalo in shame and had not been heard from in eight years. Not even Mrs. Baker knew how to find her. It was a huge gap in his investigation, but at this point, Ball believed he had enough on Cleveland to convene a summit of the city's leading Christian ministers. It was an extraordinary gathering. Thirty clergymen from every denomination, including the Catholic diocese, listened in shocked incredulity as Ball laid out the evidence he had collected. Rumors about out-of-control drinking had chased

Cleveland since his time as Erie County sheriff. His bachelorhood also made him suspect. But they couldn't have expected this. Ball argued that they could not stand by while this depraved character Cleveland ran for the highest office in the land.

As the committee dithered, Ball did what he could to get the word out. For seven years during the 1870s, he had served as editor of the *Baptist Union* newspaper in New York City, so he knew how to make his voice heard. Targeting religious publications where his name carried the utmost credibility, he sent letters to the editors of the *Chicago Advance*, the *Independent*, and the *Christian Union*. His letters were crammed with names and information—a blueprint for anyone interested in pursuing the allegations against Cleveland. They were not meant for publication, but to offer off-the-record guidance to the opinion makers who held sway over the votes of millions of churchgoing Americans.

A letter from Ball landed on the desk of the editor of the *Chicago Advance*, where the Democratic National Convention was being held:

> Dear Advance—It may be too late to do you any good, and may not be needed, but I feel moved to warn you against saying much to the credit of Grover Cleveland. He is a libertine. No Christian should condone his crimes so far as to commend his candidacy. About seven years ago he seduced the head of the cloak department of Flint & Kent's, leading merchants here. He kidnapped the woman after the boy was born, sent her to the Catholic Insane Asylum [sic] and took the child from her. She escaped, got Milo A. Whitney to help her, finally settled and gave up the child for $500. This I know to be true,

for I have it confirmed by Flint & Kent, by Mr. Whitney, her attorney, and by Mrs. Wm. Baker, where the woman boarded.

Ball's letter accused Cleveland of having a reputation in Buffalo of the "grossest licentiousness." He informed the editor of the *Advance*—a publication of the Congregational church that was said to reach the "very best class of people"—that letters had been sent to the *Independent* and the *Christian Union* because both publications had published sycophantic articles about Cleveland that Ball had found "alarming." Ball wrote that he had detected nothing objectionable in the *Advance*'s coverage of the presidential election, but "it will do no harm for you to know the facts" before writing another word that could be seen as advancing a Cleveland candidacy.

The rumor mill started churning.

Daniel Manning asked William Hudson to urgently come see him. Hudson found Manning in his office at the bank he owned in Albany, the National Commercial Bank.

"There is more work for you to do, and it is most important work," Manning told Hudson. He held three lists in his fist.

"I'm enlisted for the war, Mr. Manning, and am subject to your orders."

"You may not like this, but it must be done by someone." Manning explained that the first list was of the names of the New York delegates going to the national convention who were committed to Cleveland; on another list were names of those delegates opposed to Cleveland. It was the third list—uncommitted or "doubtful" delegates—that Manning wanted to talk about. There were six or eight names on it. Without their support,

Manning said, Cleveland could not win a two-thirds majority—the treasured "super-majority"—and without a crushing victory in New York, Cleveland could be denied the nomination.

"Now, I want you to devote yourself to these doubtful men," Manning told Hudson. "We must subject them to pressure, but first we must learn the sort of pressure which should be applied. That's your work."

Hudson, realizing the importance of the assignment, was overcome with apprehension. "It is something like detective work," he observed.

"Much like it," Manning replied, "but detective work that can be done only by a man acquainted with state and local politics."

Hudson started making inquiries, reaching out to his circle of contacts and using all the research skills he had accumulated as a political journalist at *The Brooklyn Eagle*. He looked into the background of the delegates in question, probing for vulnerabilities and susceptibilities, which Manning told him in blunt language could be political, commercial, or moral. Hudson was two weeks into the task when Manning summoned him to the bank again. A crisis was in the making.

"You must go to Chicago at once," Manning told Hudson, adding that somebody else would have to complete his work. Right now he was urgently needed on the ground in Chicago to open the Cleveland-for-President headquarters. "Stand for the cause till we get there."

When Hudson arrived in Chicago, he found the city in the grip of anti-Cleveland fervor. Emissaries from Tammany Hall were stirring up the populace and spreading poison about Cleveland such as that he was an anti-Irish bigot. There was also some crazy rumor that Cleveland had hidden away "illegitimate progeny." It didn't take any brilliant investigative work on Hudson's part to determine the source of the smear campaign: It was Cleveland's old adversary from Albany, State Senator Thomas F. Grady, recently ousted from his senate seat in a Cleveland-inspired coup. Now a full-time Tammany Hall operative, Grady was in Chicago making the rounds of the newspapers and saloons and hotels and telling anyone he could grab by the lapels that Cleveland was "bitterly hostile to anything related to Catholicity" and a dissolute drunkard besides. Intelligent people who should have known better actually believed this propaganda, and Hudson found to his bewilderment that the whispering campaign was gaining traction.

Hudson set up shop downtown at the Palmer House, in three of the hotel's largest parlors, and hung a portrait of Grover Cleveland over the entryway. He did what he could to "neutralize" Grady's mischief and privately reassured the newspaper boys and local politicos that Cleveland harbored no animosity toward the Irish.

Delegates and their cronies by the thousands started pouring into Chicago. Boss John Kelly of Tammany Hall controlled half the Manhattan delegates going to the convention. The rest of the delegation stood solid for Cleveland. But the flashy Kelly was the rogue star everybody wanted to hear from. Fearless, always the showman, Kelly and 700 Tammany "braves" pulled into Chicago on July 6 on board two chartered trains—each twenty-five cars in length, one train having tailed the other all the way from New York. Everyone climbed out wearing pearl-colored stovepipe hats and marched in formation to the Palmer House where they were staying, with Kelly and a brass band in the lead.

After he had cleaned up from his long trip, the sixty-two-year-old Kelly met with reporters and delivered his opening salvo against Cleveland.

"I would regard Cleveland's nomination very much in the light of party suicide," he said. "It would kill us."

"Will you support Governor Cleveland if he is nominated?"

Stroking his neatly trimmed beard, Kelly said, "I will not lift a hand for him."

"Will you oppose him?"

"You can print this as coming from me," Kelly said, and in case anyone missed it the first time, he repeated his declaration of utter hostility to the governor of his own state: "I will not lift a hand to aid in the election of Grover Cleveland if he is nominated." Revenge tasted sweet to Boss Kelly. Cleveland had built his good government credentials by turning his back on Tammany Hall, and for that the candidate was now paying the price.

The hub of the action was the Palmer House. Every room was taken, and the lobby and hallways were jammed with men perspiring in Chicago's summer heat. At the bars it was standing room only, and it was said that some of the New Yorkers were a "trifle careless in their use of stimulants."

Intrigue followed Kelly wherever he went. Every now and then, a rebel yell could be heard coming from his room. Kelly enjoyed being the center of attention. He stayed up well past midnight his first night in Chicago, consulting with General Benjamin Butler. He was the former governor of Massachusetts who had come to Chicago, having already won—but not yet formally accepted—the presidential nomination of two minor populist parties, the Anti-Monopoly Party and the Greenback Party. Now he was seeking the Democratic nod. Butler had an inflated sense of self-importance, but he had done some notable things in his life—as governor, he had appointed the first Irish American judge and the first black judge. But Southern delegates remembered Butler for other reasons—during the Civil War, he had been known by the epithet "Spoons," due to accusations that he had pilfered the silverware of Southern plantations in which he resided during military campaigns. He was also called "The Beast," because of his stern rule as commander of Union forces occupying New Orleans, during which he issued the notorious General Order No. 28, decreeing that a woman showing disrespect to a Union soldier would be deemed a "woman of the town plying her avocation"—that is, a prostitute.

In 1884, Butler was unelectable, his delegate strength eroding by the day. As one Southern delegate said of Butler, "We may be willing to eat crow, but we'll be damned if we'll eat turkey buzzard." The wounds of war still echoed on the floor of the convention hall, where the band played both "Yankee Doodle"— and "Dixie."

It was no accident that Butler and Kelly were occupying adjacent rooms at Palmer House. They were always in cahoots, coming out of Kelly's suite, striding arm in arm, in deep conversation. Had a pact been reached between these two wily operators? Butler running as a spoiler candidate on a third party ticket in November could siphon votes from the Democrats and throw the election to James Blaine. One conspiracy theory making the rounds was that Kelly and Butler were clandestinely coordinating everything through Blaine.

Delegates from the South and West viewed the election as their best chance since the Civil War of electing a Democratic president. With Cleveland, they had a candidate with a virtuous image who could finally retake the White House. They cursed Boss Kelly's name. He was a Democrat "for revenue only," a "national disgrace," a "tumor," and his men were "banditti." Others saw Kelly's plotting as a blessing in disguise. Tammany Hall held an unparalleled reputation for corruption, and while it controlled the votes of thousands of New Yorkers, mostly Irish immigrants, it was said that for every Tammany vote lost, Cleveland would gain the support of five Republicans or independents just on principle. *The New York Times* estimated that if Tammany bolted, the Democratic ticket would actually result in a *net gain* of a half million votes come the November election.

Victory seemed within Cleveland's grasp. Wilson Bissell was observed in the bar toasting his success before the convention even officially opened for business.

On opening day of the convention, as storm clouds rolled over Chicago's skies, delegates streamed into Exposition Hall. Just one month before, the Republican Party, which had nominated Blaine, had held its national convention in the same arena. Boss Kelly sneaked in without his usual flourish, but as he took his seat in the New York delegation, he was instantly recognizable in his stylish lightweight white summer suit, which, impeccably tailored as it was, could not conceal his husky bulk.

Back in Albany, Grover Cleveland was attending to state business and trying to ignore the fuss at Exposition Hall. Bissell, Hudson, and Apgar were all in Chicago running the political operation, although the ailing Apgar had to remain in his hotel room that first day, too frail to work the hustle and bustle of the convention floor. The only key aide who remained with Cleveland in the state capital was his private secretary, Dan Lamont. Cleveland rebuffed Western Union's offer to run a special wire into his office, so news from Exposition Hall came via a messenger running on foot from the branch telegraph office to the governor's Executive Chamber. For this historic week, Mary Cleveland Hoyt and two of Cleveland's nieces were staying at the governor's mansion to share in his glory. Cleveland remained ambivalent about the nomination—just eight days earlier he had told Manning he had "not a particle of ambition to be president." Perhaps Cleveland's keen instinct for self-preservation was alerting him to the storm that was coming his way.

U.S. Congressman Daniel Lockwood of Buffalo formally placed Cleveland's name in nomination on July 9. Lockwood was an unusual choice for the honor because he held no national reputation, but he was a sentimental favorite for the Cleveland team and a good-luck charm besides, because he had previously nominated Cleveland for mayor of Buffalo and also governor of New York.

The real spectacle came when U.S. Representative Edward S. Bragg of Wisconsin took the rostrum to second the nomination. Bragg was a retired Union general. Built like a fireplug— the "ideal size for a cavalryman"—he had a gift for spontaneous speech-making that made him a fearsome adversary on the floor of Congress. He was also cool under fire. During the battle of Antietam, he had received orders to push on, but only if it was safe—a nonsensical command because with 23,000 casualties, Antietam was the single bloodiest day in American history.

Yet Bragg issued a memorable one-word charge to his soldiers: "Forward!" That was twenty-one years before. Glaring into the New York delegation, the old warrior, his hair having turned gray in service to his country, fixed a hard expression on Boss Kelly.

"I stand today to voice the sentiment of the young men of my state when I speak on behalf of Grover Cleveland."

With a gesture of his hand, Bragg told the delegates to cease their cheers. He had something more to say.

"His name is upon their lips. His name is in their hearts . . ."

A wave of sentimentality surged forth from Cleveland's people. Here at last was the speech they had been waiting for.

"They love him, gentlemen, and respect him, not only for himself, for his character, for his integrity and judgment and iron will, but they love him most for the enemies he has made."

Tom Grady, seated next to Boss Kelly, sprang up and wagged his fist at Bragg, his face a mask of crimson fury. "In behalf of his enemies, I accept your statement!"

Bragg looked down at Grady. He let the groundswell of hisses fill the conventional hall, and then, pointing an accusatory finger at Boss Kelly, he likened the men of Tammany to the "vilest of the human species."

The roll call of the states commenced after midnight, July 11. When the votes for the first ballot were tabulated, Cleveland was way out in front with 392 votes, but still 155 votes shy of the two-thirds majority required to win. His closest opponent was Senator Thomas Bayard of Delaware, with 170 votes. The patrician Bayard didn't have a chance: He came from a small state with limited electoral clout, and he had defended the right of secession in 1861. Manning knew Cleveland was this close to victory.

Meanwhile, Kelly and Butler were working all angles. They approached Thomas A. Hendricks, the former governor of Indiana who had served as Tilden's running mate in 1876, and induced him to join their alliance. Kelly's men were sent out in force to recruit roustabouts from Chicago's most disreputable saloons. For drinks on the house and a little pocket change, these scalawags were issued tickets, personally signed by the sergeant at arms who was in Tammany Hall's pocket, and ordered to Exposition Hall at 11:00 AM sharp with these simple instructions: "Holler for Hendricks when the signal to do so is given"—and keep hollering until they were told to shut up.

Kelly and Butler were up until four in the morning in Butler's room at the Palmer House, plotting strategy.

Seven hours later, with the convention about to be called to order for the climactic second ballot, a strange thing happened. Several thousand spectators holding legitimate tickets found themselves barred from entering Exposition Hall. The doormen were permitting only Kelly's troublemakers holding those special passes to waltz right in.

The roll call commenced. For Manning, everything was falling into place. Then came Illinois—and an unforeseen hitch. Sometime during the night, Kelly had induced a single delegate from the state who had voted for Cleveland the previous day to switch his vote. The delegate stood on his chair and bellowed the words "Thomas A. Hendricks of Indiana!"

That was the signal Kelly's people had been waiting for. The next moment, Tammany delegates and Butler's men from

Massachusetts sprang from their chairs, waving their hats, while up in the gallery, Exposition Hall shook with cheers from the "spontaneous" demonstration. Manning, sitting with the New York delegation, now saw that there seemed to be an unusual number of young men up there in the best seats, shouting themselves hoarse, and they looked like a rough bunch. Someone actually yelled out for instructions: "How long shall we holler?" Kelly had stacked Exposition Hall with Tammany agents.

Right on cue, Hendricks stepped into convention hall from a side entrance. Even he looked confounded as he stood there and took a little bow. For eighteen minutes the applause kept coming.

Over at the Connecticut delegation, the state's young governor, Thomas M. Waller, was swept up by the clamor. Waller called an urgent caucus of his state right there on the convention floor. As the delegates gathered around him, Waller said the convention was clearly turning to Hendricks. Connecticut should back a winner and go with Hendricks. A consensus was reached. Waller shouted for recognition from the podium.

"Mr. Chairman! Mr. Chairman!"

Manning could not believe it. Could it be that Waller was about to switch his state's votes to the dark horse from Indiana? Manning instructed Edgar Apgar to put a stop to this nonsense. Apgar started clambering over chairs like an agile little monkey to get to Waller. At the same time, the national chairman of the Democratic Party, William Barnum, took hold of the governor's coattails. Waller wheeled around and found himself face-to-face with Barnum's wrath. Barnum had to inform the impressionable governor that he was being played for a sucker and that if he continued, he would be "making the great blunder of his life." Waller sank in his chair. How fascinating to note that Governor Barnum's cousin was the American showman P. T. Barnum, who is credited with the phrase "There's a sucker born every minute."

Cleveland pulled in 683 votes on the second ballot. Bayard was second with 81, followed by Hendricks with 45. So much for the stampede for Hendricks. Grover Cleveland was the nominee of the Democratic Party.

Word of his victory came to Cleveland in the form of a cannonball. His day had started in Albany with his usual half-mile walk from the mansion to the governor's desk. He had arrived at his office at eight. Usually, he walked back home for lunch at one, but on this day he decided to sit tight. At 1:40 PM, the telegraph announcing Cleveland as the standard-bearer of the Democratic Party came into the Western Union offices; and by prearranged signal, a cannon positioned on the dock was fired. It was said that the boom woke up every napping infant in Albany. Dan Lamont threw open the doors of the Executive Chamber, his face beaming with joy, and vigorously shook Cleveland's outstretched hand. Cleveland stood there, steady and in control. Only the sparkle in his eyes betrayed his pleasure at the news. The telephone rang a moment later with confirmation of his nomination.

"Dan, telephone the mansion. Sister will want to hear it."

Citizens started pouring in to wish Cleveland well. One laborer in short sleeves, grasping a tattered hat in his hand, came in with his clothes dusty from work. "God bless you!" he told Cleveland. The governor gave him a hearty handshake. Lamont couldn't keep up with the volume of congratulatory telegrams—there were more than a thousand. He handed only the most significant ones to Cleveland to read. The first telegram came from the editor of the *New York World.*

"Congratulate you and the cause of good government. You are nominated."

It was signed "Pulitzer."

The only sour note for Cleveland came when party bosses arranged for the nomination of Thomas Hendricks as vice president—a bone to mollify Tammany Hall and the old guard. It was seen as a cunning play because it solidified Hendricks's home state of Indiana for the Democrats. Hendricks returned to Indianapolis expressing support for the top of the ticket, although his wife, Eliza, seemed to bear a grudge over her husband's thrashing in Chicago.

"Mr. Hendricks is a man whom very few understand," she told reporters assembled outside her house. "I often tell him he ought not to be in politics, for he is as sensitive as a woman." In a crack deeply offensive to Cleveland, Eliza Hendricks added, "Thomas was put on to strengthen a bad nomination." (Mrs. Hendricks later claimed to have been misquoted.)

Tammany Hall was dust, so disgusted with the nomination of Cleveland its delegates boycotted the final session of the convention. Tammany delegates were intensely resented, and they found it prudent to remove their Tammany badges lest they be physically accosted on the streets. Kelly and his people packed their gripsacks and boarded a train out of Chicago at 6:00 PM that Friday. Thirty-seven hours later, they pulled into the depot in Manhattan. In the contemptuous words of *The New York Times,*

Tammany's braves, "shorn of their plumes . . . drank very little firewater" on the depressing train trip home.

Somebody asked John Kelly what he would do next. "I do not know," he said.

"What do you think of the nomination?"

"I think that it means defeat. I thought so before it was made, and I think so still. I am sorry that the convention was so blind as not to see it."

In Augusta, Maine, James Blaine was already immersed in preparations for the fall presidential campaign. Publicly, Blaine said he considered Cleveland to be a weak nominee because no one outside New York State knew much about the man. Privately, however, Blaine confided to his son that he was deeply concerned. Cleveland would make a formidable opponent. New York was the key to victory. The candidate who took New York would be the next president, and Cleveland had the home court advantage. Fortunately, Blaine was in possession of some dynamite. It came in the form of a letter, sent to him on June 30. A Buffalo physician, Dr. Samuel A. Warren, had written it, and the contents could have enormous consequences to the campaign. If the information was true, it could finish the Democrats. Cleveland might even have to withdraw. Blaine was enormously appreciative, and had had his private secretary, Thomas Sherman, write a thank-you note to Dr. Warren.

"I am directed by Mr. Blaine to thank you for your kindness of June 30, which he has read with interest, and referred confidentially to the secretary of the Republican National Committee."

9

"A TERRIBLE TALE"

MARK TWAIN MOVED to Buffalo when he was already a prominent writer whose masterpieces *The Adventures of Tom Sawyer* and *The Adventures of Huckleberry Finn*, yet to be written, would later bring him international fame. In 1869, he bought a one-third interest in the *Buffalo Express* newspaper for $25,000 and became co-editor of the paper.

When Twain appeared at the *Express* office building at 14 East Swan Street for his first day on the job, he was upset to see just a single soul in the entire city room. Where the hell was his staff? The city room's lone occupant stared at the squat little stranger with the shaggy mustache.

"Is there someone you wish to see?" he inquired.

Twain thought about it, then said, "Well, yes, I should like to see some young man offer the new editor a chair."

Twain had seen the *Express* as a worthy investment but had not been prepared for the stress that came with ownership. A year later, he sold his interest in the paper for $10,000, a huge loss, and left Buffalo. Like a lot of great writers, he made a rotten businessman.

Just a year after Twain abandoned Buffalo for good, Jacob Riis, who had immigrated to the United States from Denmark, was working as a day laborer doing carpentry for the railroad; he'd also started to write about the appalling social conditions that had resulted from the rapid growth of cities he'd passed through.

One day, when Riis found himself in Buffalo, he sought out the offices of the *Express* and applied for a reporting job. Told that the managing editor was at lunch, the eager twenty-one-year-old said he'd wait. After a while, a fellow strode through the lobby heading for the city room and brushed right by Riis. Assuming he was the managing editor, Riis caught up with him in the stairwell and asked him for a job. He never forgot what happened next.

"He looked me up and down, scanning my poor apparel, and then he threw his head back and laughed."

"What are you?" the editor sneered.

"A carpenter," Riis answered.

The editor turned on his heels. When he heard Riis following him, the man stopped.

Riis recalled, "I stopped too, shook my fist at him, and vowed then and there that the time would come when the *Express* would be glad to have my services."

The editor broke into a hearty belly laugh. "That editor's laugh has been ringing in my ears ever since," the great social reformer and muckraker wrote in his memoirs.

Newspapers were called rags in those days, not necessarily due to their scurrilous editorial content but because a sheet of newsprint had the consistency of a coarse dishtowel. It was an era of spirited newspaper wars and pugnacious newspapermen who appreciated the value of a good row with the competition, even if one had to be cooked up. One night a journalist afflicted with writer's block was at his desk, drawing a blank: "I wonder what I will write about tonight?" Then it struck him: "I believe I will have a controversy with the *Troy Times!*"

In the 1880s, top reporters made about $15 a week for six days of work. The *Courier*, owned by Grover Cleveland's great friend Charley McCune, was the city's leading newspaper—high-toned, leaning Democratic, and set in its ways.

Edward Willis Scripps and his half brother James Scripps were in the early stages of building their newspaper empire, having founded *The Detroit News* in 1873 and the *Penny Press* (later renamed the *Cleveland Press*) in 1878. Ed Scripps had one simple rule for decorum in the newsroom: "No man shall dress worse or get drunker than I do."

The Scripps brothers had been keeping a hungry eye on the Buffalo marketplace for several years. They settled on booming Buffalo for their launch of another penny publication, with delivery timed for the afternoon and early evening when folks at home could relax with the local newspaper. In 1880, the brothers went to Buffalo, looked at some real estate, bought office space at 153 Main Street, and declared that in a few weeks a new daily called the *Evening Telegraph* would begin rolling off the presses. Edward H. Butler, proprietor of the rival *Buffalo Sunday News*, had also been thinking about coming out with a penny afternoon paper, and the announcement by the Scripps boys accelerated his plan. Getting a jump on Scripps, Butler published the first issue of the *Buffalo Evening News* on October 11, 1880, selling it at a penny a copy when most Buffalo papers cost 2¢ or 3¢. The *Evening News* was a big hit; it sold 7,000 copies that first day, and circulation soon ballooned to 20,000.

Nineteen days later, the first issue of the *Evening Telegraph* was published; the weighty event was modestly noted in James Scripps's diary: "The *Telegraph*, our new Buffalo paper, made its appearance today."

Buffalo had not seen anything like the *Evening Telegraph*. Like its distant cousin the *Penny Press*, the *Telegraph* was edited to contain "not a line of uninteresting matter." News was conveyed in nuggets, boiled down to its essence; some stories got just a single line. Brevity was key to making the paper an easy read, but human-interest stories and exposés were given plenty of room to breathe. Like other Scripps publications, the *Evening Telegraph* was meant to appeal to all classes and political persuasions. As Ed Scripps once put it, "We have no politics. . . . We are not Republican, nor Democrat, nor Greenback, and not Prohibitionist. We simply intend to support good men and condemn bad ones."

Ed and James Scripps were absentee owners; Ed lived in Cleveland and James in Detroit. A guiding principle of the Scripps chain was that local editors knew their city best and had to be given autonomy to run the newspaper as they saw fit. Hiring the right people was vital. In the case of the *Evening Telegraph*, an able staff was engaged at a start-up cost of $25,000, not counting the purchase of the building on Main Street. Noting with envy the size of the editorial workforce at the *Evening Telegraph*, a rival publication had to acknowledge, "Everything was done to make the paper a success."

Nevertheless, it was a struggle from day one. The *Telegraph*'s first editor was Henry Little, brought in from Ohio, where he had been lured out of retirement after being laid up for a year with rheumatism. Little arrived in Buffalo vowing to "exterminate" the *Evening News* inside of ninety days. He lasted a year, and when he left, the *Evening News* was bigger than ever. Henry Griffin, a veteran of the Detroit newspaper wars, came next, followed by John A. Cresswell, the former managing editor of the *Detroit News*.

By the time Cresswell got to Buffalo, the Scripps brothers had poured $70,000 into the *Evening Telegraph*, and it was still in the red—the only newspaper in the Scripps chain to be hemorrhaging money. Cresswell was nonetheless confident that he could steer a path to profitability in the crowded Buffalo marketplace. He found a place to live on Delaware Avenue with his wife, Lief, and their six-year-old daughter; and in October 1883, Lief Cresswell gave birth to a son. Two weeks later, at the age of thirty-four, Lief died at their home from complications due to childbirth and diphtheria. A sorrow-stricken Cresswell buried his wife in her hometown of Grand Rapids, and then returned to Buffalo to resume his leadership of the *Evening Telegraph* and raise his two youngsters. The circulation of the *Evening Telegraph* was holding steady at 10,000, not a terrible failure but not yet a success.

Cresswell was thirty-four when the greatest story of his life landed on his desk.

A few days after the Democrats nominated Grover Cleveland for president, the Reverend George Ball asked Cresswell to come see him. Ball would later explain that he went with the *Evening Telegraph* rather than a more established newspaper because he knew Cresswell to be a churchgoing Christian and had high regard for the editor's personal code of ethics. As Ball laid everything out, Cresswell took careful notes. There was a tremendous amount of material to go over, and he knew that every word reported by the *Evening Telegraph* would come under attack by Cleveland partisans. The reputation, and perhaps even the existence, of his newspaper would be on the line.

Another newspaperman had also gotten a whiff of the Maria Halpin scandal.

In mid-July, Zemro Smith, the forty-seven-year-old editor of the *Boston Journal*, got word that James Blaine wanted to see him. Smith boarded the first train out of Boston and got off in Augusta, Maine, on the banks of the Kennebec River. Blaine lived in a magnificent mansion that he had purchased in 1862 as a gift for his wife, Harriet. It was one of the finest estates in Augusta, just across the street from the Maine State House. Blaine's favorite room was the study—his children called it Father's Library, and next to this was the large octagonal Billiard Room, site of a grand ball held in 1873 for President Grant. Every room in the Blaine mansion had its fitting name. There was the Ash Room, named for the color of its painted walls; Alice's Room, where Blaine's daughter Alice slept; and Aunt Susan's Room for Blaine's sister-in-law, Susan Stanwood, who for a time lived with the family.

Zemro Smith sat down with Blaine. The presidential candidate and former secretary of state had the most extraordinary document in his possession. It was a copy of the letter Reverend

George Ball had written to the *Chicago Advance* in which Ball claimed that Grover Cleveland had fathered an illegitimate son. Ball had written the letter on July 12. Five days later, it was in Blaine's hands. How the letter got to Blaine has never been determined, but one likely source was Boss John Kelly, who had apparently obtained a copy on the final day of the Democratic Convention in Chicago and may have slipped it to Blaine. It must have killed Kelly to realize that had he obtained the letter just a few days earlier, Cleveland would surely have been denied the nomination. Be that as it may, Kelly had a copy now; and given his blood feud with Grover Cleveland, he would have done anything to bury his arch-foe, even go so far as to conspire to throw the election to the Republicans.

That morning, Blaine and Smith sat in "secret consultation" for several hours. The Republican nominee had the utmost faith in Zemro Smith's discretion. Zemro's brother Joseph had been secretary of the Republican state committee in Maine when Blaine was chairman. And it was said that Zemro owed his position at the *Boston Journal* to Blaine's money and influence. As a Republican organ backing Blaine's candidacy, the *Journal* could be depended on to aggressively investigate Grover Cleveland.

Smith caught the afternoon train back to Boston, arriving late that night. The next morning he went to his offices at the *Journal* and assigned one of his reporters to the story. The reporter was on the very next train to Buffalo, arriving on July 19, a Saturday. His first stop was the obvious one—the Free Baptist Church on Hudson Street, where he found Reverend George Ball in the rectory. Ball said he was "deeply impressed" that a journalist from Boston had come to Buffalo to investigate the allegations. The minister told the reporter that he was still in a state of "outrage" that Cleveland had won the nomination. But then Ball informed him that he had already given everything he had to John Cresswell of the *Evening Telegraph*, no doubt considerably alarming the newsman. Now he had competition to deal with. All he could do was pick up his pace and hope for the best.

Ball said he was aware that the "responsibility for the disclosures" would fall on his shoulders, but he believed it was his public duty. He didn't have anything personal against Cleveland, he said. The Democratic nominee had always been an "obscure man" with a reputation in Buffalo as an "average lawyer," and like the rest of the nation, Ball said, he had been amazed at the staggeringly swift trajectory of Cleveland's political climb.

Since he'd launched his probe into Cleveland's private life, however, the minister told the reporter, he was now of the opinion that Cleveland had "low associations." Ball passed along several stories he had heard proving Cleveland's "licentiousness and debauchery." He also suggested that the *Boston Journal* investigate the circumstances of Oscar Folsom's death in 1875. The real story, Ball insinuated, had yet to be told. The reporter steered the interview back around to the contents of Ball's letter to the *Chicago Advance*, and Ball urged him to look into the allegations and determine for himself that he was speaking the truth. He also gave him the name of the man who had adopted Grover Cleveland's illegitimate son—Dr. James E. King—and added that it was Dr. King who had been "instrumental in the kidnapping of the mother," Maria Halpin. These were facts of "common repute" in Buffalo, the minister said. There were witnesses who could verify everything.

Ball remained seated as the reporter wrote his summary of the interview. It read as follows:

> That Mr. Cleveland, about seven to ten years ago, accomplished the seduction of Maria Halpin, who was in the employ of Flint & Kent of Buffalo, in charge of their cloak and lace department; that the woman, so far as known, had borne an irreproachable character up to that time; that her employers, with whom she had been about four years, had a high regard for her and considered her a virtuous Christian woman; that Mr. Cleveland had her taken to the Lying-In Hospital during her confinement; that he afterward placed her and the child, a boy, with Mrs. William Baker, on Broadway, to board; that the woman became depressed and desperate and threatened his life; that he became apprehensive that she might attempt some injury to him or herself and appealed to the Chief of Police, Col. John Byrne, to keep her under surveillance; that Mr. Cleveland had her taken by force from her room at Mrs. Baker's to the Providence Lunatic Asylum on Main Street, an institution under the charge of Sisters of Charity; that the man who took her there were one Watts, a policeman, and one Dr. King; that she was seen there by Dr. Ring, the visiting physician, who did not think her insane; that after several days she escaped, and no efforts were made to retake her; that she put her case into the hands of Mr. Whitney, Esq., an attorney, alleging kidnapping and false imprisonment; that she finally gave up the child, and received $500 from Mr. Cleveland; that the boy, who was named Oscar Folsom, in memory of a

> friend of Mr. Cleveland, is now living in Buffalo, with
> the Dr. King who was instrumental in the kidnapping of
> the mother; and that these are matters of common repute
> in Buffalo, to substantiate which numerous witnesses can
> be found, among whom are Mrs. Baker, Col. Byrne, Mr.
> Whitney, Dr. Ring, (and) Messrs. Flint and Kent.

After Ball read the statement over for accuracy, he signed it "George H. Ball," and affixed the date: July 20, 1884.

It was twilight that Saturday when the reporter bid Ball farewell. He still had a few hours left before calling it a night and decided to seek out Dr. William Ring. He found Ring at his offices on Niagara Street and informed the doctor that he had come to "inquire" about Maria Halpin.

Ring was on edge during the entire interview. He said he knew "very little about" Maria Halpin and would not recognize her if he saw her on the street today. Her case, he said, was one of hundreds he had dealt with over the years as medical director of the Providence Insane Asylum. When Reverend Ball and John Cresswell of the *Evening Telegraph* had recently queried him about Maria Halpin, Ring said, he had to look up the asylum records because he could not recall anything about the woman. The records indicated that Maria had definitely been committed: Her name was on the asylum register.

"I have seen it there," Ring said. The date of commitment was hard to make out because the record book had faded with age. He suggested that the Boston journalist speak with Sister Rosaline, who ran the institution. She could show him the records—"if she chose to." When he was asked whether Sister Rosaline would cooperate, Ring said that he didn't know, but she was a "very wise" woman.

What else did he remember from that night?

Ring recalled that Mrs. Halpin had been brought to the asylum by a police officer.

"Was the policeman's name Watts?"

"Yes, I believe so," Ring answered.

"Did he exceed his authority in taking the woman there?"

Ring said that was something for Officer Watts to "account for."

"She was not insane," Ring said of Maria Halpin, but she did appear to be "boozy," meaning under the influence, but at all times she had behaved like a lady. And that was all he wished to say about Maria Halpin. End of discussion. As the reporter was packing his things, Ring suddenly told him, "I guess you had better let Cleveland alone in these matters."

The Boston reporter stared at the doctor. "But I haven't mentioned Mr. Cleveland to you."

"Yes, I know, but I understand what you are after. Are you a newspaperman?"

"More or less."

"Well, don't say anything about me, or the asylum or Sister Rosaline." Ring said he was a Republican, and he wanted to keep his name out of the papers and out of this mess. "We shall beat Cleveland in New York by fifty thousand, without regard to such matters as this."

The reporter's next interview took him to No. 103 Broadway. He found Maria Halpin's landlady, Maria Baker, on the second floor above a store where she rented rooms. Mrs. Baker didn't want to talk. She had already spoken to the *Evening Telegraph* and didn't want to get any more involved. She had nothing left to say about Maria Halpin except that she was intelligent and principled and a good woman who had gone through misery when she lived in Buffalo.

"How long ago was she with you?" she was asked.

"About seven years," Mrs. Baker said. "I cannot tell exactly. Possibly my husband could fix the date."

"How long was she with you?"

"About a year."

"What sort of person was she?"

"Ladylike. Intelligent and fine appearing. About thirty-five years old. She was a widow and had lost her husband just before she came to Buffalo and was dressed in mourning. She had been employed in a responsible position at Stewart's in New York before coming to Buffalo. I never heard of anything in the least against her until the time of her trouble when she came to board with me."

"Was she there at Mr. Cleveland's expense?"

"Well, I wouldn't say."

"But you wouldn't say that she was not there at his expense?"

"No, of course I couldn't say that. Mrs. Halpin was very much depressed and broken down by her trouble, and she drank some, but that made it worse."

What about the night Maria Halpin was taken to the Providence Lunatic Asylum? he asked her. "Was she taken to the asylum against her will?"

"Yes, of course, she didn't want to go."

"Who took her?"

"A policeman."

"Was his name Watts?"

"Yes, it was."

"Was there anyone else?"

"Yes."

"Was it Dr. King?"

"Yes."

"How long was she at the asylum?"

"Seven days."

Mrs. Baker's recollection was faulty. Records from the asylum indicate that Maria Halpin was a patient for three days.

"Was she under the influence of liquor at the time she was taken?"

"Yes."

"What was the boy called?"

"Oscar Folsom." Mrs. Baker said it was a name chosen by Cleveland, to honor his best friend.

"Is he now in the family of Dr. King?" All Mrs. Baker could say was that she believed this to be the case.

When it was finally time to go, the *Boston Journal* reporter thanked Mrs. Baker for everything and returned to his hotel room for the night. The next morning was Sunday—perfect for knocking on doors. He went to 476 Franklin Street—an address he got either from Reverend Ball or straight out of the city directory. There, on the front porch enjoying the morning breeze, was Milo A. Whitney, Maria Halpin's former lawyer.

Whitney was now fifty-six years old. His daughter, an infant when Maria Halpin had first hired him to represent her in the lawsuit against Grover Cleveland, was now a little lady of eight. Like Dr. Ring and Mrs. Baker, Whitney did not want to say much. John Cresswell had already been to see him, and before Cresswell it had been the Reverend Ball. There were other people who knew far more than he did about Maria Halpin, and yet it was being made to seem as if the "whole matter" rested with him. It was not right. He also said his memory was hazy. He couldn't recall the year when Maria had come to see him. He thought it was sometime in 1876, but more likely 1877. In any event, the whole case struck him as an "outrage." No, he said, breach of promise was not alleged, only kidnapping and false arrest. He had to drop the lawsuit because it had been "compromised." If he had had his way, the case would have been filed and brought to trial, but he had no choice except to step aside once Maria's brother-in-law had interfered.

Whitney said that Cleveland had paid Maria Halpin $500 to go away.

The reporter closed his notebook. There were three other crucial witnesses listed in Reverend Ball's signed statement: Colonel John Byrne and the department store merchants Flint and Kent; but for some reason, the reporter decided to leave Buffalo without speaking to any of them. He may have been eager to get back to Boston to write his story and scoop the *Evening Telegraph*. He later explained, "I did not think it necessary to pursue the inquiry further." That was a strange thing for any journalist to admit. Certainly it would have been interesting to hear what these three prominent citizens had to say. Had he probed deeper, the reporter would have ascertained several interesting facts. Colonel Byrne was no longer the police chief. He was now working in the private sector—he owned the Buffalo Detective Agency. His partner in the firm was former police officer Robert Watts, who figured so prominently in the Maria Halpin scandal.

The reporter returned to Boston and presented his findings to Zemro Smith. A strange thing happened next. Smith sat on the story. He had the jump on the political scandal of the decade, and yet the *Journal* did nothing. One reason may have been that he received orders from higher up—perhaps from Blaine himself; any charges published by the *Journal* would have been suspected of being Blaine propaganda. Blaine's fingerprints were all over the paper, and especially its editor Zemro Smith. The smart move was to wait. The decision was made. Of Buffalo's newspapers, the *Evening Telegraph* was the new kid on the block. Let the "obscure" *Telegraph* have first crack at it. Then the *Journal* would pounce.

There were signs everywhere of tremendous enthusiasm for the candidacy of Grover Cleveland. In Nyack, New York, four hundred cheering citizens marched to Mr. Andrew Jackman's house to serenade him with a cornet band. What had Jackman done to deserve such a tribute? He had served as a delegate to the convention that had nominated Cleveland. Making his way home from the convention, a forty-year-old Connecticut delegate actually had to be tied into a straitjacket at a stop in Toledo when he tried to leap from the train. The cause of his derangement was said to have been ecstasy over Cleveland's victory. In Buffalo, thousands of people beaming with pleasure over their favorite son's accomplishment paraded through the streets with banners and fireworks. Special accolades were paid to Buffalo's own Wilson Bissell and his virtuoso tactics in securing Cleveland the nomination. Some in the city were calling Grover Cleveland the Man of Destiny. A fitter phrase might have been Creature of Circumstances. A trivial set of conditions had, as if by magic, lifted Cleveland into the stratosphere of national politics. Those who knew the inside story were aware that had Cleveland not been pushed into running for mayor of Buffalo just three years before, he would still be practicing law in Buffalo at the humble firm of Cleveland, Bissell & Sicard.

In Albany, Cleveland was trying hard to stay focused. Daniel Manning, the architect of the Cleveland campaign, was back from the convention organizing the fall election. Manning had been offered the chairmanship of the Democratic National Committee but declined, saying he wanted to devote himself exclusively to running the Cleveland canvass in New York.

With all this activity in progress, Cleveland was still governor of New York, with all its obligatory executive duties. On July 19, he took the Hudson River line to Westchester County for a military review of the New York State regiment at Peekskill. He had two of his nieces in tow, the daughters of his missionary sister from Ceylon who were spending the summer with him. The governor carefully stepped off the train, impeccably dressed in a black double-breasted frock known as the Prince Albert suit—standard formal business attire in the Victorian Era. A 21-gun salute greeted him. Following supper, he and his entourage returned to Albany on the 7:00 PM train. Cleveland was eager to get back. The winsome Frances Folsom and her mother, Emma, were expected in Albany any day now. Frances was on summer break from Wells College and wanted to personally congratulate Uncle Cleve on his nomination. She and her mother would be his guests at the Executive Mansion.

The Republicans were on the ropes. James Blaine was an able man, but he had a reputation as a two-faced schemer. Like the mythological Roman god Janus, one-half of Blaine was statesmanlike and honest; the other could be corrupt and sinister. As Speaker of the House in 1869, he had been accused of lining his pockets with $130,000 in bribe money to secure land grants for the Little Rock and Fort Smith Railroad Company. Blaine was never criminally charged, but the scandal had derailed his presidential ambitions in 1876 and again in 1880. Theodore Roosevelt expressed the sentiment of his generation when he announced that while he planned to vote the Republican presidential ticket in 1884, he would refuse to campaign on behalf of Blaine. To prove he meant it, Roosevelt headed off to his ranch in the Dakota Territory, where he intended to remain until November and so avoid this odious election. *The New York Times*, a reliable Republican organ, shook the party establishment by coming out with an early endorsement of Cleveland. Crystallizing the great issue of the campaign, the *Times* called Cleveland a courageous man whose "absolute integrity has never been questioned." It was a bolt from Blaine on an unprecedented scale.

And then the "great bombshell" of the election was ignited.

Before going to press, John Cresswell met with George Ball one final time and asked the minister if he would be willing to put in writing everything he had learned about Grover Cleveland. Ball said yes, provided his name was kept out of the *Evening Telegraph*'s exposé, although he authorized Cresswell to release his identity "when we deem it needful to do so."

Titled "A Citizen's Statement," Ball's account was addressed to the editor of the *Evening Telegraph*:

You ask me for facts about Mr. Grover Cleveland's moral character. Since his candidacy is being pushed on the assumption of irreproachable morals, and many are being deceived thereby, I yield to your request. . . . I give you a part of the well attested facts and place at your disposal the names of responsible citizens, both democrats and republicans who will confirm every item, if called upon.

An officer long on the police force declares that he has often seen Mr. Cleveland beastly drunk, and has indisputable evidence of his habitual immoralities with women.

Two responsible and influential citizens testify that hearing a great row in a saloon one night they rushed in and found Mr. Cleveland and another lawyer in a terrible fight over a lewd woman. Each seized a belligerent and held him fast till they both agreed to keep the peace. They were both drunk, and they had rent and torn each other till they were both nearly naked and covered with blood.

Since Mr. Cleveland was elected to the present office [as governor] he reached Buffalo one Saturday night; drove to a noted saloon; was met by three other men; laid in a stock of liquors; repaired to apartments in another building; sent out for four lewd women and spent the night and all day Sunday with them in debauchery.

Some years ago a beautiful, virtuous and intelligent young lady entered the employ of Flint & Kent, as you know, most excellent men and leading merchants in our city. She was put at the head of their cloak department and served them for some two or three years to perfect satisfaction. Mr. Cleveland made her acquaintance, won her confidence and finally seduced her. She of course lost her position, was cast out of good society, and driven to despair. Her appeals to him to fulfill his promise of marriage he did not regard. The mother and child were taken to the residence of Mrs. William Baker on Genesee Street to board and visited occasionally by Mr. Cleveland. The boy was named Oscar Folsom Cleveland. The mother was wretched and often desperate and worried Mr. Cleveland by her threats. He resolved to abate the annoyance, employed two detectives and a doctor of bad repute to spirit the woman away and dispose of the child. She refused to surrender the child or go with the detectives. Then they seized her by force and in spite of her screams and violent resistance, took her to a carriage and drove her to the Providence asylum in Main street, where she was committed as insane, for which services Mr. Cleveland paid the two detectives $50. The child was taken to the Buffalo orphan asylum. Our worthy citizen, Dr. William Ring, was the visiting physician at the Providence Asylum and on examining the new patient pronounced her perfectly sane and the authorities allowed her to depart. She had been committed without legal process and departed on her own volition. Her first move then was to employ an attorney and recover her child. Her lawyer advised her to secure it by force if necessary. She succeeded in getting the boy into her arms and at once fled, no one obstructing her flight. Then negotiations were opened with Mr. Cleveland and finally he paid her $500 to give up the child and at length succeeded in getting her to leave the city. The boy was then given to a family on Niagara Street, where he still lives and I believe bears their name. But poor Maria Halpin, for that was her name, went away broken hearted, disgraced, an outcast, while her seducer continued to revel in the realm of lust and pretend before the great American public that he is a model of virtue, pre-eminently worthy of being honored by their votes and being exalted as an example of ambitious youth to imitate. Perhaps personal character originally ought not to be involved in political discussions, but it would be criminal to allow the virtuous to vote for so vile a man as this under a false impression that he is pure and honorable.

These are a part, only a part, of the facts that have been verified in relation to Mr. Cleveland's character. It is painful to think of his offenses and shameful, infinitely shameful, to have such a man commended to the suffrages of a Christian nation. It is enough to alarm all decent people, and even cause the vulgar and profane to hesitate and demand a halt.

Ball signed the statement and dated it July 18.

Cresswell kept the handwritten original and stored it in a safe place at the *Evening Telegraph* offices. Three days later, on July 21, the *Evening Telegraph* hit the stands with one of the most famous headlines in the history of American journalism:

A TERRIBLE TALE
A DARK CHAPTER IN A PUBLIC MAN'S HISTORY
A Pitiful Story of Maria Halpin and Governor Cleveland's Son
Prominent Citizen States the Result of His Investigation of Charges
Against the Governor—Interviews Touching the Case

Cresswell personally wrote the story. The lead sentence cut right to it: "Grover Cleveland's reputation for morality has been bad in this city for some time." Whispers of a scandal in Cleveland's personal life had been an open secret in Buffalo—"freely used in private and broadly hinted at in public."

> Inquiries came to Buffalo thick and fast concerning these reports. These were addressed to ministers of the gospel, editors and business men who might be supposed to know and have the courage and candor to tell the truth about the matter.
>
> Vague stories were afloat and people wanted something definite one way or the other. We had not pursued our investigations long before we discovered that others were on the same trail.

What came next was Ball's anonymous "Citizen's Statement," which the *Evening Telegraph* published in its entirety on the front page. Cresswell described the writer as a leading minister of the city—"one of the most discreet, honored and trusted . . . worthy of all confidence," and pledged to release his name at the proper time. Cresswell said the minister had recently presented his findings before a private conclave of Buffalo pastors and had expressed to them his belief that "Grover Cleveland's immoralities are so great that his election should be opposed by all Christian people."

"The *Telegraph's* action today is taken after counsel with several of the most influential pastors of Buffalo and with their warm approval."

It was a shrewd posture. Who could condemn the *Evening Telegraph* for investigating the city's favorite son when Buffalo's own clergymen were giving their blessing?

The *Evening Telegraph* portrayed Maria as a valiant lady who had been victimized by an "infamous conspiracy." Powerful forces had thrown her into an insane asylum without due process, but her "mother's love and zeal" could not keep Maria from reclaiming her son, Oscar. The son born of that relationship "bears the governor's image if he does not now bear his name." Maria Halpin—a woman of "culture, proud spirit and hitherto unblemished life"—had been "shamed," "disgraced," and "dishonored" by Cleveland, which was code for rape.

> The woman so treated was the mother of the son of the present governor of the state of New York, who aspires to be president of the United States. The men of America, as a rule, would die to protect the mothers of their children from such treatment.

> This is the terrible story of Maria Halpin and her son.

So it was done.

Now Cresswell and the staff of the *Evening Telegraph* braced themselves for the repercussions that were sure to follow.

10

DEFAMED

IN BUFFALO, CLEVELAND'S closest advisors were going to pieces. Some of them split the city into sectors and went around to all the major newsstands trying to buy up every available copy of the *Evening Telegraph*. When the newspaper fired up its steam presses to keep up with the demand, they gave up.

Cleveland's friend Charles Goodyear urgently telegraphed Cleveland requesting a set of instructions on how to deal with the *Evening Telegraph*'s revelations. Hunkered down at the Executive Mansion in Albany, Cleveland responded to Goodyear in a telegraphed message that was destined to go down in the annals of American crisis management: "Whatever you do, tell the truth."

Daniel Manning, the state party chairman, recommended what seemed like a levelheaded course of action: Officially, say nothing. Ignore the allegations, and pray that the scandal dies a natural death. The election was still a long way off—fourteen weeks, a lifetime in politics. People forget. This made sense to

Cleveland, and he signed off on the approach. But Cleveland was very much in a state of disgrace and said to be "filled with anguish."

"I am all 'out,'" he admitted to Daniel Lockwood, the U.S. congressman from Buffalo who had placed his name in nomination as the party's presidential candidate.

On the night of July 22, eight hundred independent Republicans known as mugwumps—a word from the Algonquin language that means "person of importance"—gathered at the University Club in Manhattan. High spirits filled the hall as delegates from sixteen states marched in to make official their historic resolution to cross party lines and endorse Grover Cleveland for president. In an era when party loyalty came first, this was not an easy call to make. Predictably, Blaine was denounced as unfit for office, while Grover Cleveland was praised as incorruptible. George Curtis presided over the convention. Curtis had been there from the beginning—he was a founder of the Republican Party. Even he was defecting from the party of Lincoln and backing Cleveland. These were heady days for the cause of reform in America.

"The issue of the present campaign is moral, not political," Curtis told his fellow delegates. The platforms of the Democratic and Republican parties were virtually indistinguishable on the key concerns of the day. Both parties supported civil service reform and opposed prohibition. The fundamental question in the campaign was not policy but personality: Grover the Good of New York, or Blaine of Maine and his sketchy political history.

The motion before the mugwumps to endorse Cleveland for president passed unanimously.

When the convention adjourned for the night, everyone seemed gratified with the great and important work that had been accomplished. But as they were leaving the University Club, they heard a strange rumbling that quickly grew to a roar. Copies of the *Evening Telegraph* exposé, hot off the presses from Buffalo, were being distributed to the delegates. As they read it, their elation was quickly replaced by alarm, and even "great revulsion." Grover Cleveland—a libertine? Could this be true?

Carl Schurz, a former United States senator from Missouri, had invited several of his fellow mugwumps for a private dinner at the University Club after the convention had concluded. Schurz was renowned for the memorable speech he had once made on the floor of the Senate: "My country, right or wrong; if right, to be kept right; and if wrong, to be set right." Seated at the head of the table, he was in a deep state of depression, shell-shocked over the *Evening Telegraph*'s allegations. He had staked his reputation on Cleveland.

At the end of the glum dinner, as everyone was getting ready to leave, the door to the private dining room was flung open, and George Curtis walked in. His face was a "picture of woe." The *Evening Telegraph* was in his hand.

"Have you seen this?" he asked. Everyone nodded.

"What are we going to do?" In his prepared address to the delegates, he had said the campaign of 1884 was all about morals, not politics. Now this.

"How can we possibly continue our support of Cleveland?"

Almost everyone at the dinner table had something to say. Somebody pointed out that when Cleveland ran for mayor and governor, none of his opponents had ever alluded to this Maria

Halpin. Besides, who knew if the story was true? In this over-heated political year, with emotions at fever pitch, nothing about any candidate in any newspaper should be taken at face value.

Curtis was not persuaded. A mugwump from Chicago who was seated next to Schurz had sat there mute, absorbing everything, saying nothing—until this moment.

"Do you want to know how this matter strikes me?" Everyone encouraged him to speak his mind.

"Well, from what I hear, I gather that Mr. Cleveland has shown high character and great capacity in public life, but that in private life his conduct has been open to question, while, on the other hand, Mr. Blaine in public life has been weak and dishonest, while he seems to have been an admirable husband and father." Everyone nodded. So far, no one could disagree with his assessment of the two candidates. He was urged to go on.

"The conclusion I draw from these facts is that we should elect Mr. Cleveland to the public office which he is so admirably qualified to fill and remand Mr. Blaine to the private life which he is so eminently fitted to adorn."

They all chortled; given the quandary they faced, they welcomed the gallows humor. Whom to support for president—Cleveland, with his sexual indiscretions? Or Blaine, who had taken bribes from the railroad?

There was a consensus: The mugwumps were holding fast for Cleveland—at least for the time being.

For the governor, the publication of "A Terrible Tale" could not have come at a more mortifying time: On July 21, the day it came out, Frances Folsom turned twenty. She and her mother were in Albany to celebrate her birthday with Cleveland and the triumph of his presidential nomination. Now, all they could do was try to comfort the man who stood accused by his hometown newspaper of raping a widow, fathering her illegitimate son, and consorting with lewd women.

Surely, Cleveland felt deeply ashamed. For ten years he had lived with the fear that his dark secret could be exposed at any moment. So fearful had he been of the disclosures his presidential candidacy might precipitate that he had had to be pushed into the race—and was crestfallen when he won it. To quote the *Evening Telegraph*, "The mine that has long slumbered under the feet of Grover Cleveland has at last been exploded."

Cleveland, waiting for the inevitable fallout, got wind that his friends in Buffalo were brazenly ignoring his instructions to "tell the truth," and were taking steps to discredit Maria Halpin. He was indignant when he learned that Charley McCune, publisher of the *Buffalo Courier*, in his effort to support the paper's candidate, was spreading the venomous story that the father of Maria's illegitimate son was not Cleveland at all. According to this tall tale, the boy's biological father was actually Oscar Folsom.

"I learned last night that McCune had started the story and told it to newspapermen (one at least) that I had nothing to do really with the subject of the *Telegraph* story—that is, that I am innocent—and that my silence was to shield my friend Oscar Folsom," Cleveland wrote Daniel Lockwood. "Now is this man crazy or does he want to ruin anybody? Is he foolish enough to suppose for a moment that if such was the truth (which it is not, so far as the motive for silence is concerned) that I would permit my dead friend's memory to suffer for my sake? And Mrs. Folsom and her daughter at my house at this very time!

"This story of McCune's of course must be stopped. I have prevented its publication in one paper at least."

Maria Halpin's name swiftly circulated around the nation. Newspapers in New York, Chicago, Boston, Philadelphia, Pittsburgh, and, of course, the Scripps publications in Detroit and Cleveland all went with the story on July 22 or 23. By the end of the week, more than one hundred newspapers had reported "A Terrible Tale" or some abridged version of it. *The Sun*, under the leadership of the flamboyant editor Charles Dana, called on Cleveland to withdraw as the Democratic standard-bearer. Zemro Smith's *Boston Journal* finally published the results of its investigation on July 30. "The whole story was in our hands before any publication in detail had appeared," the *Journal* crowed. "We preferred to obtain, not through 'obscure newspapers,' but from the lips of those who ought to know, the exact situation." Unsurprisingly, the *Journal* failed to allude to James Blaine's role in tipping off the newspaper.

Many Democrat and mugwump publications refused to give the Halpin scandal much play, rationalizing their restraint on grounds that the accusations were too lurid for a family newspaper. "They would bring the blush to the cheek of every son and daughter of the Empire State who read them," explained one broadsheet in Rochester. *The New York Times* and the pro-Cleveland *Buffalo Courier* and *Buffalo Express* were also stricken deaf and dumb. Dead silence too from the *Buffalo Evening News*, whose owner, Edward Butler, was a friend of Grover Cleveland's. Daniel Manning's *Albany Argus* also suppressed the story, referencing it only in the context of an editorial that disparaged the coverage of the scandal as "beneath notice." Other newspapers rallied to Cleveland's defense. Pulitzer's *New York World* denounced the *Evening Telegraph* as "unscrupulous" and categorized the attacks on Cleveland's character as "gross, cowardly and unmanly."

In Buffalo, John Cresswell continued pouring it on.

"The *Telegraph* is little, but it is mighty and will prevail," Cresswell wrote. He called Cleveland a "moral leper" who "should never have been allowed to become governor." Cresswell claimed that his paper had performed a disagreeable but nevertheless imperative public service in stripping the mask from Cleveland and exposing the candidate's "hideous moral deformity." It also addressed the gentlemen of the press who were expressing holy horror over the graphic language used in reporting "A Terrible Tale."

"You print as bad stories as that every day—stories of rape, incest, seduction, abduction. You deceive nobody. The *Telegraph*'s story needed to be told."

Cresswell gleefully noted how Cleveland's managers seemed to have been afflicted with paralysis—"when everybody knows that they would make a fearful noise if the charge had been groundless. His partisans here do not deny it, they merely grate their teeth in rage and abuse the paper that dared to tell the truth." He had a point, and other newspapers also noted the absence of any official refutation of the facts by the governor.

"What Grover Cleveland's defense in this Halpin case may be, if he ever attempts one, I am unable to discover," declared the managing editor of the *Detroit Evening Journal*.

Letters poured into the *Evening Telegraph*. Mrs. O. K. Smith of West Eagle Street in Buffalo wrote, "All honor to the bravest paper in Buffalo! Women, if you have any influence use it." A clergyman who requested anonymity mailed this letter to the editor:

> You are to be commended for the cleanliness of your recital—it was not your fault that its details were so gross and shocking. For what you have so boldly and yet carefully done, you deserve a hearty vote of thanks from the whole American people.

But within the *Evening Telegraph*'s uncompromising posture there lay a nub of concern. The newspaper said it was confining its coverage strictly to the Maria Halpin case, leaving George Ball (whom it had yet to publicly identify as its principal source) on his own to defend the assertions—that Cleveland had been beastly drunk and had associated with lewd women—published in "A Citizen's Statement." In regard to these claims, the *Evening Telegraph* signaled that it was up to Ball to fend for himself.

It was the *Chicago Tribune* that finally outed Ball. Somehow the *Tribune* had obtained a copy of the letter Ball had written to the Christian newspaper *Chicago Advance*. The *Tribune* republished the *Advance* letter, identifying Ball as the preacher who had been the informant for "A Terrible Tale." Ball seemed to accept the leak as inevitable and wrote the *Tribune* a droll but barbed letter in which he said he did not "particularly care" that he had been named:

> I had carefully investigated the case and found the evidence of his guilt overwhelming. The sole object in writing it was to put the *Advance* on its guard and draw its attention to Mr. Cleveland's immoralities.

Ball praised the *Evening Telegraph* and John Cresswell, saying the newspaper's reporting had been truthful, thorough, and written "without exaggeration":

> The editor of that paper is a Christian gentleman who would not knowingly publish an untruth. He took great pains to ascertain the facts before disclosing anything.

Like a stern pastor scolding his wayward flock, Ball asked Chicagoans to stop writing him and instead direct their inquiries to the *Evening Telegraph* if they wanted to order a copy of "A Terrible Tale"—singly or in bulk. "If people will send for it instead of writing to me, I shall be greatly obliged."

By the first week of August, the entire country knew the name "George Ball."

It was at this point that Henry Ward Beecher found himself thrust into the maelstrom. Beecher was the flamboyant minister of the Plymouth Congregational Church in Brooklyn. His sister was, of course, Harriet Beecher Stowe, author of *Uncle Tom's Cabin*. Beecher's irreverent sermons in which he preached unconditional love and women's suffrage proved so popular that he had become New York's number one tourist attraction and, it was said, also the most famous man extant in America.

Beecher had championed Grover Cleveland's run for governor of New York in 1882, and like the other independent Republicans of his era, he had been expected to join the bolt from Blaine and, in the name of reform and good government, endorse Cleveland in the 1884 presidential race. But a letter that Beecher wrote to George Peck, a prominent lawyer from Kansas, was leaked to the press and sent the Cleveland campaign into a tailspin of concern:

"Owing to late developments from Albany, I cannot and will not now, support Grover Cleveland the Democratic nominee for President in the coming election."

The correspondence was replete with melodrama. As everyone knew, nine years before, Beecher had been sued for adultery following accusations that he seduced a married parishioner, Elizabeth Tilton. Jurors deliberated for six days but were unable to reach a verdict. It had been one of the most celebrated trials of the 19th century.

Beecher had somehow survived his sex scandal, while Cleveland was in the earliest stage of struggling to manage his own disgrace. The Cleveland campaign found itself facing yet another crisis: Beecher's defection could potentially swing the election. In Brooklyn, he was a genuine political force. And it was said that as Brooklyn went, so would go the state of New York; and as New York went, so would go the nation.

Bringing Beecher back to the Cleveland fold was now the highest priority. General Horatio C. King was designated to talk things over with the preacher.

King came from a politically connected family; his father had served as U.S. postmaster general during the last three weeks of the Buchanan administration. Horatio King had been graduated from Dickinson College in Pennsylvania and, when war broke out, was commissioned a captain in the Union Army. He fought gallantly at the Battle of Five Forks in Virginia, was discharged with the rank of colonel, and then returned to New York City to practice law. In 1871, King was named publisher of the *Christian Union* magazine—a publication whose editor in chief was Henry Ward Beecher. So King and Beecher had a history. Also, at Beecher's recommendation, Governor Cleveland had recently named King to the post of judge advocate of the New York State National Guard, with the rank of general. King, like Beecher, lived in Brooklyn. He was the perfect emissary to go before Beecher on bended knee.

King was forty-seven when he made his heartfelt appeal to the preacher to reassess his opposition to Cleveland. Speaking to Beecher as a public figure who had felt the humiliating sting of his own bout with sexual indiscretion, King's words fell on sympathetic ears. Beecher said he was open-minded and suggested that King go to Buffalo to personally look into the *Evening Telegraph*'s charges and report back to him. This King agreed to do. How a political appointee of Grover Cleveland's could be expected to conduct a credible investigation was not apparent, but in any event, King went to Buffalo on Monday, August 4, determined, he said, to get to the bottom of the case and put Beecher's mind at rest. King seems to have spent most of his time with an Erie County supervisor who personally assured King that he had never heard of any "immoral" conduct on the part of Grover Cleveland. Two days later, he was on his way to Albany to call on Grover Cleveland at the state capital. The two men had a serious heart-to-heart.

"I told him," King later said, "that Mr. Beecher was very much disturbed by these stories that have been circulated about him, and that I would like a statement from him about them." Cleveland insisted that the account published in the *Evening Telegraph* was "false and scandalous."

"I acted throughout as any honorable man should," Cleveland informed King. As King recalled, "No man could have looked at the governor and not have felt that he was speaking the truth."

Cleveland asked King to do what he could to obtain a public endorsement from Beecher.

King proceeded on to Peekskill, where Beecher owned a magnificent estate that he had christened Boscobel, set on thirty-six acres of rich farmland. He had erected the mansion in 1879 at the then-enormous cost of $70,000, money he had earned from his lecture tours and books; but over the years, he had poured another $200,000 into expanding and improving his country manor. There were twenty-three rooms with breathtaking views of the Hudson River, and wallpaper so "exquisite" Beecher couldn't bear to hang anything on them. But his favorite room was the tiny carpenter's shop where in the summer he could often be found tinkering and hammering on his woodworking projects. Beecher had personally designed the gardens; groves of trees had been artfully grouped according to species, shape, and color of foliage. He also grew his own corn, peas, and strawberries; but considering the enormous expense of running Boscobel, he liked to joke that every cabbage he raised cost him $5.

When King called on Beecher, the great preacher showed him eighteen copies of "A Terrible Tale" that had been mailed to him from friends around the country. Everyone wanted to know what Beecher thought about the scandal. George Ball had also reached out, sending Beecher a personal letter explaining his involvement in the investigation. Now Beecher was eager to hear what King had unearthed in Buffalo.

"The paper in which the slander was originally published is an insignificant, sensational sheet," King told Beecher, "and one of the strangest things is that other papers in good standing seem to give credence to the story." Beecher must have nodded knowingly, perhaps recalling the lurid coverage of his own trial for adultery in 1875. King claimed that certain unnamed "prominent men"—no doubt meaning Blaine—were behind the *Evening Telegraph*'s allegations. All of Buffalo was "indignant" over the newspaper exposé, the general sentiment being one of utter contempt for the *Evening Telegraph*.

"I went everywhere and did quite a little bit of detective work on my own account. I learned enough to convince me that Cleveland had been wrongfully accused," King said. "Like many men, Cleveland likes good living and good company, but he never goes to excess in anything." It was a deft argument that must have resonated with Beecher, as Cleveland sounded very much like Beecher himself, at least in respect to their personal shortcomings.

After Beecher considered everything King had to say, he was satisfied that the scandal had been overblown, the result of the "foolish peccadilloes of a young man committed fourteen or fifteen years ago" and should not weigh on Cleveland's current life or candidacy. He added that he was embarrassed to have been "wrongfully made to mistrust Governor Cleveland" and would now do anything to show his "appreciation" of the man.

"I am going to stand by the governor," Beecher informed King.

An ecstatic King returned to Brooklyn and promptly got the word out that Beecher had returned to the Cleveland column. When a reporter for the *New York Tribune* went to Boscobel to check out the reports of this remarkable conversion, he found Beecher's wife, Eunice, in the library. Beecher, she said, was currently unavailable. He was resting in another room.

"My husband has been quite ill for several days, and I don't think it best to disturb him." Mrs. Beecher said she had been up for forty-eight hours nursing him. Doctors said it was an attack of colic, but Mrs. Beecher suspected something else.

"The truth of the matter is, worry and anxiety about this Cleveland scandal have been the main difficulty with Mr. Beecher. It came upon him like a flash of lightning. He had always regarded Mr. Cleveland as a clean man. He was completely prostrated when he heard reports to the contrary."

There was a commotion. The great Henry Ward Beecher was awake. Mrs. Beecher jumped from her chair.

"Henry, it is another reporter."

The man from the *Tribune* apologized for the intrusion and showed Beecher clippings from recent newspaper articles asserting that he was now, with a "clear conscience" backing Cleveland for the presidency—"unless something more damaging than has yet been published is produced." Beecher impatiently tossed the articles aside.

"I know perfectly well what they contain, and in a measure they tell the truth. I wrote a hurried and private letter to an old friend, Mr. Peck, in which I said substantially that if the charges against Mr. Cleveland were proved, I should not support him. If he is such a man as this, I am done. This letter was entirely private, and I am pained that extracts from it should have found their way into print. I have now suspended judgment and am awaiting more light. You know that sometimes one gropes in the dark for a time, but the exercise of a little patience will generally show the way."

Meanwhile, Horatio King arranged for his own interview with the *New York World*. He declared that he had gone to Buffalo determined to get to the bottom of the case. The story that ran the next day was nothing short of a full-blown attack on

Maria Halpin. King had taken his cue from Charley McCune's tall tale and run with it. Here was King's account:

> The facts seem to be that many years ago when the governor was "sowing his wild oats," he met this woman, with whom his name has been connected, and became intimate with her. She was a widow and not a good woman by any means. Mr. Cleveland, hearing this, began to make inquiries about her and discovered that two of his friends were intimate with her at the same time as himself.
>
> When a child was born, Cleveland, in order to shield his two friends, who were both married men, assumed the responsibility of it. He took care of the child and mother like a man, and did everything in his power for them, and he provided for them until the woman became a confirmed victim of alcoholism and made it impossible by her conduct for him to have anything to do with her. He never separated the mother and child, nor did he do anything to injure the woman. He was throughout the affair a victim of circumstances. He accepted responsibilities that not one man in a thousand has shouldered and acted honorably in the matter.
>
> After the child was born the woman made a habit of visiting every man with whom she had been intimate and demanded money under a threat of exposure. Three of her four admirers—for she was an attractive woman—were married and the man who in reality was the father of the infant had an interesting daughter whom he idolized. He was in constant dread lest his offense should reach his wife and child, and Cleveland, being the only unmarried man, relieved him of the embarrassment by shouldering

all of the responsibility. That man is dead and the child is his perfect image in manner and looks. Cleveland acted a heroic part, suffering the obloquy that his friends might not bring unpleasantness to their hearthsides.

Then King brought in his conversations with Cleveland.

"The governor frankly told me that my version of the stories was substantially correct, and that the account published in the Buffalo *Telegraph* was false and scandalous."

The King interview created a sensation. At last the Cleveland campaign was fighting back. Here was a high-level Cleveland mouthpiece going on the record with the first spirited defense of the presidential candidate and his relationship with Maria Halpin. And what a story it was. King's portrayal of Maria could not have been more cutting. She was "not a good woman"—stinging words in the Victorian Age. The woman's morals were so loose she couldn't positively identify the father of her child. It could have been any of two or four men who were passing her around Buffalo like a sexual plaything. In King's rendering, Cleveland was a selfless hero who had assumed responsibility for the boy when he might not have been the father.

The pure malevolence of King's interview reached the peak of cynicism when, in so many words, he accused the late Oscar Folsom of fathering Maria's child. Folsom made the perfect fall guy. He was dead and couldn't defend himself. Libel laws offered no protection for the departed.

The *World* interview received national attention, even from Republican newspapers, which found the prurient details too delicious to ignore. Not only was Maria Halpin a shamed woman, she was also a harlot. *Now everything made sense.*

To everyone, that is, except Maria Halpin.

11

FINDING MARIA

SOMETIME AROUND AUGUST 1, a Western Union telegram was delivered to the offices of the *New Rochelle Pioneer* newspaper. Addressed to the publisher, Charles Banks, who was an absentee owner, it ended up on the desk of the paper's office manager.

The telegram came from a Republican Party contact in Pittsburgh, a hotbed of anti-Cleveland sentiment.

> Interview Mrs. Maria Halpin who is said to have had child by Gov. Cleveland telegraph us before two o'clock this afternoon.

The name Maria Halpin was instantly familiar to the office manager. In the two weeks since the publication of "A Terrible Tale," her name had become synonymous with the scandal that was threatening the presidential candidacy of Grover Cleveland. Everyone wanted to know what Maria Halpin had to say, but no one had been able to find her. The office manager was stunned to read that, not only had she been found—she was living right there in New Rochelle of all places, at the home of James Albert Seacord, a local carpenter. The telegram urgently asked Charles Banks to approach Mrs. Halpin and obtain an interview in which she would give a full "endorsement" of the revelations as published in the *Buffalo Evening Telegraph.*

New Rochelle had an interesting history. It was founded in 1688 by Protestants fleeing persecution in France. The Huguenot colonists were artisans and craftsmen from the French coastal city of La Rochelle. In this way, the village in the New World came to be called *la Nouvelle-Rochelle.* Even in 1884, New Rochelle retained an exotic distinctiveness. French was still spoken by many of the shopkeepers and tradesmen who were direct descendants of the original settlers. The village was also growing into a desirable town to live in for people who worked in New York City. The great showman George M. Cohan would in the not-too-distant future immortalize New Rochelle's easy proximity to Manhattan with the song, "Forty-Five Minutes from Broadway."

As luck would have it, the office manager who opened the telegram was a die-hard Democrat. Rather than hand-deliver this remarkable news about Maria Halpin to Charles Banks, he took the telegram down the block to the offices of a New Rochelle lawyer, Charles H. Roosevelt. Unlike his distinguished relative Theodore Roosevelt, this Roosevelt was a Democrat.

Roosevelt read the telegram. He knew James Seacord. Everyone in New Rochelle did. Seacord lived right on Main Street. He was a sixty-nine-year-old descendant from the line of Ambroise Sicard, one of the town's original Huguenot settlers. The spelling of the name had been anglicized over the decades to Secor, Seacor, Secord, and finally to Seacord. Roosevelt sent a messenger to Seacord's carpentry shop to tell him that Charles Roosevelt wished to see him on a matter of urgent business. James Seacord dropped everything and went right over.

Roosevelt immediately came to the point and asked Seacord whether Maria Halpin was living at his home. He responded that she was. She was the niece of his wife Harriet, a seamstress who had run a little dressmaking business out of the Seacord house. The Seacords had been childless when they took Maria in to live with them when she was a teenager. She was like a daughter to them, and under Aunt Harriet's tutelage, she had learned dressmaking skills. She had also learned to speak French in New Rochelle.

Seacord told the lawyer that Maria had been trying to deal with her troubles in Buffalo when he and his wife offered her sanctuary in their tranquil little village where no one would know of her shame. Harriet Seacord had died the previous November, and Maria was now living alone with Uncle James, serving as his housekeeper and keeping the dressmaking business going to make a little money on the side. Maria (Seacord affectionately referred to her as "Rittie") was now a woman close to fifty years of age, "well preserved" and dignified. She had been living a "quiet, decorous, unobtrusive" life as Seacord's housekeeper and always conducted herself with propriety.

Charles Roosevelt took it all in then advised Seacord to quit work for the day, return home immediately, and stay there until Roosevelt communicated with him again. In the meantime, he told Seacord, Mrs. Halpin was to remain in "strict seclusion." No one except for Roosevelt was to be permitted access to the house. As an inducement to follow these directives, Roosevelt said he would guarantee Seacord "liberal compensation."

James Seacord left the office bewildered by this turn of events. In the meantime, Roosevelt went over all the information he had gleaned from their conversation. His first order of business was to reach out to Lawrence D. Huntington, a wealthy Wall Street broker who was chairman of the Westchester County Democratic Committee. He would know what to do. Roosevelt went to Huntington's house and informed him that he had Maria Halpin in his back pocket. Time was of the essence. There was no telling when Charles Banks might learn that his telegram had been purloined. Huntington arranged for a telegram to be sent to the right people in Albany. In quick order, he got a response. It reinforced the absolute necessity that the Halpin woman be kept under lock and key.

The next day, a distinguished visitor arrived in New Rochelle. It was Wilson Bissell, Grover Cleveland's confidant and former law partner. Bissell and Huntington were joined by another Westchester County Democrat, former state assemblyman William H. Catlin, who lived in the nearby village of Port Chester. Bissell told the men that he had come to New Rochelle for the sole purpose of convincing Mrs. Halpin to issue a public statement "pronouncing the story of her alleged relations with the governor a base fabrication." A plan of action quickly came together, with Catlin in charge of coordinating everything on the local level. Pulling it off was going to be a delicate business.

The following day, another distinguished visitor from Buffalo was seen in New Rochelle. It was Reverend George Ball. The whistle-blower had learned from his Republican friends that Maria Halpin had been found alive in New Rochelle. Ball had come down to speak with the woman personally. His first stop was the law office of Charles Banks, for a "consultation." Banks was a prosperous lawyer, the senior partner in the Westchester County firm of Banks and Henderson. When he had taken ownership of the *Pioneer* two years before, he had announced that henceforth he would run the newspaper "in the interests of the Republican Party." So his political bent was evident to everyone who read his newspaper. Through Banks, the *Pioneer* had become a reliable puppet of the state and local Republican political machine. It had been three days since the telegram about Maria had been sent to the publisher of the *New Rochelle Pioneer,* and nothing had happened. When Ball told Banks the purpose of his visit, Banks must have been shocked to learn of the existence of the telegram—and the treachery of his office staff. Undoubtedly, heads would soon be rolling at the *Pioneer*. Ball took his leave, telling Banks that he wished to visit with Mrs. Halpin alone, and set for James Seacord's house.

He found the house on Main Street. It was, as the expression went, a "plain address"—an unpretentious New England colonial made of timber and clapboard siding, with a picket fence surrounding the property. It was a fitting home for a humble village carpenter. Ball walked up four steps, opened the gate, and knocked on the front door. James Seacord opened it, and Ball introduced himself. Seacord shook his head. There was no way he was letting anyone see Maria. The two elderly gents eyed each other warily. Ball tried to explain who he was and the essential role he was playing in this national crisis. He said he was there to help. But Seacord was not hearing any of it. The carpenter stood his ground, blocking Ball's path, and even though Ball used all his gifts as a communicator, Seacord would not step aside. At last, Ball turned away in "disgust" and took the next train out of town. Irritated beyond words by his encounter with Seacord, he was nevertheless more convinced than ever "of the truth of the story."

Not knowing whom to trust, Seacord was mistrustful of everyone. He was staring out the window, looking up and down the street, when he saw some curious activities. There were men who didn't look like they were from New Rochelle positioned at the corner. They seemed "very sharp" and seemed to be keeping an eagle eye on the comings and goings at the Seacord house. When the carpenter confronted them, one man claimed to be an "antiquarian" interested in researching the gravestones in the church cemetery next to Seacord's property; another acknowledged that he was a detective. Obviously, Maria Halpin was under twenty-four-hour surveillance.

Inside the house, Maria tried to make sense of the confounding turn her life had taken. This was a nightmare. Grover Cleveland was the Democratic nominee for president, and the entire country was now aware of her disgrace. It had been ten years since she had given birth to Oscar Folsom Cleveland and eight years since she had been run out of the city of Buffalo, three hundred miles to the northwest. As for the account in "A Terrible Tale," Maria had read it; and when a New Rochelle neighbor asked her whether the stories were true, she answered, "They are, and God knows they are true too."

Maria's nerves were shot to hell, and she asked Dr. Bevin, her New Rochelle physician, to do what he could to calm her. Her eldest son, Frederick Halpin, went to the Seacord house to lend his mother support. Frederick was now a fine young man of twenty-one, working for the Erie Lackawanna Railway, but with aspirations of working his way up to locomotive engineer. He stood about six foot two, with a muscular build and his mother's dark good looks. He showed her a telegram he had just received from Albany, from William Hudson, Cleveland's political counselor. In it, Hudson asked Frederick to meet with him at the Hoffman House in Manhattan.

The Hoffman House was a handsome Italian Renaissance hotel at Broadway and 24th Street. It took up an entire city block and was centrally located near all the principal New York City theaters and retail department stores. At the time it was also serving as national campaign headquarters of the Democratic Party. The food was impeccable—as good as Delmonico's—and the wine cellar was reputed to be the finest in Manhattan. The Hoffman House had a café for the gentlemen, a separate dining room for the ladies, and a seventy-foot-long carved bar paneled in mahogany that spread out a "swell" free buffet seven days a week. It was said to be the bar where the Manhattan cocktail had been concocted, though several other swanky saloons asserted the same claim.

Grover Cleveland had recently appointed Hudson to the New York State Railroad Commission, so the former political reporter for the *Brooklyn Eagle* finally had a real function in state government. But his true value was taking on these sensitive and sometimes dirty political missions. Hudson was waiting for Frederick in Room 210. Young Halpin disdained Hudson on sight; after all, he was there as the representative of the man who had violated Frederick's mother and had her committed to an insane asylum. It was a thorny conversation to say the least, and Hudson, having found it impossible to get past Frederick's personal antagonism, got down to business.

Hudson said it was in Maria Halpin's best interests to issue a public denial of the allegations concerning her relationship with Grover Cleveland. He took a sheet of paper and wrote out a statement that he said he would like Maria to sign. If she did, according to Frederick's recollection of the meeting, he would be offered a job working for the commissioner of the New York State Board of Public Works, and his mother would receive the extraordinary sum of ten thousand dollars. Hudson handed the statement he'd drafted to Frederick:

> I have read the statement published in the Buffalo *Telegram* [sic] of the date of _____, concerning myself and Mr. Cleveland, a statement which is largely false and malicious. Shortly after the death of my husband, some twelve years ago, I removed to Buffalo with my children. Some time after that I met Mr. Cleveland and made his acquaintance, which acquaintance extended over a period of some months. During that time I received from Mr. Cleveland uniform kindness and courtesy. I have now and have always had a high esteem for Mr. Cleveland. I have not seen him in seven or eight years.

Frederick read the statement, not surprised to find it a fraught with lies and falsehoods, but he knew it was his duty to bring it to his mother's attention. An enormous sum of money was at stake, and she would have to decide what to do. Frederick returned to New Rochelle with the statement in hand.

William Hudson wasn't far behind young Halpin. Now that the Cleveland camp had established a direct line of communication with Maria, nothing could keep him away from New Rochelle. On August 7, when Hudson got off the train at the New Rochelle junction, former State Assemblyman Catlin was waiting for him. They had lunch at the country club. For security purposes, Catlin introduced Hudson as his friend "Louis Delafield." (Hudson's identity only later came to be exposed because he made the blunder of traveling with a free train pass, issued in his real name by the office of the New York State Railroad Commission.)

After lunch, Hudson and Catlin climbed aboard a one-horse carriage and drove into New Rochelle where they were dropped off at Charles Roosevelt's law offices. There they waited for darkness to settle on the village. Then the three of them—Hudson, Catlin, and Roosevelt—went to the home of James Seacord.

Roosevelt knocked on the door. Having developed a trusting relationship with Maria, she let him into the house. Hudson and Catlin remained outside under a street lamp, checking a railroad timetable for the next available train out of New Rochelle. A few minutes later, Maria Halpin emerged from the house in a fetching outfit, wearing a heavy veil and carrying a satchel. She got into the carriage and was driven to the New Rochelle station where she caught the 8:07 PM to Manhattan. A New Rochelle police officer named Kane made sure she boarded without being "molested" (in other words, no reporters or Republicans were present). Hudson accompanied her on the train, and when they pulled into Grand Central Depot in New York City, a coach was waiting for them. It was last seen rattling down 42nd Street, heading for the West Side, destination unknown.

When James Seacord got home, he found Maria gone. She had left him a note, which he found on a table under the lamp. It was addressed to Uncle Albert—Albert being his middle name.

Don't worry, I am going away.

It was signed, *Rittie.*

Word had gotten out that Maria Halpin was living in New Rochelle, and James Seacord found himself in the middle of a 19th-century media frenzy. After Seacord had told all the reporters who'd come knocking that Maria Halpin had "gone away for a few days on a visit," speculation swept the country that she had been kidnapped. Even reputable newspapers such as the *Chicago Tribune* expressed concern for Maria's physical safety, reporting the bogus rumor that once again she had been thrown into a lunatic asylum against her will.

With Maria under wraps, Grover Cleveland's people were free to tarnish the woman as a prostitute and drunk. Democratic publications gleefully slammed Maria to the brink of malicious libel. A profile of Maria published in the *New York Mercury* depicted her as the village vixen of New Rochelle who, in her youth, the newspaper said had attracted a "host of admirers." She was a "magnetic girl . . . full of life . . . with a free and jolly disposition . . . the village belle." Even in middle age, according to the *Mercury* profile, Maria was said to possess bewitching charm—she was a woman with a wealth of dark hair, a pale complexion, and a "strange, fascinating power" over men; in other words, a woman with loose morals.

The pro-Cleveland *Boston Globe* claimed to have obtained an exclusive sit-down interview with Maria from inside James Seacord's house. According to this mendacious account, "Mrs. Halpin is evidently an epileptic, and she has every symptom of insanity. Her eyes are glassy; she cannot look her questioner in the face; she has the trembling twitching of the muscles and the sudden starts at every unexpected noise peculiar to insane persons."

The preposterous article went on to describe how the front doorbell rang and Maria Halpin "sprang to her feet with a shudder and trembling like an aspen leaf rushed to the hall and frantically called out, 'Mr. Seacord! Mr. Seacord!'"

It quoted Maria as saying, "I have been very sick, and am very sick now. I will not live six months I know."

The entire story was an invention, published to debase Maria Halpin and raise doubts about her sanity. "I hope that Mr. Cleveland will be elected, and I would not want to put anything in the way of his success" went one fabricated quotation. "I do not wish Mr. Cleveland any harm. I have no quarrel with Mr. Cleveland. He is a good, plain, honest-hearted, nice man who has always been friendly to me and used me kindly. It is a shame that the newspapers should have issued such lies. I would not harm a hair on the head of Mr. Cleveland."

Sadly, with the scandal at fever pitch, even Maria's family sought to distance themselves from the scarlet woman. Her father, the retired police officer Robert Hovenden, was found living at 195 Ainslie Street in the Williamsburg section of Brooklyn. In his eighties, infirm, and going blind from cataracts, until the publication of "A Terrible Tale," he had known nothing of the ordeal Maria had suffered when she was in Buffalo. The fact that he had a grandson named Oscar whose father was Governor Grover Cleveland was news to him.

When a reporter from the *Brooklyn Times* interviewed Hovenden at his home, he defended the family honor: "I am known in this city and no one can point their finger at my children here." He said he had lost contact with Maria when she moved to Buffalo following the death of her husband. "Afterwards, we learned that she was obliged to go out to work. She was, we heard, engaged as a forewoman in a millinery establishment. We heard from her occasionally but she rarely visited us. I wish she had remained home with me. This terrible trouble might then have been averted." Then he broke into sobs.

Two of Hovenden's unmarried daughters lived with him and tried to comfort the old man. "Well, Father, it is not your fault, dear. You could not have guarded against this," Maria's sister said.

"I know," Hovenden answered. "But I, her father, knew nothing of this. I do not even now know what the exact story is. I know, however, that it is bad, very bad. Here I am almost blind and we, my children, have this additional affliction. Oh, I wish I could but meet Maria. I would have her tell all. There must be some truth in the terrible accusation."

One of Hovenden's daughters wanted the reporter to understand what the family was going through. "We have known, sir, nothing whatever about this awful story. We feel the disgrace keenly." She said Maria had visited her father's home just three weeks before. It was the first time they had seen each other since the early 1860s, when Maria had married Frederick T. Halpin. She had come to call because she had heard that her father was dying. "It is indeed strange that she never confided this matter to her family," she added.

Hovenden had many questions concerning Maria's life in Buffalo and the birth of Oscar Folsom Cleveland. The newsman from the *Brooklyn Times* told them everything he knew, and the

Hovendens expressed their appreciation. It was better to know now than to read about it in cold type. Still, the information was "like knives piercing their hearts." No matter what the set of circumstances, according to the code of conduct by which they all lived, Maria was in a state of ignominy and had brought shame on her family.

Other publications, chiefly the partisan Republican type, were disposed to give Maria the benefit of the doubt. Still fuming that his newspaper had been robbed of its huge scoop, the editor of Charles Banks's *New Rochelle Pioneer* was now claiming that Maria had been "betrayed into the hands of her enemies."

When the editor was asked, "Where do you believe the woman now is?" he responded, "I do not know, but if you inquire from Mr. William Hudson, I think he can tell you."

Under pressure to account for Maria's whereabouts, Hudson wrote an open letter from his office in Albany, stating that he knew nothing about the "alleged disappearance or so-called abduction" and had no more insight into what happened to the Halpin woman than any other citizen who followed the news. His denial was met with disbelief. The *Pioneer* posed the question, "How can Mr. Hudson . . . explain his business in New Rochelle on this very night and almost the very minute that she is known to have been taken away?"

The stress of the previous week had gotten to James Seacord. In tears, he said that he missed his dead wife. "I have had trouble enough already, without more being added." It was all too much for an old man to take.

"Has Mrs. Halpin seen the story of her wrongs as published in the papers?" he was asked.

"She had," Seacord said.

"What does she say of it?"

"That it's every word true."

Around New Rochelle, Seacord was reputed to be a solid citizen—poor but honest. He was utterly opposed to Maria Halpin going public about her relationship with Grover Cleveland. All he wanted was privacy. One New Rochelle resident said Maria "idolized her uncle," predicting that if she ever emerged from hiding, she would "bow to his judgment" and remain mute.

As the days passed and nothing was heard from Maria, her family in Brooklyn started thinking the worst. Her two unmarried sisters went to New Rochelle to speak with Seacord and look into the circumstances of Maria's disappearance but, unable to make much progress, returned home and reported the dismaying news to their father. Some questioned whether Maria would ever show her face again, considering the ignominy she had brought upon her family. To this, Hovenden responded, "She is my child, I am her father, I forgive her, but I must have her with me before I die." As tears trickled into his long grey beard, the retired police officer summoned what strength he had left and declared, "If I could see as I once could, I would put a bullet through the heart of the villain who has wronged my child and brought upon us this disgrace."

Maria's brother-in-law, Simeon Talbott, was on the road in Logansport, Indiana, when he received a letter from Grover Cleveland. Talbott had not heard from Cleveland in eight years since he had negotiated the five-hundred-dollar out-of-court settlement with Cleveland on Maria's behalf. At that time,

Cleveland had found the traveling leather-goods salesman to be an even-tempered fellow you could do business with, and they had worked everything out amicably. He had no reason to believe they could not do so now. Cleveland had written to Talbott as someone he could level with, man-to-man.

When Talbott read the letter, he could not believe the arrogance of the governor of New York. In it, Cleveland urged him to make a public statement, declaring that Cleveland had always treated Maria Halpin with respect. If he did so, the governor promised him "anything I could wish for in case he was elected." In his letter, Cleveland claimed that Horatio King's smears—that Maria had been intimate with two and possibly four other men in Buffalo around the time of Baby Oscar's birth—had been "wholly unauthorized by him and were not true." He pledged that, in the event that Talbott issued the statement he proposed, the record regarding Maria's alleged promiscuity would be "corrected." Talbott felt like tearing the letter to shreds. His wife back in Jersey City had told him that Maria was offered a $10,000 enticement from the Democratic Party for her cooperation in defusing the scandal, but turned it down. According to Talbott, she said that she would rather "die" than issue any kind of public support for Cleveland. Talbott, seething with indignation, strode to the offices of the local newspaper, the *Logansport Journal*, to go public with what he really thought of Grover Cleveland.

"Yes, I know Cleveland, perhaps better than any man living. Maria Halpin is my sister-in-law. The story told in the newspapers is literally true, and the half has not been told. Grover Cleveland did seduce my sister-in-law under a positive promise of marriage, while she was living in Buffalo. This I know to be true, and Cleveland afterward paid the five hundred dollars to me for Maria Halpin when legal proceedings were about to be instituted against him. Cleveland now has possession of the child."

James E. King Jr. was ten years old and vacationing with his mother, Sarah Kendall King, in Gilmanton, New Hampshire, that summer of 1884, blissfully unaware that the circumstances surrounding his birth had become the foremost issue of the presidential campaign. James was enjoying his summer, occupying himself with simple boyhood pleasures, when he became the focus of all this national attention. The day came when his mother, in a state of mounting panic, informed him that they were ending their vacation and immediately returning to Buffalo.

Minnie Kendall took note of her sister-in-law's hasty departure with a mixture of relief and contempt. Minnie, who was married to Sarah's brother, William Kendall, had been hired by Dr. James King in 1874 to nurse Baby Oscar. The Kendalls had raised the child for the first full year of his life, until they were obliged to surrender him and get out of Buffalo because they knew too much. They had relocated to their home state of New Hampshire.

Now in 1884, a reporter for the *Chicago Tribune* had come to her door and introduced himself. Her every instinct told her to keep what she knew to herself. Minnie Kendall shut the door in his face. In spite of everything, Sarah King was still family. This plus the fact that Dr. King had warned her numerous times over the years never to say a word about Baby Oscar. It took considerable persuasion by the *Tribune* reporter to finally get Minnie to talk. When she did, she confirmed that Oscar Folsom Cleveland was now known as James E. King Jr.

"They engaged me to care for a young child. They said they would pay me for it. They both urged me to and told me several times that I would call him my twin baby. I finally consented, and they left the child." She said she was told to call the boy Jack.

Minnie recalled the day several weeks later when Dr. King came to her apartment and told her to bring "Jack" to the downtown law offices of Grover Cleveland.

"Who was present at this time?"

"Myself, Maria Halpin, the baby, lawyer, and Dr. King. It was in the forenoon that we went there."

"Have you seen a picture of Grover Cleveland?"

"I have, and I should say, by the picture, that he was the lawyer who was there. What they took me and the child there for I don't know, unless it was to ensure Maria Halpin that her child was alive and well."

Minnie said that when she was compelled to surrender the child after a year, Dr. King was "very anxious" for her to leave Buffalo.

"He charged us over and over again never to tell what we knew about Maria Halpin's child and used all manner of means to intimidate us and compel us to keep the matter quiet. Dr. King's wife said to me just before we left Buffalo, 'Maria Halpin has got that child now, but I will get him and then she will never see him again.'"

The Kendalls settled in Rochester, New Hampshire. William Kendall found work in a factory; Minnie made shoes. It was unnerving that Sarah King was still taking her annual summer vacations in New Hampshire. Three years before, when Minnie was visiting family in Gilmanton, she was shown a photo of a little boy in a checked suit. "That is my Jack," she recalled saying. She recognized him at once. But how could she be so certain? "I know it is," Minnie said. "You can't fool me. I declare it is the boy I nursed—Maria Halpin's child." William Kendall, who was present during the interview, corroborated his wife's account.

What induced Minnie Kendall to finally tell her story? She admitted that she was filled with anxiety about coming forward, but was doing so "in the interest of justice."

The past was finally catching up to James and Sarah King.

12

"A BULLET THROUGH MY HEART"

DAN LAMONT, CLEVELAND'S right-hand man, sat at his desk frowning. In his hands, he held a letter, which he was so absorbed in reading he was not even aware that William Hudson had stepped into the office. Finally, he looked up and said, "I'm glad you've come. I want to talk to you about a perplexing matter."

Lamont rose from his desk and turned the key to lock his door. He wanted no one but Hudson to hear the story he was about to convey. "I don't know what to do with these papers. If I show them to the governor, I fear he will put his foot on them. If I conceal them from him and turn them over to the managers of the campaign and he comes to know of it, he'll be angry."

Hudson presumed that this must have something to do with Maria Halpin.

Lamont continued. A letter addressed to Grover Cleveland had been sent from a tailor who lived in Millersburg, Kentucky. He was writing to let the governor know that he possessed embarrassing information concerning the private life of James G. Blaine. Lamont showed Hudson the letter. The gist of it was that when Blaine married the former Harriet Stanwood, on March 25, 1851, it had literally been a shotgun wedding. Harriet's brother had had a rifle aimed at Blaine's head during the entire ceremony. A son, Stanwood Blaine, had been born to the newlyweds eleven weeks later, on June 18, 1851. It was information, the letter writer maintained, that would "more than" offset this business with Maria Halpin.

The tailor was offering to come to Albany at once and "submit his proof as well as himself to scrutiny." It all somehow sounded plausible.

Lamont wanted to know what Hudson thought he should do.

"Turn them over to the governor, Dan, and let him deal with them. I cannot see that you can do anything else."

Lamont agreed. It might be just the thing they needed to "fight this other devilish thing." He meant Maria Halpin.

Lamont walked out of the office, and when he returned, Grover Cleveland was with him. Cleveland squeezed his bulky frame into Lamont's chair and read the letter. Then he studied the supporting documents that had been mailed with it. When he was finished, he leaned his elbow on the desk and stared out the window, pondering the view of the park in front of the State Capitol building. Then he gathered the papers into a neat little stack.

"I'll take these," he announced. "Say nothing about them to anyone. I say this to both of you. Dan, send for this man to bring his proof as soon as he can. Promise to pay his expenses. When that man does come, bring him directly to me. I will deal with him."

When Cleveland left the office, Lamont and Hudson stared at each other. They were speechless. "I'll be hanged!" Hudson said. "He's going to use them after all."

Lamont was unsure. "I don't know . . . "

Five days later, the Kentuckian was in Albany. Lamont told him to wait outside the office and went in to tell Governor Cleveland that the Kentucky tailor was there.

"Bring him to me," Cleveland said.

Lamont returned with him, and Cleveland stiffly invited him to take a seat. "Are your proofs all here?"

"Yes, sir, all of them." They were certified copies of public records, plus letters from three witnesses. Taken in total, he said, they told the sordid story behind Blaine's marriage to his wife of thirty-three years.

Cleveland asked, "Everything is here then, and you are holding nothing in reserve?" When Cleveland was assured that everything was now in his custody, the governor turned to Lamont. "Arrange with this man a proper sum for his expenses, the time he has lost and his good will in the matter, and pay him."

A brief negotiation followed, after which Lamont wrote out a check, and the fellow was on his way home.

When Lamont went back to find Cleveland, he saw that the papers were laid out on the governor's desk—Cleveland started to rip them apart. Lamont watched dumbfounded, too shocked to say a word. Then Cleveland called for a porter and ordered him to throw the scraps of paper into the fireplace and set them ablaze. He stood before the fire and watched the documents disintegrate into black soot. Then he turned to his aide.

"The other side can have a monopoly of all the dirt in this campaign," he said.

Nevertheless, the grubby story found its way into print on August 8, in the pages of the *Indianapolis Sentinel*, a rabble-rousing Democratic newspaper in Indiana. Cleveland told Lamont he was "very sorry it was printed."

"I hope it will die out at once," he said.

The backstory was this: In 1850, Blaine was just out of college and teaching at a military academy in Kentucky when he met another teacher, Harriet Stanwood, who came from a wealthy Maine family. They fell in love and, six months later, became engaged. Not long thereafter, word reached Blaine that his father had died in Pennsylvania. He made the arrangements to attend the funeral and settle his father's estate, not knowing when or if he would ever return to Kentucky. And so on June 30, 1850, in the presence of a few trusted friends, Blaine wed Harriet Stanwood in a quickie ceremony conducted by an itinerant preacher. Alas, the preacher failed to procure a proper marriage license— technically, the Blaines were not legally married. Nine months later, when Harriet was pregnant with her first child, she and Blaine decided to take their vows in church, this time in the presence of family members. The date was March 25, 1851. Their son Stanwood Blaine was born eleven weeks later.

Out of this romance, the *Sentinel*, under hard-line publisher and editor John C. Shoemaker, spun a lurid story, accusing Blaine of having "despoiled" Harriet Stanwood and only marrying her "at the muzzle of a shotgun." A layer of conspiracy was introduced when the *Sentinel* reported that somebody had crept into a cemetery in Augusta, Maine, and chiseled out the date of Stanwood Blaine's birth to make it illegible. (He died on July 31, 1854, at the age of three.) The desecration of the stone lent credence to the fable that the boy's conception had been illegitimate. James Blaine was understandably beside himself with this ghoulish violation of his son's resting place.

"As a candidate for the presidency, I knew that I should encounter many forms of calumny and personal defamation, but I confess that I did not expect to be called upon to defend the name of a beloved and honored wife, who is a mother and a grandmother, nor did I expect that the grave of my little child would be cruelly desecrated."

Even after Blaine filed a libel suit against the *Sentinel*, Shoemaker kept up the attacks. He distributed an eight-page supplement that detailed the history of the Blaine marriage; he also published a slimy attack on Blaine's practice of warmly embracing supporters at campaign stops. Blaine, said Shoemaker, was guilty of "man-kissing."

> Now, if ladies were voters, and it were ladies he practiced his osculatory art upon, we should not object—i.e., if the ladies did not. But this thing of his kissing men— of pressing his bearded lips upon bearded lips—is too aggressive. Last week, over in Ohio, Mr. Blaine kissed a man who boarded his train. No longer than last night he kissed two men in this city.

Not for nothing is the presidential election of 1884 called the dirtiest in American history.

On board the morning riverboat that pulled into Albany harbor were the most eminent leaders of the Democratic Party from all thirty-eight states and the Territory of Washington. They were there to officially notify Grover Cleveland that he had been nominated the party's candidate for the presidency. At three in the afternoon, in a drizzling rain, the men, in squads of four, climbed aboard twenty-five carriages and, with the Tenth Regiment band at the head of the procession, made their way through the capital's streets to the governor's mansion on Eagle Street. There they where shown into the drawing room and formed themselves into a semicircle to await Cleveland's appearance. On the other side of the room, enjoying this day of high honor, were Cleveland's top aides, and the women of his household: Cleveland's sisters, Mary Hoyt and Rose Cleveland; his two nieces from Ceylon, Mary and Carrie Hastings; and Emma Folsom and her daughter Frances. Daniel Manning was also there, and Wilson Bissell and Dan Lamont. Other than an immense bank of roses, carnations, and geraniums that had been grown in the governor's greenhouse, the room was empty of all furniture or ornamentation.

Cleveland descended the staircase and strode into the room to generous applause. For the occasion, he wore a new suit of black broadcloth, with a high collar and black tie. The formal certificate of notification was presented to him in a handsomely embossed portfolio bound in Russian leather. Cleveland thanked everyone and pledged to campaign on a platform of simple truths. It marked the official launch of the fall campaign season. Prolonged applause followed, and the crowd of dignitaries surged forward to shake hands with the candidate.

Frances Folsom was the prettiest young lady in the room, but none of the unmarried men on the governor's staff who attended the ceremony dared approach her. Bissell was quite amused.

"If one of you, young fellows, doesn't take an interest in Miss Folsom, the governor is likely to walk off with her himself!" Everyone laughed.

Eleven days later, around the time that Maria Halpin disappeared from her home in New Rochelle, Cleveland started out for the north woods of New York State. In this time of crisis, he was going on a two-week vacation. Accompanying him was Dr. Samuel B. Ward, an Albany physician. On August 9, Cleveland and his party took a buckboard carriage to the Prospect House hotel, a popular resort in Upper Saranac Lake. They arrived to the hearty cheers of the hundred and fifty guests who had assembled on the veranda. That evening, Cleveland had dinner at the home of a local dignitary, Paul Smith, where yet another committee of prominent citizens welcomed him with speeches and fanfare. It was all too much for Cleveland.

"I hope that brass bands and such nonsense are over for a time," he grumbled.

That night, he finally had a chance to unpack and found that Lamont, with his usual attention to detail, had stuffed the trunk with an enormous quantity of stationery. It made Cleveland chortle. "I imagine you must have thought I intended to establish the Executive Chamber here," he wrote Lamont. Once again his private secretary was proving himself to be indispensable. Cleveland informed him that he was so exhausted, he was thinking about extending his vacation into a third week.

The next night, Cleveland stayed up until 2:00 AM working on a formal letter of acceptance. He got up that same morning at six thirty and went over the letter, not quite knowing whether he liked the final product or not, but it was just about done, such as it was. He got to thinking about the duplicity of Benjamin Butler and John Kelly, which still rankled, and he had to wonder whether the members of his own party were behind the Maria Halpin scandal.

"Now this is for you privately," he wrote Lamont. "I want to tell you just how I feel. I had rather be beaten in this race than truckle to Butler or Kelly." Cleveland said he was determined to show a "stiff upper lip" and not violate his principles in his dealings with these two troublemakers.

He missed his friends. "Remember me to Apgar," he told Lamont. "Give my affectionate regards to Manning."

Cleveland and Dr. Ward spent the next two weeks hunting and "a-fishing" in the Adirondacks and dealing with the August heat and discomfort. They were steadily on the move from sunrise to sunset, with Ward boasting that they "very frequently had no better couch to sleep on than the damp ground." When Cleveland finally returned to Albany, sunburned and rested, he flat out refused to hit the campaign trail. Pressing the flesh was not Cleveland's way—he found it beneath his dignity. In addition, staying home could be a good strategy: Samuel Tilden had remained aloof from the campaign trail when he ran in 1876 and, in doing so, cemented his reputation as a great politician who stood above the fray. And when Garfield ran for office in 1880, he had not strayed far from his own backyard. Cleveland's Republican opponent, James Blaine, was a different kind of political animal. He was already slugging it out in the West, having set forth on a grueling six-week road trip. When it was over, somebody counted the number of campaign stops Blaine made—four hundred in all.

Standing in for Cleveland was a proxy of Democratic Party big shots, none more valued than the vice-presidential candidate Thomas Hendricks. Once his displeasure at being denied the top slot on the ticket was behind him, the sixty-year-old Hendricks directed most of his energy on his stronghold, his home state of Indiana, which he had to deliver. Illinois, next door, was also in play. Interest in the general election was intense everywhere in the Midwest. At a barbecue in tiny Shelbyville, Indiana, thirty thousand citizens showed up to hear Hendricks speak.

Hendricks, along with two nieces, was traveling in a private car owned by the superintendent of the Bloomington and Western Railroad to Bloomington, Illinois, for a campaign stop when the train ran into trouble. Going thirty-five miles an hour, it suddenly jumped off the tracks just outside Farmer City. The car skidded down an embankment before coming to a stop, bottom up. Amid the shrieks of the other passengers, Hendricks and his nieces managed to extricate themselves from the wreckage. Luck was with them. Twenty passengers were hurt, eight of them seriously, but Hendricks was only slightly bruised. He emerged shaken, with an injury that was described as "trifling"—and his nieces escaped unscathed. Hendricks proved himself so indefatigable a campaigner that he continued on to Bloomington and arrived in time to make his campaign appearance.

In Buffalo, George Ball remained utterly convinced of Grover Cleveland's unfitness to serve as president. The preacher launched a new line of attack, piling on the allegations against the Democratic candidate and including some shocking new charges.

"For many years, days devoted to business have been followed by nights of sin," Ball wrote of the governor. "He has lived as a bachelor . . . lodged in rooms on the third floor in a business block, and made those rooms a harem." Cleveland, claimed Ball, was a "champion libertine, an artful seducer, a foe to virtue, an enemy of the family, a snare to youth, and hostile to true womanhood. The Halpin case was not solitary. Women now married and anxious to cover the signs of their youth have been his victims. Since he has become governor of this great state, he has not abated his lecheries."

According to Ball, a German woman who lived down by the railroad tracks, and her two daughters, were eager to quench Cleveland's lust. Ball claimed that Cleveland's lascivious behavior had persisted even after his election as governor. When Cleveland visited Buffalo, he was seen at a saloon with three other men. All were intoxicated when they went to an apartment in another part of town and "sent out for four lewd women and spent the night and all day Sunday with them in debauchery."

Ball said he had the names of reliable citizens from both political parties who were willing to "confirm every item" if called upon.

"The issue is evidently not between the two great parties, but between the brothel and the family, between indecency and decency, between lust and law . . . between the degradation of women and due honor, protection, and love to our mothers, sisters, and daughters."

In a letter that was published in the *Boston Journal*, Ball had this to say to critics who questioned whether he really had the goods on Cleveland:

> As to Mr. C's drinking, take one fact. He and two other lawyers a few years since visited their club-house on Grand Island, a place of drunkenness and lust, and the three were beastly drunk on their return to the city. Oscar Folsom, esq., (one of them) fell from the carriage and broke his neck. If you desire more facts I will do my best to supply them.
> Yours truly,
> Geo. H. Ball.

The clubhouse in question, of course, was the Beaver Island Club, where Cleveland and his friends belonged to a social fraternity that came to be known as the Jolly Reefers. The clubhouse had been Cleveland's second home. When they were building it he had even helped clear the grounds with an ax and applied his lawyerly skills to write the Beaver Island Club constitution. His dearest friends, including Wilson Bissell and Oscar Folsom before his death, had all been members. This was the same thousand-acre resort where Cleveland had taken Frances Folsom for clambakes and picnics when she was a little girl. Now Ball was making the remarkable assertion that Cleveland was present when Oscar Folsom broke his neck after being thrown headfirst from a carriage. According to Ball's account, Folsom's fatal injury had come about as he was returning from a wild and "riotous party" on Beaver Island at which Cleveland had been present.

Regrettably for Ball, the facts failed to bear any of this out. In his zeal to destroy Cleveland, he gouged a hole in his own sheath of credibility. Cleveland was not with Folsom when the accident occurred; Folsom's companion had been the lawyer Warren Miller. Cleveland only appeared on the scene after Folsom was pronounced dead. Further, Folsom was not driving home after a night of revelry at the Beaver Island Club. He had been drinking, that part was true, but it was at the home of Charles Bacon, a Buffalo businessman. What really wrecked Ball's case was his contention that the Beaver Island Club was a place of booze and debauchery. The Jolly Reefers came from the most esteemed families in Buffalo; by innuendo, Ball was accusing all of them of licentiousness.

Newspapers across America ferociously attacked the George Ball. The *New York Post* launched a campaign against him that branded his anti-Cleveland letters "filthy and disingenuous." In a biographical sketch of his life, the *Post* claimed that Ball had "wandered about a good deal," making the ludicrous assertion that he had once worked at the U.S. Customs House in New York harbor. As everyone knew, the Customs House was the notorious lair of Republican political hacks, and is rampantly corrupt. The newspaper also claimed that when Ball lived in Owensville, Indiana, he had to "hastily depart, owing to an 'insult to a Christian lady.'"

"Moreover, he has, we are informed, a remarkable detective love of ferreting out low and disgusting scandals and mysteries." This was just the beginning.

Four days later, on August 12, the *Post* resumed its offensive with a vengeance. Ball and his followers were "guttersnipes" and "vampires," and Ball was a "dynamiter who plants a bomb in the waiting room of a railroad station, thronged with women and children, in order to strike terror in the hearts of other people."

The *Post's* editor, Edwin L. Godkin, wrote the articles or personally edited them and had them republished in *The Nation* magazine, which at that time was a weekly insert owned by the newspaper.

Other newspapers joined in the attack. The pro-Cleveland *Boston Herald* ran an article under the headline, "The Vile Record of 'Rev.' Ball in Gibson County, Ind."

> The "Rev." Ball, who originated the vile slander on Gov. Cleveland, it has just been learned used to live down in Gibson county, Ind. A *Courier-Journal* representative who was down in Owensville yesterday interviewed several prominent people, from whom it was learned that a number of years ago this same Ball preached to a small congregation, from whom he filched money under various pretenses. He finally became noted over the county as a great liar, and one in whom no trust could be placed. Ball not only became noted as a liar, but one who imbued [sic] very frequently a little too much bad whiskey for a preacher. He was finally expelled from the church, and he left the county. He is so well known down in Gibson county that Republicans as well as Democrats brand him as one of the monster frauds of the county. These facts are authentic and can be verified at any time.

The *Herald* later had to sheepishly acknowledge that the pastor in the story was not George Ball at all but a Reverend H. S. Ball, who had been excommunicated from his church for scandalous activities. George Ball had never even lived in Indiana. The *Herald* did run a correction and apology—two years later.

The *Post* and *Herald* articles came as a jolt to Ball and his wife, Maria Benchley Ball. They had been married for thirty-six years and raised five children. Ella, their youngest, had just graduated from Hillsdale College in Michigan, of which Ball was a trustee and benefactor. At Hillsdale, all men indeed were created equal—it was the first American college to prohibit in its charter discrimination based on race, religion, or sex. The depressing reality was that, in the raging national debate over his role in disseminating Maria Halpin's story, Ball's many worthy achievements were consigned to oblivion. According to certain newspapers in New York and Boston, he was a monster and a fraud who had finally been run out of Indiana after insulting a woman.

Ball could not let the charges against him stand. On August 10, he announced that he was instituting a $25,000 libel suit against the *Herald*. The *New York Post* would be next.

With Maria Halpin still missing in action, Cleveland's allies geared up their efforts to turn the tide of public opinion. One of these self-appointed sleuths was Kinsley Twining. A mugwump and Congregational minister from Cambridge, Massachusetts, he came from a distinguished New England family whose ancestral history could be traced back to William the Conqueror. The Twinings had arrived in America around 1641 and settled on Cape Cod. Kinsley's grandfather graduated from Yale in 1795, as did his father in 1820, and Kinsley in 1853. As the literary editor of the *Independent*, a daily religious newspaper founded by Henry Ward Beecher, Twining's ties to Beecher along with his mugwump politics disposed him to do anything he could to spin the scandal in Cleveland's favor.

Twining had just turned fifty-two when he showed up in Buffalo to speak with journalists, lawyers, clergymen, and other gentlemen of influence—"the noblest Christian men in the city." Though he spent only two days there, he called it a "most thorough" investigation. Twining's bias was obvious in the first sentence of his report, which states that he refuses to republish the "grosser" particulars of the accusations facing Cleveland. "Those who want it can get it from the publisher of the Buffalo *Telegraph*, who will be glad to sell copies."

There was a "kernel of truth" in the Cleveland scandal, Twining acknowledged, namely this: "When he was younger than he is now, he was guilty of an illicit connection." For his part, Twining said, "I can forgive it."

"But the charge, as brought against him, lacks the elements of truth in these substantial points: There was no seduction, no adultery, no breach of promise, no obligation of marriage. After the primary offense . . . his conduct was singularly honorable, showing no attempt to evade responsibility, and doing all he could to meet the duties involved, of which marriage was not one. There was no abduction, only proper legal action under circumstances which demanded it."

Twining made no effort to communicate with Maria Halpin, Dr. Ring, Milo Whitney, Mrs. Baker, or any other key witness in the affair. As for the broad assertions that Cleveland was a drunk and a libertine, Twining said, "They are, I believe, the product of the imagination of the stews. Every attempt to trace them led back into the merest gossip of saloons and brothels."

Twining concluded his report by waxing poetic about Cleveland. "He is a man of true and kind heart, a born ruler of men. He has the heartiest respect of the best families in the city."

Also snooping around Buffalo was another ostensibly impartial investigator whose objectivity was open to question. G. C. Hodges was a Boston lawyer who had been dispatched there by a board of mugwumps from Massachusetts who were calling themselves the Committee of One Hundred. They made no secret of their political convictions: A sixty-page pamphlet pointing out the "dark side" of James G. Blaine's character was in the process of being printed and distributed, at the committee's expense, to "everybody and his eldest son" in the state of Massachusetts.

Hodges spent several days in Buffalo. His investigation took him to the offices of Charles A. Gould, collector of the port of Buffalo, who didn't have much to offer but steered him to a local businessman, Henry C. French. Supposedly, French knew all about Grover Cleveland's drinking and bawdy behavior, but when Hodges asked him whether he had ever seen Cleveland drunk, French was incensed, using language so "vigorous" that Hodges fled for his physical safety.

Proceeding with his investigation, Hodges tracked down a wealthy Buffalo manufacturer who was said to have firsthand knowledge of Cleveland's debauchery. The manufacturer said he had heard the allegations from his plant foreman. Hodges interviewed the foreman who said he got it from a saloonkeeper. It was like a 19th-century game of telephone.

When Hodges departed Buffalo, he was said to be "indignant and disgusted with the people who were making such reckless and unsupported charges." Upon his return to Boston, he reported back to the Committee of One Hundred that he had given George Ball "every opportunity" to lay out the evidence and offer up supporting witnesses, but Ball had refused to cooperate.

Finally, there was the report issued by the National Committee of Independent Republicans. Its name conveyed clout and broad national influence, but it was an illusion; in truth, the committee consisted of sixteen Buffalo mugwumps. The historian J. N. Larned and the lawyers Henry Sprague and Ansley Wilcox, members of the committee, had known Grover Cleveland socially over the years or from his brief tenure as mayor. There was no question of where they were in the political spectrum.

The findings were released to the nation in mid-August with the assurances that the investigation had been "carefully and deliberately made."

"The general charges of drunkenness and gross immorality which are made against Governor Cleveland are absolutely false," the committee concluded. How had it reached such a judgment? "From personal knowledge," the committee declared, "as his acquaintances of long-standing."

As for Maria Halpin, the committee did not seem to know much about the woman at the center of the scandal. Although they professed to have made a careful and thorough investigation, they could not even pin down Maria's precise age. She could only be described as a widow "between thirty and forty" when she had made Cleveland's acquaintance. And, like Twining and Hodges, the committee had apparently made no effort to reach out to her.

"The facts of the case show that she was not seduced, and that the allegations respecting her abduction and ill-treatment are wholly false." In this rendering of the scandal, the *Evening Telegraph* was a newspaper of "no standing whatsoever," and

George Ball was guilty of spreading stories based on flimsy hearsay.

On August 11, the day the committee report was released, a wave of relief swept over the Cleveland campaign. Unshackled at last to defend its man Cleveland, the *Courier* was exceptionally venomous in its attacks on Maria Halpin.

"There was no abduction," it declared. The *Evening Telegraph* article was replete with "cheap pathos." The authorities had acted in the best interests of the child. "There was no cruelty. The mother was in a state of intoxication, and she was removed lawfully and with no more force than was necessary."

Probably for the first time since the "great bombshell" of the campaign had exploded, Cleveland had the upper hand. "Charges Wholly False," the *Boston Globe* headline crowed. The *Buffalo Courier*: "Rev. Mr. Ball Shown Up." The *New York Times*: "A Political Scandal Speedily Settled." Mark Twain added his voice to the minions defending Cleveland. "To see grown men, apparently in their right mind, seriously arguing against a bachelor's fitness for President because he had private intercourse with a consenting widow! Isn't human nature the most consummate sham & lie that was ever invented?" Of course, Twain was missing the point: Sex had not been consensual, and Twain had shut his eyes to the forcible removal of Maria from her home to an insane asylum, and of her child from his mother.

Behind closed doors, James G. Blaine's Republican campaign managers were taking robust steps to stoke the fires of scandal and innuendo around Cleveland. One endeavor was to mail reprints of "A Terrible Tale" to households across America. In Massachusetts, bundles of the *Boston Journal* investigation were sent to the state's farthest outposts. Sometimes the effort backfired. When the chairman of the Republican Committee in Franklin County, Massachusetts, received his bundle, he tendered his resignation.

"Have just received your package of *Boston Journals* containing the detail of the 'Cleveland Scandal,' which I suppose you expect me, as a Republican town committee, to distribute," he wrote back to party headquarters in Boston. "I do not propose . . . to assist in political warfare so mean and contemptible."

Letters were also sent to clergymen across the nation, pointing out the "abundant rumors" that Cleveland's immoral behavior had continued well into his tenure as governor of New York. The letters were anonymous but were believed to be the handiwork of R. W. McMurdy, a minister who ran a clandestine Republican Party agency known as the Religious Bureau. They were usually postmarked Philadelphia, the ideal location for such an under-cover operation; remote for purposes of denial, but close enough to Republican Party headquarters in New York to be supervised by Blaine's people.

The letters were clever works of propaganda. Real names were cited to enhance the credibility of the allegations. One letter in circulation attributed to William Arkell, publisher of the *Albany Evening Journal*, the statement to a friend that Cleveland frequented whorehouses in the state capital. Arkell was so offended, he went public, branding the letter a lie and challenging anyone who "has the cheek to make any such claims" to come forward.

Another letter told the story of a gentleman from Buffalo who had been invited to spend the night at the governor's mansion.

"On coming down to breakfast one morning [he] discovered a female duly installed as mistress of the Executive Mansion, who had been transferred to her position from a bawdy house," the letter went. The origin of the story was traced to John Palmer, a trustee of the old soldier's and sailor's home in Bath, New York. Moving aggressively to bury the tale, Cleveland's private secretary, Dan Lamont, commanded Palmer to come to Albany for a face-to-face confrontation. Palmer apologized and disclosed his source, James Johnson, a former newspaper reporter with close ties to the Republican state committee. When Lamont contacted Johnson, he denied responsibility. On it went.

Cleveland's friends were concerned, but in his Broad Street offices at Spencer Trask & Co., New York banker George F. Peabody (cousin of the philanthropist George Foster Peabody) was confident of victory come November. "Everything looks well for Cleveland," he reported. But he also wanted Cleveland to know that "certain parties who are troubled at the Halpin scandal but got over it are suspicious that there is some basis in truth for these whispers and they state openly that if they are true, they will not vote for him—this time they will not come back. These whispers I do not like." Peabody was a friend of Reverend Samuel Smith Mitchell of the First Presbyterian Church in Buffalo. "He writes me that the worst about Cleveland has not been published."

Observing all this drama were Henry Ward Beecher and his wife, Eunice Bullard Beecher. *He who is without sin let him cast the first stone*, went the Scripture, and Beecher, the most famous man in America—nine years after standing trial for adultery—was inclined to go with Cleveland. Mrs. Beecher was less certain.

Like Maria Halpin, Eunice Beecher had suffered the ignominy of public humiliation. Maria's story resonated with her.

Eunice Beecher's brother had been Henry's roommate at Amherst College. She was eighteen when she became engaged to Henry, and made an attractive bride, with her thick auburn hair and full-bodied figure. Eunice was raised in a strict New England household. Once when she came to dinner in what her father, a physician, observed to be a low-cut dress, he threw a bowl of hot soup at her, saying that since she must be cold, the soup would warm her up. There were seven brothers in her family who teased her unmercifully and left her an "oversensitive and insecure" woman.

Certain women found the muscular Beecher incredibly attractive, and throughout their marriage, Eunice had heard rumors about her husband's philandering. It was said that he had fathered their next-door neighbor's daughter. Imagine Eunice's misery as Henry doted on the little girl, who grew up looking more like him each passing year. So Eunice had experienced firsthand the anguish a husband's dalliances could bring to a family.

Women did not age well in the 19th century. When Henry Ward Beecher was brought to trial for adultery in 1875, his wife, seventy-two, was white-haired, stooped, and worn-out, having given birth to ten children, three of whom survived to adulthood. She was at court every day, sitting loyally behind the defense table, even on days when her husband showed his contempt for the proceedings by not bothering to be there. For six months she sat stern-faced and stoic in her simple black dress, listening to witnesses give provocative evidence about her "abysmal" marriage and philandering husband. At times the testimony was so lurid that the judge threatened to bar women from the courtroom. The case ended in a hung jury, and Beecher—somehow—resumed his life in the public arena as an esteemed minister of the faith.

Now another eminent public figure—Grover Cleveland—was facing allegations of having fathered an illegitimate child. Eunice was following all twists and turns. She clipped all the articles. She became obsessed with the story.

Without her husband's knowledge, Eunice wrote a heartfelt letter to Cleveland, stuffing into the envelope several of the stories she had clipped. One article actually listed what was said to be the address of Cleveland's favorite brothel in Albany, on 2nd Street. Another stated that Cleveland had been "grossly intoxicated" at his desk. Even his recent vacation to the Adirondacks was suspect. A Boston physician was quoted as saying it was his understanding that the true purpose of the trip was to cure Cleveland of a "malignant disease." That was why he had taken Dr. Samuel Ward with him. (Ward became indignant when he was asked if he had accompanied Cleveland because he was ill. "What! The governor took no personal physicians into the woods with him. I took the governor. I ordered him to take a rest. Treatment! The only treatment he got was plenty of exercise that kept him almost steadily on the move from sunrise to sunset. A fine story indeed. What else will the liars manufacture?")

When Mrs. Beecher's letter reached Cleveland in Albany, it made him weak in the knees. She wanted—demanded—to know whether the stories were true. Henry Ward Beecher's wife could not be ignored. As swiftly as he could, Cleveland wrote back.

"I am shocked and dumbfounded by the clippings from the newspapers that you sent me. . . . I have never seen in Albany a woman whom I have had any reason to suspect was in any way bad. I don't know where any such woman lives in Albany. I have never been in any house in Albany except the Executive Mansion, the Executive Chamber, the First Orange Club House—twice on receptions given to me, and on, I think, two other occasions—and the residences of perhaps fifteen or twenty of the best citizens, to dine.

"There never was a man who has worked harder or more hours in a day. Almost all my times [sic] has been spent in the Executive Chamber, and I hardly think there have been twenty nights in the year and nine months I have lived in Albany—unless I was out of town—that I have left my work earlier than midnight to find my bed at the mansion. I am at a loss to know how it is that such terrible, wicked, and utterly baseless lies can be invented. The contemptible creatures who coin and pass these things appear to think that the affair which I have not denied makes me defenseless against any and all slanderers."

Cleveland's letter to Mrs. Beecher was, he said, "the most I have ever written on the subject" of Maria Halpin.

In early September, four weeks after Maria Halpin had vanished, she showed up at her uncle's house in New Rochelle—"crushed in spirit and broken in health." Between fitful periods of sleep, she had quite a story to tell James Seacord. For the last month, she had been living in a house on the West Side of Manhattan. Everything had been arranged through the Democratic Party. Maria had been free to leave at any time, but she had been told that her life would be in mortal danger if she were to return to New Rochelle. She had bought into this half-truth until she had come to the realization that it was a ruse to keep her isolated from the world and out of the public arena until Election Day in November.

Now back in New Rochelle and living under Seacord's roof, Maria caught up on how the newspapers were reporting her story. It sickened her to read the extent to which her name had been smeared. Cleveland's associates were branding her a vile harlot. General Horatio King's interview with the *New York World*, in which he said in so many words that Oscar Folsom had fathered her illegitimate son, was especially tough to take.

Even Maria's son was coming under ferocious personal attack. In one report, Frederick was accused of using his mother's misfortune to lobby Grover Cleveland for a state job. According to this trumped-up story—complete with bogus quotes, courtesy once again of the zealous *Boston Globe*—Frederick, "at the suggestion of my mother," had sat down with Cleveland in Albany and "asked him for a position." Cleveland asked Frederick to send his references and he'd see what he could do.

Whoever fabricated Frederick's quotes may have thought he was being very cunning, but their effect was the opposite of what he'd intended. The *Globe* story induced Maria to give her first newspaper interview, to the *Morning Journal* newspaper in Manhattan. It was her first tentative step into the public arena to set the record straight.

"Grover Cleveland is the father, and to say otherwise is infamous," Maria declared. "The attempt to connect the dead Oscar Folsom with me or my boy, of which I hear, is cruel and cowardly.

I had but a very slight acquaintance with Oscar Folsom. It does not seem possible after all I have suffered for Grover Cleveland and my boy's sake that an attempt will be made to further blacken me in the eyes of the world."

Maria opened up about her ordeal, but just a little. She said that, in her prime, when she lived in Buffalo, men had found her attractive. "I was not as stout as I look now," she ruefully admitted. "No one knows the extent of my sufferings. After my child was taken from me, I begged Cleveland on my knees to let me have a sight of my baby. He was immovable. I found where the boy was, and one day I rushed in before his keeper snatched him up and ran away before they could stop me.

"My sufferings, subsequently my fruitless efforts to have him fulfill his promise of marriage, his neglect of myself and child, my abduction and violent treatment by his hired tools were truthfully but only partially told in the *Buffalo Telegraph* of July 21. It would be impossible to cover the events that made up those years of shame, suffering, and degradation forced upon me by Grover Cleveland."

A false rumor was making the rounds that Maria was thinking of issuing a statement clearing Cleveland of all charges. When Maria was asked about this, she exploded in anger. The reporter described what happened next. "Maria Halpin drew herself up, as preparing for a supreme effort, and replied in a most impressive and earnest manner, 'Me, make a statement exonerating Grover Cleveland? Never! I would rather put a bullet through my heart.'"

Grover Cleveland as a young man.

A woman defamed. The first photograph published of Maria Halpin.

Photo restoration by Al J. Frazza
Courtesy of New Jersey State Park Service

The Cleveland siblings. Grover is at far left. Rose is second row, far left. Cecil and Fred, seated in front row, were lost at sea in 1872.

Courtesy of Emogene Sweeney

Maria Halpin's son, Frederick Halpin, circa 1867. The back of the photo read, "Sick & expected to die." Frederick survived, and lived to come to the defense of his mother's honor.

Maria's brother-in-law, Simeon Talbott. He convinced Maria to give up baby Oscar. Young woman on right is Maria's daughter, Ada.

Maria Halpin's son, Frederick. He met with a top Cleveland aide in Room 210 at the Hoffman House hotel in Manhattan. On right, his sister Ada, Maria's daughter from her first marriage.

The boys of the Buffalo Orphan Asylum, where Grover Cleveland's illegitimate son, Oscar, was taken. The orphans are seen here harvesting potatoes for the orphanage.

From college school girl to First Lady.

The circumstances under w~~hich the~~ ruin was
accomplished is too revolting on the part of
Grover Cleveland to be made public I did not
see Grover Cleveland for ~~four~~ five or six week after
my ruin and then I was obliged to send for
him he being the proper person to whom I
could tell my trouble. I will not at ~~this time~~
detail my subsequaint sufferings, of the birth
of our boy on september 14th 1874 But will say
that the statement published in the Buffalo
Telegram in the main true There is ~~ot~~
and never was a dou ~~bt~~ as to the paternity
of our child and the attempt of Grover
~~Cleveland or his friends to~~

Excerpts from Maria Halpin's Oct. 28, 1884, affidavit denouncing Grover
Cleveland. "The circumstances under which my ruin was accomplished are
too revolting on the part of Grover Cleveland to be made public…"

any lady in the City of Buffalo. a fact which
Grover Cleveland should be man enough and
just enough to admit and I defy him or
any of his friends to state a single ~~incident~~
or give a single incident or action of mine
to which any one could take exception I always
felt that I had the confidence and esteem
of my employers messrs Finnman and Best
and Flint and Kent and this I could not

Maria Halpin defends her honor in this excerpt from her affidavit, stating that her "life
was as pure and spotless as that of any lady in the City of Buffalo—a fact which Grover
Cleveland should be man enough and just enough to admit…"

Maria Halpin says she "has been induced to remain silent."

The Halpin affidavit—"I did not believe it possible that even Grover Cleveland could attempt to further blacken me in the eyes of the world..."

The famous "I want my Pa!" cartoon from the Sept. 27, 1884, cover of *Judge* magazine. The edgy caption read, "Another voice for Cleveland."

The Wells College Class of 1885. Frances Folsom is seen in second row.

The Evening Telegraph.

NUMBER 1155   BUFFALO, MONDAY, JULY 21, 1884   PRICE ONE CENT

THIRD EDITION.

A TERRIBLE TALE.

A Dark Chapter in a Public Man's History.

The Pitiful Story of Maria Halpin and Governor Cleveland's Son.

A Prominent Citizen States the Result of His Investigation of Charges Against the Governor—Interviews Touching the Case.

Grover Cleveland's reputation for morality has been bad in this city for some time. After his elevation to the governorship his reputation became extended somewhat beyond local limits. During his campaign for the democratic presidential nomination his private reputation was used against him. Indeed this was one strong cause of the opposition to him. It was freely used in private and broadly hinted at in public.

The story that started it all—the July 21, 1884, edition of the *Buffalo Evening Telegraph*, with the famous headline, "A Terrible Tale."

The widow Emma Folsom and her daughter Frances. President Cleveland was offended when newspapers reported he was marrying Emma. "I don't see why the papers keep marrying me to old ladies."

Courtesy, Wells College Archives, Long Library, Aurora, N.Y.

Frances Folsom Cleveland, at age 22
she became the youngest First Lady
in American history.

Former First Lady Rose Cleveland,
taken in Rome.

Frances in 1886, the
year she married
Grover Cleveland and
became First Lady.

Helen Fairchild Smith, the dean, or Lady Principal, at Wells College. It was said she took it as her mission to prepare Frances Folsom for the White House.

The Goddess—Frances
Folsom Cleveland,
America's youngest
First Lady.

Rose Elizabeth Cleveland, in a studio
portrait taken in Rome, Italy.

Rose Elizabeth Cleveland served
as her brother's First Lady from
March 4, 1885-June 2, 1886.

Rose Cleveland's
"Viking" —Evangeline
Marrs Simpson Whipple.

First Lady Frances Folsom
Cleveland, depicted in an ad
for a bottle of medicine.
The unauthorized use of her
image infuriated the president.

Campaign poster from Cleveland's re-election bid, with running mate Allen Thurman. Note the presence of First Lady Frances Folsom Cleveland in center. First Ladies were rarely seen during election campaigns. Cleveland lost.

Cleveland became the first and, so far, only president to get married in the White House. The ceremony was held in the intimate Blue Room. From a 19th century hand-colored woodcut (seen here in black and white).

Another unauthorized ad using the image of the First Lady, this time for a popular laxative.

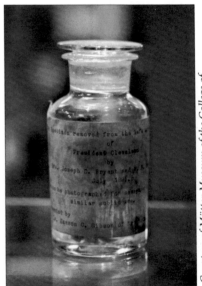

Cancerous growth removed during a secret operation on President Cleveland in 1893, now preserved at the Mütter Museum, Philadelphia.

The other side of the specimen jar preserving President Cleveland's cancerous growth.

Courtesy of Mütter Museum of the College of Physicians of Philadelphia.

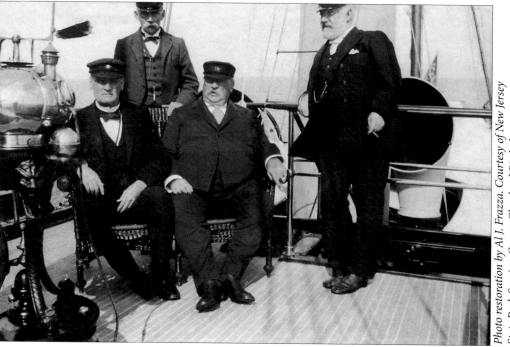

Photo restoration by Al J. Frazza. Courtesy of New Jersey State Park Service, Grover Cleveland Birthplace

Grover Cleveland on board the private yacht *Oneida*, site of his secret cancer operation during his second term as president.

The Cleveland Family. Marion (far left); Francis (Cleveland was sixty-six when he was born); Esther; and Richard. Said Cleveland of his days in retirement, "I herd the children."

The Lion in Winter. Last known photo of Grover Cleveland, taken March 5, 1908. He died fifteen weeks later.

Obituary of Dr. James E. King Jr., from 1947. The son of Grover Cleveland and Maria Halpin, revealed for the first time in this book.

Dr. J. E. King, Widely Known Specialist, Dies

Brief Illness Claims Noted Gynecologist

Associated With UB For Nearly 50 Years

Dr. James E. King, emeritus professor of gynecology at the University of Buffalo and one of the foremost women's specialist in the United States, died yesterday at his home, 1255 Delaware Ave, after a brief illness. He was 71.

Gynecologist in chief at Meyer Memorial Hospital from the time of its founding until about ten years ago, Dr. King served later as consulting gynecologist there and at Buffalo General Hospital, Buffalo State Hospital, Lafayette General Hospital and Milliard Fillmore Hospital.

DR. JAMES E. KING

13

THE AFFIDAVIT

IN MID-SEPTEMBER, CLEVELAND told Wilson Bissell, "The scandal business is about wound up. . . . I think the matter was managed in the best possible way." Cleveland credited the turnaround to a "policy of not cringing." It was a course of action, he said, which was "not only necessary but the only way."

With the worst days of the Halpin crisis behind him, Grover Cleveland was enormously relieved. Sometimes, though, he had to wonder whether his friend Horatio King had gone too far in telling the *New York World* that Maria Halpin was a harlot and that Oscar Folsom had fathered her illegitimate child. Coming to the realization that King's vilification of Maria may have been excessive, and could have consequences, "King's interview made me trouble," Cleveland admitted to Bissell. The dirty politics, he told Charles Goodyear, was making him feel "very blue," and sometimes he wished the presidential nomination were "on some other shoulders than mine."

Perhaps his political intuition was telling him that he had not heard the last of Maria Halpin.

A few voices, not many, spoke out in defense of Maria Halpin.

Judge was an upstart satirical magazine with nationwide circulation; it was modeled on *Puck*, its chief rival. *Judge* had been founded in 1881, and one of its contributing cartoonists was the gifted Frank Beard.

Beard was born "deaf as a post," as he put it, in Plainville, Ohio. The only way he could hear was through a black rubber tube, which he always wore coiled around his neck. When he wanted to carry on a conversation, Beard would unravel the hose, put one end to his ear, and hand the other end to the person he was speaking with. When Confederate batteries opened fire on Fort Sumter in 1861, triggering the Civil War, Beard was so eager to join the fight, he tried to con his way into the military by memorizing the order of the questions all volunteers were asked. An officer on the recruiting board, suspecting that Beard was deaf, switched things around. Beard had expected the first question to be, What is your name? The examination went like this:

"How old are you?"

"Frank Beard."

"What is your name?"

"Eighteen years old."

The officer burst out laughing and told Beard to go home, but a captain with the Seventh Ohio Regiment figured that if Beard wanted to sign up that badly, he'd be willing to offer him a uniform, a musket, and a posting as a private—without pay. Beard signed on and served gallantly for the duration of the war.

When peace came, he settled in New York, hoping to find work as a sketch artist. It was a struggle. Sometimes, when he couldn't afford lodging, he had to walk the streets at night. He survived on crackers and cheese for years before he eventually became one of the best-known political cartoonists in America.

Beard's most famous work appeared on the cover of *Judge's* issue of September 27, 1884. It was an unforgettable cartoon titled "Another Voice for Cleveland." Depicted was a weeping Maria Halpin holding a baby, who, with his arms outstretched, was hysterically howling, "I want my Pa!" A rotund Grover Cleveland, so shocked that his tophat was flying off, completed the caricature of a politician caught with his pants down.

Cleveland must have been mortified when he saw the *Judge* cover.

Unsurprisingly, Republicans loved it—loved anything that kept the Halpin scandal alive and kicking. "I want my Pa!" became the Republican Party battle cry, and as Cleveland campaign rallies crisscrossed America, they drew GOP hecklers, chanting "Ma, Ma, where's my Pa?" in a babylike falsetto.

James G. Blaine made a campaign swing through Western New York, and at a rally in Buffalo, seven thousand enthusiastic supporters turned up. Cleveland's hometown was now in play, and his staff told him that he had to go to Buffalo and shore up support. He still found it hard to believe that George Ball and so many other Buffalo clergymen had turned on him. The city that had made him great was causing him so much grief. Losing Buffalo would be a crushing blow.

Preparations for Cleveland's return to Buffalo got under way, and no one could predict whether it would end in triumph or embarrassment. It was his first outing on the campaign trail since his nomination. As usual, Charles McCune's *Courier* went all out, instructing its readers that it was their patriotic duty to give Cleveland a warm welcome.

"We trust the skies will smile upon our festival . . . and welcome the next president of the United States," cooed the *Courier*.

Cleveland left Albany on the Atlantic Express, with stopovers in Rochester and Syracuse to take on coal and water. It was twilight when the train pulled into the Exchange Street depot in Buffalo. The city Cleveland saw through the window was illuminated by skyrockets and fireworks—and when he stepped off the train, a steady drizzle that turned into a chilling downpour. He climbed into a carriage drawn by eight snow-white horses.

The procession passed through streets that glowed with candlelight from Chinese paper lanterns that adorned the houses. At the sight of Cleveland's carriage, cheers rang out from the crowds that gathered along the route. Cleveland's friend from Albany, Erastus Corning, who was riding in the carriage with the candidate, was pleased with what he saw. "O hell! A man don't decorate or illuminate his house unless he wants to," Corning said.

Four twisting miles later the march ended at the Genesee Hotel where a banner reading MAN OF DESTINY graced the portico. After Cleveland dried off in his three-bedroom suite, he stepped out on the balcony. It was 11:25 PM. Before him was a crowd of about fifteen thousand—soaking wet, and battling the pelting rainstorm and a bitter October wind off Lake Erie to cheer on their candidate. Above, a smoky haze hovered over the entire city, the consequence of pyrotechnics that had lit up the evening sky and bonfires that had blazed on many street corners. Cleveland, his head uncovered, looked robust; even the Republicans had to admit he seemed in fine vigor. And not one spectator dared sing out, "Ma, Ma, where's my Pa?"

"What I have seen and heard tonight has touched me deeply. It tells me that my neighbors are still my friends." The spectators roared for their favorite son.

The next morning, Cleveland took a late breakfast in his suite, and local power brokers like Charles McCune came to call. McCune was in high spirits. He thought the outpouring of adoration, and in such adverse weather conditions, was a "balm to the wounds of slander" and heralded the promise of victory in November. That fifteen thousand citizens had stood in a downpour for two hours to hear Cleveland speak also sent a compelling message to the whole country that the presidential candidate was still dearly loved in his hometown. There was more encouraging news on the home front: The *Buffalo Times*, up until then a reliable organ of the Republican Party, announced that it was endorsing Cleveland for president.

That evening, Cleveland attended a private dinner held in his honor at the Delaware Avenue mansion of Mrs. Julia Cary. The widow of a Buffalo physician, Mrs. Cary was said to be a "lady of the highest social station and of the most rigid code of social and moral ethics." The Cleveland organization made sure the word got out that Mrs. Carey would never have invited the candidate to set foot in her home unless he met the highest standards of decency.

Around 11:00 PM, Cleveland boarded a private sleeper car to make his way back to Albany. The governor went straight to the office and put in a good day's work. Overall, he thought the

Buffalo campaign swing had been successful "beyond anticipations." To Wilson Bissell he said, "And now that the Buffalo rumpus is over, I want to tell you how fully I appreciate all that you and Charles (Goodyear) have done to make it a success and how grateful I am to all my friends in Buffalo who had management of the affair."

The Rink was the largest indoor arena in Brooklyn, usually used for professional bare-knuckle boxing matches. On the night of October 22, 1884, however, it was the place where a major political rally was being held, at which Henry Ward Beecher was to officially endorse Cleveland.

On the evening of the rally, sheets of rain descended on Brooklyn. There were also rumors of an outbreak of diphtheria. No one in his right mind would venture out on a night like this. Beecher must have thought the heavenly powers were conspiring against him. But at 7:00 PM, when the colossal doors on Clermont Avenue swung open, the Rink quickly filled to capacity—five thousand—with the front rows reserved for Brooklyn's "best families." It was testament to how devoted the people of Brooklyn were to the great Beecher. One fellow, shaking off the rain, was overheard to say that nothing could have kept him from hearing Beecher's speech, even if he'd had to swim there. Every seat was filled—and even the window-sills and the aisles were solidly packed with standing-room-only humanity.

The event was scheduled for 8:00 PM, but by seven thirty, everyone who could get in had done so. Waiting in a room off stage, Beecher announced that there was no point in dithering; the speech would begin at once.

With the instincts of a born showman, Beecher strutted out just as the Twenty-Third Regiment Band came to the end of "The Star Spangled Banner." The preacher's long silver-grey hair was brushed back behind his ears, and he wore a simple broadcloth suit. His face was still ruddy from a fresh shave.

"Three cheers for Henry Ward Beecher!" somebody shouted. "Hip! Hip!"

"Hurrah! Hurrah! Hurrah!" The Rink shook. Men waved their hats and stomped their feet. Women signaled their support by delicately waving their handkerchiefs or politely applauding with gloved hands. The elderly pounded their canes. They cheered and yelled for ten minutes while Beecher looked on indifferently, a sphinx.

When the crowd finally quieted down, Beecher said, "I hope you feel better now?"

Everyone roared with laughter.

When it got quiet, forty reporters had pens poised to take down every word Beecher said.

Beecher began by laying down his credentials as a faithful Republican.

"Before many of you were born, I was rocking the cradle of the Republican Party. I fought its early battles when it was in an apparently hopeless minority. I advocated it, speaking day and night, at the risk of my health and my life itself. When the war broke out, I sent the only boy I had big enough to hold a musket, and greatly grieved was my oldest child, a daughter, that she was not a boy." The audience guffawed.

"And yet I am now opposing the party whose cradle I rocked. I am a personal friend of Mr. Blaine." More laughter "And for more than ten years I have been afraid of the man—the man that needed a congressional committee to investigate whether he was honest or not.

"Our country needed a sterling, honest man, and Cleveland is the man." At this point, the cheers were so loud that Beecher scolded the audience. "Don't occupy so much of my time. Let me go on and I will imagine you are clapping all the time, only let me go on." They quieted down. Then Beecher came to the Halpin scandal.

"In all the history of politics, we don't believe that lies so cruel, so base, so malign have ever been set in motion. The air is murky with stories of Mr. Cleveland's private life. We find that they are circulated in many cases by rash and credulous clergymen. They could not go to Cleveland with honest inquiry, so they opened their ears to the harlot and the drunkard."

Now Beecher came around to his own troubles, to the time nine years before when he had been brought to trial for adultery.

"I know the bitterness of venomous lies. I will stand against infamous lies that seek to sting to death a man. Men counsel me to ponder lest I stir again my own griefs. No! I will not be prudent. I will imitate the noble example set me by Plymouth Church in the day of my calamity. They stood by me with God-inspired loyalty. It was a heroic deed. I will imitate their example, and as long as I have breath, I will not see a man followed by hounds, serpents, or venomous stinging insects and not, if I believe him innocent, stand with him and for him and against all comers."

With that, he was done. He was seventy-one but had delivered his speech with the vigor of a lion.

"Will there be any more speaking?" somebody wondered.

"Of course not" came the reply. "Who could follow that speech?"

The Rink started clearing out.

Beecher, reported the *Brooklyn Eagle*, was simply grand. The words tumbled off of his lips like that of a great swordsman. It was the "grandest oration" ever heard in the city—"an oration such as a man is fortunate to hear once in a long lifetime."

The speech by Henry Ward Beecher left Maria Halpin confounded. It seemed to her that the great preacher had actually had the temerity to call her a harlot. She had to wonder how Grover Cleveland came to be the injured party. The scandal had somehow been twisted into a badge of honor for Cleveland.

When she told her uncle James Seacord that she thought it was time to speak out about her relationship with Cleveland, he warned her that if she did, he would kick her out of the house. He was "immovably opposed" to her going public.

But Maria could not shake off the things Horatio King had said about her in his *New York World* interview—that she had been intimate with as many as four men besides Cleveland, and that Cleveland had assumed responsibility for Baby Oscar because he was the only unmarried man among her numerous lovers. For Maria, Beecher's speech was confirmation that the American people had totally bought into these falsehoods. But her honor was at stake, and she may have come to the conclusion that she had nothing left to lose. She sent for Charles Banks, the Westchester lawyer and owner of the *New Rochelle Pioneer*, and informed him that she was finally ready to confront the scandal head-on. With his assistance, she wrote out an affidavit.

State of New York, County of Westchester:

Maria Halpin, being duly sworn, says: I reside at New Rochelle, in the County of Westchester, State aforesaid. I am the person whose name has been published in connection with that of Grover Cleveland as the mother of his son. I have been induced to remain silent while the disgrace and sufferings brought upon me by Grover Cleveland have been discussed and criticized by the public and the press, and I would most gladly remain silent even now but for the duty which I owe to my aged and afflicted father, my children, and my sisters, to whom my troubles were unknown until made public by publication a few months ago. My duty to those relatives and to those friends who knew me before my acquaintance with Grover Cleveland, whose kind assurances of love, and sympathy, and confidence have reached me, compels me to make a public statement and denial of many of the statements which have been made public concerning me and my character and actions while in Buffalo.

I would gladly avoid further publicity of this terrible misfortune if I could do so without appearing to admit the foul and false statements concerning my character and habits, especially those made by Mr. Horatio C. King and published with the alleged approval of Grover Cleveland himself.

I deny that there was anything in my actions or against my character at any time or place up to the hour I formed the acquaintance of Grover Cleveland on account of which he or any other person can cast the slightest suspicion over me up to that hour. My life was as pure and spotless as that of any lady in the City of Buffalo—a fact which Grover Cleveland should be man enough and just enough to admit, and I defy him or any of his friends to state a single fact or give a single incident or action of mine to which any one could take exception. I always felt that I had the confidence and esteem of my employers . . . and this I could not maintain if I had been the vile wretch his friends would have the world believe. He sought my acquaintance and obtained an introduction to me from a person in whom I have every confidence, and he paid me very marked attention. His character, so far as I knew, was good, and his intentions I believed were pure and honorable.

The circumstances under which my ruin was accomplished are too revolting on the part of Grover Cleveland to be made public. I did not see Grover Cleveland for five or six weeks after my ruin, and I was obliged to send for him, he being the proper person to whom I could tell my trouble. I will not at this time detail my subsequent sufferings and the birth of our boy Sept. 14, 1874. But I will say that the statement published in the Buffalo *Telegraph* in the main is true. There is not and never was a doubt as to the paternity of our child, and the attempt of Grover Cleveland or his friends to couple the name of Oscar Folsom or any one else with that of the boy, for that purpose, is simply infamous and false.

The affidavit was sworn to and signed Maria B. Halpin on October 28, 1884. It was notarized by Charles Banks and witnessed by Maria's son Frederick and two men who worked for Banks.

Frederick Halpin also submitted his own affidavit:

> Frederick T. Halpin, being duly sworn, says that he is the son of Maria B. Halpin; that about a month or a little more ago he received a telegram from William C. Hudson from Albany, requesting deponent to meet him at the Hoffman House, in the City of New York; that in pursuance of said telegram he met the said William C. Hudson at Room 210 in said Hoffman House, and conversed with him in relation to the affair of Grover Cleveland and my mother; that said Hudson then and there and in my presence prepared a statement which, as the friend of Grover Cleveland and one interested in his election, he requested me to have my mother sign; that said statement so written by said Hudson in my presence, and then and there delivered to me as aforesaid, was delivered by me to my mother at New Rochelle, N. Y., and is annexed to the statement made by my mother, Maria B. Halpin, this day . . . that my mother refused to sign the said paper, giving as her reason that the statements therein contained were not true.

Maria and Frederick's affidavits were published to great fanfare in the Republican papers—and completely ignored or dismissed as forgeries in the Democratic publications. After a day of thinking things through, Maria decided that the affidavit did not go far enough. She sent a message to Charles Banks requesting that he come to her house once again. When Banks arrived, he was surprised to see that Maria had written out a supplemental affidavit that gave more chilling details about the night she says Cleveland raped her. It contained perhaps the most graphic accusations ever to be leveled against an American presidential candidate of a major party:

> State of New York, County of Westchester, Maria B. Halpin, being duly sworn, says: In addition and supplemental to the statement made by me yesterday, I further state that on the evening of December 15, 1873 while on my way to call upon an acquaintance by the name of Mrs. Johnson at the Tiff House in the city of Buffalo, I met Grover Cleveland whose acquaintance I had formed months previous to that time. The said Cleveland asked me to go with him to take dinner—which invitation I declined because of my prior engagement but by persistent requests and urging he induced me to accompany him to the restaurant of the Ocean House where we dined.
>
> After dinner he accompanied me to my rooms at Randall's boarding house on Swan Street as he had quite frequently done from other times and where my son lived with me. While in my rooms he accomplished my ruin by the use of force and violence and without my consent. After he had accomplished his purpose he told me that he was determined to ruin me if it cost him ten thousand dollars, if he was hanged by the neck for it. I then and there told him that I never wanted to see him again and would never see him and commanded him to leave my rooms which he did. I never saw him after this until my condition became such that it was necessary for me to send for him some six weeks later to inform him of the consequences of his actions. He came to my rooms

in response to my note which I sent him and when I told him of my condition and despair by reason of it, he pretended to make light of it and told me that he would do everything which was honorable and right towards me and promised that he would marry me which promises he has never kept.

Charles Banks's law partner, Henry C. Henderson, notarized the affidavit. Frederick Halpin was the witness.

Now Maria and her uncle really had it out. James Seacord was livid at Maria for going behind his back and told her she had to "leave his house." Seacord was fed up with the attention the scandal was bringing to his household. Angry words were exchanged, and Seacord said he hoped he would never see Maria or Frederick again. A few days later, Seacord went to the village of Mount Vernon for a carpentry job, saying he would be out of town the entire day. Maria used the occasion to call in a reporter from the *Chicago Tribune*. The first question he asked was why she had decided to come forward and make her affidavits public.

"Well," Maria said, "I did not intend to say anything about the affair, for I have suffered enough already. But my father, who is aged and blind, and my two unmarried sisters, who live in Williamsburg, have urged me to do so since Mr. Cleveland and the Reverend Henry Ward Beecher had attempted to pile up mud upon me. My uncle, Mr. Seacord, is at Mount Vernon, and when he hears of these statements, he will surely send me away."

Maria suddenly burst into tears. "But I don't care, because the excitement of the last three months has broken my health and spirits, and today I am ill. I do not expect any reward from any political party, and I shall make those statements at all hazards, be the consequences what they may."

The *Tribune* reporter posed a touchy question in the most delicate manner he could muster. "It is charged that you were compromised by Mr. Oscar Folsom in Buffalo."

"I never spoke a word to that man in my life. I know his wife because she traded with me in Buffalo. The statement I made last night is true, and nothing on earth could make me sign the one offered me by Grover Cleveland, which is false in every particular."

"Where is your son?"

"God knows." Maria refused to be diverted off the subject of Grover Cleveland. "Allow me to tell you the meanness of the man. When I sent for him and informed him of my condition, he said, 'What the devil are you blubbering about? You act like a baby without teeth. What do you want me to do?' I got no satisfaction from him and never saw him again to speak to him. How he acted toward me after that the world well knows."

"So you can't tell me anything about the boy?"

"Only this: A friend of mine wrote to me from Buffalo the other day, telling me that he is there."

"Has anyone induced you to make these statements?"

"*No one. I never go out of the house.* I do not know any politicians and would not make a statement for any one. I don't want a penny from anybody. If the statements I have made will do any party any good, they may have them as freely as the air."

Grover Cleveland never uttered a single word to challenge the allegations made in Maria Halpin's affidavits, right to the end of the 1884 campaign, and beyond.

14

PRESIDENT-ELECT

IT WAS WEDNESDAY, October 29, less than a week to go before the election. Senator Arthur Pue Gorman breathed in the crisp fall air as his carriage trotted up 5th Avenue. With him was political aide William Hudson. The forty-five-year-old national chairman of the Democratic Party was not his usual upbeat self; Hudson thought he looked despondent. Gorman sighed; he was reflecting on the state of the campaign. Things were not looking promising. Maria Halpin's affidavit, which stated that Cleveland had raped her, had been the fitting wrap-up to the nastiest presidential campaign in American history.

Hudson listened as Gorman surveyed the political landscape: New England, with the possible exception of Connecticut, was solid for Blaine; out West, Kansas, Ohio, and Iowa were also likely for Blaine; the Democrats could count on Wisconsin, Michigan, and Indiana; Illinois was a toss-up. So was Colorado. The sixteen Southern states were solidly behind Cleveland. The country was evenly split. It all came down to New

York, as had been prophesized since July. Gorman spoke of the Blaine campaign with the admiration of a professional in awe of his opponent's know-how. He marveled at the efficiency of the Republican machine and extolled the energy of the fifty-four-year-old Blaine, crisscrossing America, while Cleveland sat in Albany, immobile and morose. Blaine was leading an "almost perfect organization," Blaine told Hudson, while Cleveland's efforts had been marked by a kind of artless "spontaneity."

"And spontaneity will win?" Hudson asked hopefully.

With a shrewd grin, Gorman said, "Usually organization wins."

That very day, Gorman had received some disturbing canvas reports about where things stood in New York State. Manhattan would go for Cleveland with a 40,000 plurality. It would have been 60,000 had Tammany Hall's mischief-makers not sabotaged the campaign. Brooklyn was expected to deliver a 20,000 plurality in Cleveland's corner—thank you, Henry Ward Beecher. Outside of those downstate counties, however, Blaine was expected to take the rest of New York by 63,000 votes. Hudson made his own mental calculations: "That means that Cleveland will be at least 5,000 votes behind in the whole state."

"It means that Cleveland will be beaten in the nation," said Gorman. "I regret exceedingly that I permitted myself to be persuaded to take charge of this campaign. I yielded against all my instinct." It was, Gorman said bitterly, "the mistake of my life." Hudson was distressed to hear the professed leader of the national party sulk this way, yet he could not find fault with Gorman's election-night forecast, and it plunged him into his own state of despair. Gorman continued. "It has been a scandalous campaign, with credit to nobody on either side. Cleveland has not been an easy man to handle, and I think I see that he would not be easy if he were put in the presidential office."

Gorman ordered the carriage to return to party headquarters at the Hoffman House, thinking that he should not have spoken so frankly. "Of course, what I have said is confidential," he told Hudson. "I shall keep whistling until I have passed the graveyard." That was it, Hudson thought. Blaine was going to win.

Gorman invited Hudson up to his room, where they continued their conversation. They heard some commotion in the hallway, then suddenly, John Tracy, who was in charge of the Democratic Party's press information bureau, "plunged" into the room. Tracy was out of breath and so excited, he was almost unhinged. He showed Gorman a report which had just been filed by the stenographer who had taken down the speech made by James Blaine that morning at the Fifth Avenue Hotel. (As a rule, a Democratic Party stenographer attended all Republican Party events that were open to the public on the theory that you never knew when something might happen.) Now the stenographer's account was in Gorman's hands. He looked up.

"Is this a verbatim report?"

"Every word uttered is there," Tracy assured the party boss.

Their eyes met; both men realized the great historical impact of what had occurred this morning. When Gorman spoke, his voice cracked like a whip.

"This sentence must be in every daily newspaper in the country tomorrow, no matter how, no matter what it costs. Organize for that immediately."

Tracy had his orders. He spun on his heels and left the room. Now Gorman turned to Hudson. "If anything will elect Cleveland, these words will do it. The advantages are now with us." The winds of fate had suddenly shifted in their direction.

The Fifth Avenue Hotel was the social and cultural heart of New York. The palazzo building was five stories tall and made of white marble and brick. It was the first hotel in America with a passenger elevator, powered by a steam engine in the basement and operated by a giant screw in the center of the passenger cab. All the rooms were richly appointed, with rosewood furniture, a fireplace, gilt wood, and crimson and green curtains. The hotel came with a rich history. Abraham Lincoln stayed there when he arrived in New York in 1860 to deliver the triumphant oration at Cooper Union that had set him on the path to the presidency. It was the Prince of Wales's favorite hotel in America. Stored in the cellar was a dwindling supply of bottled brandy from the vintage year 1799.

James Blaine had awakened that morning in a suite usually reserved for President Arthur and ordered breakfast. He did not want to be there. He had just completed a grueling swing through the battleground state of Ohio. His personal magnetism and statesmanlike command of the issues on the campaign trail had worked magic in the Buckeye State. All signs pointed to an upset Blaine win in Ohio, but the tour had left him exhausted. He just wanted to return to Maine and spend the final days of this epic election at home with his family, but the national committee was imploring him to make one final road trip through New

York. It would be his last hurrah before election night, and could be just what was needed to ensure victory on November 4.

In his room, Blaine could hear applause. Five hundred clergymen who had been invited to meet Blaine had gathered in the hotel parlor. Invitations had been extended to all denominations, but only two Catholic priests and one rabbi had shown up. The bulk of the guests were Presbyterians and Methodists. Resolutions were passed, calling Cleveland's nomination an "insult to Christian civilization," and declaring that, for the sake of "virtue in the home," he had to be defeated.

With his wife at his side, Blaine descended the staircase. Wearing a long black coat, Blaine looked like one of the assembled preachers cheering him on; the only thing that distinguished him from the clerics was his jaunty polka-dot necktie. Blaine folded his hands and waited to be introduced.

Standing next to Blaine was the master of ceremonies, Dr. Samuel D. Burchard, a Presbyterian minister from New York. He was a last-minute replacement for a minister from Philadelphia who was supposed to introduce Blaine but had been delayed. Burchard had been given the duty because, at age seventy-two, he was the oldest minister present, and deemed to be a nonthreatening compromise with the clergy of other denominations who were angling for the role. Not much was known about Burchard. He came from an obscure redbrick church in the Murray Hill section of Manhattan. He was bald, with a long pair of side-whiskers, and weighed about two hundred pounds.

When Burchard took the podium, everyone quieted down.

Burchard spoke directly to Blaine. "We are Republicans, and don't propose to leave our party and identify ourselves with the party whose antecedents have been rum, Romanism, and rebellion. We are loyal to our flag. We are loyal to you." The remark didn't register with most people in the crowd. Supposedly, just one fellow hissed. Associated Press correspondent Frank Mack, apparently the only reporter present, wasn't sure he'd heard what he thought he heard. He turned to the Democratic Party stenographer who was at his side and asked in a whisper, "Did you get that?"

"Bet your life—the old fool."

Blaine later claimed that he never heard the phrase, "Rum, Romanism, and Rebellion," explaining that Burchard was an old man with a shaky voice and he, Blaine, had been focused on thinking about the remarks he had been about to make, not on what Burchard was saying. Blaine must have known he was facing a political calamity because right after the event, he sought out Frank Mack to get the AP reporter to confirm the contents of Burchard's speech. When Mack said that a stenographer had already left, a "flicker of annoyance" passed over the candidate's face. All Blaine could do then was hope for the best.

"Rum, Romanism, and Rebellion" spread like a virus across the nation. Burchard was denounced as a Know-Nothing bigot while Blaine was assailed for failing to immediately disassociate himself from Burchard's anti-Catholic sentiments. Disregarded in the abuse heaped on Blaine were these relevant facts about his personal history: Blaine's mother was a devout Catholic, his father had converted to Catholicism on his deathbed, and his sister was the mother superior at a Catholic convent. Blaine didn't speak out about the controversy until seventy-two hours later, at a speech in New Haven. By then, there was very little that he could do to stem the damage.

"I am the last man in the United States who would make a disrespectful allusion to another man's religion." He called Catholicism an "ancient faith in which my revered mother lived and died."

Until the morning of "Rum, Romanism, and Rebellion," Blaine had been steadily chipping away at the half million voters of Irish descent who appreciated Blaine's Catholic heritage and his anti-British foreign policy sentiments. All that was now in the past. Wavering Irish Catholic voters stampeded back to the Democratic fold. Tammany Hall's Boss Kelly also came around, decreeing that he must "now swallow the Cleveland pill" and urged his Tammany braves to go all out for the Democratic ticket.

At Wells College in Aurora, New York, Frances Folsom was giddy with anticipation as she diligently followed the final days of the 1884 election. Her friendship with the Democratic presidential candidate was the talk of the campus.

"I must tell you about one girl here, a Miss Folsom (not to be at all conceited, she is 'gone' on me, to use a common expression), who is awfully nice," a gossipy Wells student wrote her friend on October 23, 1884. "She is very handsome and, my dear, I want you to understand Governor Cleveland is perfectly devoted to her. Sends her flowers all the time and writes her regularly every week. Of course, she is very much excited to know how the election is coming off, as it will in one case be *slightly* agreeable to her."

Sometimes, Cleveland stopped in Aurora to visit Frances on his way to Buffalo. One recent evening, Frances had been caught in a downpour. She had gotten out of her wet clothes, dried off, and snuggled into bed for a good night's sleep when she got word that the governor had unexpectedly shown up and was waiting for her in the parlor. Frances quickly put on a frock and made herself presentable, but it wasn't quick enough for Cleveland. When she finally descended the staircase, she found him impatiently pacing the floor. He was pretty peeved to have been kept waiting, and Frances had come down just in time. Years later, Cleveland was able to laugh off the incident. "Five minutes more that time and we should never have been married."

Frances herself could only wonder at the attention Cleveland showered on her and what it all meant. Her dorm room was still fragrant with roses sent weekly from the governor's greenhouse. Cleveland also sent fruits and mailed her campaign pamphlets that he thought she might find interesting. For now, she accepted everything and glowed in the aura of his attentions. A framed photograph of Cleveland hung in her dorm room. When another student asked her if it was her father, No, Frances responded, it was Grover Cleveland. Did anyone suspect a romance? Perhaps not. On the surface, Cleveland seemed like a devoted stepfather or caring uncle.

Frances followed every new lurid development in the Maria Halpin scandal. The only daily newspaper available on campus was a Republican sheet published in Auburn that aggressively covered the Halpin case in a way that Frances found deeply offensive. She considered the reporting so one-sided she couldn't look at the paper without throwing a fit. She said it "disgusted" her. When another student got up the nerve to ask her about the scandal, Frances bristled, but handled the query like a lady. If "you" only knew Grover Cleveland like she did, she said, the man was, in her opinion, "more sinned against than sinning."

Frances asked around and found somebody on campus who subscribed to the rival *Auburn Bulletin* newspaper and was willing to share it with her. At least the *Bulletin* slanted its news Democratic, the way Frances liked it. One can only imagine her distress when Cleveland's own people planted the story that so conveniently linked her much-loved dead father to Maria Halpin. Many Americans were now of the opinion that Oscar Folsom had had an extramarital affair with the Halpin woman and was Baby Oscar's biological father. And yet, right through the drama, neither Frances nor her mother Emma wavered in their affection for Cleveland.

As Election Day neared, at Wells, Frances became the center of attention. At that time the campus was a stronghold of Republican activism, and even though Frances and her room-mate Katherine "Pussy" Willard were the only Democrats there, the other girls were encouraging Frances and, even if their hearts weren't in it, rooting for Blaine. One night, as November 4 loomed, Frances gathered her friends around her.

"Girls, wouldn't it be pretty nice for me to spend a winter at the White House?" she wondered dreamily.

"Why, of course," one student answered. "But you must be sure to invite all of us to see you."

The prospects for victory seemed dim, however; Frances's friend confided as much in a letter home. "I am sadly afraid she will never spend such a winter, aren't you?"

Time would soon tell. The election was almost here. Frances told everyone she was on her way to Albany. She and her mother had been invited by Grover Cleveland to await the returns at the governor's mansion.

The day before the election, Grover Cleveland made a stealthy return to Buffalo, arriving in the city at 7:00 AM. Only a few citizens who happened to be at the depot greeted him. Cleveland shook their hands, declined a ride uptown, and walked to one of his favorite restaurants, Gerot's, for breakfast. On the surface, he seemed serene and in good spirits.

Cleveland spent the rest of the morning with Bissell at the law firm. He also got a haircut at Barthauer's barbershop, where he told an old friend who happened to be sitting in the chair next to his that he was confident of victory but would accept defeat if that was to be the outcome. At noon, he took lunch at the Tifft House. Word had gotten out that he was in town, and throngs were now following him everywhere. He had a cheery word for all who came to shake his hand; he could hardly take a step without running into some acquaintance from the old days.

At 6:00 PM, Cleveland dined at the City Club with Bissell, Charles Goodyear, John Milburn, and several other dear friends. Later that evening, he went to the theater, sitting in a box at the Academy of Music for a production of the comedy fittingly titled *Our Governor*, starring the popular actor William J. Florence. Cleveland left before the play was over and checked into his room at the Tifft House. When he awoke the following morning, Election Day, he went to his designated polling place in the Ninth Ward to cast his ballot. There were six men ahead of him in line, and they made way for the governor to go first.

When several ballots were thrust in his hand, he said good-naturedly, "A fellow can't cast but one, you know." Cleveland finished in time to catch the 9:00 AM train to Albany. Nine hours later, he was back in the Executive Mansion.

Just the menfolk were invited to join Cleveland for dinner: Lamont, Apgar, and a few other intimates. Cleveland's two sisters, Mary and Rose, kept the Folsom ladies company. Then Cleveland and his political team gathered in a room on the second floor to await the returns. A telephone was the only direct means of communication with the outside world, but unfortunately, early in the evening, a deluge knocked out phone service. From then on it took a steady stream of messengers from the telegraph office to keep them informed of how the election was faring.

The first reports from downstate were encouraging. Mugwumps were turning out in force in prosperous Republican neighborhoods like Murray Hill and Brooklyn Heights, although Blaine was performing better than expected in the Irish slums. It was like reading tea leaves: The election could go either way. When returns from the upstate counties started drifting in, the news from Jefferson County was disappointing. "That hurts," Cleveland said. William Sinclair laid out a buffet supper for everyone. It was going to be a long night.

In this black hole of information, Cleveland's assistant secretary, William Gorham Rice, was sent to the offices of the *Albany Argus* newspaper. As Daniel Manning owned the *Argus*, Rice was assured full and unfettered access to the Associated Press wire services. After he'd reviewed the fragmentary election data coming into the newsroom, Rice surmised that New York was going to be a squeaker. The "drift," as he put it, favored Cleveland, but only by a slender margin, perhaps 2,000 votes in total out of more than 1,000,000 votes cast. That was all. Everyone back at the Executive Mansion had assumed that the state would give Cleveland a large majority. The numbers startled Rice. He jotted them down and ordered a special messenger to deliver his handwritten analysis directly to Lamont.

Up in Maine, Blaine was spending election night at his mansion in Augusta, where Western Union had strung a special wire into the family library. As Blaine looked at the numbers coming in, even with twenty-five years of experience in national politics, he couldn't tell which way the night would go. Outside, a storm was rolling in. A vast front, roaring its way east, was making this a soaking-wet Election Day from Chicago to New England. Rain was usually a bad omen for Republicans; it was asking a lot for traditionally Republican farmers to toil their way into town in a storm over muddy country roads to cast their ballots. Blaine, stressed out, had had enough and said, "I'm going to bed," to his private secretary. "Don't disturb me unless something decisive comes in."

A remarkably similar scene was playing out in Albany. Around midnight, Cleveland stretched, saying, "If you stay up much longer, you will be counting me out." Then he announced that he was going to bed and advised everyone to do the same. They watched the candidate retire for the night. The moment he was gone, the wily Apgar and Lamont leapt into action. Now they were free to play some hardball politics. Something was definitely up. Returns from the Republican counties seemed "suspiciously slow," and the two men suspected that the tabulations were being withheld until GOP leaders could determine to what extent the ballot boxes had to be stuffed to make up the difference. Apgar and Lamont divvied up the list of every Democratic Party county leader in the state and sent telegrams to all of them:

"The only hope of our opponents is a fraudulent count in the county districts. Call to your assistance today vigilant and courageous friends, and see that every vote is honestly counted. Telegraph me at once your estimate."

To this telegram they affixed Daniel Manning's name, for added weight. Across the state, party leaders were ordered to head to their respective county clerk's office and remain there until the votes were tabulated and certified. No one wanted a replay of the election theft of 1876.

The morning after the election, Americans were bewildered; the Democratic newspapers projected Cleveland as the next president while the Republican papers assured their readers that Blaine had emerged triumphant. No one knew for certain. Unofficially, in New York State, Blaine was ahead by just 988 votes, with thirteen election districts yet to report. Outside Democratic Party headquarters at the Hoffman House and GOP headquarters at the Fifth Avenue Hotel, vast partisan crowds gathered as the official count trickled in. Two bellwether states, New Jersey and Indiana, went for Cleveland. So had Connecticut—which cut into Blaine's lock on New England. California was up in the air. Of course the entire Deep South had voted for Cleveland.

Outside the Hoffman House, the shout went up, "Give us New York!" Everyone was waiting for the results from the Empire State; without his home state, Cleveland was done for. The propaganda machines went into overdrive, and accusations flew on both sides. The Western Union Telegraph Company, which was owned by the Republican robber baron Jay Gould, issued a communiqué, claiming that Blaine had taken New York by a plurality of 11,000 votes, but most people assumed it was just dust being thrown in the electorate's eyes. In retaliation, an angry mob marched to Gould's mansion on 5th Avenue, chanting, "We'll hang Jay Gould to a sour apple tree." Bulletins posted at the nation's leading Republican newspaper, the *New York Tribune*, proclaiming Blaine victories in Virginia, Maryland, and Tennessee were laughed off as "simply idiotic," and a throng of outraged Cleveland supporters stormed the *Tribune* building on Nassau Street. Had a quick-thinking janitor not slammed the iron doors shut just in time, the *Tribune* would have been taken over before reinforcements from the city hall police precinct got there and dispersed the horde.

"I believe I have been elected president," Cleveland informed the mayor of Troy, New York. "And nothing but the greatest fraud can keep me out of it, and that we will not permit." Dan Manning even hinted at inaugurating Cleveland by force of arms if necessary.

Writing to his father from his desk at the judge advocate's office on Broadway, Horatio King said the anxiety of the people "equaled anything I ever felt in the war."

"Cleveland is elected," King declared, and any attempt to deny him the office "will be met by force. The people here are greatly excited, and it will take but a spark to create a riot."

On the Friday following Election Day, Cleveland finally took the official lead in New York. A recount for the entire state was ordered. When Cleveland learned that he had been defeated in

Erie County—that the voters of his hometown, who knew him best, had gone for Blaine by a plurality of 1,490 votes—it was a bitter pill. Even the voters in his own ward had turned on him. Cleveland had George Ball to thank for that.

Downstate, it was another story. In Manhattan, the Board of Aldermen met as board of canvassers. The air was so thick with tobacco smoke, it seemed to envelop everyone in a toxic brown haze. Democratic ward heelers and the rank and file sat on one side, Republicans on the other. Everyone watched as the sergeant at arms carried in armfuls of immense manila envelopes stuffed with the original election-night ballots. To the surprise of many who had feared Tammany Hall mischief, only a few were found to be defective. It was a rout for Cleveland—he took Manhattan by 43,000 votes.

When the recount was finally certified, Cleveland had won the national popular vote by just 25,000 out of 10,000,000 cast. He had taken New York State by a scant 1,246 votes. A turn-over of just over 600 votes would have made Blaine the president. As it was, New York went to Cleveland, giving him a total of 219 votes in the Electoral College, versus Blaine's 182. One observer estimated that Reverend Burchard's "Rum, Romanism, and Rebellion" crack had cost Blaine 50,000 votes in New York alone. Others put the figure at 30,000. In any event, it turned the tide in New York, New Jersey, and Connecticut. A shower of insults came down on Burchard, and no one held him in more contempt than the man whose presidential ambitions he had unintentionally dashed. "An ass in the shape of a preacher" had cost him the election, said Blaine. Overnight, Burchard became a pariah. On Broadway, actors tossed his name into their routines for an "easy laugh"; his own congregation abandoned him, and church elders forced him into early retirement. To his dying day, in 1891, Burchard maintained that "Rum, Romanism, and Rebellion" should never have been regarded as more than a clever turn of phrase; he just liked its alliteration. But he came to be indelibly marked as the man who "opened his mouth and swallowed a presidency."

As for Maria Halpin, joyous Democrats took to the streets, chanting this memorable couplet:

> *Hurray for Maria, hurrah for the kid!*
> *We voted for Grover, and damned glad we did!*

Another little verse also swept the country, a spiteful, in-your-face rhyme that turned on its head that famous *Judge* cartoon caption from the early days of the campaign:

> *Ma, Ma, where's your pa?*
> *Gone to the White House, Ha Ha, Ha!*

The Southern states celebrated. In Richmond, the old capital of the Confederacy, crowds sang hymns. In Atlanta, five thousand people poured into the state legislative building and cheered the rebirth of the Democratic Party. But Southern blacks expressed real anxiety, and some of them even fear, that slavery would be restored.

In Albany, Cleveland could finally relax. He was the president-elect. It was official, and Blaine finally conceded defeat. "I am glad they yield peaceably," Cleveland remarked. "If they had not, I should have felt it my duty to take my seat anyhow."

But the bitterness of the Halpin scandal and its chief architect George Ball were still in his thoughts even in these days of triumph.

"It's quite amusing to see how profuse the professions are of some who stood aloof when most needed," he wrote his truest friend, Wilson Bissell. "I intend to cultivate the Christian virtue of charity toward all men except the dirty class that defiled themselves with filthy scandal and Ballism. I don't believe God will ever forgive them, and I am determined not to do so."

Cleveland also aimed his wrath at the *Evening Telegraph* and asked Bissell, "Is there any chance of having a decent and ably conducted Democratic paper in Buffalo?"—overlooking the fact that he already had the *Courier* and the *Evening News* in his corner. Ten days later, the issue still nagged him. "How much would it cost to start an evening Democratic paper in Buffalo? Something ought to be done, but I suppose the expense will stand in the way." Apparently, he wanted to hit the *Evening Telegraph* where it would hurt most, in the bottom line, by starting up a competitive afternoon publication. At the forefront of his concern was what future grief the *Evening Telegraph* might be intending. The matter was of such great consequence to Cleveland, he was actually thinking about making a clandestine trip to Buffalo so that he and Bissell could discuss it in person.

In the meantime, Cleveland had to adjust to life as the president-elect. He found the social demands on his time grating. He woke up one morning to the irritating sight of a Buffalo socialite who had invited herself to breakfast. She was there to insist that Cleveland have dinner with her family before he left for Washington. "Did you ever see such work?" Cleveland asked Bissell. One night in late November, he arrived home to find that a grateful citizen had sent him a sweet-tempered black Newfoundland dog. Cleveland sent the hound back by express rail at his own expense, saying he was "averse" to accepting gifts from admirers. Cleveland saw the next four years as a "dreadful self-inflicted penance for the good of my country."

"I can see no pleasure in it and no satisfaction . . . "

He couldn't get Buffalo out of his head. It wasn't just George Ball. He took the fact that the city had turned on him in the presidential election as a personal betrayal.

"I am overwhelmed with all kinds of things and perplexed more than I can tell you, but nothing is so annoying to me as my thoughts connected with Buffalo.

"I feel this moment I would never go there again if I could avoid it," he confessed to Bissell. "Elected president of the United States, I feel I have no home *at my home.*" He had to shut down his Buffalo bachelor apartment, but he so dreaded going back, he wondered whether he could conduct his business in one day and leave before anyone knew he was there. They were "scum"—this "dirty and contemptible portion of the Buffalo population."

"I wish you'd try to put yourself in my place and imagine how all this thing seems to me."

It was a bitterly cold and lonely Christmas Day for the president-elect. The Folsom women had gone, leaving him without companionship except that of his sisters'.

"I wish you a very 'Merry Christmas' from the bottom of my heart," Cleveland wrote Bissell. He had apparently sent Bissell a wool sweater for Christmas several days before—a gift that Cleveland said could not possibly match what Bissell meant to him. "If I had the world, I'd give you half of it at least."

The two men again exchanged correspondence on New Year's Eve. Bissell's letter arrived first. Cleveland retreated to his den to write a reply.

It was time for Cleveland to set about the task of selecting a cabinet and reading up on the great policy issues of the day. He was determined to take Dan Lamont with him to the nation's capital. That other Dan—Daniel Manning—would be rewarded for his loyalty with his appointment as secretary of the treasury. Cleveland had another critical choice to make. He would be the second president in American history, after James Buchanan, to enter the White House a bachelor. But even a bachelor required a first lady.

At Wells College, Frances Folsom was giddy with excitement. She had received a special invitation to attend the inauguration of Grover Cleveland, and she was determined, come March, to be at the ceremony—even if it meant missing exams.

In Buffalo, George Ball could not let go. The election had left his reputation in tatters. In the not-too-distant future, he would seek his vengeance.

In New Rochelle, Maria Halpin passed into history, her name forever soiled. Like George Ball, she was not yet through with Grover Cleveland.

15

ROSE

PRESIDENT-ELECT CLEVELAND CONSIDERED naming his even-tempered married sister Mary Hoyt his First Lady, but in the end, he decided that his youngest sister, Rose, would be more suitable.

Rose Elizabeth Cleveland lived in Holland Patent, nestled in the foothills of Oneida County, about a dozen miles from the city of Utica. It was a charming but isolated hamlet, populated by just five hundred people. Holland Patent's winters were harsh, with January temperatures that rarely rose above eighteen degrees and Nor'easters that could bury the place in snow. Forty years after Samuel Morse had revolutionized American communications with his immortal message, "What Hath God Wrought," in 1884, Holland Patent still had no telegraphic connection with the outside world.

Rose was the mistress of the Cleveland homestead and its sole inhabitant. The house was filled with carefully placed family heirlooms: her father's armchair in the library, her mother's easy chair in the bedroom, and in the dining room a great mahogany side-board dating back to the Cleveland clan's early days in America. A special treasure was the piano her mother Ann Cleveland had once played, and all the parlor furnishings that had been her mother's were now Rose's. A visitor would have been hard-pressed to find any evidence of feminine interests or endeavors in Rose's home—no sewing basket or cookery manuals—but there were plenty of books and literary magazines.

Rose was a creature of rigid habit. She took breakfast at eight and by nine was in her library where she spent the morning reading literature or history; her specialty was the Middle Ages. In the afternoons, even when the weather was harsh, the solitary figure of Rose Cleveland could be seen climbing the surrounding hills, crossing the meadows, or disappearing into the woods, defiant of wind and rain.

The townspeople had known Rose since she was a preco-cious seven-year-old, the youngest child in the Cleveland family of nine. She had been educated at the Houghton Seminary, taught history and English at a girls' school in Pennsylvania, and returned to Holland Patent to take care of her ailing mother in Ann Cleveland's final years. She remained there after Ann's death in 1882 and built for herself a tranquil if solitary life, but for attending the church where her late father had once served as pastor and teaching the girls' Sunday school Bible class.

Grover Cleveland's announcement naming his sister his offi-cial White House hostess came on January 17, 1885.

Washington was eager to hear all about this interesting intel-lectual who had been anointed First Lady of the land. A thirty-eight-year-old spinster, with coiled hair already slightly tinged with grey, she, like her brother, possessed genuine brainpower and an extraordinary capacity for total recall. It was said that she never forgot a name, or the face that went with it. She also had a one-of-a-kind talent illustrative of her capacity to lose herself into another world: She could conjugate ancient Greek verbs in her head. Moreover, it was a skill she made use of on public occasions whenever she was flustered or found herself getting bored.

The inauguration of the new president was set for March 4, 1885, as prescribed by the Constitution. (The Twentieth Amendment, changing Inauguration Day to the twentieth of January, would not go into effect until 1933.) Rose, Mary Hoyt, their sister Louisa Bacon, their brother the Reverend William Cleveland, his wife and three nieces, all accompanied Grover Cleveland on the journey to Washington. Joining them were Mr. and Mrs. Daniel Manning—the incoming secretary of the treasury—and Mr. and Mrs. Dan Lamont. Lamont was going as Cleveland's private secretary, having initially resisted Cleveland's many efforts to persuade him to take the position. Cleveland had finally won him over by saying, "Well, Dan, if you won't go, I won't, that's all."

Everyone boarded a modest little train with an engine car, one baggage car, and two sleepers, and it quietly slipped out of the Albany station at 6:45 AM sharp, without so much as a toot or whistle. The only people to see them off were Cleveland's personal physician, Dr. Ward, a military adjutant, a police officer, and several inquisitive youngsters from town who had come to observe this moment of history. There were no stops scheduled between the state capital and Washington except to take on water.

The entire trip took exactly twenty-four hours. When the train pulled into the Baltimore & Potomac Depot at 6th and B Street NW in Washington, six newspaper reporters were standing on the platform to witness the arrival of the president-elect. Security consisted of a police inspector and a squadron of soldiers under the command of an army colonel who wore a flashy scarlet bandana around his neck. What followed was anything but a formal ceremony. No one seemed to know the proper protocol. It was an awkward scene, with Rose and the other ladies on board the train seen staring out the windows as porters scrambled to unload the Clevelands' trunks and boxes. Finally, President-elect Cleveland stepped off the train. In his beaver overcoat and high hat, carrying a small leather satchel, more bookkeeper than president, he failed to make much of an impression. His face was homely and he had a double chin and he was not as tall as everyone had expected. The general consensus of those who witnessed the event was that the Cleveland campaign posters that had been plastered across the land during the election were "considerably flattering" when compared to what he looked like in the flesh. Cleveland was shown to the B Street exit where he found a team of carriages waiting for his party, and when everyone was comfortably seated, the convoy trotted off on a fifteen-minute drive to the Arlington Hotel on H Street.

A doorman held the door for Cleveland and said, "How d'ye do, Mr. President?"

Cleveland was shown to his rooms on the second floor of the Pomeroy House, which was connected to the Arlington Hotel by private corridor. The suite faced Lafayette Square, with the White House looming in plain view. President Arthur made the thoughtful gesture of sending over the chief White House door-keeper, Sergeant E. S. Dinsmore of the Washington city police. Dinsmore knew every important personage in the capital by sight, and Dan Lamont, quickly assessing the sergeant's value, positioned him at the H Street entrance to control the stream of distinguished visitors who came to call on Cleveland. Senator Gorman of Maryland, Horatio King, and a score of other politicians all showed up to pay their respects.

The next day, Grover Cleveland was inaugurated twenty-second president of the United States. He wore his Prince Albert coat, a high old-fashioned standing collar, and a black tie and bore the honor with becoming dignity. Cleveland had committed his entire speech to memory, only occasionally consulting notes he held in his right hand. His only regret on this great day was the absence of Frances Folsom whose midterm exams at Wells College unfortunately coincided with the inauguration. Lady Principal Helen Fairchild Smith had refused to grant Frances special leave, even to attend this never-to-be-repeated historic spectacle. Surely Frances found it a challenge to focus on her exams while the man who was romancing her with flowers was being sworn in as commander in chief, but the strict disciplinarian of Wells College could not be swayed.

As the powers of the executive branch of government were transferred to a new administration, Rose Cleveland began to acclimate herself to her role as First Lady.

A relation rather than a wife serving as First Lady was not without precedent in Washington. Rose's predecessor, Mary Arthur McElroy, was President Arthur's sister. (Arthur's wife, Ellen, had died of pneumonia at age forty-two, twenty months before Arthur became president.) Andrew Johnson's shy and sickly wife, Eliza, had made only two official appearances as First Lady and had delegated all hostess duties to their daughter Martha. And Harriet Lane had served as hostess for the only other bachelor in American history to be elected president, her uncle James Buchanan. Rose was in distinguished company.

Rose moved into a bedroom on the second floor of the White House, facing south, with a commanding view of the Virginia hills. She could also see the tallest structure in the city, the Washington Monument. The White House living quarters had undergone a complete renovation during the Arthur Administration, so Rose found her rooms in perfect condition and comfortable in every way.

Washington got its first real look at Rose and the rest of the family at the inaugural ball that night. As First Lady, she should have been the center of attention, but it was Vice President Hendricks's stylish wife, Eliza, a veteran of the Washington social scene, who assumed that status. With her white brocaded satin gown with beaded pearl front, Mrs. Hendricks won the evening's accolades from the *Washington Post,* followed by the wife of the commanding general of the United States Army, then President Cleveland's three nieces, Mary Hoyt, and finally, the First Lady. Rose's low-waisted gown of white silk, edged with plaited ruffles, was depicted without editorial comment. Some may have seen this as exceedingly insulting.

Four days later, Rose held her first reception at the White House. She must have been anxious because she asked her sisters Mary and Louisa, and her sister-in-law, for assistance. They stood in the East Room greeting a throng of high-society ladies who were there to observe the First Family firsthand. It was an uncomfortable occasion for the four Cleveland ladies because even the most inconsequential social gaffe could potentially be blown up into an embarrassing situation by the hostile press. Rose wore her hair in stylish little curls to enhance the framing of her intelligent face. This time her outfit—a plain green velvet dress—received favorable notices. It was remarked that she was "in every way fit to preside over the social ceremonies at the famous mansion."

Then the rumor mill started churning. The *Washington Post* pointed out how Rose was so like Anna Dickinson in the way she wore her hair short and sensible. Anna Dickinson was a well-known suffragette and lecturer who, in 1864, became the first woman to speak before the House of Representatives. In those days, she was known as a fierce abolitionist—the Joan of Arc of the Civil War—but as the years went on, she struggled with mental health, and her sister would one day have her committed into a state hospital for the insane. There was also the scuttlebutt that Anna was a lesbian. Having made the comparison, and its inescapable insinuations, the *Post* was quick to point out "there is nothing mannish" about Rose Cleveland.

The capital's leading socialites treated Rose cordially, but some snarky comments hinted at something amiss. One had to read between the lines to get the message. The *Boston Herald* praised Rose for bringing to Washington much needed "earnestness" and applauded her "clean-cut" face. Then came this dig: "If she has the courage of her convictions she will lead in her *natural bent* [italics added] rather than be led by the stereotyped ways of so-called fashion."

When Rose invited a delegation from the Woman's Christian Temperance Union to tea at the White House, she showed that she had a mind of her own. This was bold of her: The Prohibition Party had fielded a candidate against her brother in the election of 1884, winning 150,000 votes. When the ladies arrived wearing white ribbons denoting their devotion to the cause of prohibition, there was quite a scene. To Rose, wine was "poison," and drinking a national curse. When an article Rose had written for a temperance magazine back in 1882, when she was an unknown academic, found its way back into print now that she was First Lady, it's easy to imagine President Cleveland's irritation at her words: "It is only a strong man who can keep his wine glass upside down." Rose also let it be known that she had great admiration for Rutherford B. Hayes's wife, Lucy, known by the sobriquet "Lemonade Lucy" after she banned alcohol at all White House functions. Rose did not go that far—wine continued to be served at dinner in the Cleveland White House—but whenever a toast was made, the only drink Rose hoisted was water.

Mary Hoyt remained in Washington until the end of March, when she returned to her family in Fayetteville, New York. Louisa Bacon, who was married to an architect, also went home to Toledo. Rose was on her own, but she was not without companionship. A woman she knew from Albany, Miss Annie Van Vechten, arrived at the White House on March 19 for an extended stay.

Annie came from a distinguished Dutch family that had settled in America in the 1600s. She was a statuesque forty-year-old brunette with queenly shoulders and a commanding physical presence—a finished woman of the world, and just the right antidote to Rose's taciturnity. At least she wasn't conjugating Greek verbs in her head to pass the time on the tedious reception line, as was said of Rose. A few days after Annie moved into the White House, she assisted Rose in hosting an afternoon tea. Two days later, she attended Sunday services at Rose's side at the First Presbyterian Church on Fourth Street—the house of worship where President Cleveland had just purchased a pew. No one knew what to make of Annie. Was she Rose's companion? Or was this a cover and was President Cleveland courting her?

The following week, Annie Van Vechten had to take a backseat to another fetching visitor: Frances Folsom had been invited by President Cleveland to stay at the White House for her Easter break from Wells College. Frances may have missed the inauguration, but she was finally able to savor her first sweet taste of life in the Washington limelight. She was given a room in the family quarters on the second floor, overlooking the North Portico entrance. She could not believe she was actually here. It was like a storybook. Schoolgirl that she was, she opened her heart to her diary.

"I can't realize it is Washington. I can't realize it is the White House—or if it all is, I think I can't be I, but must be some other body."

That first night, dinner was served with all of President Cleveland's favorite ladies at the table: Frances, her mother Emma, and Rose. Somehow he managed to lose the mother and his sister and invited Frances to accompany him on a private tour of the White House, where they could be alone. The time had come to take his courtship to the next level. Cleveland showed his former ward all the points of interest until they found themselves in the East Room, the site of most formal state dinners and other presidential ceremonies, and to this day, the largest room in the presidential mansion. Surely, Cleveland showed Frances a most treasured work of art—the Gilbert Stuart portrait of George Washington that, according to legend, had been saved by Dolly Madison when the British burned the White House to the ground in 1814. Romance was definitely in the air as Cleveland and Frances made tender small talk. He told her that he tried to come to the East Room every night and walk its length for exercise, and they playfully calculated how many times they had to walk from one end to the other to make a mile. It came to forty-eight. The president escorted Frances to the south window, and as lovers have always done, they gazed at the moon. Words danced from his lips, and they were "very romantic." Cleveland had now crossed the line, and he had probably never felt more vulnerable.

The new few days were a whirlwind of activity for Frances. She was officially presented to Washington society on March 28 at an afternoon reception at the White House. Emma Folsom and Annie Van Vechten were also there, but it was Frances, her lush chestnut hair and charming sincerity free of affectation, who became a sensation—a "decided favorite," according to the *Washington Post*, by far the "prettiest girl that Washington society has seen this winter." Frances wore a simple short skirt of white silk and cascades of lace. Her tight-fitting collar covered her neck so entirely it seemed to bellow the essence of virginity. Her corsage of Jacqueminot roses matched the blush that graced her cheeks. Among the guests were an exceptional number of the capital's most alluring debutantes, but the Wells College senior was "the belle of the assemblage." When Cleveland sneaked a peak at the reception and saw Frances's sparkling debut, he was said to have exclaimed, "She'll do! She'll do!" Also keeping a watchful eye was that "handsome matron," her mother Emma Folsom. Emma hovered over Frances, whispering words of encouragement in her daughter's ear, and Rose also made a special fuss, referring to Frances as "my little schoolgirl."

Dan Lamont's wife, Juliet, who was also at the party, found herself standing next to a gossipy Washington socialite to whom she said of Frances, "Isn't she the loveliest, the sweetest little beauty you ever saw?"

"Charming, charming," the socialite agreed. Then she said something she would one day come to regret. "How perfectly ridiculous it is to talk of the president marrying that child. The mother is even a trifle young for a man of his years and seriousness, and he will never marry while he lives in this house, I know. That sort of thing is not in his line and not in his mind, now that he has the duties of this great office on his shoulders." It was this woman's opinion that that other fetching White House visitor, Annie Van Vechten, would make a far more appropriate bride for the president.

There was genuine curiosity about President Cleveland's romantic life. Already there were rumors afloat that the forty-eight-year-old president was thinking about taking a bride, an as-yet unidentified "Buffalo belle." Scuttlebutt settled on four contenders, first among them Emma Folsom, although it seemed to many that Cleveland was smitten with Emma's daughter. Another prospective bride was said to be Maria Maltby Love, heiress of a prominent Buffalo family. Annie Van Vechten also found herself on the short list. Meanwhile, Cleveland's friends were quick to shoot down the reports, assuring everyone that the president was a confirmed bachelor. Those in the know, however, were putting their money on the winsome Frances Folsom.

Everyone wanted to get to know Frances. She and her mother were invited to a dinner party at the home of Senator George Pendleton of Ohio where she was introduced to the ambassadors of Great Britain, France, and Germany. Frances also saw all the sights and went shopping with her mother for a formal white gown for her college graduation. For this purchase, she wrote a letter to her grandfather asking for eighty dollars, assuring the flinty old man that it was a "fine gown," which she would get plenty of use out of—"if I shall receive another invitation to Washington, as Miss Cleveland intimates I shall." Even so, she was a little embarrassed about asking her grandfather for the cash. "Have you come to think that your oldest grandchild never writes you very much without tacking on a request for money—I believe that is almost so. But you know when that grandchild is going to the White House, money is rather inevitable, for one must have clothes. . . . Do you want any messages delivered to our good president?"

Cleveland took Frances on drives around Washington in his Victorian carriage, drawn by two seal-brown bays, with veteran White House coachman Al Bird at the reins, and it was, Frances wrote in her diary, a thrill to be sitting next to the president. After Cleveland pulled a few strings, Frances got to be taken to the top of the Washington Monument which—though it had been completed in 1884 following thirty-six years of on and off construction—had not yet been opened to the public. Emma tagged along.

It was finally dawning on the widow Folsom that Cleveland had no interest in taking her as his wife. How Emma learned that it was her daughter who was the object of the president's romantic desire and not herself has been a closely guarded family secret for more than a century, but it was said that when she was given the bracing news, Emma was "not pleased." At some point, she came to an accommodation and, finally, gave her blessing to the union. Perhaps she was able to appreciate the fact that, though she could not be First Lady, she could at least be the mother of the First Lady.

After six weeks in office, President Cleveland had settled into a daily routine. He awoke at eight, had breakfast at nine, and by ten was starting his workday in the library. In the morning, the first order of business in the president's office was sorting the mail. This was the duty of Dan Lamont, Cleveland's indispensable private secretary, who usually selected eight or ten letters worthy of the president's personal attention. The rest of the correspondence was distributed to the various branches of government. Letters from cranks and strange characters were placed in a file informally marked "eccentric." Once the morning mail was dealt with, Cleveland was ready to receive callers. In those days, formal appointments to see the president were not necessary. A distinguished gentleman with the right pedigree could present his card to the White House doorkeeper, who would take it to Lamont. No one got to see the president without Lamont's say-so. Almost every day, Cleveland made sure to check in with Rose to see how she was doing. Weather permitting, at 5:00 PM,

Cleveland would climb aboard the White House coupe, almost always with Lamont at his side, for a drive around Washington to get to know the capital. Sometimes the tour would last ninety minutes.

Dinner was always served at seven, followed by a mild cigar, usually his favorite brand, Reina Victoria, sometimes a Maduro. In those early days, Cleveland found the food indigestible and came to detest the French-born chef, Alexander Fortin, who had run the kitchen since the Garfield administration. Cleveland scornfully referred to Fortin as "that man who cooks," and longing for those unfussy meals in Buffalo—"pickled herring, Swiss cheese and a chop"—he finally fired him. He then brought in Eliza, his cook from the governor's mansion in Albany, and she was able to keep the husky president content with her basic steak-and-potatoes fare.

By 8:00 PM, Cleveland could be found back at his desk in the library, reading through mounds of paperwork that would keep him occupied until midnight, when he retired. A single telephone number serviced the entire mansion, and after hours, when all the clerks had gone home, it was not unusual for President Cleveland to answer the phone himself.

Frances's presence in the White House seemed to be softening Cleveland's hard-edged personality; for the first time in his political life, he came to enjoy the ceremonial functions of office—to a point. He was working in the library one Monday morning when he looked out his window and saw hundreds of children, accompanied by their mothers and nurses, gathered on the White House lawn for the traditional Easter egg roll. The spectacle lifted his spirits, and he instructed the ushers to collect all the children who were interested in meeting the president and bring them to the East Room. When Cleveland strode in, accompanied by Frances, Emma, and Rose, his attention was drawn to the littlest boy there, whose outstretched hand held a brilliantly colored egg that he was offering to the president. He wanted Mr. Cleveland to have it, he said, because he had "plenty more in the box," and Cleveland patted the boy on the head.

Alas, Frances's Washington fairy tale was coming to an end. Cleveland tried to talk her into extending her stay, but she had the good sense to insist that she had to return to Wells College and complete her senior year. Frances and Emma had stayed at the White House for eleven days, and on April 8, they stretched out their final hours—neither wanting to leave this fantasy-land—until they bid their farewells to President Cleveland and, in a driving rainstorm, boarded the last train back to New York.

Rose had cancelled all her appointments for that day and refused to receive any callers so that she could spend the Folsoms' last day in Washington with them. Her brother had let her in on a state secret—that he had made an "arrangement" with Frances and would ask for her hand in marriage. Rose had seen it coming for at least a year, and having found Frances to be a promising young lady, "capable of great development," she approved of the match despite the twenty-seven-year disparity in age. No one, Rose came to realize, should underestimate Frances. Underneath that veil of 19th-century femininity, she was a "much-stronger character" than people supposed. She was, in Rose's opinion, a "superior person." So Rose was encouraging, though she had to have understood that in grooming her successor as First Lady, she herself would inevitably be shown the door.

Annie Van Vechten finally departed the White House in mid-April and returned to her home in Albany where she lived with her mother. Rose missed her very much and apparently sank into a state of melancholia. She started scaling back her social duties and let it be known that she was canceling all White House receptions for the rest of the social season. Washington's elite found the entire situation exceedingly disquieting. It seemed that after a mere two months as First Lady, Rose had had enough. She had once contemptuously equated upper-crust society to a salivating and servile dog, specifically a spaniel. Like the spaniel, fashionable people obediently tagged along, drooling at the mouth. Some of the formalities required of her position as First Lady were, in Rose's estimation, nonsensical; conversely, some of the women who came into contact with Rose regarded her as "rather terrifying." Was she really conjugating Greek verbs while they were trying to engage her in chitchat?

On April 29, Rose left Washington bound for New York to "recuperate and rest." The White House would only say that she was taking some time off. The truth was that Rose and her brother had had a major blowout of an argument. To her shame, Rose had told the president that his administration was appointing too many Catholics to high-level government posts. The nation, she said, was facing a "Romanist peril." It was anti-immigration bigotry straight out of the Know-Nothing party handbook. Cleveland found it "annoying."

With Rose gone, Dan Lamont's wife, Juliet, moved into the White House temporarily to run things. Cleveland, writing to his sister Mary, tried to downplay the situation, saying that Libbie, as he called Rose, had gone to New York for "a little rest."

"She'd had a pretty hard time here," Cleveland admitted.

Reverend Byron Sunderland, pastor of the Presbyterian church where Rose and the president worshipped, offered himself as peacemaker and tried to patch things up, without success. The White House worked overtime to keep a lid on the family turmoil. The stories two newspapermen had written about it may have been accurate, but all the same, the men were banned from covering the administration for having had the nerve to report accounts of the falling out between the Clevelands. Charles A. Hamilton, a reporter for the *Buffalo Express*, and later the dean of White House correspondents for the *Washington Post*, found his access to the White House jeopardized when he was accused of spreading the tale that Rose and the president were at each other's throats. Hamilton became so concerned that he went to Lamont and informed him that he had no intention of writing a word about this "scurrilous" story. Once he had Hamilton's pledge, Lamont did a good turn and told the reporter he would be "always welcome at the White House."

The family drama was an authentic crisis for Cleveland, coming as it did on the heels of the Maria Halpin scandal the year before and the misgivings it had raised about Cleveland's fitness for office. Cleveland had to wonder whether he had blundered in naming his maiden sister First Lady. Perhaps Mary Hoyt would have made the more prudent pick. Like her brother, Mary held to the old-fashioned conviction that "a good wife is a woman who loves her husband and her country with no desire to run either." The president called on his most trusted aide,

Lamont, dispatching him to New York to talk things over with Rose. It was a delicate mission. Obviously, Rose was on the edge, but whatever words and assurances Lamont used, he was persuasive enough to bring Rose back with him to Washington. Once again, Lamont had come through in a pinch.

16

THE BRIDE

GRADUATION FOR WELLS College, class of 1885, took place in June. It was a small ceremony—only six girls were receiving their diplomas. Frances Folsom wore a white dress, the one she had purchased during her stay at the White House. The commencement program listed her as Frank Folsom. Cleveland could not attend; common sense and the duties of office were keeping him tied to his desk in the White House. Instead, he sent Frances a huge hamper of roses. He also arranged for the class ivy to be delivered to Wells College in his name. Frances and her classmates planted the ivy against the wall at Morgan Hall during a gentle June shower, and in the generations to come, the ground-creeping plant would make its sturdy climb up the brickwork.

Her family gave Frances an amazing graduation gift: a trip to Europe. Some have suggested there was an ulterior motive behind Emma Folsom's generosity. After all, for a disapproving mother who frowns on her daughter's beau, putting an ocean between the couple can do wonders. Before Frances departed, she spent a lazy summer at the family farm in Folsomville, New York. Then she journeyed to Scranton, Pennsylvania, to spend some time with her college chum, Grace Storrs. Grace had black hair and cobalt eyes, and a serious expression set on a very pretty face. Her father was the general superintendent of the Delaware, Lackawanna and Western Railroad, so the Storrs family stood at the apex of Scranton's social pecking order, and Frances had a grand time mingling with the other young swells in town. During her stay in Scranton, Frances received a letter that changed everything. It came from the president of the United States. Wrote Cleveland, "Would you put your life in my hands?"

It was a formal proposal of marriage.

"Yes," Frances wrote back.

Everyone was sworn to secrecy. She told only her mother, grandfather, and cousin, the Buffalo lawyer Ben Folsom. None of her kin raised any objection about the propriety of the match, even though Cleveland had known her from babyhood. By now, despite her misgivings, Emma was coming to the realization that nothing could keep Frances and the president apart.

"Frank made a hero out of him before she was out of short dresses," Emma would later explain. Her daughter, she ruefully remarked, "looks at him through the glamour of love's young dream."

So it was done. Frances wanted a quickie wedding, but Cleveland told her she should take the time to think things through. Did she really want to be Mrs. Grover Cleveland? He even expressed remorse for their infatuation to have reached this stage and said, from the bottom of his heart, how he wished that he were not president of the United States and thus not subjecting his "darling" to the harsh glare of life in the public arena. "Poor girl," Cleveland would remark some time later, "you never had any courting like other girls."

Women in that era rarely traveled abroad without a male escort, hence Ben Folsom wrote Cleveland a letter, assuring the president that he would accompany Frances and Emma Folsom to Europe and serve as their guardian. It would be Ben's third tour of the Old World. A thirty-eight-year-old bachelor, Ben was fairly tall for those times, about five foot eight, with narrow shoulders, and a pleasant face marked by a trimmed brown beard that gave him the look of an English prince. His reputation in Buffalo was that of a bon vivant.

Frances's grandfather, Colonel John Folsom, paid all the expenses for the European voyage and told Frances that when she found herself in Paris, she had to shop for a trousseau befitting the bride of the American president. She was under instructions from her grandfather to buy "as fine a costume as possible" for her wedding. Family honor required nothing less.

President Cleveland heartily approved of Frances's adventure. He saw the experience as an invaluable education for the future First Lady. The nine-month separation would also give her a stretch of time to ponder whether she truly wanted to be his wife. In the meantime, the president kept a photograph of her in his bedroom. Just before she boarded the transatlantic ship, Cleveland sent Frances a telegram, wishing her a bon voyage. It was addressed to "Miss Folsom" and sprinkled with expressions of adoration and undying love. A Western Union operator slipped the telegram to a reporter who made the erroneous assumption that the Miss Folsom in question had to be the mother, Emma. Once again, there was a flurry of newspaper stories about the bachelor president, this time predicting a White House wedding on the horizon—but to the widow Emma Folsom. Speculation about Emma cut Cleveland where it hurt—his ego. "I don't see why the papers keep marrying me to old ladies. I wonder why they don't say I am engaged to marry her daughter," he grumbled to an aide.

In November, President Cleveland made a trip to Buffalo, still his legal residence, to cast his vote in the New York State gubernatorial race. He was in his old law offices, chatting with Wilson Bissell and several other cronies when Ed Butler of the *Buffalo Evening News* came in with some unsettling information. None other than George Beniski, the illiterate Polish-born sailor who had served as Cleveland's substitute in the Civil War, had approached the publisher to see if a meeting with the president could be arranged. Beniski was in fact just outside the office, waiting for Butler's answer.

Cleveland agreed to meet with the man, and when he saw the army veteran ushered in, it was quite a shock. Beniski was now fifty-four, and it was a struggle for him to walk. Cleveland greeted him effusively.

"This is the man who went to war for me," he declared.

Cleveland showed Beniski to a chair in the corner and pressed him to be seated. Then the president asked everyone else to leave. When he was alone with Beniski, Cleveland asked him what it was he wanted. Beniski said he was "unwell and destitute," and he was embarrassed to say that his current place of residence was the Erie County Poorhouse. He needed a helping hand, he told Cleveland.

Beniski didn't get much sympathy from the president. For some reason, Cleveland found his story of absolute destitution far-fetched. "That is not true," he responded gruffly. Then he reached in his pocket and handed him five dollars. With that, Beniski was dismissed.

Cleveland could only hope that this would be the last time he would hear from the inconvenient George Beniski.

Frances Folsom's tour took her to England, France, Belgium, Italy, and Germany. In Berlin, Frances met up with her college roommate, Kate Willard, who joined Frances, her mother, and Ben on an excursion to Italy where they explored the streets of Pompeii and stared into the "boiling seething lava of Vesuvius." Frances was so moved, she let her guard down and found herself telling Kate that she was secretly engaged to President Cleveland. Kate must have recalled the portrait of Grover Cleveland that had hung in their dorm room, the regular delivery of fresh roses, and the playful, almost flirtatious way they talked with each other when he came to visit Frank on campus. Yet it hadn't registered then—and even now, Kate could not quite believe it. He was old and unattractive and Frank was young and beautiful. Kate tried to talk Frank out of the engagement, but she just shook her head. She loved the man, she told Kate. She had found true happiness with Cleveland and her "mission" in life was to be his wife.

In April, they went their separate ways, Kate returning to Berlin while Frances, her mother, and her cousin Ben continued their tour of Italy. But in Rome, Emma contracted malaria, and by the time they got to Genoa, she could barely function. The fever and debilitating chills confined her to bed for the next six weeks, convalescing in Naples while Frances and Ben walked the city's ancient cobbled streets and visited its landmarks. They were joined by another young American socialite, Jennie Davis, the daughter of Henry Gassaway Davis, a self-made railroad tycoon recently retired after twelve years as the United States senator from West Virginia. Naturally, Jennie was completely plugged into Washington society, and when she and Frances had really gotten to know each other, she boldly asked Frances whether it was true that she and President Cleveland were thinking about an engagement. Frances shrugged it off, saying "Those foolish newspaper stories." But Jennie didn't buy it. "Well, then," she said, "will you answer this question: If you do marry the president, will you promise to honeymoon near me at Deer Park?" Deer Park was a resort town in Western Maryland where Jenny's father had built a beautiful summer cottage near the world-famous boiling springs. Frances skirted the cunning trap. "Yes, if anything of that kind ever occurs, I will go to Deer Park."

Jenny returned to America while the Folsom women, Emma having recovered from her bout with malaria, and Ben moved on to Paris. Frances planned to shop for her trousseau there, and Dan Lamont had arranged to have the American consul from Antwerp and his wife meet up with the Folsoms to lend a hand. John Steuart made the perfect guide; he was not only an experienced public servant but also a well-regarded antiquarian with excellent taste.

Back in Berlin, Kate Willard reflected on the Grover Cleveland situation and put her thoughts in a letter, which reached Frances at her Paris hotel.

"I should have begged you wildly never, never to marry Mr. Cleveland," Kate told her friend. Frances deserved "another life and love"—anyone but Grover Cleveland. Kate was so sure of her ground, she put their friendship on the line: "I don't know *what*, only not this."

Frances then made another blunder. In Buffalo, New York, Cora Townsend, the mother of Frances's former fiancé Charles Townsend, was having breakfast with her family, including young Charles, now an ordained Presbyterian minister and married, when Cora announced that she had received a letter from Frances Folsom. Charles bore Frances no hard feelings, and Frances adored the Townsends, especially Mrs. Townsend. As it was a family custom so that one and all could enjoy the latest news from the people they knew, everyone urged Cora Townsend to read the letter out loud. The last time Charles had had a letter from Frances, the ring he had placed on her finger asking for her hand in marriage had fallen out of the envelope.

Mrs. Townsend read from Frances's latest that she was in Paris with her mother on the final leg of their European adventure and having a grand time, although these last few weeks had been a little rough because Emma Folsom had malarial fever, and now Frances was afflicted with a case of shingles and in a state of complete "misery." She would be coming home in late May. And by the way, she was getting married to President Cleveland, but Mrs. Townsend had to promise not to breathe a word to anyone. All this had flooded out before Cora had grasped the fact that she was being let in on a fabulous secret. Now the secret was out, and everyone at the table sat dumbfounded as Mrs. Townsend finished reading: "I wish all you dear girls could have such a devoted sweetheart as I have. Grover Cleveland is the finest man in the world."

Not long thereafter, Cora Townsend was in Troy, New York, visiting her daughter, who was married to George Wellington, an up-and-coming assistant United States attorney. She showed her daughter and son-in-law Frances's letter, and in no time, the news spread through Troy. Pretty soon, a reporter from the *New York Sun* came knocking on their door, and George Wellington confirmed that he had read Frances's letter, and "there was not the slightest doubt but that it was genuine." From what he had gathered, Wellington said, the wedding "would be of the most quiet character possible."

Meanwhile, Cleveland thought it was time for him to let his sister Mary Hoyt in on his wedding plans. He wrote,

> I expect to be married pretty early in June—very soon after Frank returns. I think the quicker it can be done the better and she seems to think so too. . . . I want my marriage to be a quiet one and am determined that the American Sovereigns [Cleveland's acid expression for newspaper reporters] shall not interfere with a thing so purely personal to me. . . . I have thought of having no one but the family, hers and mine, present at the ceremony. Hers is not large. Her mother has two sisters and two brothers and her mother. Then I have thought that it might be well to have the Cabinet people at the ceremony. They have been so devoted to me and on all occasions that it seems almost as though they should be with me there.

"I have my heart set on making Frank a sensible, domestic American wife," Cleveland wrote Mary. His main concern was preserving Frances's sweet nature, he said, and he would be very displeased to hear her referred to as First Lady because it might give her "notions." "But I think she is pretty level-headed."

Cleveland ended his letter by asking Mary to "think of all these things and let me know how they strike you." He may have been a control freak who stewed over the most inconsequential details of the wedding, but he was sensible enough to realize that he needed a woman's perspective.

Three weeks later, Cleveland settled on a wedding date, writing Mary, "It looks as if Frank would reach New York about the 28th of May, stay there a few days, and then come here and be married the next day or the day of her arrival—say the 2d or 3d of June. Have the ceremony at 7 o'clock, with no one present but the two families; have a dinner immediately after the ceremony."

As matrimonial rumors swept the nation, Cleveland grew incensed over how the newspapers were intimating that Frances had found a father figure in Grover Cleveland, a man to replace her father who had fallen. And the president must have squirmed when he read the analysis of a socialite quoted in the *Washington Post* who claimed to have inside knowledge of the romance:

"To him she was nothing but a child; he watched her develop and . . . become the beautiful woman she is, and yet only in a dim, unconscious way realized that the little thing whom he had at one time carried in his arms was now a woman, with a woman's heart and a woman's love."

Once again, reporters were looking into his personal affairs, except now, his fiancée's had become the target of relentless snooping. Nothing outrageous was uncovered—Frances was only twenty-one and had an unblemished history. But from Cleveland's point of view, the reporting was unbearably intrusive—a repeat of the Maria Halpin scandal. One profile he found exceptionally impertinent claimed that during recess in high school, Frances enjoyed the company of boys more than girls. And at Wells College, Frances had to be "admonished" about the "perfidious" nature of young men who had only one thing on their minds. Her failed engagement to Charles Townsend also came under scrutiny. Cleveland referred to newsmen sniffing around Buffalo as a "dirty gang" and said he loathed them all.

"I have changed my ideas entirely in regard to the wedding," he informed Mary. "I am decidedly of the opinion now that the affair should be more quiet even than at first contemplated." A grand wedding was not going to happen, Cleveland said, because he didn't "care to gratify" the newspapers.

"I am very indignant at the way Frank has been treated and mean to give the 'gang' as little chance at us hereafter as possible."

At around four o'clock, a cluster of correspondents were strolling up to the White House when President Cleveland's low-hung Victorian coach came trotting by. There sat the president, wearing a black silk hat, with Lamont next to him, off on their regular afternoon jaunt around Washington. The correspondents doffed their hats, and Cleveland lifted his in acknowledgment. No newsman dared ask whether the reports of his engagement to Miss Folsom were true. To do so would have risked banishment from the White House, where access meant everything. Reported the *New York Times*, "No one here seemed to think there was any ground of possibility for such a match." Miss Folsom, said the *Times*, was a "mere schoolgirl." The *Washington*

Post also expressed incredulity. It quoted a Buffalo gentleman as saying that Cleveland was "such a stickler for propriety," there was not a chance in the world he would marry his former ward that he had helped raise from girlhood.

Other publications were still speculating on a matchup with Annie Van Vechten or Emma Folsom ("a handsome matron with a gentle, amiable countenance"). Congressman John Weber, who had lost the race for sheriff when he ran against Cleveland in 1870, had this to say: "I have no reason to believe that Mr. Cleveland is about to be married, but if it should happen, then I say, God bless them both!"

Cleveland could have done without the public support of Frances's uncle, H. F. Harmon, a Boston flour dealer, who said Cleveland's "acquaintance with the lady began when she was hardly knee high. She used to climb up on his knee and call him 'Uncle Cleve.' Mr. Cleveland was very fond of her as a child."

When one reporter had the temerity to corner Lamont and straight-out ask him about Frances Folsom, the president's secretary responded with a voice that oozed disdain, "What is the matter with that story? Isn't that sensation good enough for a week's run at least? I'd keep it going for a while." Was it a denial or sarcasm or confirmation? No one could tell. Lamont bristled when another reporter wondered how President Cleveland could consider marrying Frances Folsom. Wasn't she just a schoolgirl?

"Miss Folsom is considerably more than a schoolgirl, I can assure you," he growled.

In Paris, Frances carried on with her shopping spree. She had to be fitted for outfits for travel, balls, dinners, walking excursions, and of course the most important event of all, her wedding. For this, she settled on a simple ivory satin gown with a long train and a bridal veil nearly seven yards in length that was to be worn high on the head and fall gracefully over the train. Frances was also getting a taste of what was awaiting her back home. Reporters from America and the European newspapers were staking out her hotel and following her everywhere, and Ben Folsom found himself running interference. Before he became a lawyer, Ben had worked as a cub reporter for the *New York World,* but nothing in his experience as a journalist had prepared him for this blitz of attention. It galled him to read that President Cleveland had paid for the Folsoms' European tour, and he called these reports "rubbish and nonsense."

The time came to commence the long voyage home. The itinerary called for Frances, Emma, and Ben to sail the English Channel and make their way across England to the port city of Liverpool where they had booked passage on the transatlantic ship *Servia.* But at the last minute they rerouted to Belgium and booked passage on the Red Star Line's *SS Noordland* out of Antwerp. Six Saratoga trunks went with them while eleven more, filled with Frances's trousseau, continued on to the *Servia.*

The *Noordland* was set to sail at 11:00 AM on May 15, a raw and rainy day. Just before the clock struck ten, two carriages swung around the crooked streets of Antwerp and came to a stop in front of the great steamship. Out stepped a statuesque beauty wearing a straw hat. It was the American princess Frances Folsom. She strode up the gangplank followed by her mother, her cousin Ben, and a dachshund named Miss Vollopoo that Ben had purchased from a kennel in Brussels. A team of porters and stewards trailed the party, bearing their luggage. The local manager of the Red Star Line was there to make certain that all the needs of the First Lady-in-waiting were taken care of. Precisely at eleven, Frances and her companions stood on deck as the lines were cast off and the *Noordland* moved away from the dock and steamed up the Scheldt River to the North Sea and homeward.

The *Noordland* was a four-mast vessel with one funnel and accommodations for sixty-three passengers in first class, fifty-six passengers in second, and five hundred in steerage. Frances and Emma were assigned cabin no. 20, the bridal chamber. Mother and daughter suffered seasickness during the first day of the crossing, but when the waves settled, Frances was finally able to enjoy the passage. All eyes were fixed on her when she strode into the dining hall, and she and her party were seated at the captain's table. How the food flowed! Eight courses at breakfast and twelve at dinner. Frances passed the days taking pleasurable turns on the deck, sometimes walking the dachshund, or on the lounge chair wrapped in layers of rugs to keep warm. Wearing either a feathered bonnet or a merry polo cap, "She possesses no airs; she is remarkably humble," a fellow passenger later reported.

On Monday, May 24, Frances and the other passengers awoke to a frigid day, and she asked Captain Nickels how it could be so cold that time of year. The *Noordland*, Nickels explained, was in northern waters, off the coast of Newfoundland, and he in fact had to be alert for icebergs that were too close for comfort. On Tuesday, the weather was warmed by the Gulf Stream, and Frances occupied herself writing a short story for the ship's newspaper, the *North Atlantic Spray*. When the story, "Little Moll," was read to the passengers, she tried to keep a straight face, but everyone knew that she had written the yarn, which had as its main characters Moll, a well-behaved waif, and Bartley, a redheaded and "very ugly" newspaper reporter for a New York daily.

The *Noordland* was 280 miles from New York harbor, and Frances was on the bridge, having been invited by Captain Nickels, when the Red Star Line's pilot boat no. 22 pulled along the port side with news from America. Following the captain's directive, Frances signaled the engine room to come to a full stop, and when the ship came to a standstill, a crewman from the pilot boat climbed on board with a bundle of newspapers. Then Frances, with a gentle nod from Nickels, gave the signal for the engineer to fire up the engines.

When the captain got a chance to read the papers, he called Ben Folsom to his cabin to tell him some distressing news: Colonel John Folsom was dead. According to the accounts, Frances's grandfather had passed away on May 20 at the age of seventy-three on his two-hundred-acre farm in Folsomdale, the hamlet in Wyoming County, New York, that had been named for him. Folsom had been a colonel in the New York State militia and had died a wealthy man, with a reputed net worth of nearly half a million dollars from interests in milling, trading, farming, and the mining of potash. He also owned real estate in Omaha. Everyone in the family was aware that Frances had been the colonel's favorite of his five grandchildren. Ben decided to keep Colonel Folsom's death from Frances and Emma for the time being, and the next day, when the *Noordland* dropped anchor off Sandy Hook, New Jersey, Ben finally informed the

Folsom ladies of Colonel Folsom's death. Predictably, they took it hard, but after the immediate shock wore off, there were practical matters to think through. One plan under consideration had been for the wedding to take place on Colonel Folsom's farm, but obviously that was now out of the question.

Now that the ship had reached port, as Frances wondered what would happen next, the United States revenue cutter *William E. Chandler* came alongside, with Dan Lamont on board.

Ben seized Lamont's hand. "Why, old man, how are you?" Then he led the president's emissary to the stateroom occupied by Frances and Emma. The Folsoms were given the full VIP treatment. Frances bid a quick farewell to all her *Noordland* friends and hurried down the gangplank. Miss Vollopoo, the dachshund, was left behind with the ship's butcher, who promised to take care of her and keep her well fed until arrangements could be made to reunite her with the Folsoms.

As hundreds of Frances's fellow passengers watched from the deck, the cutter, after some puffing and blowing, pushed off from the *Noordland* with Frances and her party on board and steamed to the U.S. Custom House on the tip of Manhattan for processing. They were stunned when an inspector named J. B. Haynes insisted that all their bags and trunks be subjected to routine examination. He dug his hands through everything, looking for dutiable items, and only then did he permit the Folsoms to pass through. When the Custom House superintendent learned of the episode, he was so embarrassed that he fired Haynes two weeks later on grounds of "offensive partisanship." Apparently, the inspector was a die-hard Republican.

Under cloak of darkness, at two in the morning, Lamont spirited Frances, Emma, and Ben to the Gilsey House hotel at 29th and Broadway where they checked into a four-bedroom suite. Lamont could not let them rest without first resolving the issue of the time and location of the wedding. Frances said she believed her grandfather would not want his death to stand in the way of her happiness. Lamont communicated to her the president's reluctance to be married in a hotel, and his objection to a church wedding. That left the White House. Frances concurred that the wedding should take place "as soon as possible," and the following Wednesday was deemed the earliest practical date. It would be in the Blue Room, the most intimate parlor in the White House. So it was settled. Lamont telegraphed an anxious President Cleveland:

ARRIVED SAFE. ALL IN GOOD HANDS.

17

DEATH OF A NEWSPAPER

THERE WAS NOT a moment to lose. At 3:00 AM, Lamont boarded a train for the nation's capital, and when he arrived in Washington, he went directly to the White House where he briefed the president on his mission. Only then did Cleveland learn the particulars of his own wedding. A White House announcement that President Cleveland would marry Frances Folsom was issued at 8:00 PM. At last it was official. If Cleveland feared he'd come under attack for robbing the cradle, he needn't have worried. Not a single member of Congress raised his voice in public opposition to the marriage; as one after another rose to offer congratulations, Speaker of the House John G. Carlisle declared the discussion closed with the words: "The chair hears no objection." Even the Republican opposition took pleasure at the prospect of a White House wedding. There had been nine previous weddings within the walls of the White House, but never before of a president. (John Tyler, the tenth president, was a widower when he married Julia Gardiner in New York City, in 1844.)

After getting a few hours' sleep that first night at the Gilsey House, Frances and Emma awoke and went to pay a courtesy call on Rose Cleveland, who was in New York, doing what she could to help out. When they returned to Gilsey House, New York City Mayor William Grace came to pay his respects. So did three friends from Wells College whom Frances hadn't seen in a year since graduation. Ben had to admit that his cousin wasn't "quite herself yet." The ocean voyage, her grandfather's death, the rushed wedding, and all the attending "racket" had understandably left her "a little nervous." Later, a huge bouquet from the White House conservatory, delivered by night train, cheered her up.

On May 30, 1886, President Cleveland left Washington on the 4:15 PM train bound for New York and the Decoration Day parades. This year, Decoration Day had taken on special meaning because in the intervening year, three great Union generals had died—Grant, McClellan, and Hancock. The holiday was also fraught with political complications. It was supposed to be a day of remembrance for those who had fallen during the Civil War, but Southerners did not recognize Decoration Day; they honored their dead in other ways, on other dates.

Cleveland spent the night in New York at the mansion of his secretary of the navy, William C. Whitney, and the next morning, after a 7:00 AM breakfast, he stepped out in his frock coat, buttoned up to the chin, and a glossy silk hat to the hurrahs of an enormous crowd that had gathered at 5th Avenue and 57th Street to congratulate the groom-to-be. There was a healthy color to his cheeks and a merry twinkle in his eyes when, seeming surprised at the hearty reception, he lifted his hat and bowed before the cheering multitude. Then the president boarded a handsome carriage that had come to convey him to the Decoration Day parade route. At the same time, another carriage was picking up Frances at the Gilsey House to take her to the same location—the Fifth Avenue Hotel on 23rd Street. She was shown to a second-floor room where she joined the wives of several of Cleveland's cabinet officers who had come to New York to observe the parade. Frances wore a becoming grey suit tailored very high to the neck. In her hands, she held the bouquet of flowers Cleveland had sent her. The wives made way for her, and she positioned herself on the window ledge that afforded the best view of the marching soldiers. As she looked down at a sea of high hats and waving handkerchiefs, right below her she could make out the portly figure of President Cleveland. Next to him on the grandstand were the men he held in the highest esteem: Dan Lamont, Secretary Whitney, the secretary of the interior, the postmaster general—and Horatio King, his political ally whose defamation of Maria Halpin during the presidential campaign of 1884 had done so much to sully her good name and rescue the Cleveland candidacy from defeat. A coincidence that did not escape Cleveland's attention was that the Fifth Avenue Hotel where he now stood was the scene of the infamous "Rum, Romanism, and Rebellion" misstep that had wrecked Blaine's candidacy in its final days and helped ensure Cleveland's victory.

As the veterans of the Civil War marched by, the president doffed his hat when each regiment passed before him, dipping its colors. Cleveland kept his right hand in the breast of his coat as Frances heartily applauded with gloved hands. Everyone seemed to be watching her. It was quite a spectacle—commemoration of the fallen giving way to admiration of the fine figure of Frances Folsom, perched on that second-floor window ledge.

"Long live President Cleveland and his bride!" toasted the crowd. Three loud hip-hip hoorays were offered to "our bridegroom president." When the Twenty-second Regiment passed, the band ceased their marching music and broke into Mendelssohn's "Wedding March." Cleveland glowed with a "warmth" he had never felt before in public. In all, with the various parades, on this day alone the president would be seen by a half million people.

Frances did not move from her place on the ledge for a moment, and only after the entire procession had passed by did the president look up. Frances acknowledged him with a coquettish little wave of her dainty handkerchief and he, in turn, doffed his hat to her. That fleeting encounter was the first time they had seen each other in fourteen months. Modesty required that they not be seen together in public. Cleveland was careful to observe all the proprieties of Victorian courtship; his engagement to his former ward was already fraught with worry, and the slightest breach in etiquette now could lead to embarrassing questions. Later that day, at 3:30 PM, Cleveland met his betrothed face-to-face at Gilsey House, where they could greet each other with a warm embrace. That evening, they dined with Emma Folsom, Ben Folsom, and the Lamonts.

The matter of the honeymoon had been put on the back burner, but now Frances showed Cleveland a letter she had received that day from Jennie Davis, the daughter of the former U.S. senator from West Virginia who had befriended her in Italy. Jennie had written to remind Frances of her promise to honeymoon in Deer Park, Maryland, should she ever marry President Cleveland. That was good enough for Cleveland. Deer Park it would be. It just so happened that the trout fishing in Deer Creek was excellent.

At eleven o'clock, Cleveland took his leave. He had a train to catch back to Washington. He was getting married in just fourteen hours.

The next morning, Frances did not get up until ten. She had a late breakfast with her mother in a private parlor at the Gilsey House and caught up with her correspondence. When it was time to leave for Washington, the full concierge services of the hotel were put at her disposal. Eleven Saratoga trunks stenciled with the name Folsom were piled onto a wagon for the trip while the other trunks were sent off to 394 Main Street in Buffalo where her mother lived. There were so many hatboxes, it was difficult to gather them all. Deluxe accommodations welcomed them at every step. The president of the railroad had made available his personal drawing-room car, now hitched to the rear of a four-car train. Not taking any chances, the railroad's most dependable engineer was put at the controls. The train lumbered out of the station at nine twenty that night, and at five twenty the next morning, Frances, Emma, and Ben (wearing a foppish white derby) were in Washington. Lamont was there to greet them and escorted them all to the White House where, in a gentle rain, Frances bounded up the steps and crossed the grand threshold of the presidential mansion like a "radiant vision of young springtime."

She was shown to the south room where she dressed for her wedding before Dolly Madison's mirror.

Cleveland was still focusing on every detail of the ceremony. He had personally written out the invitations: *"I am to be married Wednesday evening at seven o'clock at the White House to Miss Folsom. It will be a very quiet affair and I will be extremely gratified at your attendance on the occasion."* Lamont was a big help. Working with the conductor of the Marine Band, John Philip Souza, he timed out the exact number of steps Frances would have to take down the staircase to reach the correct position in the Blue Room at the climax of the "Wedding March." Sousa, the great composer of "Stars and Stripes Forever," was also ordered to submit his musical selections for the president's approval. When Cleveland saw that the title of one number was the quartet, "The Student of Love," a Sousa standard, he flinched and ordered Sousa to make a change. "Tell Sousa he can play that quartet, but he had better omit the name of it," he told Lamont, concerned that the spicy title might fan any lurking flames of derision. Rather than censure his own work, Sousa decided to simply omit "The Student of Love" from the evening's performance.

The time for the wedding was now at hand, and in her last hours as First Lady, Rose was to receive every guest as they made their way into the Blue Room. Cleveland's brother William and his sister Mary were also there, and from Buffalo, just two old friends had been invited, Wilson Bissell and the lawyer Sherman S. Rogers. All the members of the cabinet came with their spouses, with the exception of the curmudgeonly attorney general, Augustus Hill Garland, who detested all social functions and refused to attend any gathering that required him to wear a dress suit. Ben Folsom was there of course, and Dan Lamont and his wife. Rose had invited a Miss Nelson who, now that Annie Van Vechten was out of the picture, was the First Lady's steady companion. In all, there were just twenty-eight guests.

At seven fifteen, a hush fell over the gathering. Sousa lifted his baton, and the scarlet-and-gold bedecked members of the Marine Band launched into the "Wedding March." With Frances, President Cleveland came down the staircase—not only the groom but also the father figure giving the bride away. He wore a fitted black broadcloth suit. A low-cut vest displayed a wide expanse of dress shirt closed by three flat white studs. His shoes were patent leather. On his left hand he wore a white kid glove, so-called because it was made from young goat leather. In his right hand he held the other glove. There was no best man or maid of honor.

Sousa kept his eye on the couple, and when Cleveland and Frances reached the center of the Blue Room, the Reverend Byron Sunderland stepped forward to greet them. The president nodded, and at the signal Sousa directed the band to cease playing. There was a moment of silent prayer, then Sunderland, speaking resolutely, said, "If you desire to be united in marriage, you will signify the same by joining your right hands." With his ungloved hand, Cleveland took his bride's pretty little hand in his own.

"Grover, do you take this woman whom you hold by the hand to be your lawful wedded wife, to live together after God's ordinance in the holy estate of wedlock? Do you promise to love her, cherish, comfort, and keep her in sickness and in health, in joy and in sorrow, and forsaking all others, keep you only unto her so long as you both shall live?"

"I do," said the president.

Sunderland recited the same oath to Frances, who responded in a low but clear voice, "I do."

Sunderland pronounced them husband and wife. Then William Cleveland, who had been standing behind and to the left of Sunderland, came forward to offer a benediction for life everlasting. With those tender words, Emma Folsom was the first to kiss her daughter on the cheek, the moment both sweet and sad for Emma. Rose and Mary offered their congratulations, Rose with tears in her eyes. Ben Folsom was next, followed by Secretary of the Treasury Daniel Manning, first among equals, and then the other members of Cleveland's cabinet and their wives. Frances offered kisses to just the wives. Sousa's band struck up a march, and President and the new Mrs. Cleveland led the way into the East Room where the guests spent just a few moments in conversation before Cleveland, escorting his wife, ushered everyone into the family dining room. At the supper table, the newlyweds stood in front of a huge wedding cake. Frances took a pearl-handled knife and buried it into the rich cake. It was the signal for the banquet to begin. Champagne glasses were raised to the bride's health. Cleveland quaffed his drink; Frances, a teetotaler, put her lips to her glass for just a taste. Rose had made sure a bottle of Appollinaris, sparkling water from Germany, would be at her sister-in-law's place setting, and a grateful Frances emptied an entire glass. In the overheated room, the water, chilled by chunks of ice, was deliciously refreshing. At the plate of each guest was a wedding favor—a box of bonbons. After a simple meal of spring chicken and terrapin, each guest was given another outstanding souvenir: a dainty satin box containing a slice of wedding cake wrapped in silver foil and placed inside a layer of lace. A small card bore the autographs of the bride and groom. On the box, the date had been artistically painted, *June 2, 1886.*

Early in the evening, President and Mrs. Cleveland took their leave and went upstairs to the second floor. Cleveland disappeared into his bedroom while Frances and her attendants—her mother and Rose Cleveland—followed her into her sitting room. All the guests remained seated. When Cleveland emerged, he had changed into a black Prince Albert frockcoat. Then Frances came out. Standing there on the landing for everyone to see, she had changed into a deep gray traveling dress and double-breasted waistcoat decorated with rows of steel buttons. A magnificent hat lined with velvet and trimmed with picot ribbon and ostrich feathers completed the ensemble. The Clevelands descended the staircase, and all the guests gathered around to bid the couple farewell and good wishes. Emma and Frances said a tearful adieu. Cleveland gently tugged at his bride, saying they were behind schedule. Rose dabbed at a burst of tears that had flooded her eyes as she bid her brother good-bye. The First Couple climbed into a closed carriage that awaited them outside the south balcony, and the horses started off in a shower of rice and old slippers as the guests waved, shouting, "God speed!"

Everyone lingered for a moment on the balcony and watched the carriage wind its way through the White House grounds without escort then take an unused road up 17th Street to outwit the small army of newspaper reporters who were massed at the southwest entrance in hired cabs, ready to give chase.

Cleveland and his bride were off to Deer Park, Maryland.

The honeymoon had begun.

Maria Halpin also got married, in the year following President Cleveland's White House wedding. She became a bride for the second time, and her choice of a groom was truly shocking: It was her uncle-in-law, James Albert Seacord, the carpenter in whose house Maria had sought sanctuary after she was run out of Buffalo. Seacord, who was sixty-nine when he married Maria, walked with a stoop and was so frail he could no longer ply his trade. Their twenty-three-year age gap eerily echoed that of Cleveland and Frances. Whether it was true love for Maria or the act of a woman who had nowhere else to go, no one can say. She and Seacord married quietly and moved into a yellow frame cottage on Hudson Street in New Rochelle.

There had been another milestone worthy of attention—not a marriage, but the demise of a newspaper.

On the afternoon of August 17, 1885, the staff of the *Buffalo Evening Telegraph* was shocked to see Ed Butler, the owner of the rival *Evening News*, in the newsroom. Butler appeared there with his business manager, his brother J. Ambrose Butler. Everyone gathered around.

"Gentlemen," Ed Butler said, "I have purchased the *Telegraph*, and after today, it will be issued from the office of the *News*."

What followed was the wholesale slaughter of the *Evening Telegraph* staff. Allen Bigelow, the editor, was asked to resign. So were the state editor and the paper's three top reporters. John Cresswell, the editor responsible for "A Terrible Tale," had resigned four weeks earlier after the Scripps brothers privately informed him that they were putting the *Evening Telegraph* on the market. Negotiations had otherwise been conducted in the strictest secrecy, and Cresswell's brother, Harry, a reporter on the *Telegraph*'s staff, was now also informed that his services were no longer required. Everyone pulled together and put out one final edition. The lead story was the publication's own obituary.

And so the *Evening Telegraph* ceased to exist. Had the 1884 election gone the other way, it would have gone down in history as the gutsy little newspaper whose exposé had brought about Cleveland's defeat and ensured Republican rule for another four years. But it's greatest scoop, "A Terrible Tale," became its undoing. Advertisers had been running away from the newspaper. No Buffalo business could afford to be associated with a newspaper that topped the president's enemies list. Circulation had stagnated at ten thousand, and the *Telegraph* was $70,000 in the hole. Now it had been killed off by Grover Cleveland's chum, Ed Butler. The sale was absolute and unconditional. It included everything in the building, even the cast metal type-face and the four-cylinder rotary press. The subscription list was folded into the *Evening News*.

The first edition of the consolidated newspaper rolled off the presses on August 18, 1885.

Four weeks after her brother's marriage to Frances Folsom, Rose Cleveland moved out of the White House. Her era as First Lady had lasted fourteen months. She also left Washington—"simply because her heart was not there." She was when she departed as she had been when arrived—an enigma. Rose returned to Holland Patent and, in July, published her first novel, a romance titled *The Long Run*. The central character, Emeline Longworth, seemed to be drawn from the life of Frances Folsom. Emeline was a rich and "haughty beauty" from Philadelphia society who was being courted by a priggish theological student, Rufus Grosheck— shades of Charles Townsend? The book received solid reviews, and not long after, Rose published a collection of essays, *George Eliot's Poetry and Other Studies*, in which intriguingly, one of the essays dealt with the life of Joan of Arc. So Rose was reflecting on two great sexually ambiguous historical figures: George Eliot, the pen name of the English novelist Mary Anne Evans; and Joan of Arc, who dressed as a man to conceal her true sex.

The Cleveland family home in Holland Patent was a humble little cottage, but befitting her new social status, Rose now christened it with a whimsical name, the Weeds. One day in late September 1886, she smelled a whiff of smoke coming from the fireplace and went to sleep thinking that the chimney needed cleaning. At five in the morning, she woke up and realized that her house was on fire. She ran out and sounded the alarm. Volunteers saved the Weeds from total destruction, but it was considerably damaged by smoke and water. It was a double blow because Rose had spent the previous three months renovating the Weeds to make it a proper residence. That all around her lay the ashes of her home was a depressing situation.

Around this time, Rose was being recruited to serve as editor of the monthly magazine *Literary Life*. The publisher of *Literary Life* was Abram P. T. Elder, a colorful Chicago businessman who saw in Rose a way to reap attention for his publication. Elder wrote her effusive letters, offering her the position.

"Your reception in Chicago would be the greatest literary and social event that has ever taken place in this country," he told her. Elder's overbearing language should have alerted Rose that something was amiss with this fellow, but she continued to negotiate the terms of the position.

Rose drove a hard bargain. She insisted on approving all advertisements and refused to allow her name to appear on the title page or the masthead. *Literary Life*, she informed Elder, should stand or fall on its merits and not her celebrity. Elder agreed to all her conditions, but he put his foot down when Rose sought to hire her twenty-five-year-old nephew—Reverend William Cleveland's boy—as her deputy editor. He found young Cleveland to be a "callow youth," so Rose backed off then finally signed a five-year contract at a good salary—$350 a month.

Rose and Elder butted heads from day one. When she was sent page proofs for her first issue, she banned all "quack" advertisements for wrinkle removers, beautifying elixirs, and patent medicines. Elder could not believe it; some of those ads ran a full page. He had granted her full control over the editorial content of *Literary Life*, but he had never imagined she would shrink his bottom line. "I am not publishing the magazine exclusively for the editor's benefit," he complained. Elder designed a new title page with the words "Edited by Ms. Cleveland" and sent it to Rose, hoping the classy illustration would appeal to her artistic sensibilities. By return mail came this tart response: "My name shall not appear—this is final." Then Elder had an inspired notion. He got the idea from seeing Frances Folsom Cleveland's image adorning so many storefront windows in Chicago. Elder hired an artist to sketch an engraving of Rose for the magazine's cover. Rose was appalled and again said no.

"The difference between us is this—I mean what I say—you do not," she wrote him.

It didn't help that Rose lived in an inaccessible village in the interior of New York State. They disagreed on everything, even the little things. Elder considered the Weeds a preposterous name for a residence. It vexed him to be addressing his correspondence to Rose Elizabeth Cleveland, The Weeds, Holland Patent, New York. He made the silly suggestion that perhaps she should consider changing the name.

"The Weeds it will remain," Rose responded.

Then Rose's attempts to commission works from the most famous writers in America sometimes backfired. In terms of popularity, the poet John Boyle O'Reilly was Longfellow's successor, and Rose suggested a fee of twenty dollars for him to write two thousand words. O'Reilly's blood boiled. He found her offer to be disgraceful and a "humiliation," even though a cent a word was the going rate for writers working for *Harper's Weekly* and *Frank Leslie's Illustrated*, two popular magazines of the era.

In November 1886, Elder went to Holland Patent to work things out. He rang the doorbell at The Weeds, but Rose instructed her maid to refuse him entry. Four months into the job, with both sides weary of the endless hostility, Rose and Elder parted company. Stirring things up right to the end, Elder asserted that Rose was on the verge of a physical and mental collapse.

"Ms. Cleveland has been in poor health and really unable to attend to the demands made upon her. Then her home at the Weeds was burned and that affected her in a depressing way."

He publicly questioned her competence in business and claimed her editorial leadership had plunged his once-profitable magazine into debt. Quoting Tennyson, Rose countered that

Elder's blatherings were half-truths, which were "the worst of lies." Rose came to believe that Elder had used her fame as a publicity stunt to bring attention to his magazine, and she was probably right. Five years later, the huckster publisher found himself in jail on mail fraud charges.

President and Mrs. Cleveland came to visit Rose to lift her spirits. The train from Washington rolled into the Utica station at five fifteen on the morning of July 12, 1887. The postmaster from Utica was an old acquaintance, and when Cleveland saw him at the station, he called out, "Hello!" Then the presidential car was uncoupled and switched to the Rome, Watertown and Ogdensburg railroad line. A special engine was at the ready to haul the presidential party twelve miles to Holland Patent. It was good to be home.

The president tucked a bundle under his arm, picked up a satchel, and the Clevelands got off at Holland Patent. The Weeds stood only a block from the station, and Cleveland led the way. Rose, looking plump and flushed, met them at the door and welcomed them in. After inspecting the damage from the fire and cleaning up after the long trip from Washington, President Cleveland took a drive with an old friend, Dr. Delos Crane, while Rose showed Frances around the village in her pretty one-horse carriage. At the reins, Rose proved herself to be an experienced horsewoman, in complete control of the spirited animal. Frances sat in the traverse seat, set back-to-back to Rose. Later in the day, everyone met up at the village cemetery where President Cleveland's parents were buried beneath a granite tombstone, and for the first time, Frances got to see the family monument to Cleveland's two brothers who had been lost at sea in 1872.

Rose had big news. She informed the president and her sister-in-law that she had found a new job in New York City, teaching history at Mrs. Sylvania Reed's School for Girls at 6 East 53rd Street, starting in September.

Mrs. Sylvania Reed was a Mayflower descendant; her father, Albert Gallup, had been a congressman from Albany. All of New York's elite sent their daughters to Mrs. Reed's school, and Rose had problems from the outset dealing with the "highbred" student body. She refused to allow the girls to see a production of Shakespeare's romance, *Cymbeline*, on grounds that the bedchamber scene in which a Roman soldier tempts Imogen to commit adultery was "utterly unfit for young girls."

Predictably, Rose also came into conflict with the obstinate Mrs. Reed, who had founded the fashionable school in 1864. The headmistress was already in her sixty-seventh year when she hired Rose for a salary of $100 a month, plus board and lodging. Rose, who absolutely believed she could run things better if she were in charge, made a move to take control of the school. She asked Mrs. Reed to sell it to her, proposing a small down payment and paying out the rest in yearly installments. To this, Mrs. Reed responded that her asking price stood at $200,000 in cash up front. It was a far-fetched amount, well beyond Rose's reach. That settled things. She resigned after a year.

Once again, Rose was adrift. She considered a vacation in the south of France. Then she settled on Florida, where she would meet the love of her life.

18

THE TRIAL

F**RANCES FOLSOM CLEVELAND'S** time as the youngest First Lady in American history was brief but unforgettable. Her youth and exquisite beauty earned her the affection of an entire nation. Frances found her image adorning sewing machines, bars of soap, luggage, liver pills, and even tobacco products. Any association with the popular Mrs. Cleveland spiked sales. The commercialization of the First Lady infuriated President Cleveland. When he saw an advertisement featuring his wife's likeness in the *Albany Evening Journal,* Cleveland denounced it as "dirty and disreputable." Frankie Folsom Cleveland clubs sprang up across America, but the president considered the clubs a "perversion" and a waste of time—"a direct menace to the integrity of our homes."

The memory of the Maria Halpin scandal never ceased to loom. It was the story that would not die. Cleveland seemed to be eternally tainted by his past. Once again, he was facing a whispering campaign.

"The place is full of rumors about Mrs. Cleveland," wrote Sir Cecil Spring-Rice, a British diplomat stationed in Washington. According to the gossip, Sir Cecil was hearing Frances Cleveland had "fled" Washington because of the president's loutish behavior. Frances's maid, so the story went, had been hit on the head with a broomstick when she stepped between Frances and the president. Sir Cecil found the gossip mongering hard to believe. In his opinion, Cleveland was the victim of a political smear campaign.

In December 1887, accounts of domestic violence in the White House started to show up in print. Chauncey Depew, a Yale-educated lawyer who represented Cornelius Vanderbilt's railroad interests, went public with a story claiming that Frances had gone to the theater one night escorted by a dashing former congressman from Kentucky, Henry Watterson. Supposedly, President Cleveland simmered with jealousy, and when Frances returned to the White House, he went berserk—"called her wicked names and finally slapped her face." When Watterson was asked about the episode, he begged to differ. By his account, the president had been very gracious and even thanked Watterson for taking the First Lady out to the theater.

Five months later, the Reverend C. H. Pendleton, a Baptist minister from Worcester, Massachusetts, returned from Washington, where he had gone to attend the national Baptist convention, and delivered a shocking sermon. He had had heard stories about President Cleveland, he said, that his congregation needed to hear.

"Mrs. Cleveland had been forcibly abused by her husband," claimed Pendleton. What's more, the president's mother-in-law, Mrs. Folsom, had been "driven from the White House and had gone off to Europe to prevent a further scandal." Pendleton's sermon, published in the *Worcester Telegram*, went nationwide. Cleveland must have felt cursed. Once more, a Baptist clergyman was leading the charge, and this time, the accusation was that he was a wife beater.

Margaret Nicodemus, a factory worker from Worcester, wrote the First Lady, asking whether the stories were true. In the envelope, she enclosed Pendleton's sermon and an interview he had given the *Worcester Telegram*. On June 3, Frances sent the following stinging rebuke:

Dear Madam:

I can only say in answer to your letter that every statement made by the Rev. C. H. Pendleton in the interview which you send me is basely false, and I pity the man of his calling who has been made the tool to give circulation to such wicked and heartless lies.

I can wish the women of our country no better blessing than that their homes and their lives may be as happy, and that their husbands may be as kind, as attentive, considerate and affectionate as mine.

With Election Day 1888 just five months off, the last thing Cleveland needed was another reminder of Maria Halpin. Cleveland's proxies went on the attack. Pendleton found himself depicted as a clueless dandy, said to wear "stylish" layman's clothes. He was unmarried and "giddy." According to *The New York Times*, his "tongue is considerably longer than his judgment."

Pendleton got the message and quickly began to backpedal. "Of course, I don't believe these rumors and had no desire to circulate them," he declared. "I have only the most humble apology to make if I have innocently been the cause of doing the President and Mrs. Cleveland an injury." He said he had not voted for Cleveland in 1884 but would support him in 1888, but only as penance for having made a "grievous sin."

Grover Cleveland was renominated by acclamation at the Democratic National Convention in St. Louis. Frankie Cleveland Clubs held rallies across the United States to bring out the vote. The First Lady's popularity was certainly one of the president's great political assets. Cleveland's opponent was Indiana's Benjamin Harrison, the grandson of William Henry Harrison, the ninth president of the United States, who died in 1841 after serving just thirty-two days in office, the briefest presidency in history. Cleveland, with his wife and mother-in-law, waited for the results in the White House library. At midnight, Secretary of the Navy William Whitney came in with the returns.

"Well, it's all up," he told them.

It was a narrow defeat. As in 1884, the outcome hinged on New York, but this time, Cleveland's home state went for the Republican candidate. Cleveland won the national vote by 90,000, but was beaten in the Electoral College 233 to 168.

After getting a few hours sleep, Dan Lamont found the president at his desk, having just eaten lunch. Cleveland gave his aide a wan smile. He wondered how he had lost his home state.

Lamont frankly replied, "I do not know."

All Cleveland could do was laugh. He thought he had the answer: "It was mainly because the other party had the most votes." He advised Lamont not to take it personally. "One party won and the other party has lost—that is all there is to it." Lamont observed that the president "never looked more calm or self-possessed."

Frances said what she was required to say. "I am sorry for the president and, for his sake, wish it had been otherwise, but what cannot be helped must be met." As the First Lady and her husband pondered what to do next, Emma Folsom gave a candid interview, divulging for the first time intimacies about her daughter's married life, which had been the subject of so much speculation. Emma had for a spell lived at the White House, assisting Frances in her duties as First Lady, so she knew all about the marriage.

"The president had the greatest blessings in his young wife, and he is in his heart too happy to be long cast down by political fortune. Though older, considerably, than she, he does not permit her to realize it, and her affection for him is extreme." The marriage was sturdy, Emma said. Frances had found in Cleveland "the tenderness of a father with the devotion of a husband."

"Mrs. Cleveland looks up to her husband with the trust and confidence she felt as a child in him." It had to be obvious to anybody reading the interview that Cleveland's rejection of Emma in favor of her daughter was still galling.

As to the reports that Frances had been the victim of domestic violence, Emma had this to say: "The only comfort I find in the defeat of the president is that the public will have the opportunity to correct some misapprehensions entertained toward him and his wife. He is a peculiar man, but one of the noblest in the world."

Emma surprised Frances with the announcement that she would be marrying Henry Perrine, a distant cousin and genial widower from Buffalo with three grown children.

President Cleveland came to a decision: He and his wife would settle in Manhattan. Buffalo was not even in consideration. It was, Cleveland told William Vilas, his secretary of the interior, "the place I hate above all others." He still could not forgive his hometown. Frances supervised the move to New York. The White House attic was a "jungle of gifts" that had to be cleared out, and Cleveland sold off his team of seal brown horses. "I am now eagerly counting the days till March 4, when I shall be free," he told a confidante. Finally, the time came when Mr. and Mrs. Cleveland had to depart. It was the morning of Benjamin Harrison's inauguration, March 4, 1889. Frances was coming out of the family living quarters when she saw Jerry Smith, a White House steward. Smith stood as erect as a grenadier and held her handbag out for her.

"Now, Jerry," Frances told him, "I want you to take good care of all the furniture and ornaments in the house, and not let any of them get lost or broken, for I want to find everything just as it is now, when we come back again."

Smith was aghast. "Excuse me, Mis' Cleveland, but just when does you all expect to come back, please—so I can have everything ready, I mean."

"We're coming back just four years from today."

Frances and her husband moved into a four-story brownstone at 816 Madison Avenue near 68th Street, and Cleveland's faithful servant William Sinclair accompanied them as their butler. Cleveland became of counsel to the blue chip Manhattan law firm Bangs, Stetson, Tracy and McVeigh. Frances supervised the new house and raised funds for Wells College in her spare time, but she found readjustment to civilian life challenging.

Her days as the indulged First Lady, when White House stewards catered to her every whim, were over. Her mother offered zero sympathy.

"This will be an opportunity to see if you can run a household by yourself," Emma acidly informed her.

Emma had told Frances that her wedding ceremony to Henry Perrine would take place in June 1889, but in May came word that Emma and Perrine had gotten married in Jackson, Michigan. When Frances found out, she took off for Michigan to see the newlyweds. Cleveland chose to stay behind in Manhattan.

"Things are getting into a pretty tough condition when a man can't keep his mother-in-law in the traces," Cleveland said. He sounded bemused yet also offended.

Tension escalated between mother and daughter. "Why hasn't Lena sent my corsets," Emma wrote. Lena was Frances's maid. Emma scolded Frances for not writing enough; her new stepdaughter, Cornie, she tartly reminded Frances, "is *never* neglectful of me."

Even the little things got between them. Emma complained about the size of the coffee cups Frances had given her as a wedding gift. "They hold so little—only half of what an ordinary after dinner coffee cup holds . . . They are *very* pretty but not exactly practical." Emma wondered if Frances wouldn't mind if she exchanged the gift.

On the third anniversary of the Clevelands' marriage, Emma failed to send them her best wishes.

As Emma and Frances went on squabbling, Cleveland was plotting his political comeback.

Then everything was put on hold.

Cleveland's future hinged on the outcome of *Ball v. The New York Evening Post.*

Six years after the Reverend George Ball filed his libel lawsuit against the *New York Evening Post,* which had condemned him for his role in the Maria Halpin scandal, the case finally came to trial. The day was February 4, 1890, Justice Charles Daniels presiding. The Buffalo courtroom was packed. With so much at stake in the outcome of the trial, it was the hottest ticket in town. At the plaintiff's table sat Ball, now seventy-one, and next to him his lawyers, Adelbert Moot and Frank Ferguson.

Three men sat at the defense table. There was the defendant himself, the fifty-nine-year-old editor of the *New York Post* Edwin L. Godkin, and his two lawyers, John Milburn and Franklin Locke.

Ball and the *Post* may have been the named parties in the litigation, but no one had more on the line in *Ball v. The Evening Post* than Grover Cleveland. Having been defeated for reelection in 1888, he was contemplating another run for the presidency in 1892. Should he win, Cleveland would become the first American president to serve two nonconsecutive terms in the White House. If the jury found for Ball, Cleveland would in all probability be politically finished.

Jury selection took all morning—an unprecedented length of time for voir dire in a trial that did not involve a capital offense. So many challenges were raised that Moot and Milburn came close to exhausting the pool of potential jurors. Finally, just before noon, the last man was named, and the panel was sworn in.

Moot rose and presented his opening statement. Moot was thirty-six, with a reputation as a plain-speaking and unrelenting advocate for his clients, which may explain his readiness to take on the former president who still commanded so much influence over the Buffalo bar.

Moot began with a brief history of Grover Cleveland's whirlwind political career—his election as mayor, governor, and then while still a newcomer to the national political arena, his nomination as the Democratic candidate for president. George Ball had learned of "certain charges," the upshot of which was the publication in 1884 of "A Terrible Tale" in the *Buffalo Evening Telegraph*. Moot went to the plaintiff's table and stood over Ball. The *New York Post* had published wicked and malicious articles about his client, Moot told the jurors, written with the intent of destroying Ball as payback for his role in exposing the Maria Halpin scandal. He read from one of the *Post's* articles:

> The accounts of Mr. Ball, "the highly respected Baptist minister" who wrote the filthy and disingenuous letters which appeared in the Boston Journal about Governor Cleveland continue to grow worse. He appears indeed to be a sort of politico-clerical adventurer. He is not a Baptist minister at all, a leading Baptist minister in the City informs us, but a Free-will Baptist.
>
> He has wandered about a good deal, being various things by turn and nothing long. He once had a place in the Custom House, and has tried his hand at Journalism in this City, was once in Owensville, Indiana, from which place, the *Indianapolis Sentinel* says, "he had to depart hastily, owing to an 'insult to a Christian lady.'" In Buffalo, he seems to have been running a little independent

machine of his own, the services of which he has been offered for money to both parties indiscriminately, and not much money either, for he takes as little as $25.00 at a time. Moreover, he has as we are informed, a remarkable detective love of ferreting out low and disgusting scandals and mysteries.

This article was published on August 8, 1884.

Moot read to the jurors the next attack by the *Post*, published three days later. It accused Ball of concocting "extremely disgusting" stories about Cleveland and having a "passion for notoriety which seems to be his most powerful motive."

The last allegedly libelous article, Moot told the jurors, was published the next day under the headline, "The Rev. Mr. Ball and His Kind." It reported the results of the independent investigation by sixteen prominent citizens of Buffalo who had cleared Cleveland of wrongdoing in the Halpin matter. In this story, the *Post* called Ball and his supporters "guttersnipes," among other choice words.

What shall be said of the vampires, clerical and others, who have been exploring the haunts of infamy to find material for blackening private character and bringing sorrow to households in no way concerned in the present political campaign? It is the common characteristic of such rascals that they care no more for the feelings of innocent persons than a dynamiter who plants a bomb in the waiting-room of a railroad station thronged with women and children, in order to strike terror in the hearts of other people who are out of danger miles away.

They have exposed themselves as persons of depraved taste and imagination as well as liars by instinct. They have done all this without accomplishing the end they had in view, which was to hold Governor Cleveland up as a habitual profligate, a hardened criminal, a deliberate betrayer of women, and a monster of cruelty to the victims of his depravity.

Until the publication of these articles, Moot continued, no one had questioned Ball's standing as a "God-fearing Christian minister and gentleman." The articles, he said, had "wounded" Ball's reputation, "crippled" his work as a teacher and minister, and led to his "utter ruin."

Moot asked the jury to return with a verdict for Ball in the amount of $25,000 in damages.

Court was recessed for lunch. At two in the afternoon, the trial resumed. Moot called his first witness. It was Edwin Godkin.

The Irish-born Godkin had come to America in 1856 as a correspondent for the *London Daily News,* and in 1865, he founded *The Nation,* then as now a weekly magazine with a small but influential readership. In 1881, he sold *The Nation* to the *New York Post* and became the *Post's* editor-in-chief and an eloquent force in the mugwump political movement. Such was his renown, the reporters who worked for Godkin regarded him as a kind of "remote deity." On the occasion when he found himself riding in the elevator with a member of his staff at the *New York Post* building, which then stood at Broadway and Fulton, Godkin never spoke a word. Although he stood on "friendly footing" with his managing editors and the city editor, he could not recognize most of his reporters. His temper was as mighty as his pen. Once, when the great muckraker Lincoln

Steffens was a young journalist starting off at the *Post*, Godkin thought the front-page story Steffens was assigned to write, on the death of a music teacher, "smacked of sensationalism." Godkin fired him, and later grudgingly capitulated, but only after several editors had gone to bat for the talented young Steffens.

Moot asked Godkin about the circulation of the *Post*. Godkin said it reached about twenty thousand people daily. *The Nation*, which had reprinted several of the *Post's* articles about Ball, had a weekly circulation of nine thousand. Godkin acknowledged that he had personally written or edited all the articles regarding Ball. He said this without equivocation or discomfit. In point of fact, his authorship gave him pleasure. Surprisingly, after just a few minutes, Godkin was off the stand and back in his seat at the defendant's table.

That was all. Moot rose and announced that the defense rested. It had taken only one afternoon to present the evidence. Moot had not even called Ball to the stand. His strategy had been daringly straightforward: The articles published in the *Post* and *The Nation* spoke for themselves. No further evidence of libel was necessary.

John Milbank's partner, Franklin Locke, gave the opening statement for the defense. Locke was a forty-seven-year-old graduate of Hamilton College. Such was his knowledge of the law that it was said he could dictate an entire corporate charter without a reference book. Locke was also a voracious reader. Gibbon's six-volume *History of the Decline and Fall of the Roman Empire* was his favorite work.

Locke stood before the jury, with his noble forehead crowned with a thicket of white hair, looking like an Old Testament prophet. Addressing the panel, he recalled the time of the presidential election of 1884, six years before. Until that political campaign, Locke said, "Not one word had been spoken against [Cleveland's] character." The man was a "saint upon this earth." Then came the day when George Ball stepped onto the political stage—"this crank," as Locke contemptuously called him.

Locke produced the letter Ball had written to the *Boston Journal* about the Beaver Island Club and the circumstances surrounding the death of Oscar Folsom in 1875. In it, Ball had claimed that on the night Folsom had been killed, he and Cleveland had been "beastly drunk" on their return from the Beaver Island Club—which Ball called a "place of drunkenness and lust."

Locke looked at the jurors. "The Beaver Island Clubhouse was just as pure and reputable a place as Dr. Ball's church!"

Locke closed by asking the jurors to find in favor of the *Post* and against Ball. A message had to be sent. Ball should stick to the business of education and religion. "Tell him to keep out of politics, for which he is evidently unfitted."

With that, Locke was finished. It was now John Milburn's turn to take over the defense. Milburn called his first witness. It was George Ball.

Ball took the witness chair and faced the well of the courtroom. He looked vexed and weary. His rimless glasses were planted on the bridge of a long sharp nose, and his face was framed in a heavy beard of iron grey. His upper lip was clean-shaven, and the top of his head was entirely bald.

Milburn got right to it. He showed Ball the *Boston Journal* letter. Ball owned up to the fact that he had been in error; Cleveland had not been with Folsom the night of the buggy collision. Milburn demanded to know where he had heard the story that Cleveland had been drunk.

Just then the clock struck five. Court was adjourned for the day. Ball would be back on the stand the next day.

On the second day of George Ball's testimony, the courtroom was filled with the city's leading clergymen, there in force to show their support for their beleaguered colleague. Ball braced himself. He was going up against Buffalo's leading lawyer, a master at courtroom tactics and the technique of cross-examination.

People were surprised when John Milburn spoke because he had a cultivated British accent. He was born in England and had come to America when he was eighteen, settling in Batavia, not far from Buffalo. Like Grover Cleveland, he learned the law by clerking and developed a reputation as a cautious and able litigator. During the 1884 campaign, he was one of Cleveland's key aides, who had advised the candidate to hang tough when the Maria Halpin scandal erupted.

Milburn picked up with Ball's damaging admission that he had been in error when he accused Grover Cleveland of having been present when Oscar Folsom broke his neck.

"I want to ask how you came to learn that the Beaver Island Clubhouse was a place of drunkenness and lust?"

"I do not know. I did not understand that there was a club. That is, I did not know the nature of the organization."

Milburn kept at it. He was intense and very persistent. He wanted to know how Ball had come to characterize the Beaver Island Club as a disreputable place when "respectable citizens were in the habit of taking their wives and children there."

Ball finally admitted that he got the information about the goings-on at Beaver Island from Dr. Alexander T. Bull, a physician who served as house doctor at the Iroquois Hotel. Dr. George

W. Lewis had also been present during the conversation, which was held in Alexander Bull's medical office at the Iroquois.

What about the publication of "A Terrible Tale" in the *Evening Telegraph*?

Ball admitted that he had turned over the findings of his investigation regarding Grover Cleveland to the *Evening Telegraph*.

"Did you give facts for it?" he asked.

"Yes, sir."

"To whom?"

"To Mr. Cresswell."

"Did you visit him?"

"No, sir, he came to see me. I gave him the points, and he wrote the article. He made notes of what I said. But I did not write it."

"Did you not recommend people to read it?"

"Yes, sir."

Was it not a fact, Milburn asked Ball, that he had gone to Vine Alley "hunting up" the janitress who used to work for Cleveland? The question caused a stir in the courtroom. Everyone knew that Vine Alley was a notorious neighborhood where vice and wickedness were more or less condoned by authorities. The question was intended to establish that Ball was not just a source for the *Evening Telegraph* but had also played an active role in the newspaper's investigation.

Ball said yes, he had gone to Vine Alley in search of Mrs. McLean, Cleveland's "colored" maid, to question her about Cleveland's drinking habits and the company he kept. Reverend E. S. Hubbard had accompanied him. It was an awkward moment for Hubbard, who at that moment was sitting in the courtroom.

"Did you visit with this negress?"

"I did."

"And you visited her for the express purpose of finding out about Mr. Cleveland's habits?"

"Yes, sir."

"You were in the habit of running down people to learn all about Mr. Cleveland, were you not?"

That was not the case at all, Ball said. He accused Milburn of trying to give the impression that he was a snooping detective. "These visits were made at the solicitation of our ministers."

Milburn turned to another subject.

"You lived in Owensville, Indiana?"

"At one time, yes."

"And you had trouble with a lady of your congregation?"

"I had some difficulty there."

The unpleasant incident had taken place on May 15, 1881. Ball had been invited to give a guest sermon at the General Baptist Church in Owensville. He was delivering the sermon when an esteemed lady, Mrs. James Montgomery, caught up in the Holy Spirit, praised God in a manner that Ball found offensive. But he let it go. A moment later, she did it again—it was described as an "ejaculation." This time Ball turned to Mrs. Montgomery and told her, "Hush up!" She just sat there, indignant at this public rebuke. The rest of the congregation became incensed at what they construed to be the humiliation of one of the town's leading citizens. The next day, with righteous anger mounting, Mrs. Montgomery's son went to see Ball and "compelled him to make an immediate apology to his mother." Ball was threatened with a whipping if he refused. Ball went to Mrs. Montgomery's home, got down on his knees, and prayed for forgiveness. Afterward, his standing in Owensville was in shambles. He cut short his stay and returned to Buffalo. The petty episode involving Mrs. Montgomery had been forgotten until the *Indianapolis Sentinel* took Ball on in 1884. In the hands of the rabble-rousing *Sentinel*, Ball had to "depart hastily" from Owensville, "owing to an insult to a Christian lady."

Milburn read the *Sentinel's* account into the record. Then he turned to Ball. "Now, did you make an apology to any lady or person in Owensville?"

Ball stammered, "I . . . I . . . "

"This question calls for a direct answer—yes or no."

"Well, yes, I did."

Milburn was done. Ball looked drained. One reporter who was in the courtroom said of Ball's experience on the stand, "It was torture." He wrote that Ball looked exhausted in "flesh (and) spirit" by the assault on his integrity.

Now it was Adelbert Moot's turn. It was going to be a challenge to recoup some of the damage caused by Milburn's skillful interrogation. Under Moot's guidance, Ball gave the jurors a sense of his distinguished career. He said he'd earned his doctorate of divinity from Bates College in Maine. He explained the theological diversity in the Baptist church. He came from the church's Free Will denomination, which placed autonomy in the hands of the local house of worship. It was important for Ball to clarify what it meant to be a Free Will Baptist, lest anyone on the jury think this somehow was a lesser branch of the church.

Moot brought the witness around to the mayoral campaign of 1881. Ball said he ran a local independent political club.

"That body supported Mr. Cleveland?"

"It did."

"Was any question raised as to his moral character then?"

"There was not," Ball answered. "One member did object to him, but I made no investigations."

Ball acknowledged that he had received fifty dollars from Cleveland, but he denied the donation was in exchange for a political endorsement. He said he spent the money on a church construction project. Moreover, he noted, the check had been sent to him *after* the mayoral election.

"Did you ever ask or receive a dollar for political services of anyone?"

"No, sir. Every dollar I received for the church was used to build it."

"Was the independent club a little political machine of your own?"

"No, it was not." He downplayed his influence in Buffalo, saying that if he ran a political machine, then it was a "party of one." He said he would never endorse anyone for fifty dollars or for any amount of money.

"Coming down to the time when Mr. Cleveland ran for governor, did your club have anything to do with that campaign?"

"No, sir."

"Did you learn anything about the history of Grover Cleveland's life at that time?"

"No, I did not."

"When did you get your first information against Mr. Cleveland?"

"Just before the political convention, which nominated Mr. Cleveland for president."

"Who told you these facts first?"

"Dr. George W. Lewis."

Lewis came from one of Buffalo's most esteemed pioneer families. His brother, Dr. Diocletian Lewis, was a famous physical fitness advocate. Another brother, Loren Lewis, was a judge.

"Did you learn them from others?"

"Yes, a Mrs. Baker of Huron Street."

Moot showed a letter that Ball had written to Dr. Lyman Abbott, the editor of a Christian newspaper in New York City. The Abbott Letter—one of three that Ball had sent to religious publications in July 1884—laid out the allegations that Cleveland had had an illegitimate son with Maria Halpin. Moot read the letter out loud, and as he did, murmurs rippled through the courtroom. The facts of the Halpin case were familiar to everyone, but the Abbott Letter contained a sensational new accusation: Cleveland had been courting a "respectable young lady" when he arrived at her home with a bottle of champagne and invited her to have a drink. She immediately grabbed the bottle and threw it out the window. That was the last time Cleveland was permitted in her home.

"Did you believe the statements contained in this letter?"

Ball said he did. He went on to detail his investigation of Cleveland, including his interviews with Maria Halpin's lawyer, Milo Whitney, and with her former employers at the Flint & Kent department store. Ball said a committee of thirty Buffalo clergyman had authorized him to look into Cleveland's life. He said he never desired publicity or notoriety.

Moot came around to the Vine Alley excursion in search of Mrs. McLean. "Did you go anywhere else [on Vine Alley] except to see Mrs. McLean?"

"I am not certain whether we did or not."

Ball apologized for dishonoring the late Oscar Folsom and the Beaver Island Club. In Ball's words, he was "off about the whole affair generally." But he also pointed out that a correction under his name had been published in the *Buffalo Commercial Advertiser* back in 1884, just three days after he realized he had committed a grave blunder.

Moot then asked Ball to give the jurors his version of that unpleasant business in Owensville.

"I was preaching to a crowded congregation in the evening and there was someone who screeched during the service." He said at first he thought the woman was having a "fit."

"Then I went on and heard the screech again and I thought someone was interrupting the service. I said in substance that I hoped no one would disturb the meeting and closed the service." Right after, Ball said, he was informed by the other worshippers that what he had assumed to be screeching had actually been an "outburst of religious fervor."

"I had never heard of such manifestations of religious fervor before," he said, and it was his idea to go to Mrs. Montgomery's house to ask for forgiveness. He did get down on his knees to pray, but he denied that he had ever been threatened with a whipping. "The meeting was very pleasant. We joined in religious services and that was all."

Moot was done. Now John Milburn rose to commence his re-direct. He tore into Ball for failing to get Cleveland's side of the story before going public with the allegations regarding his relationship with Maria Halpin and the birth of his illegitimate son.

"You have sworn that you went to Flint & Kent. Did you go to Wilson S. Bissell or George Sicord, longtime friends of Mr. Cleveland, for confirmation?"

"I did not go to them."

"Who brought up these matters in reference to Mr. Cleveland's character at the minister's meeting?"

"I can't say."

"Were you not the prime mover?"

"No." Ball's baritone voice shook. Was it defiance—or equivocation? "I don't know as I was."

With that, his testimony was over.

Milburn called Dr. Alexander Bull to the stand. The sixty-three-year-old physician wore rimless glasses. He had long sideburns connected to a bushy white mustache that left his chin clean-shaven. Bull was one of Buffalo's finest healers. Once he had treated the son of a tribal chief for a life-threatening abscess, and when, in a matter of days, it had disappeared, the grateful chief adopted Bull into the tribe.

Dr. Bull said he knew George Ball only slightly. He knew Grover Cleveland much better—they had been friends for more than twenty years. He recalled the day in 1884 when Reverend Ball came into his office accompanied by Dr. George Lewis. Milburn asked for his recollection of the conversation the three men had regarding the death of Oscar Folsom.

"I don't know much about it, and I don't think I gave Dr. Ball any information on the subject."

Moot shot up from his chair for re-direct. He could not shake the physician's story. Bull said he could not recall the subject of Oscar Folsom's death ever coming up. And he said that whatever he may have told Ball about Folsom or Maria Halpin was a "street story," meaning just gossip, not to be taken as factual.

Dr. Lewis was the next witness.

"Did you have a conversation with Dr. Ball in 1884 in regard to the private character of Grover Cleveland?" asked Milburn.

"I really have no recollection of it," Lewis said. He took the jury back to the day when Mrs. Baker brought her neighbor Maria Halpin into his office. This occurred just a few days after Maria Halpin's illegitimate son had been forcibly taken from her arms. "I don't think the name of Grover Cleveland was mentioned."

Sitting at the defense table, Ball was confounded. He could not believe that Bull and Lewis were not backing his story.

Milbank recalled Edwin Godkin to the stand. The *Post* editor swore under oath that before writing the articles about Ball, he had dispatched a reporter to Buffalo to look into the preacher's background. Godkin said the research had established that Ball had been a political operator in Buffalo and had a record of making "inquisitive" investigations into the affairs of other people, which could be interpreted as prying. He called Ball a "fussy, credulous person who dabbled in politics." As for the Maria Halpin story, Godkin said he believed it had been "substantially true" but that all the rest of the allegations regarding Grover Cleveland and his licentious behavior had been a "pack of lies." Godkin said the *Post* articles had been written and published "entirely without malice."

Milburn was done with Godkin. Now it was Moot's turn to take a crack at the editor. He faced the defendant and showed him the 1884 *Post* articles that had been introduced into evidence. "I see that you wrote that, 'The accounts [about] Dr. Ball grow worse and worse.' What can you recall that is detrimental to Dr. Ball's character?"

"I considered that the slanders he was spreading of Grover Cleveland were detrimental to the highest degree."

"If the story Dr. Ball tells in the Abbott letter were true, would you still have a feeling against him?"

Godkin considered this. "I should, for I think a minister is unqualified to pursue such a line of business. I think that on such lines as the Maria Halpin story, ministers are especially disqualified, for they are very credulous and not likely to conduct an investigation in a judicial manner."

Moot pointed out that in one *Post* article, Ball had been referred to as a "politico-clerical adventurer." Could not the venerated Henry Ward Beecher be subject to the same insulting characterization? Godkin shook his head. Beecher, he said, was too great an orator and his thoughts were too "well defined."

"This phrase you use was a direct thrust at Dr. Ball's character?"

"It was."

Moot hammered away at the witness. Regarding the incident in Owensville, Godkin acknowledged that when the *Indianapolis Sentinel* had accused Ball of "insulting a Christian lady," he had jumped to the assumption that Ball had committed a morally offensive act of a sexual nature. "Did you think that Dr. Ball had been undertaking something in the line that Mr. Cleveland was accused of?"

"I thought it very likely," said Godkin. "I thought it all went together with what Dr. Ball was doing in Buffalo," Godkin sneered; his contempt for Ball was evident to everyone in the courtroom. Moot asked Godkin about his charge that Ball had an aptitude for "ferreting out low, disgusting scandals." Godkin admitted that outside of the Halpin scandal, he could not find any evidence that Ball was involved in investigating political scandals.

In the *Post* article under the headline, "Dr. Ball and His Kind," Ball was called a "miscreant." Did Godkin regret using that word?

Godkin said it was a strong word but warranted.

"Guttersnipes," said Moot, reading from the same article. "Doesn't this make charges of low character to Dr. Ball and his kind?"

"It refers to people engaged in low occupation," Godkin agreed.

"Vampires," Moot read. "These are bloodsuckers, spirits that return after death and roam over the earth." He wanted to know whether Godkin still believed Ball could be compared to such a creature.

Godkin would not back down.

"Rascals," Moot said, still reading from the article. "Do you know that the term a rascal indicates a criminal?"

Godkin retorted that sometimes it did and sometimes it did not.

Moot said that based on the testimony he had just heard, he could only conclude that in Godkin's estimation, George Ball was all these things: a miscreant, a guttersnipe, a vampire, and a rascal. If this was the case, suggested Moot, then Ball must also be a cad, unfaithful to his wife, and a horrible father.

Godkin said, "I didn't know whether he had wife or child."

"Or to his church?"

"I think anybody who did as he did was unfaithful to his church."

Moot was done. He seemed confident of victory. Then Milburn got up and asked Godkin one more time whether he considered the words "miscreant, guttersnipe, and vampire" too strong as applied to George Ball.

"I should not," Godkin said.

Milburn looked at Judge Daniels. "That's our case, Your Honor." At the moment, the clock struck five. Court was adjourned for the day.

The next morning, a pallid George Ball sat at the plaintiff's table. Looking around, he saw that every seat was taken, but it was disappointing to see that the clergymen who had been filling the courtroom for the past two days to show their support were not there. Ball fidgeted in his chair, and his eyes shifted to the twelve men sitting in the jury box. John Milburn was about to begin his closing argument.

In an even-toned voice no louder than was necessary to be heard in the courtroom, Milburn said it was regretful that the case of *Ball v. New York Evening Post* had ever come to trial. President Cleveland had administered the affairs of state with "ability and manliness," and he had taken a wife who had won the admiration and affection of the American people for the "dignity, courtesy, and simplicity with which she presided over the White House." It was a nimble manipulation of the goodwill the jurors had for their hometown idol, Frances Folsom Cleveland.

The Maria Halpin scandal was "long gone by," Milburn said, and it was unfortunate that the passions of 1884 had to be "raked over by this minister and his greed for money." Milburn said he had considered and then rejected the idea of calling President Cleveland as a witness. "It would not be fair to him and his family," he said.

"Now this action was brought for defamation of character, to get money, when it appears that (Ball) has not suffered at all in either character or purse. What an opportunity for a minister to be gracious, and say that as the campaign was passed and the heat of it was over, he would let the matter drop. But no, he must drag it into court and rake up things so painful to many."

George Ball, Milburn conceded, may have stepped into the campaign of 1884 in the spirit of "public duty," but that same spirit had moved Godkin to write his articles denouncing Ball. The two men had engaged in a war of words that required the widest privilege available under the law. "There can be nothing done about it unless a malicious motive can be shown."

"Dr. Ball is the libeler, we are not."

Milbank turned now to Ball's excursion to Vine Alley when he interviewed Cleveland's maid for evidence of drunken behavior and lewd associations. "That," said Milburn, "is the work of a guttersnipe. Do you want such a man to officiate at your wedding, to preach the Gospel to you! He is with you to baptize your children, to visit you when you are sick, and to officiate at your funeral. His business is to do good, to lift up society and protect it from debasement. But our papers were for months filled with the scum of the gutter, scraped up by this man who now wants damages. He so debased the reputation of Buffalo that it will take a quarter century to recover."

He poured on the bile. He compared George Ball to a "fish woman" and an assassin. He said it was shameful for Ball to have linked Cleveland to the death of Oscar Folsom. "In this an attack had been made not only upon the living but upon the dead, upon a man who had been in his grave for years."

Court recessed for lunch, and when it went into session again at two o'clock, Milburn resumed his closing arguments. Bristling with sarcasm, he went over the *Post* articles sentence by sentence. They were "mild" compared to the language Ball had used in his attacks on Cleveland. And who could object to "vampire" when Ball was bringing shame on a "fellow townsman who was a candidate for high office." If the *Post* had erred in accusing Ball of insulting a Christian woman in Owensville, it had done so in good faith with the best information available at the time.

Then Milburn put everything on the line. He was not interested in a compromise verdict, he told the jurors. It was all or nothing. Either his client was guilty or Ball was not entitled to a single dollar bill in damages.

Two hours after he had begun, Milburn completed his closing arguments. He had put forth a masterful performance.

It was now Adelbert Moot's turn to face the jury. How strange, Moot said, that two-thirds of John Milburn's closing address had been about a man who was not on trial and who had not taken the witness stand. That man, of course, was President Cleveland, now a private citizen and qualified to defend himself—"if he chose." Fear had kept Cleveland away from the trial, Moot said. "If he did, he might speak of the boy who could never have the same chance as other boys, and of the mother who was disgraced by her motherhood."

The case boiled down to this, said Moot. Could a newspaper use the language aimed at Ball and "go unpunished"? What had George Ball done that had been so egregious? He had come into possession of certain facts concerning Grover Cleveland "as would prevent you or me from introducing this man to a wife or daughter." He had communicated the information to the editors of several newspapers. Was he not entitled? Moot alluded to the illegitimate birth of Oscar Folsom Cleveland—"the boy who had no right to use his father's name." Moot pointed out that Cleveland was nearly forty years old when his son was born out of wedlock, so his conduct could not be excused by the irresponsibility of youth. Moot said he had not intended to raise the specter of Oscar's birth during the trial, and only did so when the other side kept bringing it up. Why, he wondered, had the defense not called to the stand Mrs. Baker, who was still alive and could speak as a witness with firsthand knowledge of Cleveland's illegitimate son and of the woman who had been "wrongfully" locked up in an insane asylum?

"I told you that we were not trying Governor Cleveland's libel suit. He can do that himself. But if these stories had been lies, Dr. Ball and the others who told them could have been thrown into prison and punished."

The question before the jury was this: "May a minister of the gospel think? May he say whether the chief magistrate of the nation shall be clean? The defendants should be made to sweat. I submit you ought to find a verdict that would teach a substantial lesson."

A strange thing happened when Moot finished his summation. John Milburn's law partner, Franklin Locke, announced that a surprise witness, James C. Fullerton, had come forward during a break in closing summations with evidence concerning George Ball.

"If it pleases Your Honor, we desire to reopen our side of the case for the purpose of placing James C. Fullerton upon the stand."

Judge Daniels looked down from the bench. "What is the nature of the testimony you purpose to introduce?"

"We expect to prove by Mr. Fullerton that Dr. Ball applied to him for money during the campaign of 1881."

The judge pondered. With so much on the line, he was inclined to give the lawyers on both sides plenty of latitude. Besides, Adelbert Moot was raising no objection to reopening the case. "I think we will hear the testimony of Mr. Fullerton," the judge said.

James Fullerton was sworn in. He looked as if he definitely did not want to be there.

Fullerton testified that in 1881, he had considered running for city attorney of Buffalo. George Ball had come to his law office and offered to put Fullerton's name on the ballot of the independent party that Ball controlled—if Fullerton handed over a $250 donation. If he did so, Fullerton claimed, Ball was willing to replace the lawyer who was already on the ballot with Fullerton.

"Did you give it to him?" Locke asked.

"I did not," Fullerton answered. "I was a poor boy and did not have much money."

"Did your name go on Dr. Ball's ticket?"

"It did not."

It was blockbuster testimony that appeared to stain Ball as a grubby political boss ready to sell a slot on his independent ticket to the highest bidder, just as the *Post* had represented in its articles.

"Well," said Judge Daniels when Fullerton concluded his testimony. "Does the plaintiff desire to introduce any testimony?"

"Just a moment," said Adlebert Moot. His brow was deeply furrowed as he carried on a whispered consultation with his law partner Frank Ferguson. Finally, Moot said he was recalling their client George Ball to the stand.

Ball looked nervous. Moot asked, "Dr. Ball, did you visit with Mr. Fullerton in his office during the campaign of 1881?"

"I have no definite recollection of such a visit." But as he said this, he sounded evasive.

Franklin Locke handled the cross-examination. He asked Ball straight-out, "Will you swear that you did not have a conversation with Mr. Fullerton in his office during the campaign of 1881?"

"I think I might have had some conversation with Mr. Fullerton, but I am certain that I did not ask for money. We talked about the management and general expenses of a campaign."

"And what possible object would you have had in talking with Mr. Fullerton about the general expenses of a campaign?"

Ball hesitated. "I would like to have the language of some of my previous answers read to see exactly what I said." Ball had tied himself into an awkward knot of equivocation. Titters broke out in the courtroom. Judge Daniels looked sternly at the spectators, and his glare told everyone to be quiet.

It was now five o'clock. Judge Daniels cautioned the jurors not to say anything about the case and then he dismissed them for the night. His final instructions to the panel would take place the next day. Ball looked shell-shocked. Godkin was grinning for the first time in three days.

On the morning of February 7, 1890, Judge Daniels delivered his charge to the jury. Daniels had deep-set hazel eyes and a long thin mouth with a kindly expression that suggested an impish wit. He had only dim recollections of his early years and could not say when or where he was born. It could have been in 1825, which would make him sixty-five, in Wales or New York City. He just did not know. His father was an itinerant shoemaker who, as Daniels dryly recalled, "had certain habits which stood in the way of his success." Daniels was sixteen when he happened to hear a lawyer plead a case before a jury. Then and there he was determined to become a lawyer. For the next five years, his books were lying on his cobbler's bench as he hammered away, making shoes, to earn 25¢ a day—just enough to stay alive and buy more books. Every free hour he had he would slip into the county courthouse and watch the law play out. He lived by the adage that "labor conquered all." He clerked nights for a Buffalo lawyer, was admitted to the bar in 1847, and elected to the bench in 1863. Frail but wiry, he hardened his body with calisthenics. Even in the coldest winter weather, he went without an overcoat and wore low shoes and thin clothes. His reputation as a jurist was one of absolute impartiality. He told his son that he could not make friends for fear his objectivity would be bent if a friend came before him in court. Railroad companies sent him free passes, but he would never use them because the railroads frequently appeared in court as litigants.

Now he was presiding over a case with historic repercussions. As usual, his charge to the jury was utterly evenhanded— "without the slightest leaning one way or the other." He laid out the mass of evidence that had been presented. Sentence by sentence, he read for the jurors the articles in dispute and dwelled on their impact, implicit or not. He said that George Ball had a constitutional right to probe Grover Cleveland's personal life, and it was for the jury to determine whether the investigative measures Ball had taken, such as interviewing Cleveland's maid, warranted the *Post* calling him a guttersnipe. If Ball had libeled Cleveland in asserting that he had been drunk the night of Oscar Folsom's death, that in turn was no justification for the *Post* to libel Ball. It was for the jury to determine whether the *Post's* articles had been written with actual malice and whether they were intended to injure Ball. For ninety minutes, Daniels systematically laid everything out. Finally, at eleven ten, the jury retired to the deliberation room.

The spectators gathered into small clusters of conversation. A general consensus was reached: The jurors would either be hung or vote for Godkin and the *New York Evening Post.* No one expected a victory for Ball.

The panel was out for less than four hours. At 2:45 PM, a court officer announced that the jurors had come to a verdict. Everyone scrambled to find seats. The jurors filed back into the courtroom.

"Gentlemen, have you reached a verdict?" asked the clerk of the court. A hush fell.

"We have," said the foreman. He rose. "We find a verdict of no cause of action."

Ball sank in his chair, crushed. Characteristically, Godkin exhibited no visible reaction, even in his moment of victory. Ball left the courtroom without saying a word. Moot vowed to appeal. Later, it emerged that when the jurors began deliberations, they had taken a secret ballot to see where things stood. Eight men had voted in favor of Godkin and three for Ball. One ballot was blank. It had taken six more ballots before reaching a unanimous verdict.

One month later, Godkin was back at the editor's desk at the *Post* in Manhattan. Before him was a check in the amount of $856.82, signed by none other than Grover Cleveland. The former president had made good on a private pledge he had made five years before to pay a substantial portion of Godkin's legal fees. He had full faith in the editor's eagerness to keep the transaction strictly confidential. A grateful Godkin took pen to paper.

My Dear Mr. Cleveland,

I have to acknowledge the receipt of your check for $856.82 being half the bill of Rogers Locke Milburn [the full name of Milburn's law firm.]

Let me add that we all here think your contribution to the expense of the suit ample and in all respects satisfactory to us. Allow me at the same time to congratulate you most humbly on the result of the trial, for it was a triumph for you as well as for us.

Two years later, Grover Cleveland won the Democratic nomination for president. His running mate was Adlai Stevenson, the former congressman from Illinois who had served as his assistant postmaster general. The general election of 1892 was a replay of the 1888 campaign, but this time, Cleveland emerged triumphant, defeating President Harrison with 46 percent of the vote to Harrison's 43 percent, and becoming the first and only United States president to serve nonconsecutive terms of office.

19

KEEPER OF THE FLAME

DEATH CAME TO Maria Halpin on February 6, 1902, at the age of sixty-six.

Maria had known when the end was near, and there were things she had to take care of before she passed on. The first was to notify her son, Frederick Halpin, now forty-nine and living in Matamoras, Pennsylvania. A telegram informed him that his mother was dying and he must come at once to New Rochelle.

Two days before she passed away, Maria wrote out a will. It was a simple document—her personal property was a paltry two hundred dollars, and her real estate holdings amounted to $2,000. That was all. She bequeathed everything to her third husband, Wallace Hunt, whom she had married three years earlier.

On her deathbed, Maria gave Hunt specific instructions regarding her interment.

"Do not let the funeral be too public. I do not want strangers to come and gaze on my face. Let everything be very quiet. Let me rest."

Frederick arrived in time to bid his mother farewell. Then she was gone, the cause of death recorded as bronchial pneumonia by her doctor, Samuel Beyea. In the little parlor of her home at 47 Hudson Street, she was laid in repose in a stained pine coffin, costing $75. Her sister sat with her, sobbing.

It was a plain funeral, conducted without a church service. Then a hearse carried the coffin down a rain-slicked country road to the Beechwood Cemetery where Maria was buried next to her second husband, the carpenter James Albert Seacord, who had died in 1894 at age seventy-six. Three dozen chairs had been placed at the gravesite to accommodate the turnout. Eighteen years had passed since the notorious mudslinging election of 1884, and it was said that many of Maria's neighbors who attended her funeral were unaware of the eventful role she had played in the life of President Cleveland. They knew her as Maria Hunt and never connected her with *that* notorious Maria Halpin.

In the local New Rochelle newspapers, Maria's obituary warranted just a single paragraph in the *Press* and three paragraphs in the *Pioneer*, which identified her only as Mrs. Maria B. Hunt, wife of Wallace Hunt—"the well-known stove and furnace dealer." The newspapers, which were surely aware that she was the Maria Halpin involved in the Cleveland scandal, made no mention of it in all probability because they didn't want to offend Hunt, whose hardware store was a steady local advertiser.

Others, however, remembered Maria's place in history, and even in death the insults kept coming her way. In a retrospective of the Halpin scandal, the *Brooklyn Eagle* made this mean-spirited commentary: "Never of a strong nature, mentally and physically, she was disturbed and frightened to such a degree that her nerves were nearly wrecked. The sprightliness which had been her youthful charm had given way to a subdued, even a shrinking manner." For some mystifying reason, the *Eagle* chose the occasion of Maria's death to scold her old friend from Buffalo, Maria Baker. According to the *Eagle*, Mrs. Baker was an "evil genius," and her husband a "night hawk" who never "enjoyed the best of reputations."

"But for this woman [Mrs. Baker], it is doubtful whether there would have been heard anything of the stories in which subsequently the names of Cleveland and Maria Halpin were involved."

In the years that followed Maria's death, she was not the only person touched by the scandal who came to a sad end.

Colonel John Byrne had been Buffalo's superintendent of police when two detectives under his command seized the infant Oscar Folsom Cleveland and threw Maria Halpin into an insane asylum. On October 30, 1909, Byrne was sitting in the stadium at West Point, bursting with pride as he watched his son, Eugene, a fourth-year cadet, play in the Harvard-Army football game. Ten minutes into the second half, Eugene, a robust 175-pound left tackle, was brought down by two Harvard guards. When the gridiron was cleared, he was found to be paralyzed from the neck down. His snow-haired seventy-year-old father wept as he was carried off on a stretcher. Eugene, aged twenty-one, died the next morning, and West Point cancelled the remainder of the football season, including the army-navy game.

Six weeks later, Colonel Byrne suffered an incapacitating stroke at his home in Buffalo. He died on December 30 without regaining consciousness.

Dr. Alexander Bull, the physician whose testimony had done so much damage to Reverend George Ball's case during the *New York Post* libel trial, also came to an unexpected end. He was boarding a trolley in front of the Iroquois Hotel in Buffalo and was on the second step when the conductor sounded the signal to proceed, and the trolley lurched forward. The doctor lost his balance and fell backward, hitting his head on the pavement. Bull lingered at death's door for two weeks before he died. All Buffalo mourned his passing.

John Milburn, the lawyer who had successfully defended the *New York Post* in the George Ball libel trial, found himself at the center of a national tragedy.

Buffalo in the early 1900s was the eighth largest city in America, with a population exceeding 350,000. In recognition of the city's prominence, it was named host of the Pan-American Exposition. Buffalo would take its just place next to London, Paris, Vienna, Philadelphia, Chicago, and the other great municipalities of the world to have hosted world fairs. The 342-acre site opened on May 1, 1901, featuring the X-ray machine, hydroelectric power, and other technological marvels of the industrial revolution. As a leading citizen of Buffalo, John Milburn was named president of the exposition, and in this capacity, he had extended an invitation to President William McKinley to visit the fairgrounds.

On September 6, there was a vast throng at the Pan-American Exposition's concert hall, the Temple of Music, where President McKinley was holding a public reception. He was standing in the great arena, shaking hands with visitors, when Leon Czolgosz, a twenty-three-year-old anarchist, opened fired with a .32 Iver-Johnson six-shooter. The first bullet grazed the president's chest. McKinley took the full blast of the second shot in the stomach. He was taken by ambulance to the hospital and, later that night, was transported to a private residence at 1168 Delaware Avenue—the home of John Milburn. For the next eight days, the world was focused on Milburn's house. Delaware Avenue ("Mansion Row") was roped off, an armed camp, with absolute silence ordered for the president's comfort. McKinley lingered until September 14, when he uttered his final words, "It is useless, gentlemen. I think we ought to have a prayer."

The assassination of McKinley was a calamity for Buffalo, the nation—and for Milburn on a personal level. The bullet that killed McKinley would forever link Buffalo to a presidential assassination; when the Pan-American Exposition officially closed in November, it was found to have lost more than $6 million. Milburn was crushed and could see nothing but enduring heartbreak if he remained in Buffalo. Like his friend Grover Cleveland, he forsook the city that had given him his start and resettled in Manhattan. The vagaries of history passed Buffalo by. In 2010, it was ranked the sixty-ninth largest city in the United States, with a shrinking population of 270,000.

Rose Cleveland was mesmerized. Before her lay seven miles of sugary white beach and a turquoise bay of exquisite tranquility. For Rose, having been raised in the blustery climate of upstate New York, it was a revelation.

Rose was in the town of Naples, in the old Confederate state of Florida, where she was accorded a special privilege. It was January 22, 1889, and she had been invited to register as the first guest at the opening of the sixteen-room Naples Hotel. The hotel was the social hub of the new town, founded only three years earlier, with a name designed to evoke the sunny peninsula of Italy. Her room was charming and cozy, and like the other guests, she promptly lost her heart to the town's simple diversions. She wandered for miles down the beach, gathering pretty shells, and when she returned to the hotel, she rested under the shady porch until it was time for dinner. In the dining room, she feasted on oysters, turtle steaks, wild turkey, and venison and a mouth-watering tray piled with local tropical fruit.

Other distinguished guests were also checking in. There was a Judge Meier, the railroad tycoon Bennett Young, and a Miss Hattie Snyder from Chattanooga. Then Evangeline Marrs Simpson arrived in town, the beguiling widow of Michael Simpson, a millionaire merchant from Boston who had made a fortune in hide and leather. Simpson had died in 1884 when he was seventy-five, and had left Evangeline, just twenty-seven, enormous assets that afforded her the luxury of traveling the world in high style. The Naples Hotel was for her a stop on a never-ending tour of the world's pleasure spots.

Rose Cleveland and Evangeline Simpson clicked. The young widow had a flare for drama that some people considered excessive but Rose found enchanting. There was chemistry between the two, and Rose fell in love. She called Evangeline her Eve, or "my Viking." Rose threw herself into the relationship, and Eve reciprocated. The private correspondence between the two women lays bare one of the great forbidden romances of the Victorian Age.

"Ah, Eve, Eve, surely you cannot realize what you are to me— what you must be. . . . Oh, darling, come to me this night, my Clevy, my Viking, my—Everything. Come!"

When Florida's winter season came to an end, Rose had to return to Holland Patent, and Evangeline continued her world travels. The separation cut both women. Rose, sitting in the train's parlor car in the "home stretch" of the trip to Holland Patent, ached with longing when she took pen in hand and wrote Eve.

"Oh, Eve, Eve, this love is life itself—or death. I love you, love you beyond belief—you are all the world to me. God bless you."

When Rose arrived at the Weeds, she found things a little disorganized after all her months away, and she missed Eve terribly. That night she wrote her again, "You are mine, and I am yours, and we are one." Rose said she dreamed of being embraced in her lover's "enfolding arms."

"I shall go to bed, my Eve, with your letters under my pillow. I wonder if I will feel alone. God bless thee and keep thee safe."

The next day, Rose went to the country store to purchase a supply of ink and stationery and prepared to "attack" another round of letters. In a rush of longing for Eve, she reached back to ancient times for lovers who epitomized their own love: Evangeline was Cleopatra and Rose was Antony.

"Ah, my Cleopatra," Rose wrote that day, promising to "crush those Antony-seeking lips." The letter ended with this erotic possibility: "How much kissing can Cleopatra stand?"

Rose picked up a book of poems by Robert Browning that must have put her in an amorous mood as she looked forward to the arrival of the afternoon mail—and two letters from Eve. In them Rose read that Eve was wondering whether they would ever see each other again. Rose wrote back, assuring her that their future together was real.

"Yes, darling, I will be with you, surely, in the Autumn." Until then, Rose said, she was prepared to drown herself in work—"while I wait." They solidified plans to rendezvous in New York City. Rose knew she'd be expected to stay at her brother Grover's townhouse, but she wrote that she could also lodge with Evangeline, if Evangeline so desired. She was teasing. Of course they'd stay together.

"I could spend most of the time at your hotel—in your room. Ah, how I love you, it paralyzes me—It makes me heavy with emotion. . . . I tremble at the thought of you—all my whole being leans out to you. . . . Ah, Eve, Eve . . . you are mine by every sign in Earth and Heaven—by every sign in soul and spirit and body."

Rose gazed at Evangeline's photograph and could not take her eyes away—"the look of it making me wild."

In 1893, after Grover Cleveland was sworn in for his second term as president, Rose's relationship with Evangeline cooled off. One reason may have been that Rose, as the sister of the incumbent president, had to be cautious. Any whiff of a scandal questioning Rose's sexual orientation had to be avoided. None of the Clevelands wanted a replay of the whispered innuendos aimed at Rose when she lived in the White House as First Lady. Around the same time, Evangeline told Rose that she was thinking about settling down and getting married—to a man. The gentleman in question was Henry Benjamin Whipple, bishop of the Episcopal Diocese of Minnesota, a celebrated churchman with a national reputation as a champion of Native American rights. The Sioux called him "Straight Tongue" because he was always honest with them. A widower with six children, he was also thirty-eight years older than Evangeline.

Naturally, Rose was conflicted. While she was on a visit with her brother at the White House, when night fell and he had gone out, Rose thought things through, and part of her understood Evangeline's desire for conventionality. She put her thoughts down on stationery embossed *Executive Mansion*.

"I wish for your happiness and good," Rose wrote. While appreciating everything she was going through ("I know you suffer"), she implored Evangeline not to "decide hastily." But she also promised to "act gracefully" and would support anything that would "give you joy and peace. . . . I love you enough for anything. . . . That means to take myself out of your way—for a while at least."

"God bless you," Rose told Eve. "You can depend on me."

Evangeline was married at St. Bartholomew's Church in Manhattan. As the wedding was an unexpected interlude during a convention of Episcopal bishops in the city, Whipple's fellow bishops were surprised to say the least. He was seventy-four and Evangeline just thirty-six, although as *The New York Times* charitably pointed out "the Bishop is in vigorous health, and looks much younger than he really is." In terms of age, it certainly echoed Evangeline's first marriage to the aged Boston textile manufacturer Michael Simpson. Whipple and his bride checked into the Buckingham Hotel for their honeymoon.

To try to forget Eve, Rose traveled to Europe and the Middle East, but wherever she was, she kept in contact with Evangeline, marking time until the day came when they would be together again.

On May 5, 1893, Cleveland was in the ninth week of his second term in office when he became aware of a "rough spot" on the roof of his mouth. It was in the precise place where he liked to chew his daily cigar. It did not go away, and his discomfort increased until finally, on June 18, he called for the White House physician. Dr. Robert O'Reilly examined Cleveland's mouth and found an inflamed ulcer about the size of a quarter. The doctor also saw evidence of diseased bone. Cleveland winced as O'Reilly scraped a section and sent it to the Army Medical Museum for a biopsy. He did not identify the patient as the president of the United States. The report came back "strongly indicative of malignancy."

Dr. Joseph Bryant, Cleveland's personal physician from New York, was summoned to Washington. First he read the medical reports, then he conducted his own examination. "What do you think it is, Doctor?" the president casually asked. He had the utmost confidence in Bryant's medical judgment.

Bryant looked at his friend. "Were it in my mouth, I would have it removed at once." He explained that it was a fast-growing malignancy for which the need for an operation was urgent. Bryant refused to take responsibility if Cleveland delayed the procedure by even a month.

The diagnosis could not have come at a more unfortunate time. The Philadelphia and Reading Railroad had recently filed for bankruptcy, a step that had precipitated a run on the banks and a credit crunch that was rippling through the economy. Panic was in the air. Businesses were paralyzed, and the stock market had crashed. Stabilizing the country's currency was the Cleveland administration's uppermost priority. An announcement that the president had cancer of the mouth could trigger a full-scale economic depression, and the 1885 death from throat cancer of Ulysses S. Grant—another habitual cigar smoker—was still fresh in the American people's collective memory. Hence the president consented to the operation, but only under the strictest confidentiality. No one outside his inner circle must know, not even his cabinet, with the exception of Dan Lamont, who was now serving as secretary of war. The White House issued a low-key statement that President Cleveland was leaving Washington for a few days to join his wife at their summer house in Buzzards Bay in Cape Cod.

Dr. Bryant coordinated the medical team that would treat the president. He wrote to Dr. William Williams Keen, a surgeon from Philadelphia, to tell him that he was seeking a consultation on a "very important matter." Keen was renowned in medical circles for his skill with the surgeon's scalpel. He was also credited with introducing the concept of antiseptic surgery to America at a time when operations were performed without gloves or sterilization of instruments. Bryant and Keen met on a deserted dock in New York City. Only then did Bryant inform Keen, who was sworn to secrecy, that the patient in question was Grover Cleveland. To ensure privacy, Keen agreed to perform the operation on Commodore Elias Benedict's yacht *Oneida,* which was moored in New York harbor. The stateroom of the *Oneida* was disinfected, and an operating table and all necessary instruments and dressings were brought on board. Arrangements were made with a New York dentist, Dr. Ferdinand Hasbrouck, to assist in anesthetizing Cleveland. He was considered the nation's leading authority on nitrous oxide, also known as laughing gas. Keen returned to Philadelphia and packed his bags, keeping his family entirely in the dark about his mission. He told his wife only that he was going away for an "important operation" and would not be returning for several days.

On the evening of June 13, Keen appeared at Pier A in New York and was taken by launch to the *Oneida*, anchored off the battery in Lower Manhattan. The entire medical team was already on board, plus a tank of nitrous oxide and a supply of ether. An hour later, the presidential party consisting of Cleveland, Lamont, and Dr. Bryant arrived. Cleveland tried to put everyone at ease. He was introduced to Keen and invited all to sit on deck and enjoy the night breeze. He even lit up a cigar! They chatted for an hour and Keen, who had never met Cleveland, observed that the president seemed anxious about one thing: Would he be able to carry on the duties of office and speak in public without anyone knowing about the operation? Keen explained that if everything went well, his appearance would be normal, though he might have a defective speech pattern. Cleveland seemed to accept this. He spoke about the burdens of the presidency.

"Oh, Dr. Keen, those office-seekers. Those office-seekers. They haunt me even in my dreams."

Cleveland slept well that evening, having declined the offer of a sedative. The next morning, Keen examined the president. Cleveland said he was positive that the rough spot inside his mouth was of recent origin and had not been present when he took the oath of office on March 4. Probing the ulcerous growth, Keen said it was "unquestionably malignant." Surprisingly, though Cleveland weighed almost three hundred pounds, Keen found little evidence of arteriosclerosis. His pulse was ninety, within normal range. But Keen was worried—not necessarily about the operation itself, but the administration of anesthesia. The president's corpulence aside, there was the age factor—he was fifty-six—and physically drained. The team was seriously concerned that Cleveland might suffer a heart attack and die on the operating table.

Throughout the morning, with the yacht proceeding up the East River at half speed, Cleveland's mouth was repeatedly cleansed and disinfected. As the *Oneida* sailed past Bellevue Hospital on 26th Street, all the physicians abruptly went below deck lest their colleagues at Bellevue, who might be gazing out at the passing vessel, recognize them and suspect that something was up.

With the yacht continuing its progress up river, the operation commenced. Imagine the steady hands of the physicians involved. No one wanted to think about the consequences if something terrible happened. All their reputations were on the line. "If you hit a rock, hit it good and hard," Dr. Bryant informed the ship's captain. That way, at least, "we'll all go to the bottom." It was dark humor at its most macabre.

The cabin had been cleared of furnishings except for the organ, which was fastened down. Cleveland was placed on a chair that was propped up against the mast. A dose of nitrous oxide put the president under, and Hasbrouck, the dentist, went at it, extracting the two left upper bicuspids. They were having trouble rendering the president fully unconscious and an additional dose of ether was ordered. Ether was more potent than nitrous oxide but also riskier. The problem with ether was that while it knocked a patient out, sometimes the patient never woke up. They monitored Cleveland's vital signs as an incision was made and the entire left upper jaw was excised with a cheek retractor, a "most useful" instrument that Keen had discovered while attending a medical convention in Paris in 1866. The physicians peered into the exposed hollow cavity of the upper jaw and found that it was filled with a gelatinous mass, evidently a sarcoma. A small section of the soft palate was also removed. Thank goodness the cancer had not spread into the orbit of the eye socket, which meant that Cleveland's left eye would remain in place, and the president would be spared any external disfigurement. The physicians worked at a fast pace, and the entire procedure lasted only thirty-one minutes. Cleveland hemorrhaged a mere six ounces of blood—just enough to fill a tumbler. The large cavity inside the president's mouth was packed with gauze and cotton, and while he was still out, he was injected with a hypodermic needle of morphine to manage the pain. The patient was lifted onto a bed.

"What a sigh of intense relief, we surgeons breathed," Keen said many years later as he recounted the experience. They all shared a toast of whiskey in celebration of a successful operation.

When Cleveland opened his eyes, he saw a physician standing over him who he did not recognize. It was Bryant's assistant, Dr. John Erdmann, taking first turn on the watch. With his mouth packed with dressing, the ill-tempered president grumbled, "Who the hell are you?"

Erdmann identified himself. Cleveland asked where he came from.

"Chillicothe," Erdmann answered, in Ohio.

"Oh, do you know Mr. Nigbe there?"

"Yes, he's the druggist."

A woozy Cleveland, his mind not really functioning, wondered whether the druggist was interested in a government job. When Erdmann assured Cleveland that the druggist was doing just fine, Cleveland snapped, "Then he won't get one!"

Keen and the other doctors took turns sitting by the president's bedside. To pass the time when he was awake, they read to him. The next day, Cleveland wobbled out of bed. By the third day, he was socializing with his old friend Commodore Benedict and Secretary Lamont. Dr. Hasbrouck was anxious to leave— he had another operation scheduled—and was dropped off at New London, Connecticut. Then the yacht crossed Long Island Sound bound for Sag Harbor, where Keen got off and made his way home to Philadelphia. The next day, the *Oneida* reached Buzzards Bay. Somehow, Cleveland found the strength to walk from the launch to his summer house, Gray Gables.

Newspaper reporters smelled something was up, but during an impromptu news conference held inside the barn at Gray Gables, Lamont deflected suspicions with out-and-out falsehoods and the usual scorn for anyone who questioned the official White House line. All he conceded was that the president had been stricken with a tooth infection and had to have two teeth pulled on his way to Buzzards Bay. But that was all. Specifically asked about a malignancy, Lamont snapped that it was a "preposterous" question.

For the next several days, Cleveland was kept out of sight while he recuperated. A New York orthodontist, Dr. Kasson Gibson, was brought in to fit the president with an artificial jaw made of vulcanized rubber. When the appliance was mounted into the hole inside his mouth, it had the effect of reinforcing the underpinning of Cleveland's cheek and thus averted the appearance of a sunken jaw. Cleveland tried it out. His speech was labored, but no one would have suspected that much of his jawbone had been surgically removed. Later, when the rubber plate gave him some trouble, Cleveland was fitted with a more comfortable appliance.

Even the greatest healers can sometimes slip up. Cleveland was still recuperating at Gray Gables when Dr. Bryant found something disturbing. It was now evident that not all the diseased tissue had been cut out. Because the mouth had been bathed in blood during the operation, the surgeons had apparently overlooked a small mass of it. Word went out to the team of surgeons, and once again, everybody assembled on the *Oneida* for another round of clandestine surgery. Keen took the train to Greenwich, Connecticut, where Commodore Benedict lived. The *Oneida* was waiting for him at dockside and crossed the sound to Buzzards Bay. Cleveland boarded the yacht on July 17 and, just to be safe, a second operation was performed, and the suspicious tissue excised.

As the president convalesced, it was crucial that he attend to the national economic crisis. Cleveland called for a special session of Congress to be held on August 7 to repeal the Sherman Silver Purchase Act, which required the United States to purchase a set quantity of silver every month with a special treasury note that could be redeemed in gold. The misguided law, which had been passed in 1890 during the Harrison administration, was now threatening to deplete the nation's gold reserve. Charles Hamlin, the assistant secretary of the treasury, went to Gray Gables on July 23 with an important statistical analysis prepared by the treasury department to update the president on the status of the gold supply. Confiding to his diary, Hamlin wrote, "Cleveland appeared not well at all. Had his mouth packed with some kind of bandage. Could not speak distinctly . . . looked thoroughly tired out." When Attorney General Richard Olney called on Cleveland, he was shocked to see at how much weight the president had lost. His mouth was still stuffed with antiseptic wads, and he could barely speak.

"My god, Olney, they nearly killed me!" Like the rest of the country, Olney had no idea that the president had cancer. He found Cleveland depressed, resigned to imminent death. Olney wondered how the removal of two molars could have caused him to be in this state.

As Cleveland's mouth healed, he found a peach in the kitchen and ate it—much to his wife's annoyance, since he was supposed to take only liquids during his convalescence. But his physical endurance was nil, and his hair had thinned out and turned white. He seemed to have become an old man overnight.

E. J. Edwards, a reporter who wrote under the pseudonym Holland for the *Philadelphia Press*, got a whiff of the president's true condition. In a roundabout way, the leak had come from Dr. Hasbrouck, the dentist who had administered the anesthesia. Hasbrouck explained to another doctor that he had been unavoidably delayed because he had to operate on a very important patient, none other than President Cleveland. That was quite a name to drop. The doctor who heard the story happened to be a friend of E. J. Edwards. The reporter went to see Hasbrouck and, bluffing his way through the interview, claimed that he only wanted to double-check some of the facts he already knew. Hasbrouck ended up telling him everything. He even gave him the names of all the physicians who were on the president's surgical team. Even with this solid foundation for a story, Edwards held back. To accuse the Cleveland administration of lying to the American people in this time of national crisis could have historic repercussions, and it could jeopardize the congressional vote to repeal the Sherman Silver Purchase Act. Keen, Erdmann, Bryant, and O'Reilly were approached by Edwards, but they all stuck to the story that the president had had routine dental work and nothing more. Erdmann later said he "did more lying" than he had done in his entire life put together.

The White House denials were so vehement that Edwards's editors had second thoughts and spiked the story for the time being. On August 28, the House of Representatives voted in favor of repealing the silver act, handing Cleveland a major victory. The next day, the *Philadelphia Press* finally "summoned the nerve" to run with Edwards's scoop—that the president had a malignancy and part of his jaw had been surgically removed. Once again, Cleveland's people assailed the messenger. Edwards and the *Philadelphia Press* were attacked with all the gusto that had been aimed at the long-departed *Buffalo Evening Telegraph*. The rival *Philadelphia Times* accused Edwards of writing fiction.

"Mr. Cleveland had suffered so much at the hands of untruthful newspaper correspondents . . . that he felt compelled to seek a quiet spot even to have his teeth looked after," spewed the *Philadelphia Times*. Cleveland's neighbor in Buzzards Bay was quoted as saying, "I have never seen him in better health."

It took a quarter of a century for the truth to come out. In 1917, at the age of eighty, Dr. Keen decided it was time for the American people to be told the real story. He wrote an article for the *Saturday Evening Post* and later published a monograph, *The Surgical Operations on President Cleveland in 1893*.

On Cleveland's last day as president, he suffered an attack of gout and walked with a limp as he escorted President-elect McKinley up the steps of the Capitol building to his inauguration. In one hand, Cleveland carried a tightly rolled umbrella, which he held at the ready in the event that he required something to lean on. He left office a pariah in his own party, his policies held in low esteem for having brought economic malaise to America. Nevertheless, there was grudging admiration for his steadfastness and rigid honesty. With the passage of time, Cleveland has come to be regarded as a well-thought-of if not a great president. His administration restored good feelings between North and South. He successfully opposed adoption of the silver standard, and many credit him with rescuing the nation from bankruptcy. He also stood firm against British imperialist designs in South America by embracing the broadest possible definition of the Monroe Doctrine. His was one of the most eventful peacetime presidencies in American history. In reviewing the hapless line of presidents who followed the martyred Abraham Lincoln, Daniel Lamont offered an interesting summary. For Andrew Johnson there was sorrow, for Grant scandal, for Hayes humiliation, for Garfield death, and for Arthur unpopularity.

As for Cleveland, Lamont had this uncomplicated observation: "Herculean toil."

Cleveland lived out the final years of his life in the charming village of Princeton, New Jersey, where he bought a Georgian-style estate surrounded by lovely lawns. He became a trustee of Princeton University and wrote letters, hunted rabbits and quail, and sometimes went fishing for bass. Now and then he spoke out on national issues. In 1905, he wrote an article for the *Ladies Home Journal,* still stubbornly denouncing the women's suffrage movement. Sensible and responsible women "do not want to vote," he maintained. The status of women in civilization was "assigned long ago by a higher intelligence."

Frances Folsom Cleveland gave birth to five children during their marriage. Their first child, Ruth—Baby Ruth as she came to be called—was born in 1891, at the Cleveland townhouse on Madison Avenue in Manhattan. Esther came next, in 1893, the only child in history ever to be born in the White House. Marion was delivered at Buzzards Bay in 1899. A son, Richard, came in 1897, followed by the last born, a boy, Francis, in 1903, when Grover Cleveland was sixty-six years old. Fatherhood agreed with Cleveland. He was no longer scowling and harrumphing all the time. "I sit on the piazza a good deal and herd the children," he said about his days in comfortable retirement.

The Clevelands suffered a terrible loss when Baby Ruth was stricken with what seemed like a mild case of tonsillitis the day after New Year's 1904. Five days later the twelve-year-old was diagnosed with diphtheria. On January 7, she was dead. Her death came as a staggering loss for the former president and his wife.

President Cleveland died of a heart attack on the morning of June 24, 1908, in a large room on the second floor of his home in Princeton. At his side were Frances and three physicians. His death came six years after Maria Halpin's passing. His last words were, "I have tried so hard to do right."

Emma Folsom died of pneumonia at the age of seventy-six, in 1915, also in Princeton, where she had gone to live in 1901 after the death of her second husband, Henry Perrine.

Rose Cleveland lived to the age of seventy-two. Her greatest days were her last. She was living in Tuscany when the influenza epidemic of 1918 swept through the village of Bagni di Lucca on its way to killing fifty million people worldwide. Rose organized the village's medical response. Working at her side was the great love of her life, Evangeline Simpson Whipple, their romance having been rekindled following the death of Evangeline's husband, Bishop Henry Whipple, in 1901. The two women acted heroically. As villagers began to "die like sheep," Rose sent urgent telegrams to the regional capital of Florence, appealing for nurses. She also cabled her friends in America to send money and medicine. The air, Rose ominously reported, was "heavy with germs" with a virulent pestilence out of the Dark Ages. Rose and Evangeline rented an empty house in Bagni di Lucca as a dwelling for the youngsters in the village whose parents were infected with the flu. They scoured the shops, securing every bit of available clothing to make into bed linen for the sick. It was said that Rose exhausted every lira she had.

Rose was stricken with fever in late November. Six days later, the former First Lady was dead. Evangeline gave a moving account of these final days, calling Rose "one of the noblest, truest, and really greatest characters I have ever known." Her coffin was draped in the American flag, and by edict of the mayor of Bagni di Lucca, all shops and places of business were closed and flags were flown at half-mast. Evangeline rode in a carriage behind the hearse followed by a silent procession of Italian villagers. Rose was buried in a cemetery on the banks of the Lima River, and when Evangeline died in 1930, she was laid down in a grave next to Rose. Eve's will stated that her personal letters remain sealed for fifty years. Only then was her forbidden romance with the former First Lady made known.

Frances Folsom Cleveland was raising her four surviving children when, four years after Grover Cleveland's death, she made the surprising announcement that she was remarrying. Her fiancé was Thomas Jex Preston, a fifty-year-old professor of archeology and art history at Wells College. Preston had had an unusual career path. He had studied at Columbia and the Brooklyn Polytechnic Institute and gone to work for the family kerosene business in Newark, but in his late thirties, he quit and moved to Paris to study at the Sorbonne for two years. Afterward, he enrolled at Princeton University, where he met Frances. In time he earned a doctorate. Frances used her connections at Wells College, where she was a member of the board of trustees, to obtain a professorship there for Preston, and after less than a year on the faculty, lo and behold, he was named acting president. Eight months later, he and Frances announced their engagement. Preston, after grumbling that he could find no suitable accommodations for himself and his bride-to-be in rustic Aurora, New York, except for a vacant apartment over Hickey's store, resigned his post at Wells. He returned to Princeton to be with his fiancée.

Preston was six feet tall and broad shouldered, with jet-black hair streaked with gray and a black mustache. He had a sarcastic sense of humor and was quite the connoisseur, smoked cigarettes, and played a "rattling good game of tennis." He was also the subject of much chatter among the young ladies at Wells who were intrigued by the racing car he drove and his reputation for being "light on his feet." The girls called him "Arty," because he taught art history. They could not believe he was approaching fifty—he looked a decade younger. It was remarked that Frances Cleveland had endowed an art history chair at Wells specifically for Preston—"where she knew she could find him."

Stout but still winsome at age forty-eight, Frances said her engagement to Preston gave her a sense of contentment. She told her friend Helena Gildor, "I feel sure you will like him . . . This is not the enthusiasm of a girl—it is the settled conviction of a mature woman—whose standards of men you know." Frances indicated that all her children approved of the match.

Others were not so sure. Jean S. Davis, who had been a playmate of Baby Ruth Cleveland, found it distressing that President Cleveland's widow was marrying. No fan of the groom, Jean Davis recalled the "unpleasant shock when I read the headlines reporting the engagement. . . . And that it was Mr. Preston!" Frances Cleveland was to her a "national monument, and it distressed many of us to learn that the base was of clay."

Preston could be eccentric and fussy about his clothes. During his brief tenure at Wells, the students kept count—he wore twenty-eight suits. Even the worshippers at the First Presbyterian Church in Princeton had something to say about his clothes when he took President Cleveland's seat in church.

"The Cleveland pew was third in front of ours," recalled Jean Davis. "The broad back of the ex-president had long been familiar to me. So now his place was taken by a younger, less corpulent man, with shiny black hair, who wore a shepherd's plaid suit to church in an era when we were accustomed to gentlemen who dressed in Sunday morning formality." Another source of umbrage for Jean Davis was the unpleasant realization that Preston had failed to correct his profile in *Who's Who in America* that erroneously identified him as a professor of archeology at Princeton, when his only association with the university was that of alumnus. Another ingredient of Preston's quirky character was that he was fond of crocheting. Needlework was a pastime he shared with Frances; the moment she'd pull out her knitting, Preston would reach for his crochet. A man's man in the Grover Cleveland mode Preston was not.

Preston stepped into his new social life with ease. Two weeks after he'd resigned from Wells College, he was at Frances's side when Esther Cleveland presented herself to society. President Taft feted the couple at a White House dinner. (Frances held back tears when they were shown the Blue Room, where she had married Grover Cleveland nearly thirty years before.)

Frances's wedding to Preston took place on February 10, 1913, at the home of Princeton University's president. It was a small affair, nothing like her White House wedding, with only a handful of guests present, including her servants. Frances walked into the main drawing room wearing a white silk gown and carrying a bouquet of her favorite flower, white Killarney roses. Preston's father gave her away. The 10:30 AM ceremony, followed by a wedding breakfast, had been so hurriedly arranged that Frances's son, Richard, a student at Phillips Andover Academy, could not make it in time. The three other Cleveland children were in attendance, though it seemed to Jean Davis that a brick wall of antipathy had been erected between Preston and his youngest stepson, nine-year-old Francis.

The reason that had been given for the hasty ceremony was said to be the groom's physical condition; he was reported by Frances to be "very ill," ordered by his doctor to spend the winter in Florida for reasons of health. However, several of the guests could not help but notice how nimbly he ducked under a shower of rice when he slid his lean six-foot frame into Grover Cleveland's old steel-grey motor car and drove off with Frances. His bearing, according to one observer, didn't seem to be "that of a man who needed to go to Florida for his health."

After Frances remarried, she took up the cause of ensuring President Cleveland's place in history and devoted the rest of her life to it. She was the keeper of the flame, standing guard over her late husband's papers and granting access to them only to those historians in the academic establishment who could assure her of their devotion to the man's greatness.

The first authorized biography, *Recollections of Grover Cleveland*, by George F. Parker, was published in 1909, the year after Cleveland's death. Parker had been a loyal political aide who Cleveland had appointed U.S. consul in Birmingham, England. Every word of his book was written with reverence and regard for the late president. According to Parker, Cleveland was "a good and pure man in his private and domestic life." Like all hagiographies, Parker's *Recollections* offered a one-dimensional portrait of the man. How did Parker deal with the Maria Halpin scandal? He ignored it. Even so, Frances, who had been granted complete editorial control of the book, found some things in it that she didn't appreciate.

"I went over his book before it was published," Frances confided to her late husband's private secretary, William Gorham Rice. She had hacked away at some of the language, Frances said, and "cut out a good deal."

Exalted men require big biographies, and in Robert McNutt McElroy, a distinguished professor of history at Princeton University, Frances believed she had found the perfect collaborator. The Princeton connection aside, Frances and McElroy were also friends. McElroy served with her on the board of trustees at Wells College, and in 1913, she recruited the historian for the presidency of Wells, an offer he declined. Frances gave McElroy her complete endorsement of his Cleveland biography and called on all her late husband's colleagues to cooperate with him. McElroy commenced work in 1919, and the two-volume *Grover Cleveland: The Man and the Statesman* was published in 1923. In its 786 pages, there is not one mention of Maria Halpin. McElroy alludes to the scandal only in this roundabout way. "When his friend, Charles W. Goodyear, reported that a particularly violent attack was to be made upon him by the enemy press the following day, regarding an incident in his earlier life, and asked what to say in reply, Cleveland telegraphed: 'Whatever you say, tell the truth.' And his friends told the truth."

In 1932, the historian Allan Nevins published his biography of Grover Cleveland. Nevins taught at Columbia University and wrote more than fifty books during his celebrated career, his most acclaimed work, the epic eight-volume Civil War history *Ordeal of the Union*. But the book that won him the first of two Pulitzer Prizes was *Grover Cleveland: A Study in Courage*. In his preface, the first person Nevins thanks is Cleveland's widow, "who threw open his papers and gave invaluable advice."

Unlike McElroy, Nevins chose not to ignore the scandal, understanding that for the sake of his credibility, it had to be dealt with. He tackled it head-on, but with the unmitigated vilification of Maria Halpin that set the tone for all historians to come. According to Nevins's account, the *Evening Telegraph* was a "despised Buffalo rag" whose article, "A Terrible Tale," was garnished "with unctuous detail" and revealed nothing more than that Cleveland had once "maintained a connection with a Buffalo woman named Halpin whose illegitimate son was later placed in an orphan asylum."

"After reciting the initial charges, the *Telegraph* gradually added a series of allegations venomous in their falsity." Nevins wrote that these accusations emanated from the owners of "saloons and dives" who were out to get Cleveland for his clean-government crusade to root out corruption in Buffalo. As for George Ball, Nevins says the Baptist minister "made himself a national nuisance," and by posing as "Buffalo's exponent of decency, he actually gave currency to indecent falsehood."

In the Nevins book, Cleveland makes a common sense decision in decreeing that his associates tell the truth because "from the truth he had little to fear." Maria Halpin, Nevins concludes, was a sexual plaything, passed around among the leading lawyers of Buffalo, a harlot who drank to excess and neglected her illegitimate son Oscar. Uncertain about the identity of the father, she fixed on Cleveland because he was the only bachelor among her paramours and "she hoped to make him marry her." Cleveland did not question paternity because "the other men in the scrape were married."

"A weaker or more callous man in his place would have tried to, with some prospect of success, deny responsibility for the child; but Cleveland saw the matter through in the most courageous way." Cleveland, concludes Nevins, "never flinched" and his "subsequent indifference to the child was due to his doubts about his fatherhood." Put another way, Cleveland conducted himself selflessly, and the Halpin scandal was a high mark in Cleveland's long life of personal integrity.

When Frances completed reading Nevins's work, apart from some minor reservations, she pronounced herself satisfied, as well she should have been. It offered, she said, a "true picture—of the man and his meaning."

To this day, Nevins's work is regarded as the definitive Cleveland biography. Every subsequent Cleveland book has trod the path he set down. But as we have seen, this time-honored version of the scandal borders on being a fairy tale. And the falsehoods continue to this day. In 2008, when the tabloid *National Enquirer* revealed that a love child had been born to Rielle Hunter and Democratic presidential candidate John Edwards, *New York Times* columnist Gail Collins noted how it was "weirdly reminiscent" of what Grover Cleveland had experienced, in that a "scurrilous newspaper from his hometown of Buffalo accused him of being the father of a love child born to Maria Halpin, a store clerk. She later took to drink, and Cleveland, a bachelor, arranged to have the baby adopted by friends.

"It probably wasn't Cleveland's child. . . . But Cleveland stolidly refused to defend himself . . . "

Gail Collins does not merit any blame for recapitulating this fundamentally dishonest account of the Halpin scandal. It is, after all, how so many esteemed historians have presented it. It is said that history is written by the victors, which certainly holds true in the defamation of Maria Halpin.

In October 1946, an extraordinary spectacle took place in Princeton, New Jersey. Under a brilliant October sun, several hundred of the world's leading scholars, dressed in vividly colored academic robes representing the foremost universities in the United States and Europe, paraded through the campus of Princeton University. It was Princeton's bicentennial celebration, and in the long line of intellectuals who were to receive honorary degrees in science, law, and letters were some of the most brilliant minds of the 20th century. The Danish physicist Niels Bohr was there. So was Trygve Lie, the secretary-general of the United Nations, and the Nobel Prize–winning chemist Linus Pauling.

At a dinner celebrating the event, President Harry Truman, his daughter Margaret, and the new army chief of staff, General Dwight David Eisenhower, were all seated at the head table, along with another dignitary—a white-haired old lady nearing the end of her days. Frances Folsom Cleveland Preston had been diagnosed with cataracts, and she was told that she might lose her sight. She accepted her fate and had begun to learn Braille and prepare herself for progressive blindness when an operation mercifully restored her vision. Time had ravaged the former First Lady of the United States, although it could not erase the essence of her graciousness. Even in old age, she remained a beautiful and self-assured woman.

Mrs. Preston was introduced to General Eisenhower. It was sometimes forgotten that Mrs. Preston had once been Mrs. Grover Cleveland. At some point during their conversation, she remarked that she had once lived in Washington. Eisenhower was intrigued.

"You did?" he asked. "Where?"

One year later, Frances died in her sleep.

EPILOGUE

AND **SO** **WE** come to the fate of Oscar Folsom Cleveland, the bastard child of Grover Cleveland and Maria Halpin. For more than a century, mystery has shrouded his life story. One enduring myth was that he became an alcoholic and died homeless somewhere in upstate New York. The truth of what happened to Oscar can at last be answered in this book.

Records show that Oscar was born September 14, 1874, at a hospital for unwed mothers. At age two, he was taken by force from his mother's arms and thrown into an orphanage. Although his formal legal adoption papers have been sealed in perpetuity, we know from contemporary accounts that he was taken in by the physician James E. King and his wife Sarah. They gave Oscar a new name—James E. King Jr.—and raised him in a fine house with a picket fence at 93 Niagara Street in Buffalo.

James E. King Jr.'s life after that was exceptional and productive. Like his adoptive father, he became a doctor. In 1896, he graduated from the University of Buffalo School of Medicine and then pursued postgraduate studies in Munich, London, and Dresden. When he returned to Buffalo in 1898, he became a pioneer in the field of gynecology when it was rare for a physician to specialize in women's medicine; in all of Buffalo, there were only three doctors practicing gynecology. King was a cautious healer who was said to be unusually devoted to his patients. He also took on numerous charity cases. Not surprisingly, considering the circumstances of his birth, King was a zealous enthusiast of the work of Charles Dickens, the great English writer. The story of the orphan boy Oliver Twist must surely have resonated with him. King even set up a Dickens Room in his house in which wallpaper and every piece of artwork and furniture depicted characters from Dickens's novels.

King was devoted to his adoptive mother, Sarah, who outlived her husband by thirty-five years. She and her son lived together until her death in 1923. No matter the sinful manner by which the Kings came to adopt James, they were good parents to him.

King married once, in 1910 when he was thirty-five. His bride was Rose Weber, a German-born divorcee who had a seventeen-year-old son. The marriage did not last the decade, and they had no children, but King went on to live a full if lonely life. He enjoyed horseback riding, a favorite pastime, loved opera, and had an excellent art collection. Dr. King traveled to Europe seven times during his life, chiefly to attend lectures and medical conventions. For fourteen years, he was a professor of gynecology at the University of Buffalo School of Medicine.

The doctor had a devoted household staff that attended to all his comforts, but as an employer, he had some quirks. Saimi Pratt worked as his cook and live-in housekeeper for five years, but when she got married, he told her that her services were no longer required. It was King's policy to have only single women working for him. The cook bore him no hard feelings and in fact thought so highly of him that his picture hung in her house long after he had dismissed her. The feeling was mutual; James King generously gave her $500 for her son's education.

Dr. Milton Kahn, a promising young gynecologist, became King's protégé. He and his bride, Ruth, were favored Sunday guests at King's stately home at 1255 Delaware Avenue, a five-bedroom colonial decorated in high-end Kittinger furniture. Sunday dinners with King were formal events, with the full-course meal starting at one in the afternoon. Ruth Kahn found herself somewhat intimidated in his presence. "I was a new bride and very nervous. I listened more than I talked," she recalled. Back in 1938, when the Kahns were newlyweds, there were rumors that King was Grover Cleveland's out-of-wedlock son, but understandably, the couple never once raised the subject with him. Gossip about James King's heritage persisted into his old age. It is an interesting footnote that notwithstanding his biological father's historic importance to the Democratic Party, King was a Republican.

King was active until the end. In 1946, at age seventy, he attended a medical conference in faraway Peru. On March 9, 1947, he died at home. Preserving his privacy to the end, he told his nurse the day before his death, "If anyone calls, just say I am improving." A funeral procession took his coffin to the King family plot in Warren, Pennsylvania, where he was buried next to his adoptive parents. So far as is known, he never reached out to Maria Halpin, or she to him.

Dr. King's will was a carefully thought out document. All his possessions were doled out with a purpose. To his medical school he left the considerable sum of $480,000, plus Pliny the Elder's *Naturalis Historia*, the world's first encyclopedia. The treasured work remains at Buffalo University to this day. King also remembered Dr. Kahn, bequeathing his protégé ten needles of radium. In those days, gynecologists in private practice had to have their own source of radium, which was used to treat ovarian cancer by injection of the radioactive element directly into the cancerous tissue.

King showed remarkable generosity to Mary Meek, a nurse who cared for Sarah King in the final years of her life. In recognition of her devotion to his mother, he permitted Ms. Meek to live at his home for six months without rent and bequeathed her all his household furnishings and a monthly income for the rest of her life. Other people who were special in his life were also remembered in his will. To his former laundress, he left $500. A poor patient's six-year-old son was given $500 for his education.

But to the very end, Dr. James E. King Jr., born Oscar Folsom Cleveland, kept the family secrets.

THE END

ACKNOWLEDGMENTS

R ESEARCHING *A SECRET LIFE* has been a challenge.
Published biographies of Grover Cleveland have whitewashed the Maria Halpin scandal or treated it only superfi-
cially. As happens occasionally to authors, there came a eureka
moment for me when I realized I had found a treasure trove of
material that previous writers had overlooked. These were the
court proceedings of the 1890 libel trial of *Ball v. The New York
Evening Post Corporation*. For the first and only time, many of
the key people connected to the scandal were compelled to testify
under oath about what they knew of Maria Halpin and Grover
Cleveland. I found these records in the archives of the New York
State Appellate Division, Fourth Department Law Library, in
Rochester, New York. Although Maria Halpin was never called
as a witness at the *Ball* trial, I also obtained her handwritten
affidavits, sworn to in October 1884, when the attacks on her
character compelled her to go public with her version of events.

Grover Cleveland's lifetime of correspondence has been collected by the historian Allan Nevins and published in the *Letters of Grover Cleveland, 1850–1908*. The letters, particularly those written in the 1850s, offer priceless detail of time and place when Cleveland was on the cusp of manhood. The Cleveland Papers at the Library of Congress were another vital source of information for the White House years. Fortunately, the papers and correspondence of several key Cleveland aides who were involved in managing the Maria Halpin crisis—including Horatio C. King, Wilson Bissell, and Daniel Lamont—have been preserved in the Library of Congress and various archives and special collections. Allan Nevins also left much of his research into the life of Grover Cleveland archived at Columbia University.

Maria Halpin's family put into my hands cherished family photographs passed down through the generations. No photograph of Maria Halpin has ever previously been published. With *A Secret Life*, we finally get a look at this woman who I believe has been terribly disparaged in history. I especially want to thank two of Maria Halpin's direct descendants, Emogene Sweeney and Jennifer Hawkins, for guiding me through their family history and encouraging me in my research and writing so that Maria Halpin's story could finally be told.

I want to thank Doris Cross for her invaluable editorial contributions to the final manuscript. She has my sincere appreciation for another great job. Tamie Rovnak served as my research associate in Buffalo for more than two years of indefatigable endeavor.

William Kendall III and his son, William Kendall IV, descendants of Minnie Kendall and Sarah Kendall King, were also generous with their time and advice. And Ruth Kahn Stouroff was kind enough to offer me firsthand memories of Dr. James E. King Jr.

Many dedicated archivists and librarians were extraordinarily helpful, especially Cynthia Van Ness of the Buffalo and Erie County Historical Society, Sister Mary Grace Higgins of the Sisters of Charity Hospital in Buffalo, John A. Edens of the University at Buffalo Libraries of the State University of New York, and Barbara Davis of the New Rochelle Public Library. I also want to express my gratitude to Jarrod Cushing for creating some of the graphics used in this book, and David Voisinet and Robyn Carlton of the Appellate Division, Fourth Department Law Library, in Rochester for their essential efforts in locating the files of *Ball v. The Evening Post Corporation*. Also, Tim Freeman, Utica Public Library; Wendy Edwards, Ludington Library, Bryn Mawr; Daniel DiLandro, college archivist and Special Collections librarian, E. H. Butler Library, Buffalo; Malinda Triller, Dickinson College; Jennifer B. Lee and Tara C. Craig, Rare Book & Manuscript Library, Butler Library, Columbia University; Muriel Godbout, Wells College; and Jeanette Cafaro, Historical Society of Princeton.

Also, Paul Toomey and Vanessa E. Higgins in Boston; Rick Moody in New Rochelle, Beverly Hermes in St. Paul, Patti Cottingham of the Scripps Howard Foundation, and the historians Dr. Mary Block and Dr. Merril Smith. The historian Barbara Bair of the Library of Congress went beyond the call of duty in guiding me through the Cleveland Collection.

In Buffalo, Karen Spencer, Archives & Special Collections, Charles B. Sears Law Library at the University of Buffalo; Jeannine A. Lee, senior law librarian, Buffalo City Court Library; and

Michael Nowakowski, Erie County Clerk's Office. Buffalo lawyers Glenn Murray, Maryann Saccomando Freedman, Courtland R. LaVallee, and Chief Judge Carl L. Bucki of the Western District of New York Bankcruptcy Court were all enormously generous.

Any errors or omissions in the writing of *A Secret Life* are mine alone.

Thanks to the Minnesota Historical Society for making available the correspondence between Rose Cleveland and Evangeline Marrs Simpson Whipple. Although I have cast a critical eye on the historian Allan Nevins, this relates only to his biography of Grover Cleveland. None of the conclusions in this book should diminish the great body of work in Nevins's illustrious career. I want to acknowledge my reliance on his Cleveland biography, which, despite its flaws, remains the definitive work on President Cleveland's life. *A Secret Life* should not be seen as a biography of Cleveland but, rather, as the story of the Maria Halpin scandal. Anyone wishing to explore the full, rich life of Grover Cleveland and his two presidential administrations are advised to read Nevins's work.

Thanks to my colleagues at *Inside Edition* and CBS Television Distribution and Charlie Carillo, Eric Fettmann, and Lisa Sharkey for all their encouragement. I owe yet another debt of appreciation to my literary agent, the great Larry Kirshbaum, and everyone at Skyhorse Publishing, particularly Herman Graf and Jennifer McCartney.

Finally, to my wife, Nancy Glass, whose loving support through these years of research and writing were so important in the completion of this book. Her editorial eye greatly contributed to the final product. And to our children—Max, Pamela, and Sloane—for all that they mean to us.

BIBLIOGRAPHY

APPLEGATE, DEBBY. THE *Most Famous Man in America: The Biography of Henry Ward Beecher.* New York: Three Leaves Press, 2006.

Armitage, Charles H. *Grover Cleveland as Buffalo Knew Him.* Buffalo: Buffalo Evening News, 1926.

Bailey, George M. *Illustrated Buffalo, the Queen City of the Lakes.* Buffalo: Acme Publishing and Engraving Co., 1890.

Baker, William Spohn. *American Engravers and Their Works.* Philadelphia: Gebbie & Barrie, 1875.

Barnum, Augustine. *The Lives of Grover Cleveland and Thomas A. Hendricks: Democratic Presidential Candidates of 1884.* Chicago: A. G. Nettleton & Co., 1884.

Bassett, Norman L. *Sprague's Journal of Maine History,* vol. 8. New York: Lewis Historical Publishing Co., 1909.

Batterberry, Michael and Ariane. *On the Town: The Landmark History of Eating, Drinking, and Entertainments From the*

American Revolution to the Food Revolution. Oxford: Routledge, 1998.

Bigelow, John. *The Life of Samuel J. Tilden.* New York: Harper & Bros., 1895.

Block, Mary R. Block. *An Accusation Easily to be Made: A History of Rape Law in Nineteenth Century America.* Lexington: University of Kentucky, 2001, PhD dissertation.

Brands, H. W. *The Reckless Decade: America in the 1890s.* Chicago: University of Chicago Press, 1995.

Brodsky, Alyn. *Grover Cleveland: A Study in Character.* New York: St. Martin's Press, 2000.

Browne, Ray Broadus and Lawrence A. Kreiser. *The Civil War and Reconstruction.* Oxford: Greenwood Press, 2003.

Chudacoff, Howard P. *The Age of the Bachelor: Creating an American Subculture.* Princeton: Princeton University Press, 1999.

Crook, William H. *Memories of the White House: The Home Life of Our Presidents from Lincoln to Roosevelt.* Boston: Little Brown and Co., 1911.

Davis, Jean S. *A Rambling Memoir of Mrs. Grover Cleveland and Some Related History.* Aurora, New York: Wells College, 1969.

Dieckmann, Jane M. *Wells College: A History.* Aurora, New York: Wells College Press, 1995.

Dunlap, Annette. *Frank: The Story of Frances Folsom Cleveland, America's Youngest First Lady.* Albany: SUNY Press, 2009.

Faderman, Lillian. *Odd Girls and Twilight Lovers: A History of Lesbian Life in Twentieth-Century America.* New York: Penguin, 1992.

Farquhar, Michael. *Treasury of Great American Scandals*. New York: Penguin Books, 2002.

Field, George W. *Field's Medico-Legal Guide for Doctors and Lawyers*. Albany: Banks & Brothers, 1887.

Goldman, Mark. *High Hopes: The Rise and Decline of Buffalo, New York*. Albany: State University of New York Press, 1983.

Gould, Lewis L. ed. *American First Ladies*. New York and London: Garland Publishing Inc., 1996.

Gullan, Harold I. *Faith of Our Mothers: The Stories of Presidential Mothers from Martha Washington to Barbara Bush*. Grand Rapids: William B. Eerdmans Publishing Co., 2001.

Harmon, Isabel F. *Glamour Girl*, Buffalo: Buffalo & Erie County Historical Society, 1949.

Howe, M. A. DeWolkfe. *Portrait of an Independent*. Boston: Houghton Mifflin Co., 1932.

Hudson, William C. *Random Recollections Of An Old Political Reporter*. New York: Cupples and Leon Co., 1911.

Jamro, Ron and Gerald L. Lanterman. *The Founding of Naples*. Naples, Florida: The Collier County Museum, 1985.

Keen, William Williams. *The Surgical Operations on President Cleveland in 1893*. Philadelphia: George W. Jacobs & Co., 1917.

Leary, Thomas E. and Elizabeth Sholes. *Buffalo's Pan-American Exposition*. Charleston, South Carolina: Arcadia Publishing, 1998.

London, Jack. *The Road*. New York: Macmillan Company, 1907.

Lynch, Denis Tilden. *Grover Cleveland: A Man Four-Square*. New York: Horace Liveright, Inc., 1932.

McElroy, Robert McNutt. *Grover Cleveland, the Man and the Statesman: An Authorized Biography.* New York: Harper & Brothers, 1923.

Nevins, Allan. *The Evening Post: A Century of Journalism.* New York: Boni & Liveright, 1922.

Nevins, Allan. *Grover Cleveland: A Study in Courage.* New York: Dodd, Mead and Co., 1933.

Nevins, Allan. ed. *Letters of Grover Cleveland.* Boston and New York: Houghton Mifflin Co., 1933.

Parker, George F. *Recollections of Grover Cleveland.* New York: The Century Company, 1911.

Peck, Harry Thurston. *Twenty Years of the Republic, 1885–1905.* New York: Dodd, Mead and Co., 1920.

Rapp, Marvin. *The Port of Buffalo.* Duke University doctoral thesis, 1947.

Rice, William Gorham and Francis Lynde Stetson. *Was New York's Vote Stolen?* New York: The North American Review Publishing Co., 1914.

Richardson, Jean. *A History of the Sisters of Charity Hospital, Buffalo, New York 1848–1900.* Lewiston, New York. The Edwin Mellen Press, 2005.

Robar, Stephen F., *Frances Clara Folsom Cleveland.* New York: Nova History Publications, 2004.

Seacord, Morgan H., *Biographical Sketches and Index of the Huguenot Settlers of New Rochelle, 1687–1776.* New Rochelle, New York. The Huguenot and Historical Association of New Rochelle.

Frank H. Severance, ed., *The Periodical Press of Buffalo* vol. 19. Buffalo: The Buffalo Historical Society, 1915.

Smith, Henry Perry. *History of the City of Buffalo & Erie County: 1620–1884,* vol. 1. Syracuse, New York. D. Mason and Co.

Summers, Mark Wahlgren. *Rum, Romanism, and Rebellion: The Making of a President 1884.* Chapel Hill and London: University of North Carolina Press, 2000.

Trimble, Vance H., *The Astonishing Mr. Scripps: The Turbulent Life of America's Penny Press Lord.* Ames, Iowa: Iowa State University Press, 1992.

Vogel, Michael N., Ed Patton and Paul Redding, *America's Crossroads: Buffalo's Canal Street.* Buffalo: Western New York Heritage Institute, Canisius College, 1993.

Willard, Frances Elizabeth and Mary A. Livermore, eds. *A Woman of the Century.* Buffalo: Charles Wells Moulton, 1893.

NOTES

PROLOGUE

IX. The child was born on September 14, 1874, United States Federal Census, 1880; Buffalo, New York. The census approximates the year of the child's birth as 1875. Later census records (see 1900 Census) clarify James E. King Jr.'s date of birth as September 1874.

X. The baby had a "sore" on the top of his head: Account of Minnie Kendall, *Chicago Tribune*, "Maria Halpin's Terrible Experience Related By Her Child's Nurse," 1 October 1884.

XII. "Yes, it does look like its father," Ibid.

1. BUFFALO

1. "I am kind of fooling away my time here," Grover Cleveland (GC) to Mary Cleveland Hoyt, undated, winter 1853–1854, Allan Nevins, ed., *Letters of Grover Cleveland* (Boston and New York: Houghton Mifflin Co., 1933), 3–4. Hereafter Nevins, *Letters*.

2. "like an inspiration," Allan Nevins, *Grover Cleveland: A Study in Courage* (New York: Dodd, Mead and Co.,1958 edition), 27.

2. "It's just the place for a young man to establish himself in," *New York Times*, 24 January 1892.

3. "I was attracted by the name," Denis Tilden Lynch, *Grover Cleveland: A Man Four-Square* (New York: Horace Liveright, Inc., 1932), 31.

4. "my start in life," GC to Ingham Townsend, 23 January 1867, Nevins, *Letters*, 10.

6. "proper location for me," Richard Cleveland to Dr. A. B. Cleveland, 12 October 1841, Cleveland Papers, Library of Congress.

6. "His modesty killed him," Nevins, 13.

6. not a "single friend or acquaintance," Letter to editor from Lewis Allen to *Buffalo Courier*, 14 July 1884.

8. he came close to losing two fingers: GC to Mary Cleveland Hoyt, 29 October 1850, Nevins, *Letters*, 9.

8. The two-story Allen house, constructed of stone: Charles H. Armitage, *Grover Cleveland as Buffalo Knew Him* (Buffalo: Buffalo Evening News, 1926, Kessinger Publishing Edition), 4.

8. "Who's the new fellow?" Ibid, 2–3; 7.

11. "high-spirited boy," Armitage, 15.

17. Lewis Allen was probably Buffalo's leading citizen, Nevins, 32–33.

13. Grover was trapped inside (Author's note: This incident is murky. Some books say Cleveland was locked out only during lunch hour (Nevins, 36); Armitage says it happened overnight.)

13. "Pay him what they could afford," Armitage, 15.

13. "very satisfactory," GC to Mary Cleveland Hoyt, 18 October 1855, Nevins, *Letters*, 4–5.

14. pocket was feeling "light," Ibid, 14 November 1855, 5.

15. "though sometimes I find it pretty hard," Ibid, 31 December 1855, 6–7.

16. "I am so ashamed of myself after allowing such a swindle," Ibid, 14 February 1856, 8; 1 January 1858, 8–9.

16. "The truth is I have a great deal to do nowadays," Ibid, 27 May 1858, 20.

17. "Politically, we differed," *New York Times*, 24 April 1887.

18. "sad in the eye," *Buffalo Commercial Advertiser*, 18 February 1861.

18. "You must save the Union," *Buffalo Courier*, 18 February 1861.

19. "lukewarm," Nevins, 48.

20. even Grover Cleveland said that was a myth, ibid, 50.

20. behind drum and bugle, ibid, 47.

22. "I have my man," *Buffalo Democrat and Chronicle*, 3 September 1884. Author's note: The spelling of Cleveland's substitute has been spelled in various ways, including Benninsky and Brinske. The spelling of Biniski is from Army records.

23. "I told him if he would . . . help me out if I came out alive: *Buffalo Sunday Times* interview with Beniski, 10 July 1887.

24. "The terms . . . were distinctly repeated by me: GC to John E. Hale, 13 September 1887, Nevins, *Letters*, 52.

25. "frightfully filthy," Testimony of Dr. George W. Edwards, U.S. Army surgeon, 6 June 1864.

25. Beniski's medical records show: Application for pension signed by Beniski (with his mark, the letter X) 3 June 1886, National Archives and Records, Pension no. 561–108.

2. THE BACHELOR

27. Hovenden gave chase, *Brooklyn Eagle*, 16 November 1858.

28. The Halpins had immigrated to the United States in 1842, William Spohn Baker, *American Engravers and Their Works* (Philadelphia: Gebbie & Barrie, 1875), 79.

28. "Is that all?" Fletcher Harper paid the bill, *The Dial*, 1912 (*The Dial* was a literary review published in Chicago; the incident involving Fletcher Harper and Frederick Halpin took place in 1869.)

29. In general, he was in "poor health": *Chicago Tribune*, 18 August 1884. Interview with Robert Hovenden.

30. "Well, Cleve, I have been offered: Lynch, 48.

31. "Grover! Do you realize we have by now 'anticipated,'" *Saturday Evening Post*, "Grover Cleveland's Career in Buffalo, 1855–1885, 28 August 1920. Lyman Bass's background is from Henry Perry Smith, *History of the City of Buffalo and Erie County: 1620–1884,* vol. 1 (Syracuse, New York, D. Mason & Co.), 481.

31. Bass's electoral strength lay in the towns: Nevins, 53.

32. A favorite was, "There's a hole in the bottom of the sea," ibid, 57;

32. "hammer and tongs," Lynch, 51.

33. "Boas used to say he preferred to have his patrons. Armitage, 67.

33. forced to "lose a day," Lynch, 48.

34. It was the dawning of the Age of the Bachelor: Howard P. Chudacoff, *The Age of the Bachelor: Creating an American Subculture* (Princeton: Princeton University Press, 1999), 35. Author's note: Chudacoff's book offers an excellent analysis of the era.

34. "How doth the little busy B": GC to Mary Cleveland Hoyt, 14 February 1856, Nevins, *Letters*, 7–8.

35. "Let's dance the step-over," Armitage, 35.

36. "queer people": Nevins, 55–56.

37. "They needed it, too," Level said. Armitage, 24.

37. "lock, stock or barrel," ibid, 27.

37. My Dear Mr. Townsend: GC to Ingham Townsend, 23 January 1867, Nevins, *Letters*, 10.

38. "As thy days are, so shall thy strength be," Nevins, 56.

38. "livery-stable set," ibid. 58.

40. "sink of iniquity," ibid, 59.

43. "Can't do it, Louis" Lynch, 58–61.

44. Patrick Morrissey was short, about five-four: *Buffalo Commercial Advertiser*, 6 September 1872.

47. "No, I have to do it myself. I am the sheriff," Lynch, 65.

50. "I do not know how it is, but I have an impression: the story is recounted by Colonel William C. Church in *The Century* magazine, undated, "Midwinter Resort."

52. an "estimable lady": *Utica Morning Herald*, 4 November 1872.

52. "a servant of Mr. Cleveland, the lessee of the R.V. Hotel, *New York Times*, 23 November 1872.

53. "When the boats were filled there was no room for them: Augustine Barnum, *The Lives of Grover Cleveland and Thomas A. Hendricks: Democratic Presidential Candidates of 1884* (Chicago: A. G. Nettleton & Co., 1884), 186.

3. MARIA

57. Alexander Stewart's showcase: Ray Broadus Browne and Lawrence A. Kreiser, *The Civil War and Reconstruction* (Oxford: Greenwood Press, 2003), 59–60.

59. "remarkable beauty and rare accomplishments": *Buffalo Evening Telegraph*, interview with Maria Baker, 21 July 1884.

59. "pure and spotless," Maria Halpin affidavit (hereafter Halpin Affidavit), 28 October 1884, signed by Maria Halpin, notarized by Charles G. Banks.

61. "unbelievable and monstrous," Jack London, *The Road* (New York: Macmillan Company, 1907), 97.

61. Disease was omnipresent: Smith, 275. For the depiction of Buffalo in the 1880s the author is also indebted to Michael N. Vogel, Ed Patton and Paul Redding, *America's Crossroads: Buffalo's Canal Street* (Buffalo: Western New York Heritage Institute, Canisius College, 1993), 65–68; and Marvin Rapp, *The Port of Buffalo* (unpublished doctoral thesis, Duke University, 1947.)

63. "What shall be done with these poor creatures," Mark Goldman, *High Hopes: The Rise and Decline of Buffalo, New York* (Albany: State University of New York Press, 1983), 83. Author's note: Goldman's book offers an excellent account of Buffalo's history.

64. Buffalo was the preeminent inland port: Goldman, 121.

65. The busiest time of day at Flint & Kent: Flint & Kent records, Buffalo & Erie County Historical Society archives, MSS A. 70–62.

65. "proper hours," *Buffalo Times*, 1 November 1932.

65. The founding partner, William Flint: *Buffalo Courier*, 12 November 1887.

67. "Send them to Barnum's," *Buffalo Times*, 1 November 1932.

70. "He sought my acquaintance: Halpin Affidavit.

68. "John Gaffney, stand up": *Buffalo Evening Times*, 15 February 1873; *Buffalo Commercial Advertiser*, 14 February 1873.

4. WITHOUT MY CONSENT

74. "Grover told me that night that," Armitage, 58; Nevins, 64.

74. The Metcalfes were celebrated in Buffalo, *New York Times*, 1 December 1893.

75. Cleveland decorated his suite of rooms, Nevins, 66.

75. "fondness for children," Barnum, 82.

76. "Uncle Jumbo," Nevins, 66.

77. "I want you to know that I practice," ibid., 70.

77. "Grant's re-elected, and the country's gone to hell," Lynch, 66.

88. "very pleasing in appearance" Stephen F. Robar, *Frances Clara Folsom Cleveland* (New York: Nova History Publications, 2004), 2–4.

80. The Tifft House on Main Street: George M. Bailey, *Illustrated Buffalo, the Queen City of the Lakes* (Buffalo: Acme Publishing and Engraving Co., 1890), 226; *Buffalo Express*, 21 May 1903.

81. He was "persistent," and "urging": Halpin Affidavit.

82. "He told me that he was determined to ruin me. Ibid.

82. Julie Dow was riding a horse: The author is indebted to the work of the historian Mary R. Block and her PhD dissertation, *An Accusation Easily to be Made: A History of Rape Law in Nineteenth Century America* (Lexington: University of Kentucky, 2001)

83. a woman of "easy virtue," ibid., 28–30 (*People v. Brown*).

83. "did not earnestly resist it," ibid., 75.

83. "ultimately yielded," ibid., 123–124 (*State v. Hartigan*).

84. "fullest extent of her abilities," ibid., 15.

86. "he being the proper person to whom I could tell my trouble," Halpin Affidavit.

86. "What the devil are you blubbering about?" *Chicago Tribune*, 30 and 31 October 1884.

87. "told me that he would do everything which was honorable," Halpin Affidavit.

87. "Was she there at Mr. Cleveland's expense?" *Chicago Tribune*, 30 July 1884.

87. "I cannot ask your love in advance," *Buffalo Democrat & Chronicle* 11 April 1872 (Avery is sometimes spelled Arey.)

88. "I do not wish to palliate his offense: *Boston Daily Globe*, 31 October 1884. Avery is apparently quoted but goes unnamed in the article.

89. "Mr. Cleveland wanted him to have that name," *Chicago Tribune*, 30 July 1884, quoting *Boston Journal* interview with Maria Baker.

89–94. "I don't want to take it," ibid., 1 October 1884, interview with Sarah Kendall. Author's note: Some of the quotes from the 1884 interview have been put in the present tense for purposes of the narrative.

5. THE ORPHAN

95–97. It was a Friday afternoon, July 23, 1875: account of Folsom's death from *Buffalo Commercial Advertiser* and *Buffalo Morning Express*, 24 July 1875.

97. The adolescent Frances, who was considered to be too young. Robar, 5.

99. Marriage was the "only step possible: *Buffalo Evening Telegraph*, 21 July, 1884.

99. "After the birth of her child she led a blameless life. Ibid.

100. Byrne was born in Ireland and came to America: *New York Times*, 27 May 1879; *Buffalo Commercial Advertiser*, 30 December 1909.

103. Received from MB Halpin: Buffalo Orphan Asylum records, courtesy Buffalo & Erie County Historical Society Archives, C821–1.

104. "Thoroughly cleaned," Mrs. M. L. Hopkins, *Charities in Western New York: A Record of Examinations*, 1893, 23. Author's note: No record exists of Oscar Folsom Cleveland's specific experience at the orphanage. This description is based on state inspection reports from the era.

106. "Poor and shiftless," ibid., 21.

106. Overcrowding was a serious problem: *Buffalo Express*, 23 May 1909.

107. "Stolen by M. B. Halpin—mother," Buffalo Orphan Asylum records, vol. III, Admissions and Departures, 4 January 1875–20 March 1882. Buffalo & Erie County Historical Society, C82–1.

108. Because of her purported alcoholism, he informed Level. Lynch, 70.

108. Level, forty-three, liked to boast: *Buffalo Times*, 1 March 1925; 25 February 1925.

109. "Attendant publicity," Lynch, 70.

109. Detective Watts "surreptitiously" broke into the apartment: *Buffalo Evening Telegraph*: 21 July 1884.

110. evidence that Oscar was being neglected was "not lacking," Lynch, 70.

110. "It was a hell of a time," *Buffalo Evening Telegraph*, 21 July 1884.

110. There she was registered as patient No. 1050: Register, Providence Lunatic Asylum, History of Patients, Sept. 23, 1861–Jan. 13, 1897, 35.

111. "A peculiar form of insanity," George W. Field, *Field's Medico-Legal Guide for Doctors and Lawyers* (Albany: Banks and Brothers, 1887), 71.

111. She utterly "loathed" the man: *Chicago Tribune*, 19 September 1884.

112. "Pray that I may meet some good soul," Jean Richardson, *A History of the Sisters of Charity Hospital, Buffalo, New York 1848–1900* (Lewiston, New York The Edwin Mellen Press, 2005)

113. "Guarantee against destructive tendencies," *Buffalo News*, 5 May 1901.

113. "I went through all the halls and rooms and saw all of the patients," *State of New York, Eighteenth Annual Report of the State Board of Charities, 1885*, 311–312.

113. He came to the asylum once a week to offer: Sisters of Charity Hospital Archives, 75 Years Providence Retreat, 1860–1935, 26.

114. "Without warrant or form of law": *Buffalo Evening Telegraph*, 21 July 1884.

114. "Long enough to get straightened out," Lynch, 71.

115. Cleveland had "plotted" her abduction and "hired the men to carry it out," *Boston Journal*, 30 July 1884, interview with Milo Whitney.

116. Appearing under the name *The Misses Kendall*: Author interview with William H. Kendall III, 12 June 2009.

119. Grover Cleveland was a "seducer": *Chicago Inter-Ocean*, 29 September 1884.

120. The Halpin family was not willing to risk a "public scandal," *Buffalo Evening Telegraph*, 21 July 1884.

121. The lawsuit had been irrevocably "compromised," *Boston Journal*, 30 July 1884.

121. The sun could one day "blaze up" and destroy the earth. *New York Times*, 2 January 1877.

122. "Taken by his guardian," Buffalo Orphan Asylum archives, Buffalo & Erie County Historical Society, C82–1.

6. PATH TO THE PRESIDENCY

125. Finally, Cleveland said, "All right, I'll run," Lynch, 79.

125. Sheehan had a reputation for shiftiness and political malfeasance. *New York Times*, 1 November 1894.

125. "I'll be damned if I'll run with that Irishman," Lynch, 79; Armitage, 82. In John B. Weber's biography, he says the actual quote was, "None of that Irishman for me."

126. The "boy judge," Armitage, 59.

126. "I think you'd better accept," ibid., 86–87.

127. "Great unwashed," *Buffalo Commercial Advertiser*, 26 October 1881.

128. "lordly manners," ibid.

129. A Buffalo policeman stood outside each polling station: *Buffalo Morning Express*, 6 November 1881.

130. His reputation for pugnacious honesty. Nevins, 80.

130. "But now that you have taken upon yourself the burdens," Barnum, 185.

132. "I cannot remember a time when interest," Armitage, 101–102.

132. "While I was your attorney I was loyal," ibid., 105.

132. "I have made the greatest mistake of my whole life," Nevins, 86.

133. "Gruff as a mastiff," Armitage, 141–142.

134. "Best available engineering skill," Nevins, 87.

135. "Has always been devotedly attached to her," *Buffalo Morning Express*, 20 July 1882.

135. "Her children arise and call her blessed," Harold I. Gullan, *Faith of Our Mothers: The Stories of Presidential Mothers From Martha Washington to Barbara Bush* (Grand Rapids: William B. Eerdmans Publishing Co., 2001), 137.

136. "I shrink from it every time with just the same reluctance you would feel," Moses Coit Tyler, *In Memoriam Edgar Kelsey Apgar* (Ithaca, New York, *Ithaca Democrat Press*, 1886), 133.

137. An "ugly-honest man": Nevins, 98–99.

138. "Men come here daily from all parts of the state," Armitage, 166–167.

138. "I am gratified with the interest you take in my candidacy," GC to Edgar K. Apgar, 29 August 1882, Nevins, *Letters*, 15.

139. "A man for the hour," Armitage, 169.

140. "I'll do that and better," Mahoney said. Armitage, 153; Lynch, 97.

141. No one here expresses any confidence in his nomination," Lynch, 103.

141. "Deposits placed in his mind were as safe as those made in a bank," William C. Hudson, *Random Collections of an Old Political Reporter* (New York: Cupples and Leon Co., 1911). The description of Hudson is from the introduction by St. Clair McKelway, 9.

142. "Mr. Cleveland, you will be the nominee. Ibid., 132–134.

143. "John B. Manning has been in to see me tonight," GC to Wilson S. Bissell, 19 September 1882, Nevins, *Letters*, 17.

144. "He's our kind of people," Armitage, 154.

144. "It was almost beyond my understanding what to do," George F. Parker, *Recollections of Grover Cleveland* (New York: The Century Company, 1911), 52.

145. A "chance to look me over," ibid.

145. "His features are regular and full of intelligent expression," *New York Times*, 21 September 1882.

146. "He had achieved that rare result in a political convention," Nevins, 103.

147. Still confident of victory, Congressman Flower buttonholed. Armitage, 156.

148. Grinning like a "conqueror," *New York Times*, 24 September 1882.

149. "My friends . . . I cannot but remember," Ibid, 22 September 1882. Some reports say the speech took place in front of Democratic Party headquarters. Dranger's saloon is sometimes spelled Drainger's.

7. THE GODDESS

152. Indisputable glamour: Isabel F. Harmon, *Glamour Girl*, paper presented 14 December 1949 before the Buffalo chapter of the Daughters of the American Revolution, courtesy, Buffalo & Erie County Historical Society.

154. "Advanced standing," Robar, 6.

155. Her roommate, Ms. Katherine "Pussy" Willard: Frances Elizabeth Willard and Mary A. Livermore, eds., *A Woman of the Century* (Buffalo: Charles Wells Moulton, 1893), 781.

156. "Do you know that if Mother were alive," GC to William Cleveland, 7 November 1882, Nevins, *Letters*, 17–18.

157. Cleveland said he was "unable to understand it," Parker, 244–245.

159. "I propose the health of Governor Grover Cleveland," *New York Times*, 6 December 1882.

160. "We come to you as the king," Nevins, 92.

162. Governor Cleveland's inaugural address impressed everyone: *New York Times*, 2 January 1883.

163. "The governor might just as well place his desk on the grass," Hudson, 138.

164. "Blunder of great dimensions," Hudson, 141–142.

168. "When I marry it must be someone more than a year older than I am," Robar, 12.

170. "Specifically for the White House," Ibid, 13.

8. STIRRINGS OF A SCANDAL

172. "My boy, don't you see it is impossible?" Nevins, 146.

172. "Cleveland is not yet a candidate." Hudson, 151.

173. "What makes me puff so?" *New York Times*, 5 August 1886.

173. "I ought not to assume a task which I have not the physical: John Bigelow, *The Life of Samuel J. Tilden* (New York: Harper & Bros., 1895), 280–282.

175. "I wish I might not hear my name mentioned." GC to Mary Cleveland Hoyt, 23 March 1884, Nevins, *Letters*, 32.

175. "Good heavens, Governor, how can you potter," Hudson, 152–154.

176. Dr. George W. Lewis could still remember the day: *Buffalo Evening News*, 5 February 1890. The anecdote is based on Lewis's testimony at the trial of *Ball vs. New York Evening Post Corporation*. Lewis claimed on the stand that he could not recall whether Cleveland's name was brought up when Maria Halpin came to see him, but it seems unlikely that Halpin would have told Lewis her story without referencing Cleveland.

177. Ball was sixty-five years old. *Buffalo Commercial Advertiser*, 22 February 1907; *Buffalo Express*, 10 March 1904.

178. Ball went to see William Flint and Henry Kent: *Buffalo Evening Telegraph*, 21 July 1884.

179. Had a notorious reputation, second only to Canal Street: *Buffalo Courier*, 7 March 1926; *Buffalo Times*, 26 May 1929; *Buffalo Express*, 29 July 1902.

181. "Grossest licentiousness," *Boston Journal*, 6 September 1884.

181. "I'm enlisted for the war, Mr. Manning," Hudson, 162–163.

182. He found the city in the grip of anti-Cleveland. Ibid., 180.

180. "You can print this as coming from me," *New York Times*, 8 July 1884.

184. Every now and then a rebel yell could. Nevins, 151.

186. "For revenue only," a "national disgrace," a "tumor," *New York Times*, 8 July 1884; 9 July 1884.

187. "Not a particle of ambition to be president," GC to Daniel Manning, 30 June 1884, Nevins, *Letters*, 149.

187. "Ideal size for a cavalryman," Lynch, 198.

189. "Holler for Hendricks." Ibid., 203.

189. Kelly and Butler were up until four in the morning. Nevins, 153–154.

190. "How long shall we holler?" *New York Times*, 12 July 1884.

191. "Making the great blunder of his life." Ibid., 13 July 1884.

192. "Congratulate you and the cause of good government." Ibid.

192. "Mr. Hendricks is a man whom very few understand": ibid, 12 July 1884.

193. "Shorn of their plumes," ibid., 14 July 1884.

193. "I am directed by Mr. Blaine to thank you." *Boston Daily Globe*, 28 September 1884.

9. "A TERRIBLE TALE"

195. "Is there someone you wish to see?" Frank H. Severance, ed., *The Periodical Press of Buffalo* vol. 19, (Buffalo: The Buffalo Historical Society, 1915), 335.

196. "He looked me up and down," ibid., 340.

197. "I wonder what I will write about tonight?" Ibid., 173, quoting Joseph O'Connor, editorial writer of the *Buffalo Courier*.

198. "We have no politics . . . We are not Republican, nor Democrat," Vance H. Trimble, *The Astonishing Mr. Scripps: The Turbulent Life of America's Penny Press Lord* (Ames, Iowa: Iowa State University Press, 1992), 75.

199. "Everything was done to make the paper a success," *Buffalo Morning Express*, 18 August 1885.

200. It was one of the finest estates in Augusta: Norman L. Bassett, *Sprague's Journal of Maine History*, vol. 8 (New York: Lewis Historical Publishing Co., 1909), 342. Author's note: Blaine's mansion is now the official residence of the governor of Maine.

200. Zemro Smith sat down with Blaine: *New York World*, 19 May 1885.

201. "Secret consultation," ibid.

202–209. "Responsibility for the disclosures," *Boston Journal*, 30 July 1884.

209. The cause of his derangement: *New York Times*, 15 July 1884.

211. Theodore Roosevelt expressed the sentiment. Ibid., 21 July 1884.

211. "Absolute integrity has never been questioned," ibid., 16 July 1884; 22 July 1884.

211. "Great bombshell," Nevins, 162.

211–216. Titled "A Citizen's Statement," *Buffalo Evening Telegraph*, 21 July 1884.

10. DEFAMED

217. Went around to all the major newsstands trying to buy. *Utica Herald*, undated.

217. "Whatever you do, tell the truth," GC telegram to Charles Goodyear, 23 July 1884, Nevins, *Letters*, 37.

218. "Filled with anguish," Nevins, 168.

218. "The issue of the present campaign is moral, not political," *New York Times*, 23 July 1884.

219. "Great revulsion," *Buffalo Evening Telegraph*, 23 July 1884.

220. "The conclusion I draw from these facts is that." M. A. DeWolkfe Howe, *Portrait of an Independent* (Boston: Houghton Mifflin Co., 1932), 150–152.

221. "I learned last night that McCune had started," GC to Daniel Lockwood, 31 July 1884, Nevins, *Letters*, 38.

222. "They would bring the blush to the cheek of," *Rochester Herald*, 23 July 1884; *New York World*, 24 July 1884; *New York Morning Journal*, 24 July 1884.

223. "The *Telegraph* is little, but it is mighty and will prevail," Buffalo *Evening Telegraph*, 23 July 1884.

223. "All honor to the bravest paper in Buffalo!" *Buffalo Evening Telegraph*, 27 and 28 July 1884.

226. "Owing to late developments from Albany," *New York Times*, 7 August, 1884.

226. Beecher had been sued for adultery," Debby Applegate, *The Most Famous Man in America: The Biography of Henry Ward Beecher* (New York: Three Leaves Press, 2006), 462.

227. "I told him," King later said. *New York World*, 8 August 1884. The headline accompanying Horatio King's interview was, "Cleveland's Vindication."

228. He had erected the mansion in 1879: *New York Times*, 17 March 1889; 8 December 1889.

228. Wallpaper so "exquisite," Applegate, 457.

229. "My husband has been quite ill for several days," *New York Tribune*, 7 August 1884.

231–232. The facts seem to be that many years ago when. *New York World*, 8 August 1884.

11. FINDING MARIA

233. *"Interview Mrs. Maria Halpin who is said to have had child,"* *Buffalo Evening Telegraph*, 14 August 1884.

234. Roosevelt read the telegram: *Buffalo Evening Telegraph*, 14 August 1884.

234. Secor, Seacor, Secord, and finally to Seacord. Morgan H. Seacord, *Biographical Sketches and Index of the Huguenot Settlers of New Rochelle, 1687–1776* (New Rochelle, New York, The Huguenot and Historical Association of New Rochelle, 1941), 47.

235. She had been living a "quiet, decorous, unobtrusive" life: *Boston Globe*, 6 August 1884.

235. Mrs. Halpin was to remain in "strict seclusion," *New York Morning Journal*, 14 August 1884.

236. "Pronouncing the story of her alleged relations," *Buffalo Evening Telegraph*, 14 August 1884.

237. "Henceforth" he would run the newspaper "in the interests of the Republican Party," *New York Times* 5 August 1884.

238. "Of the truth of the story," *Buffalo Evening Telegraph*, 14 August 1884.

238. "They are, and God knows they are true too," *New Rochelle Pioneer*, undated.

239. A "swell" free buffet seven days a week. Michael and Ariane Batterberry, *On the Town: The Landmark History of Eating, Drinking, and Entertainments from the American Revolution to the Food Revolution* (Oxford: Routledge, 1998), 145.

240. His mother would receive the extraordinary sum of ten thousand dollars. *Chicago Inter-Ocean*, 29 September 1884.

240. I have read the statement published in the Buffalo. *Chicago Tribune*, 30 October 1884.

241. Without being "molested," *New Rochelle Pioneer*, undated.

242. *Don't worry, I am going away*. Note published in *Tell the Truth, or the Story of a Working Woman's Wrongs* (New York: Popular Press, 1884). The pamphlet was distributed by the Republican Party and consisted of reprinted articles from the *Evening Telegraph* and other anti-Cleveland newspapers.

242. She was a "magnetic girl . . . full of life. *New York Mercury*, as quoted in *Chicago Tribune*, 13 August 1884.

242. "Mrs. Halpin is evidently an epileptic," *Boston Globe*, 2 November 1884.

243. "I am known in this city and no one can point," *Brooklyn Times*, undated, reprinted in *Tell the Truth* pamphlet under the headline, "Maria Halpin's Parent Relates the Story of his Daughter's Career."

245. "Betrayed into the hands of her enemies," *New York Star*, undated, as quoted in *Tell the Truth*.

245. "I have had trouble enough already, without more," *New York Star*, undated, reprinted in *Tell the Truth*.

247. "Yes, I know Cleveland, perhaps better than any man living," *Chicago Tribune*, 30 September 1884. Cleveland's letter to Talbott does not survive.

249. "They engaged me to care for a young child," ibid., 1 October 1884.

12. "A BULLET THROUGH MY HEART"

251. "I'm glad you've come. I want to talk," Hudson, 184–190.

254. "I hope it will die out at once," GC to Daniel Lamont, 14 August, 1884, Nevins, *Letters*, 40–41.

255. "As a candidate for the presidency I knew that I should," Harry Thurston Peck, *Twenty Years of the Republic, 1885–1905* (New York: Dodd, Mead and Co., 1920), 234–236, Blaine withdrew the lawsuit in December 1884, complaining that the "law gives no adequate redress" in cases of libel involving a public figure.

256. Cleveland descended the staircase and strode. *New York Times*, 30 July 1884.

257. "If one of you young fellows doesn't take," Nevins, 175.

257. "I hope that brass bands and such nonsense," GB to Lamont, 10 August 1884, Nevins, *Letters*, 39.

258. "Remember me to Apgar," ibid., August 11 1884, 40.

258. "Very frequently had no better couch to sleep on," *New York Times*, 27 October 1884; Nevins, 177.

259. Hendricks, along with two nieces, was traveling. *Chicago Tribune*, 18 September 1884.

260. "For many years, days devoted to business," Michael Farquhar, *Treasury of Great American Scandals* (New York: Penguin Books, 2002), 166.

260. "The issue is evidently not between the two great parties," *Buffalo Evening Telegraph*, 21 July 1884.

262. "Filthy and disingenuous," *New York Post*, 8 August 1884.

262. "Moreover, he has, we are informed," ibid., 12 August 1884.

263. The "Rev." Ball, who originated the vile slander. *Boston Herald*, 10 August 1884.

264. The Twinings had arrived in America: *Modern History of New Haven and Eastern New Haven County*, vol. II (New York and Chicago: The S. J. Clarke Publishing Co., 1919), 282–286.

265. "When he was younger than he is now," Twinings's report published as, *The Facts and Evidence Concerning the Private Life of Grover Cleveland*, 27 October 1884.

266. "Everybody and his eldest son," *Boston Globe*, 30 August 1884.

266. "Indignant and disgusted with the people," *Buffalo Courier*, 31 October 1884.

267. "The facts of the case show that she was not seduced," ibid., 11 August 1884.

268. "There was no abduction," ibid.

268. "To see grown men, apparently in their right mind," Twain quoted in Farquhar, 166.

269. "Have just received your package of *Boston Journals*," *New York Post*, 13 August 1884.

269. "Abundant rumors" that Cleveland's immoral behavior. Mark Wahlgren Summers, *Rum, Romanism, and Rebellion: The Making of a President 1884* (Chapel Hill and London: University of North Carolina Press, 2000), 279.

270. "On coming down to breakfast one morning," *New York Times*, 27 October 1884.

270. "Everything looks well for Cleveland," George F. Peabody to William Gorham Rice, 7 September 1884; Box 7, Folder 1, William Gorham Rice Papers, New York State Library, Albany, New York.

271. An "oversensitive and insecure" woman. Applegate, 85. Applegate relates the story of the hot bowl of soup on page 84.

271. Provocative evidence about her "abysmal" marriage, ibid., 444.

272. "What! The Governor took no personal physicians," *New York Times*, 27 October 1884.

273. "I am shocked and dumbfounded by the clippings," GC to Mrs. Henry Ward Beecher, undated but around 20 October 1884, Nevins, *Letters*, 45. The letter was read by Reverend Beecher before a large rally in Brooklyn the night of 23 October 1884.

273. "Crushed in spirit and broken in health," *New Rochelle Pioneer*, 13 September 1884.

274. Frederick, "at the suggestion of my mother," *Boston Globe*, 2 November 1884.

274. "Grover Cleveland is the father," *New York Morning Journal*, 14 August 1884, reprinted in *Tell the Truth*, 31.

275. "I would rather put a bullet through my heart," ibid.

13. THE AFFIDAVIT

277. "The scandal business is about wound up," GC to Wilson Bissell, 11 September 1884, Nevins, *Letters*, 42.

277. "On some other shoulders than mine," GC to Charles Goodyear, 14 September 1884, ibid., 43.

278. Beard was born "deaf as a post," *Morning Oregonian*, 15 September 1895. *Judge* ceased publication in 1947.

280. "We trust the skies will smile upon our festival," *Buffalo Courier*, 2 October 1884.

280. "O hell! A man don't decorate or illuminate his house," GC to Bissell, 5 October 1884, Nevins, *Letters*, 44.

281. "Balm to the wounds of slander," *Buffalo Courier*, 3 October 1884.

281. "Lady of the highest social station and of the most rigid code," *The Facts and Evidence Concerning the Private Life of Grover Cleveland,* a political pamphlet distributed by the Cleveland campaign, 44.

282. "Beyond anticipations," GC to Bissell, 5 October 1884, Nevins, *Letters,* 44.

282. "And now that the Buffalo rumpus is over," ibid.

282. Brooklyn's "best families," *Brooklyn Eagle,* 23 October 1884.

283. "Before many of you were born I was rocking the cradle," ibid.

285. "Immovably opposed" to her going public, *Boston Globe,* 10 August 1884.

288. Frederick T. Halpin, being duly sworn. Affidavit in possession of author. It was also published in several newspapers 30 October 1884.

289. Maria B. Halpin, being duly sworn. *Chicago Tribune,* 31 October 1884. Affidavit in possession of the author.

290. "Leave his house," *Boston Globe,* 2 November 1884.

290. "I did not intend to say anything about the affair," *Chicago Tribune,* 31 October 1884.

14. PRESIDENT-ELECT

294. "And spontaneity will win?" Hudson, 205–210.

296. The Fifth Avenue Hotel was the social. *New York Times,* 4 April 1908.

297. An "insult to Christian civilization," Summers, 280.

298. "Flicker of annoyance," ibid., 282.

299. "I am the last man in the United States," ibid., 285.

299. "Now swallow the Cleveland pill," Nevins, 171.

299. "I must tell you about one girl here," W. F. Lampton, "Mrs. Cleveland as a College Girl," *Ladies Homes Journal,* March 1904, 12.

300. "Five minutes more that time and we should never have been married," Nevins, 302.

300. Her dorm room was still fragrant with roses. Annette Dunlap, *Frank: The Story of Frances Folsom Cleveland, America's Youngest First Lady* (Albany: SUNY Press, 2009), 22.

301. Frances asked around and found somebody. *New York World*, 8 November 1892.

301. "Girls, wouldn't it be pretty nice for me to spend a winter," Lampton, *Ladies Home Journal*, May 1905.

302. "A fellow can't cast but one, you know," *New York Times*, 3 November 1884.

304. "Don't disturb me unless something decisive," Summers, 9.

304. "Suspiciously slow," ibid.

305. "The only hope of our opponents is a fraudulent count," William Gorham Rice and Francis Lynde Stetson, *Was New York's Vote Stolen?* (New York: The North American Review Publishing Co., 1914), 83.

306. "I believe I have been elected president," Summers, 11.

306. "Cleveland is elected," King declared. Horatio King to his father, also named Horatio King, 8 November 1884, Archives and Special Collections, Waidner-Spahr Library, Dickinson College, Carlisle, Pennsylvania, MC1999.9, Box 1, File 11.

307. The air was so thick with tobacco smoke. *New York Times*, 14 November 1884.

307. "An ass in the shape of a preacher," Summers, xi; 296; 301.

308. "Opened his mouth and swallowed a presidency," Summers, 282.

308. "It's quite amusing to see how profuse," GC to Bissell, 13 November 1884, Nevins, *Letters*, 47–48.

309. "I can see no pleasure in it and no satisfaction," ibid., 13 November 1884, 47–48.

310. "I feel this moment I would never go there again," ibid., 5 December 1884, 50–51.

310. "I wish you a very 'Merry Christmas,'" Ibid., 25 December, 51.

15. ROSE

314. Rose was a creature of rigid habit. *Washington Post*, 14 January 1887.

314. Grover Cleveland's announcement naming his sister. Ibid., 28 December 1884; 18 January 1885.

315. She could conjugate ancient Greek verbs. Ibid., 14 January 1887, quoting Laura C. Holloway's *The Ladies of the White House.*

315. "Well, Dan, if you won't go, I won't, that's all," Nevins, 198.

316. "How d'ye do, Mr. President?" *Washington Post,* 4 March 1885.

318. Rose moved into a bedroom on the second floor. Ibid., 26 April 1885.

318. Mrs. Hendricks won the evening's accolades. Ibid., 5 March 1885.

318. Rose held her first reception. Ibid., 8 March 1885.

320. When Rose invited a delegation: Ibid, 14 March, 1885.

320. "It is only a strong man who can keep his wine glass upside down," ibid., 10 May 1885, quoting Rose Cleveland's 1882 article from *Youth's Temperance Banner.*

320. Ms. Annie Van Vechten arrived at the White House, ibid., 23 April 1885.

321. "I can't realize it is Washington," Lewis L. Gould, ed., *American First Ladies* (New York and London: Garland Publishing Inc., 1996), 247. Sue Severn, whose husband, William I. Severn, had researched an unfinished biography of Frances Folsom Cleveland and conducted extensive interviews with her youngest son, Francis G. Cleveland, and other family members, wrote the chapter.

322. They playfully calculated how many times they had to walk from one end. Robar, 15.

322. "Very romantic," Robar, 17.

322. "Decided favorite," *Washington Post,* 29 March 1885.

323. "She'll do! She'll do!" Nevins, 311.

323. "Handsome matron," *Washington Post,* 30 May 1885.

323. "How perfectly ridiculous it is to talk of the president," ibid., 30 May 1886.

323. "Rumors afloat," ibid., 17 November 1884.

324. "Have you come to think that your oldest grandchild," Frances Folsom to Col. John Folsom, 23 March 1885, Nevins Collection, Columbia University, Box 106.

326. It was not unusual for President Cleveland to answer the phone. Alyn Brodsky, *Grover Cleveland: A Study in Character* (New York: St. Martin's Press, 2000), 157.

326. "That man who cooks," *New York Times*, 3 April 1911. The quote is from Alexander Fortin's obituary.

327. "Plenty more in the box," *Washington Post*, 7 April 1885.

327. "Capable of great development," ibid., 9 April 1885; 6 June 1886 ("Echoes of the Wedding.")

328. Equated upper-crust society to a salivating and servile dog. Ibid., 10 May 1885.

328. "Rather terrifying," Nevins, 300.

328. "Romanist peril" and "annoying," ibid.

329. "She'd had a pretty hard time here," GC to Mary Cleveland Hoyt, 30 April 1885, Nevins, *Letters*, 63.

329. This "scurrilous" story. *Washington Post*, 26 January 1939, from an interview with Charles A. Hamilton.

16. THE BRIDE

331. Frances and her classmates planted the ivy. Robar, 16.

332. "Frank made a hero out of him. Dunlap, 4.

333. Not subjecting his "darling," Severn in Gould, 248.

333. "Poor girl," Cleveland would remark some time later. Nevins, 303.

334. "I don't see why the papers keep marrying me to old ladies," Robert McNutt McElroy, *Grover Cleveland, the Man and the Statesman: An Authorized Biography* (New York: Harper & Brothers, 1923), 184.

334. "This is the man who went to war for me," GC to John E. Hale, 13 September 1887, Nevins Collection, Columbia University, Box no. 102. Cleveland spelled Benisky's name Benninsky.

335. "Boiling seething lava of Vesuvius," Severn in Gould, 248.

336. "Well, then," she said, "will you answer this question," *Washington Post*, 7 June 1886.

337. "I should have begged you wildly never, never," Katherine Willard to Frances Folsom, 13 March 1886, GC Papers, LOC.

337. In a state of complete "misery," Robar, 19.

337. "I wish all you dear girls could have such," *Utica Herald*, quoted in *Washington Post*, 18 May 1886.

338. "There was not the slightest doubt but that it was genuine," *Washington Post*, 18 April 1886.

338. "I expect to be married pretty early in June." GC to Mary Cleveland Hoyt, 21 March 1886, Nevins, *Letters*, 103–104.

339. "It looks as if Frank would reach New York," ibid., 14 April 1886, 106.

339. Frances had found a father figure. Brodsky, 162.

339. "To him she was nothing but a child," *Washington Post*, 30 May 1886.

340. Frances had to be "admonished," ibid., 18 May 1886.

340. "I am very indignant at the way Frank," GC to Mary Cleveland Hoyt, 19 April 1886, Nevins, *Letters*, 106–107. See also GC letter to Mrs. Hoyt, 26 April 1886.

341. "I have no reason to believe that Mr. Cleveland is about to be married," *Washington Post*, 19 April 1886.

341. Cleveland's "acquaintance with the lady began when she was hardly knee high," ibid., 27 April 1886.

341. "Miss Folsom is considerably more than a schoolgirl," ibid., 18 May 1886.

342. "Rubbish and nonsense," ibid., 4 May 1886.

343. "She possesses no airs; she is remarkably humble," *New York Times*, 29 May 1886. A reporter from the *Times* happened to be a passenger on board the *Noordland* and wrote his account when he reached shore.

344. Colonel John Folsom was dead. *Buffalo Evening News*, 20 May 1886.

345. "Offensive partisanship," *Washington Post*, 14 June 1886.

346. "Arrived safe. All in good hands," Brodsky, 172.

17. DEATH OF A NEWSPAPER

348. His cousin wasn't "quite herself yet," *Washington Post*, 30 May 1886.

349. Frances acknowledged him with a coquettish little wave. *New York Times*, 1 June 1886. Author's note: Decoration Day became Memorial Day after World War I.

349. "Radiant vision of young springtime," William H. Crook, *Memories of the White House: The Home Life of Our Presidents from Lincoln to Roosevelt* (Boston: Little Brown and Co., 1911), 170.

352. Dolly Madison's mirror. Robar, 27.

352. Augustus Hill Garland, who detested all social functions. *Washington Post*, 26 June 1908.

354–356. Sunderland pronounced them husband and wife. The account of Cleveland's wedding comes primarily from an excellent article in the *Washington Post*, 3 June 1886.

356. Maria Halpin also got married. *Chicago Tribune*, 2 July 1887.

356. "Gentlemen," Ed Butler said, "I have purchased the *Telegraph*: *Buffalo Express*," 18 August 1885; Smith, 46.

357. "Simply because her heart was not there," *Washington Post*, 29 June 1886.

357. A romance titled *The Long Run*. Ibid., 19 July 1886.

358. She smelled a whiff of smoke. *New York Times*, 22 September 1886.

358. "Your reception in Chicago would be the greatest literary," *Washington Post*, 16 January 1887.

359. A "callow youth," ibid., 7 October 1886.

359. "The difference between us is this," ibid., 16 January 1887.

360. "The Weeds it will remain," Ibid, 25 July 1886.

360. He found her offer to be disgraceful and a "humiliation," ibid., 23 September 1886.

360. "Miss Cleveland has been in poor health," ibid., 19 October 1886.

361. "The worst of lies," Rose Cleveland, letter to *Washington Post*, ibid.

361. Mail fraud charges. *New York Times*, 5 September 1891.

361. When Cleveland saw him at the station he called out, "Hello!" Ibid., 13 July 1887.

362. "Utterly unfit for young girls," *Washington Post*, 12 February 1888.

18. THE TRIAL

363. "Dirty and disreputable," Dunlap, 42–43.

363. "A direct menace to the integrity of our homes," *Ladies Home Journal*, May 1905.

364. "The place is full of rumors about Mrs. Cleveland," Dunlap, 52, quoting Sir Cecil Spring-Rice.

364. "Called her wicked names and finally slapped her face," *Chicago Tribune*, 7 December 1888.

365. "I can only say in answer to your letter." *New York Times*, 8 June 1888.

365. His "tongue is considerably longer than his judgment," ibid., 10 June 1888.

366. "Of course, I don't believe these rumors," ibid., 8 June 1888.

366. "It was mainly because the other party had the most votes," Lamont scrapbook, Nevins Collection, Box 104.

367. "I am sorry for the president," Dunlop, 58.

367. "Mrs. Cleveland looks up to her husband," *Atlanta Constitution*, 25 November 1888, quoted by Dunlap, 58.

368. "The place I hate above all others," GC to William Vilas, 20 May 1888, Nevins, *Letters*, 207.

368. "Jungle of gifts," Nevins, 448.

368. "We're coming back just four years from today," Crook, 197–198.

369. "Things are getting into a pretty tough condition," GC to Vilas, 20 May 1888, Nevins, *Letters*, 207.

369. "Why hasn't Lena sent my corsets," Dunlap, 63.

370. Moot rose and presented his opening statement: *Four Great Lawyers of Our Time*, amemoir privately published by the Buffalo law firm Kenefick, Cook, Mitchel, Bass and Letchworth, undated, 10.

370–395. Author's note: No official transcript of the *Ball vs. New York Evening Post Corporation* trial exists. The Q and A and opening and closing arguments in chapter 18 are taken from a variety of sources, primarily contemporary newspaper accounts published in Buffalo in February 1890 and court papers on file at the New York State Appellate Division Law Library in Rochester.

373. "Remote deity," Allan Nevins, *The Evening Post: A Century of Journalism* (New York: Boni and Liveright, 1922), 529. Nevins once worked at the *Evening Post*.

374. "Smacked of sensationalism," *New York Times*, 22 May 1902.

374. Locke was also a voracious reader: *Four Great Lawyers of Our Time*, 3–5.

379. "It was torture," *Buffalo Times*, 5 February 1890.

383. Once he had treated the son of a tribal chief. *Buffalo News*, 14 August 1910.

387. A pallid George Ball sat at the plaintiff's table. *Buffalo Times*, 6 February, 1890.

389. "In this an attack had been made not only upon the living but upon the dead." Author's note: The quote is from the *Buffalo Commercial Advertiser* account of the trial (6 February 1890.) Although there are no quotation marks, it appears to be directly taken from John Milburn's closing arguments.

391. "If it pleases Your Honor we desire to reopen our side of the case," *Buffalo Times*, 7 February 1890.

394. "Without the slightest leaning one way or the other," *Buffalo Commercial Advertiser*, 7 February 1890.

394. No one expected a victory for Ball. *Buffalo Courier*, 8 February 1890.

395. It had taken six more ballots before reaching a unanimous verdict: *Buffalo Courier*, 8 February 1890.

19. KEEPER OF THE FLAME

397. Two days before she passed away, Maria wrote out a will. *New Rochelle Pioneer*, 22 February 1902.

397. "Do not let the funeral be too public," *Utica Journal*, 10 February 1902.

398. Then a hearse carried the coffin down a rain-slicked country road. Records from the Davis Funeral Home, New Rochelle, New York, courtesy Rick Moody of New Rochelle.

398. "The well-known stove and furnace dealer," *New Rochelle Press*, 8 February 1902. Also see *New Rochelle Pioneer*, same date.

399. "But for this woman [Mrs. Baker]," *Brooklyn Eagle*, 9 February 1902.

399. On October 30, 1909, Byrne was sitting. *Buffalo Courier*, 1 November 1909; death of Byrne from *Courier*, 31 October 1909.

400. He was boarding a trolley in front of the Iroquois Hotel. *Buffalo News*, 14 August 1910; 16 August 1910. Bull was eighty-three when he died. Some accounts put his age at eighty-five.

400. The 342-acre site opened on May 1, 1901. Thomas E. Leary and Elizabeth Sholes, *Buffalo's Pan-American Exposition* (Charleston, South Carolina, Arcadia Publishing, 1998), 110, 117.

401. The hotel was the social hub of the new town: Ron Jamro and Gerald L. Lanterman, *The Founding of Naples* (Naples, Florida, The Collier County Museum, 1985), 41.

402. "Ah, Eve, Eve, surely you cannot realize what you are to me," Rose Cleveland (RC) to Evangeline Marrs Simpson Whipple (EMSW), postmarked 23 April 1890, *Whipple/Scandrett Family Papers*, Minnesota Historical Society (MHS), P789, Box 2, File 1890. Author's note: An account of the relationship between Rose and Evangeline can also found in *Odd Girls and Twilight Lovers: A History of Lesbian Life in Twentieth-Century America* by Lillian Faderman (New York: Penguin, 1992), 32–33.

402. "Oh, darling, come to me this night, my Clevy, my Viking," RC to EMSW, 22 April 1890, ibid.

403. "Oh, Eve, Eve, this love is life itself—or death," RC to EMSW, 5 May 1890, ibid.

403. "I shall go to bed, my Eve," RC to EMSW, 6 May 1890, ibid.

403. "Ah, my Cleopatra," Rose wrote that day. RC to EMSW, 9 May 1890, ibid.

404. "Yes, darling, I will be with you, surely," ibid.

405. "I wish for your happiness and good," Rose wrote. Postmarked 25 April, apparently in the year 1893. P789, Box 3, ibid.

405. "The bishop is in vigorous health. *New York Times*, 24 October 1896.

407. Seeking a consultation on a "very important matter." William Williams Keen, *The Surgical Operations on President Cleveland in 1893* (Philadelphia: George W. Jacobs and Co., 1917), 30–31.

409. "If you hit a rock, hit it good and hard," Nevins, 530.

411. Lamont snapped that it was a "preposterous" question: H. W. Brands, *The Reckless Decade: America in the 1890s* (Chicago: University of Chicago Press, 1995), 83. Author's note: Brands's book offers an excellent account of the Panic of 1893.

412. Dr. Bryant found something disturbing. Keen, 36–44.

413. "My God, Olney, they nearly killed me!" Nevins, 532.

414. Erdmann later said he "did more lying," Nevins, quoting Erdmann, 533.

414. "Mr. Cleveland had suffered so much at the hands," *Philadelphia Times*, 31 August 1893.

416. Sensible and responsible women "do not want to vote," *Ladies Home Journal*, October 1905, 7–8.

416. Baby Ruth as she came to be called. Author's note: The Baby Ruth candy bar made its first appearance some seventeen years after the child's death. Although the Curtiss Candy Company maintained it was named in honor of Ruth Cleveland, some have speculated that it was a ruse to avoid paying royalties to the baseball great Babe Ruth.

419. "Where she knew she could find him," Dunlap, 129; Jean S. Davis, *A Rambling Memoir of Mrs. Grover Cleveland and Some Related History*, unpublished manuscript, Louis Jefferson Long Library, Wells College, 23.

419. "Unpleasant shock when I read the headlines reporting the engagement," Davis, 24.

420. "The Cleveland pew was third in front of ours," ibid.

420. He was fond of crocheting. Dunlap, 133.

421. "That of a man who needed to go to Florida for his health," *New York Times*, 11 February 1913; also noted by Davis, 26.

422. "I went over his book before it was published," Frances Cleveland Preston to William Gorham Rice, 13 August 1918, Rice Papers,

Folder 8, Manuscripts and Special Collections, New York State Library.

422. She recruited the historian for the presidency of Wells. Jane M. Dieckmann, *Wells College: A History* (Aurora, New York Wells College Press, 1995), 101.

422. "When his friend, Charles W. Goodyear, reported that a particularly violent," McElroy, 91–92.

423. "Who threw open his papers and gave invaluable advice," Nevins, v.

424. "A weaker or more callous man in his place," Nevins's account of the Halpin scandal can be found in his Cleveland biography, 162–169.

424. A "true picture—of the man and his meaning," Frances Cleveland Preston to Rice, 23 December 1932, Rice Papers, Folder 9.

424. "It probably wasn't Cleveland's child," *New York Times*, September 8, 2008.

424. Author's Note: If Nevins's meticulous scholarship closed the door on divergent accounts of the Cleveland-Halpin story, it also opened a window, albeit a small one. He claims that in 1895, Maria Halpin made a crude attempt at blackmail in a letter she addressed to President Cleveland at the White House. She demanded money from Cleveland, Nevins says, and threatened to "publish facts in her possession" unless she was paid off. Nevins cites a date for this letter— September 9, 1895—which he says can be found in the collection of Grover Cleveland's presidential papers in the Library of Congress. The Library of Congress has no record of such a letter. One can only presume that Frances Cleveland, or someone acting on her behalf, removed Maria Halpin's letter before consigning the Cleveland Papers to the Library of Congress in 1923. One can also wonder whether it was the only item to have met that fate.

425. In October 1946, an extraordinary spectacle. *New York Times*, 22 October 1946.

426. "You did?" he asked. "Where?" Davis, 30.

EPILOGUE

428. King even set up a Dickens Room in his house. *Buffalo Evening News* obituary on King, 10 March 1947.

428. Saimi Pratt worked as his cook. E-mail from Ronald Pratt to author, 28 July 2009.

429. "I was a new bride and very nervous," interview with Ruth Kahn Stouroff, 21 October 2008.

429. "If anyone calls, just say I am improving," *Buffalo Evening News*, 10 March 1947.

429. A funeral procession took his coffin. Warren (Pennsylvania) *Times Mirror*, 10 March 1947.

430. Pliny the Elder's *Naturalis Historia*: This edition of *Naturalis Historia* was published in 1634 or 1639. The nameplate indicates it was a Christmas gift to King from Beulah Hood. John Edens, University of Buffalo Libraries, SUNY. Via e-mail, 27 July 2009.

430. To his former laundress he left $500. *Buffalo Evening News*, 28 May 1947. The laundress was Marie Bazinski; the six-year-old boy was James Millard Riley.

INDEX

471